Thomas J. Wood

ALSO BY DAN LEE
AND FROM MCFARLAND

*The L&N Railroad in the Civil War:
A Vital North–South Link
and the Struggle to Control It* (2011)

*Kentuckian in Blue: A Biography of
Major General Lovell Harrison Rousseau* (2010)

Thomas J. Wood

A Biography of the Union General in the Civil War

DAN LEE

McFarland & Company, Inc., Publishers
Jefferson, North Carolina, and London

LIBRARY OF CONGRESS CATALOGUING-IN-PUBLICATION DATA

Lee, Dan, 1954–
    Thomas J. Wood : a biography of the Union general in the Civil War / Dan Lee.
    p.   cm.
    Includes bibliographical references and index.

    ISBN 978-0-7864-7130-0
    softcover : acid free paper ∞

    1. Wood, Thomas John, 1823–1906. 2. United States— History — Civil War, 1861–1865 — Campaigns. 3. United States. Army — Biography 4. Generals — United States — Biography.
I. Title.
E467.1.W87L44 2012
973.7'41092 — dc23
[B]   2012026211

BRITISH LIBRARY CATALOGUING DATA ARE AVAILABLE

© 2012 Dan Lee. All rights reserved

No part of this book may be reproduced or transmitted in any form or by any means, electronic or mechanical, including photocopying or recording, or by any information storage and retrieval system, without permission in writing from the publisher.

Front cover image: Thomas John Wood, 1845–1906, a career United States Army officer and a Union general during the American Civil War (Civil War Photograph Collection, Library of Congress)

Manufactured in the United States of America

McFarland & Company, Inc., Publishers
   Box 611, Jefferson, North Carolina 28640
   www.mcfarlandpub.com

To Linda

Table of Contents

Introduction 1

1. The Making of a Professional 5
2. Mexico 16
3. The Crisis 37
4. From Camp Nevin to Nashville 47
5. Shiloh and Corinth 55
6. The North Alabama Campaign 64
7. The Contest for Kentucky 74
8. Murfreesboro 90
9. Winter Quarters at Murfreesboro 102
10. Tullahoma and Beyond 115
11. Chickamauga: Along La Fayette Road 129
12. Chickamauga: The Day of Days 138
13. Chattanooga 152
14. East Tennessee 171
15. The Atlanta Campaign 183
16. Nashville 201
17. War's End 219
18. Post-War Duty 231
19. Dayton 241

Appendix. Wood in Command: An Organizational Chart 248
Notes 251
Select Bibliography 261
Index 267

Introduction

On November 18, 1896, Thomas J. Wood, Major General, U.S. Army (Retired), limped into the library of his comfortable home on North Main Street in Dayton, Ohio. He was seventy-three years old. His close-cropped hair and his moustache were silver, but he was soldierly in his bearing, as erect and trim as when he was a West Point cadet, a half century before. One would think that he was perfectly fit, despite his years, until he was in motion. Then, his limp was impossible to ignore. It was the result of war wounds, and he walked painfully with the aid of an ivory-headed cane, which he carried in his left hand. His features were straight and sharp and his eyes were clear. Easing into the chair behind his desk, he could glance around the room and see on the walls the familiar reminders of his long career, souvenirs of the Mexican War, of the western frontier—Texas, Utah, Kansas—and of the War of the Rebellion. More important to him than his trophies of war was his framed commission to the rank of major general. This was the proof that he had reached the pinnacle of his profession, an honor he had earned, but one for which he had had to petition over a period of years before the final promotion was granted. He still considered himself subject to the rules and regulations of the War Department, though he had been out of active service for thirty years. The army had been Wood's life, and sending divisions of men into battle the richest use of his talents and training.

However, it was politics, not war, that occupied Wood's thoughts as he spread before him a sheet of stationery. A presidential election had just ended and though he had no personal ambition for public office, he followed politics closely, and even more closely this year, for a friend of his had been on the losing Democratic ticket of Palmer and Buckner. They were the Gold Democrats, conservatives who were opposed to the free-silver platform of William Jennings Bryan, who was the candidate of both the Silver Democrats and the Populists. The Palmer-Buckner ticket was an oddity in that John M. Palmer was a former Union general and Simon Bolivar Buckner was a former Confederate general. Thomas J. Wood knew them both. He had served with Palmer in the Army of the Cumberland in Tennessee and in the Atlanta Campaign, but he had known Buckner since boyhood, had grown up with him and gone to school with him. At times, they had lived under the same roof. It was to Buckner that Wood was writing. He dipped his pen in the inkwell and began, "My dear Bolivar...."

For years they had been estranged. Wood had bitterly resented Buckner's choice to side with the Southern Confederacy and had turned against him entirely after the 1862 Rebel occupation of their mutual hometown, Munfordville, Kentucky. Wood's son George H. Wood later recalled, "Very frequently my father got very hot on the subject of Bolivar Buckner ... but with the passage of years this feeling quieted down and his remarks about Buckner became those of an old boyhood friend."[1]

The ice dam between the two old soldiers seems to have broken in 1890 when a mutual friend returned to Dayton from a trip to Frankfort, Kentucky. There he had seen Buckner, who gave him a message for Wood. Wood wrote Buckner the same day, "I assure you, Bolivar, that message touched the chords of memory in a way that men of your age and mine do not often feel ... I am quite certain that each of us now is the oldest living friend and acquaintance the other has ... Let us cherish, then Bolivar, the friendship found sixty years ago on our native hills of Green River!"[2]

Now, six years after the resumption of their friendship, Wood's old affection for Buckner had fully reasserted itself, and on this day he was writing Buckner a letter of encouragement following his loss to the Republican ticket headed by William McKinley. The defeat was not a complete surprise, the Democrats being split as they were between the Gold and Silver wings of their party. Still, the Republicans' margin of victory was embarrassing. McKinley had beaten the Silver Democrat Bryan, but he had utterly thrashed the Gold Democrats Palmer and Buckner, with a gap of nearly six and a half million votes. Palmer's and Buckner's total of 134,645 votes was only slightly more than that of the Prohibitionist ticket.

Nevertheless, some good had come of it. Bryan and Populism were quashed. Wood wrote to Buckner, "As you well say, the contest through which we have just passed was, truly, a most momentous one, and I trust the Democratic party has preserved for centuries more of usefulness. In another Olympiad may it bury the Republican party as deep as it buried Populism."[3]

Wood continued in a more personal vein. Responding to an invitation from Buckner, he wrote, "I will try to arrange a visit to you spring next. I do, indeed, wish to look once more on the 'Knobs' of dear old Hart County." In return, he extended an invitation to Buckner and his family to pay a visit to Dayton. He ended the letter, "As ever, the friend of your childhood, boyhood, and manhood to life's end."[4]

Wood fancied himself a writer. He liked words and used them in abundance. His Civil War reports were long and flowery and his letters were often similarly long, but this letter to Buckner was uncharacteristically brief. The clock was ticking. He could faintly hear it as he folded the letter and slid it into its envelope, addressed it in his angular hand to Buckner at Glen Lily, Hart County, Kentucky, and limped out to post it.

Wood's reference to "dear old Hart County" was a rare expression of sentimentality. He rarely looked back to his early years and had no particular love for his boyhood home in Munfordville. It was Simon Bolivar Buckner who returned to live in Hart County and who had served Kentucky as governor before his unsuccessful foray into national politics. The past interested Wood only insofar as it reflected his own accomplishments. From the time of his boyhood his focus had been on moving ahead, away from Hart County and out to the larger world. Once he left Hart County, he was done with it. He never lived there again and very infrequently did he even return to visit his father and siblings. Buckner's invitation to Wood to come visit at his Hart County home was politely accepted, but there is no evidence that he ever acted upon it. Hart County was the ancient past.

Wood's ambition was fierce and single-minded in its focus and his career path had consequently been straightforward. Ambition, combined with sizable reserves of energy and a sharp intelligence, had propelled him forward like a cannon-shot, clean and undeflected. Wood had used his talents with the alert skill of a battlefield tactician in order to advance in his chosen profession. The most dangerous element of Wood's personality was always his pugnacious sense of pride. He had barely been able to contain it, yet he had almost always done so. His discipline was exquisite. Only once had his offended pride broken its bonds to overwhelm his judgment, and his resulting actions in that one ill-considered moment in 1863 had nearly cost him everything. Yet he overcame it to win battles and the respect of his fellow officers and, ultimately, his civilian superiors in the War Department.

Thomas J. Wood was the consummate professional, totally absorbed by his military career. He served the country with devotion to duty, with personal valor, and with enough skill as a division commander that he was finally honored with that precious, long-sought after, long-delayed promotion to major general. This was the climax of his life. He was satisfied now. Everything that followed was simply the fading light following a long and glorious day. After retiring from the U.S. Army in 1868, he never worked again, not in business, not in politics, and not in philanthropy, even though he had another thirty-eight years to live. To Major General Thomas J. Wood, there was no other conceivable profession than the army.

This is the story of a professional during the great crisis of U.S. history.

Chapter 1

The Making of a Professional

Thomas J. Wood was not compelled to seek a life outside of Hart County. In this region of West-Central Kentucky, he and his family were counted among the elite. His father was George Twyman Wood, a Virginian who had come to Kentucky in 1799 with his family. They settled in Barren County. As a young man, George T. Wood moved to the Green River region. There he prospered. When Hart County was formed in 1819, he became the first circuit court clerk, a position he held for decades. At times George T. Wood was the circuit court clerk and the county court clerk simultaneously.

Hart County's rolling land was good not only for burley tobacco and grain but also for all breeds of livestock. In addition, the land had industrial potential, for it was shot through with iron ore. There would be two iron furnaces in Hart County by the start of the 1840s — the Henry Clay Furnace and the Buckner-Churchill Furnace. At the height of the antebellum period, land in Hart County sold for $3.15 an acre, which was above the average of the surrounding counties. George T. Wood bought a farm on the edge of Munfordville and built his home there. It was on a high hill, the highest in town, and its yard sloped gently down to the town center. Going out his front door in the morning for the short stroll down to the courthouse square, Wood could gaze over the rooftops of Munfordville and could see piercing the distant horizon the dramatic eminence of Summerseat Knob.

Munfordville was a raw young community, bustling with activity. It was situated to take advantage of intersecting transportation arteries. The Louisville and Nashville Turnpike, linking two of the most important cities of the Upper South, bisected the town. Cracking whips and the jingling trace chains of stagecoaches added a counterpoint to the chopping thud of axes shaping timbers for the homes and shops of the county seat. The Green River flowed on the southern edge of town and paddle wheelers docked there, bringing all manner of interesting travelers and rich cargoes of merchandise and household goods from New Orleans, Louisville, and Cincinnati.

George T. Wood had chosen a promising setting for his life and his career in local politics, but he had also married well. His wife was Elizabeth Helm, a daughter of the pioneering Helm family of Hardin County. Among her close kinsmen were celebrated lawyers, members of the Kentucky General Assembly, and a future two-time governor of the commonwealth. Her father was Charles Helm, a veteran of the War of 1812, a state senator, and a close associate of Henry Clay. The early Hardin County historian Samuel Haycraft, Jr., recalled Charles Helm as "the most popular man in the county."[1]

Elizabeth Helm Wood's sons would show that they had inherited her family's varied talents. The firstborn son, Henry C. Wood (born in 1821), went on to attend Centre College in Danville, Kentucky. He became an attorney and represented Hart County in the Kentucky General Assembly before removing to Louisville in 1850. He became a judge on the Kentucky Court of Appeals in 1858. Based on his adult accomplishments, Henry C. Wood must have been a gifted child, and he set a high bar for his younger brother, Thomas John Wood, born September 25, 1823.

George T. Wood's future seemed bright. He owned a farm and several town lots. He had a position of trust in the county government and was a leader in the Masonic Lodge and in the Presbyterian Church. He was married to a socially prominent wife and was the father of two healthy sons. But, for all of his hard work and good fortune, George T. Wood could not escape personal tragedy. Not long after the birth of her second son, Elizabeth Helm Wood suddenly died. It is unlikely that Thomas J. Wood had any memories of his mother. Two stepmothers would follow (and five half siblings), but as the son of a privileged family Thomas was probably closer to his slave "mammy" than to either of his father's subsequent wives.

Though the number of slaves owned by George T. Wood at the time of Thomas J. Wood's birth is uncertain, the number would eventually reach twenty-one, a tally that put the Wood family in the planter class. As with most slave-owning families in Kentucky, the relationship between whites and their black servants was a tangle of contradictions.

In 1834, George T. Wood built a new house for his family, a fine two-story brick home on the same hill where the original dwelling stood. It was a model of symmetry, with a central door topped by a graceful fanlight and flanked by two windows on each side. Six white columns framed the entry. The effect was one of elegance and orderly living. But there were secrets within those brick walls, and the architectural evidence suggests that George T. Wood could be a harsh master.

Of the Wood residence (which still stands), Hart County historian Susan C. Lafferty wrote:

> The George T. Wood home has two identical cellar-like rooms approximately 10' × 20'. These rooms are located on the same side of the main house. They are

close together, have no windows, and each has its own entrance from the outside.... Whether these rooms were used to contain slaves for some reason, or if they were used for some other purpose such as food storage is not known. Other homes in the state have been built with such masonry walled cellars for punishing slaves. One [such] well known home was that of Edward Stone, a slave-trader of Bourbon County, Kentucky. Most likely he is an extreme example to compare to George T. Wood, but the large dual cellar rooms are of interest and worthy of study.[2]

While there is evidence that George T. Wood could be a stern, possibly even cruel, slave-master, there is also evidence that proves that he was a considerate one as well. For instance, some favored slaves were buried in the family cemetery, which was located about seventy-five yards behind the big house. One of them, Aunt Sarah, was given a headstone engraved with the epitaph: "Aunt Sarah — Sometime Slave, Always Our Friend." In addition, George T. Wood left property to one of his former slaves in his 1876 will. The freedman Elisha was bequeathed six acres.[3]

It was in this environment of the alternately brutal and benevolent slave system that Thomas J. Wood grew up. As an adult, he owned at least one slave of his own, and he was slow to recognize the end of slavery as a desirable goal of the Union in the War of the Rebellion. It seems certain that, when he was a youth the injustice of American slavery never entered his head. Not only did his family own slaves, but so did that of his closest friend, Simon Bolivar Buckner.

Desiring that Bolivar receive the best education available, Aylett Buckner sent his son from their rural estate to attend a village academy called the Seminary in Munfordville with his chum T. J. Wood. Because the roads outside of town were so bad, young Buckner sometimes stayed for extended periods with the Wood family, and because it was not fitting for a young squire to tend his own needs, Bolivar always brought along his valet, a slave named Shelburne Matthews. One supposes that T. J. Wood had a body servant of his own and that the white boys and the black boys engaged in all of the adventures of boyhood together: roaming the woods searching for persimmons and pawpaws, fishing and swimming in Green River, smoking corn silk behind the barn, chasing after the stagecoaches as they rumbled into town, and learning to curse from the riverboat pilots and the rough-hewn stage drivers. The companionship of white and black children of a certain age was common in the South, but they parted company at the schoolhouse door.

The Seminary must have been a quite good school. By 1840, the instructors there had trained Simon Bolivar Buckner so well that he was accepted as a cadet at the U.S. Military Academy at West Point. It may have privately galled Thomas J. Wood that his friend Bolivar was the first to achieve the goal they had both set for themselves, but he was gracious about it and wrote his soon-to-be-absent friend a letter of congratulations, "for what can yield to a human soul more pleasure than to hear of the success of a cherished and beloved friend." He also admitted his own disappointment in not being able to enroll at West Point at the same time as his friend. "Nothing would afford me more real satisfaction than obtaining a commission and going on in company with you at this time," he wrote. "The pleasure we would experience in traveling together and the engagement of each other's society after our arrival at West Point would be very great." Wood suggested that Bolivar send him copies of West Point's rules and regulations, so that he could study them and be ready when his own time came. Meanwhile, he would have to content himself with a job as junior clerk in his father's courthouse office. The circuit court was scheduled to begin on the first Monday of the month, so at least he would be busy.[4]

As it turned out, the volume of work for a junior clerk was not enough to keep Wood from brooding. By the end of May he despaired of ever getting an appointment. He recounted to Buckner how deeply he longed for the chance to begin training for his life's work but concluded, "It may be in the course of events that all the fondest expectations of my life may be blasted, and the field of advancement, enjoyments and improvements which I have pictured, may never be realized by me." However, his prospects were about to brighten. In mid-June he learned from Buckner that a cadet named G. B. Tyler was very likely to resign. If he did, Wood could probably win the appointment. Wood agreed that his chances were good and wrote, "I flatter myself that ere long we will be permitted to meet at West Point, and there lay the foundation and commence the work of distinction and usefulness: Usefullness to ourselves and our beloved country."[5]

Anxious to enlist all the help he could in the campaign to win an appointment, Wood sent his qualifications to Willis Green, the Democratic congressman from Kentucky's Second District. An uncomfortable month passed. About the first of August, Wood wrote again to Congressman Green, repeating his list of qualifications and explaining the situation of Cadet Tyler, and received the encouraging reply that he, Green, had passed the letter on to the secretary of war.

In late August, a letter addressed in an unfamiliar hand came to the Wood residence. Tearing it open, Wood saw that it was from G. B. Tyler. The news was all that Wood had hoped for. Tyler wrote that he had begun the process of resigning from West Point. Unconcerned that he might appear grasping, Wood immediately wrote to the secretary of war — wrote too soon, as it turned out — that he wanted the appointment. The secretary's reply was both prompt and deflating. The War Department had not yet received Tyler's resignation, and the secretary added that "at any rate the vacancy caused by his resignation would not be filled before next spring, the regular time for making appointments." Wood reviewed the unfolding events in a letter to Buckner and thanked him for the copy of West Point's rules and regulations that he had sent. Aside from career news, the most interesting thing that had happened in Wood's recent life was that Henry Clay had passed through Munfordville on his way to Nashville. Harry of the West spoke to the admiring crowd in a voice Wood described as "rich and eloquent" and was greeted with the accustomed cheers.[6]

After a final letter to Willis Green in mid–December, there was nothing left for Wood but to be patient. He relieved the tedious wait for news of his appointment by a December trip to Frankfort. It cannot be coincidence that he decided to pay a visit to the Kentucky capital while the General Assembly was in session; influential friends in the legislature would help guarantee his appointment. Besides, with the legislators in town, the Christmas season in Frankfort would be a glittering round of dances and fancy dinners. Wood took advantage of them. He wrote to Buckner on January 2, 1841, that the social scene was exciting in more ways than one. "Saw lots of pretty girls, and fine company, which you know is not hard to take at any time."[7]

By the first week in February, Wood was back in Munfordville, where disturbing news reached him. Willis Green wrote that there was another applicant for the West Point vacancy, John B. McLarty of Breckinridge County. For a young man of privilege, one who was not used to disappointments or setbacks, the effort to win an appointment to West Point was proving to be uncomfortably difficult. This news about the competitor McLarty was yet another irritation.

Another month of anxiety followed. Then, in early March, Wood received the news that changed his life: he was appointed to the U.S. Military Academy. He announced the appointment in a jubilant letter to Buckner: "All uncertainty and doubt is now at an end. On last Thursday I received a notification that I had been appointed a Cadet in the Service of the United States.... I will leave home about the middle of May next, so as to be at West Point by the first of June." He wanted advice. One of his concerns was money. He knew that Aylett Buckner had given Bolivar $150 at the start of his trip to New York; was that "sufficient to begin with? If not, how much money?" Also, should he buy the things he would need before leaving Munfordville or wait until he got to West Point? He wanted to know, "in short, everything which you think will be of advantage to me to know...." Within ten days, Wood had a reply from Buckner, containing at least part of the information he requested. In his return letter Wood said, "I will take your advice, and leave home about the 15th of May so as to be enabled to get to West Point by the 1st of June."[8]

So it was that in the second week of May 1841 seventeen-year-old Thomas J. Wood stepped out of the front door of his father's fine brick house for the short walk down to the stagecoach stop, the first steps of his long life's journey. In the far distance he could see Summerseat Knob, the highest point on the horizon. The high points on his own horizon were waiting for him. They were too far away to see, but he was confident that they were there.

Thomas J. Wood traveled by stagecoach on the Louisville and Nashville Turnpike north to Louisville. There he booked passage on a riverboat that bucked the current to Wheeling, Virginia, where he transferred his baggage to another stagecoach, which carried him to Washington, D.C. From there, he traveled to Philadelphia, thence to New York City. He did a bit of sightseeing in each of the three biggest cities he'd ever seen (Munfordville had three hundred people; New York City had three hundred thousand), but not so much as to delay his departure for West Point on a Hudson River steamer. He debarked at West Point on June 1.

Wood had arrived at the military academy at a fortunate time. This was near the beginning of what Stephen Ambrose called "The Golden Age" of the Academy. Despite the perennial problem of underfunding by the U.S. Congress, West Point had just emerged from a period of reform and expansion that enhanced considerably the quality of the education offered to the cadet corps. This was largely the work of Joel Poinsett, the secretary of war under President Martin Van Buren. Poinsett had overseen the construction of several badly needed buildings, including new classrooms, a barracks, a library, and, most impressive, an observatory. In addition, Poinsett insisted on an expanded and improved curriculum. As James L. Morrison observed, "It was largely through his efforts that equitation, or horsemanship, was introduced into the curriculum, [and] that the professorship of chemistry, mineralogy, and geology was established." Though Poinsett was out of office by the time Thomas J. Wood arrived at the Point, his spirit still motivated those who were in charge of the curriculum, and in 1841 the effort began to add logic to the curriculum as well as a course in "practical military engineering."[9]

The superintendent was Richard Delafield (Class of '18), a sarcastic, large-nosed man whose busybody interference in every aspect of life at the Academy and tendency to be rigid and punitive made him unpopular with cadets and instructors alike. Delafield seems to have had the well-being of the cadets at heart, though his methods were heavy-handed and often misunderstood. For instance, when he canceled the clothing credit of plebes (what the rest of the world called freshmen) at the cadet store, it meant that they could not replace their worn-out uniforms. It also meant that they could no longer engage in their favorite form of barter, which was to trade their duds for liquor and then buy new outfits on credit at the store. Thus, he was sparing both the Academy and the cadets the trouble caused by quantities of readily available whiskey. But the young men did not see it in that light. All they knew was that they had to mend their old clothes and could not get fresh ones in a world turned suddenly dry.

Delafield was a strict man, but he was not an unreasonable one. He was approachable and would listen to sensible suggestions. For example, at the request of Cadet E. P. Alexander, the future Confederate artillery officer, Delafield ordered an extension of "the period between parade and supper so cadets would have time to bathe and also ordered that both tea and coffee be served in the mess hall every night." The superintendent also did away with the cadets' side-button trousers and replaced them with britches that buttoned up the front. This reform, at least, was popular with the cadets, but it offended deeply Mrs. Delafield's modesty, and she afterward forbade cadets to come to her house.[10]

Thomas J. Wood was entering an institution in which failure could be achieved more easily than success. The standard of expected behavior was almost inhuman and demerits were handed out for the most insignificant error; one hundred demerits in any six-month period was cause for dismissal.

Then there was the class work. The course of studies at West Point was so demanding that the graduation rate was less than 50 percent. In addition to the earth sciences mentioned earlier, there were civil and military engineering, the art of war, French, rhetoric and moral philosophy, drawing, ethics, and—the colossus that overshadowed all—mathematics. All of the various forms of mathematics were drilled into the cadets and, for many, became the most burdensome of their already-heavy load. Stephen Ambrose pointed out, "Those who had been to other colleges before coming to West Point were amazed at how much they were expected to know and how well they were required to know it." West Point was an exercise in mental stamina, if not downright masochism.[11]

Added to the demands of the classroom were what might be called the extracurricular activities, chapel and debating. Participation in one of the two debating societies was voluntary, but it was expected. Thomas J. Wood had the confidence to argue and a personality that enjoyed dispute, and debating could not have been too difficult for him. Chapel was another matter. The two-hour Episcopal service at chapel must have been hard to endure for a Kentucky Presbyterian.

The pressure at West Point was never-ending and it surrounded the cadets, pushing on them from all directions. The upperclassmen barked at them and hazed them, the Tactical Department spied on them, and their classmates competed with them not only to survive but also to excel. Privacy was non-existent and there was no free time, save on Sunday afternoons, which most cadets used for more study, mostly math. Cadets were allowed no money and they were restricted to the campus.

West Point was not a prison, but it was a reasonable facsimile and, for some of the young men, homesickness must have been nearly crippling.

During the summer, when students at other institutions were allowed to return home on vacation, West Point cadets endured a summer encampment, where from June through August they practiced their engineering skills and received instruction in artillery, cavalry, and infantry tactics (depending on their class level). It was in the summer encampment of 1841 that Thomas J. Wood began and might well have ended his West Point experience.

On arriving at the Academy, Wood walked from the Hudson River landing up the steep path to that high, flat bench known as The Plain, to report and sign in at the adjutant's office. Then he proceeded to the treasurer's office where he turned over all of his money. He would earn a small stipend while at West Point, but the money was held for him and he never saw it; he could only draw on it at the various commissaries. Neither was he allowed to receive money from home.

Next, Wood was directed to his room in the barracks and may have been surprised at its tiny dimensions, only twelve by twelve feet. Wood went next to the quartermaster for his furnishings. In his interesting book *The Best School: West Point 1833–1866,* James L. Morrison inventoried the Spartan effects of a cadet's life: "A pair of blankets, a chair, an arithmetic text, a slate, a blanket, a tin or cocoanut dipper, a tin wash basin, a lump of soap, a candlestick, a tallow candle, and a supply of stationery." By T. J. Wood's time, it appears that the list also included an oil lamp.[12]

Wood passed his entrance and physical exams, but since classes did not begin until the fall, he and the other cadets went into their first summer encampment. There Wood became seriously ill, and he was still in the hospital when it came time to move into barracks. Once again, he called on his friend Simon Bolivar Buckner for help. In a long and imperious letter dated August 22, Wood wrote Bolivar:

> I understand that it is probable the battalion will move into Barracks on tomorrow or the next day, if so I want you to take charge of my things in camp. You will find my trunk key in my locker, my trunk is in the room with D Company's trunks. It is a tolerably large fine leather trunk and my name fastened on each end. It is plenty large to hold all my things. Take everything out of my locker and put them into my trunk and lock it up, and keep the key. Be certain not to lose my trunk. Keep or pocket books. Take good care of my bedding for me, as I shall need it all when I get into Barracks and a good deal more.[13]

A week later, still in the hospital, Wood again wrote Buckner. This time, Wood's tone was somewhat more modest. He confessed that he had "troubled you so often during my unfortunate illness that I [am] almost ashamed to ask for anything more of you," but he overcame his reluctance. Without slowing down for commas, he asked Buckner to go to the Company D deposit room and "get my table chair wash stand and oil camm [?] and put them in your room until I can get up to Barracks." He feared that the returning furlough men — those who were returning from the two-month leave that was granted to cadets at the end of their Yearling (sophomore) year—would take his things, for he had been told that they "will seize on anything that is left whether theirs or not."[14]

One of those furlough men turned out to be one of Wood's roommates. He was a quiet, round-shouldered fellow named Ulysses Simpson Grant, though everyone called him Sam. Grant entered the Academy in 1839 and was about to begin his Cow (junior) year, but cadets were not required to room with men in their own class.

Wood knew that he would have to endure two years of rigorous study and carefully controlled conduct before he would get his furlough. By then, he would have become resigned, if not quite accustomed, to the poor and often adulterated food, to the indignity of assigned seats in the mess hall, to quarters that got all of its heat in the summer (the coal grate was an insufficient source of wintertime heat, even in a room so small), to the uncomfortable and monotonous uniforms of "Cadet Gray," and to the strict daily schedule: a drumroll reveille at 6:00 A.M., classes all morning, followed by study and official duties until a 6:00 P.M. supper, which was followed by more study until the drums sounded taps at 9:30. Wood, like many other cadets, undoubtedly crammed in still more study after lights-out by means of a lit candle under a propped-up blanket, a dangerous and officially forbidden practice. If he was lucky, he mastered his lessons well enough to close the books and snuff the candle by the wee hours. The immutable routine repeated itself the next morning, after a short night's sleep. Certainly by the summer between his second and third years Wood was ready for his furlough.

Predictably, he wrote to Buckner about his brief time away from the Academy. His first stop was New York City, where he and his fellow cadets palled around together, attending performances at the Park Theatre and enjoying the restaurants. Some of them—and Wood made no confessions—"paid a visit to some ladies of no very good fame. You know it is the way of Cadets on furlough and will not wonder at it." He did reassure his friend that "whatever else I may have done wrong in New York or elsewhere I kept entirely sober." Apparently, drunkenness was more to be avoided than debauchery.[15]

After two days of pleasure in New York City, Wood left for Baltimore and, a day later, boarded a train for Cumberland, Maryland. There he took a stagecoach over the mountains to Brownsville, Pennsylvania, on the Monongahela River. A small boat carried him to Pittsburgh, where he booked a cabin on a river packet to Cincinnati. A mail boat conveyed him thence to Louisville. He arrived at the City at the Falls on the morning of June 30, took a stagecoach for a fast trip down the Louisville and Nashville Turnpike to Munfordville, and stepped out of the hack in his hometown, dusty and tired, later that same day.

"You have enjoyed the inexpressible pleasure of meeting with dear friends and relations after so long a separation," he wrote to Buckner. "I found all my father's family well, and anxiously expecting me home. All my friends of both town and country gave me a most hearty reception, such an [*sic*] one as gratified me very much."16

The uniformed cadet who stood before them had attained his adult height of five feet, eight inches and stood with painfully erect posture, so straight that his back was practically bowed. He filled his uniform as if he were born to be a soldier. Physically, he strongly resembled his father: the same high forehead, aristocratic brow, the same dark eyes and thick brown hair. Even the shape of the ears was the same. The gathered family may have noticed, however, a subtle haughtiness in their young relative, a nascent air of superiority that would only grow through the years and which was based on the undeniable fact that he had endured hardships and met a standard that they had not. They were civilians, and though they were his blood, they were no longer quite his equals.

If his family expected him to stay at home and visit with them, they were quickly disappointed. .The next two months were a whirl of barbecues and dances in Munfordville, Greensburg, Glasgow, and Bowling Green. As always, he took special notice of the girls, referring to them as "the bewitching fairness" and assuring Buckner, "None of the handsome ladies I have seen have been able as yet to seduce me into ... love."17

That changed for the outwardly cool and debonair young man during the middle of July. On August 1, while eating a yellow apple — and wishing that they had such good fruit at West Point — he wrote a letter to Buckner in which he announced, "A fair lady from the sunny south, who has been at our house for some time on a visit to my [half] sister, has completely entrapped me in love's silken meshes. She left us on last Wednesday for home and it is somewhat in 'dubio' whether I will come North or go South about the last of this month." Surely, Wood did not mean that he was seriously considering giving up his appointment. Probably, he quickly cooled off and proceeded directly to West Point. Still, he might have gone to see her. If Wood did make a trip south to visit with his "fair lady," it must by necessity have been a flying trip, for he reported back about the first of September for his final two years at West Point.18

The next two years passed with the now-familiar patterns of cadet life. In the spring of 1845 Wood passed his final examinations before the Board of Visitors, and on July 1 he graduated fifth in his class. It was not a particularly distinguished class, but there were a handful of names that would earn a place in the history books. Wood saw proceed across the stage to accept a diploma Cadet Bernard Bee, who would give Thomas J. Jackson his immortal nickname of "Stonewall" at First Manassas and who would die there from a Yankee bullet moments later. There was steely-eyed Louis Hébert, another classmate who would renounce his oath to defend the Constitution and lead his Confederates against the Federal forces in Missouri, Arkansas, and Mississippi. There was Gordon Granger, one of the future heroes of the Battle of Chickamauga, who would serve in the Army of the Cumberland as Wood's superior. And here were the two Smiths: William Farrar ("Old Baldy") Smith, who graduated fourth in the Class of 1845, one notch above Wood, and who would help break the Confederate siege of Chattanooga in 1863. The other Smith, Edmund Kirby Smith, would someday wear the collar stars of a Confederate general, lead an infamous invasion of Kentucky, and end the war in command of the vast Department of the Trans-Mississippi. Now Fitz John Porter was crossing the stage. He would be called "the most magnificent soldier in the Army of the Potomac" in 1862—and would be court-martialed and dismissed from the army in 1863. Fortunes could change in an instant, but that possibility was not in the thinking of the graduating cadets today. On this day they were on the top of the world and ready to go out and conquer.[19]

At last, the name Thomas John Wood was called. This was the great moment of his young life. He had scaled the heights to do more than succeed at the military academy; he had excelled. He had his diploma, a commission as brevet second lieutenant, U.S. Topographical Engineers, and he had a circle of friends and contacts who would figure into his career for as long as he served and in his life for as long as he lived. With them, he had been fully immersed in the West Point experience and had been reborn with a new outlook on life. It was called the "West Point attitude," and as explained by historian Stephen Ambrose, its components were a "cool contempt for civilians, especially civilian soldiers, and an exalted view of the United States Army and its officers."[20]

Traditionally, the new West Point graduates were given a three-month furlough in which to go home, there to wait for further orders. Wood was offered the choice to return to Munfordville (and the last chance he would probably ever have for an extended visit with his family) or to go to Texas, where he would be assigned to General Zachary Taylor's staff. Wood chose Texas. He lingered at West Point for a few weeks, perhaps helping with the summer encampment, and then he left the Hudson for a duty along a new river, the Nueces in South Texas, and the beginning of his life as a professional soldier.

Chapter 2

Mexico

In September 1845, Lieutenant Thomas J. Wood reported to General Zachary Taylor, whose army was assembling at Corpus Christi, Texas. It was an exciting first assignment for Wood. Trouble was brewing with Mexico and General Taylor was in command of the American forces on the border. Traveling with Wood was Lieutenant George G. Meade, another army engineer.

Lieutenants Wood and Meade stowed their gear in the tent that they would share, then reported to General Taylor's headquarters. They saw before them an unpretentious man with a face as tan and wrinkled as a tobacco leaf. Wood and Meade might have been West Point neat in their striped trousers and frock coats with the shoulder straps and brass buttons, but their commanding general was disheveled, with hair like a haystack and dressed in a blue-checked gingham coat and blue overalls. They would become used to seeing him poking around camp in a straw-brimmed farmer's hat or in an even broader-brimmed Mexican sombrero, the living, breathing personification of the cliché that looks could be deceiving, for Taylor was a soldier.

Taylor was unflappable, alert, sincere in his concern for the well-being of his men, and if he was ignorant of the finer theoretical points of military science, such as might be learned in the lecture halls of West Point, he was steeped in common sense and in the practical aspects of army command. He was also stubborn. It was told that a woman asked one of Taylor's troopers, "Is the general a Christian?"

The soldier answered, "I don't know, but if he makes up his mind to go to heaven, all hell cannot keep him out."[1]

Thomas J. Wood might have done worse in acquiring his first field experience under a general like Zachary Taylor.

Four days after their arrival at Corpus Christi, General Taylor handed the engineers their first assignment. Captain Thomas J. Cram and Lieutenants Wood and Meade were ordered to make a scouting expedition up the Nueces River to San Patricio. Wood grew sick on the second day and returned to

Taylor's camp. The others ascended the sluggish Nueces in Mackinaw boats with a guard of thirty infantrymen and two officers. They found that all was quiet at San Patricio; in fact, the village was completely deserted, so they turned around and were soon back in Taylor's peaceful camp.

The illness that Wood suffered on the second day of the reconnaissance to San Patricio developed into a violent fever, and sometime before the second week in November he left the army on sick leave. He recuperated at his father's home in Munfordville and did not return to the army until April 9, 1846.

When orders came in late January 1846 for the army to move south to the Rio Grande, the roads were so mushy from the winter rains that it was impossible to comply. Weeks passed before General Taylor could begin to advance. On March 9, 1846, the army of thirty-eight hundred moved out. Along the route, wildflowers bloomed. Songbirds filled the mesquite thickets and the soldiers caught glimpses of wild mustangs and antelope dashing across the plain. James Longstreet, who would go on to become a corps commander in Robert E. Lee's Army of Northern Virginia, was a young lieutenant on the march south and he recalled in his autobiography, "The army was well instructed, under good discipline, and fully prepared for field work, the weather was fine, and the firm turf of the undulating prairie made the march easy."[2]

Naturally, the Americans could not expect to move south unopposed. Wood's old roommate Lieutenant U. S. Grant remembered that when the enemy was found blocking the way at the Arroyo Colorado there was a council between General Taylor and the unnamed Mexican commander. The Mexican warned that he was obliged to obey his orders to keep the Americans on their own side of the Colorado and that if they attempted to cross he would fire upon them. Taylor replied that he was going to cross in fifteen minutes; if the Mexicans tried to oppose him, he would give them all the fight they wanted. Convinced that Taylor was not bluffing, the Mexicans fell back and offered no more trouble.

On March 24, the American column struck the road that ran between Point Isabel and Matamoros. The army turned west, led by General William J. Worth, while General Taylor, with his staff and escort, turned east toward the coast. Their goal was the port of Point Isabel, a few miles north of the mouth of the Rio Grande. The town itself was on a small bluff, prominent in that flat land, and consisted of a customs house and a small residential community of houses made of "twined reeds, timber from wrecked ships, and grass thatching." Here Taylor would make his forward supply base.[3]

Upon their arrival, Taylor ordered the construction of defensive works and storage sheds for the perishables that were being ferried ashore from supply ships. Then "Old Rough and Ready" rode hard to rejoin the bulk of his army, now approaching a spot on the north bank of the Rio Grande opposite Mata-

General Zachary Taylor (Library of Congress).

moros. There they set up a camp in an open square, wagons in the middle, and a band played while the national flag was hoisted. Alerted that their enemies had arrived, the Mexicans in Matamoros began to erect defensive works that night.

The next day, Taylor's soldiers commenced work on an earthen fort that they named Fort Texas. U. S. Grant remembered, "The fort was laid out by the engineers, but the work was done by the soldiers under the supervision of their officers, the chief engineer retaining general direction." When the fort was finished, it was commodious enough for five regiments. There were five walls, nine feet high, and on each corner were gaping gun emplacements, ready for action when the big guns came up the dusty trail from Point Isabel on the fifth of April. The cannon were a welcome sight, for the situation was becoming more tense. There had been a few shooting incidents.[4]

On April 11, the Mexican garrison in Matamoros was reinforced by two hundred men under General Pedro de Ampudia. The Americans heard the bells of Matamoros ringing, soon followed by the roar of two hundred guns firing in salute and the strains of martial music. A day later, Ampudia signaled that he wanted a parley. His representatives were shown to Taylor's headquarters, where they presented a flowery demand for the Americans to withdraw within twenty-four hours. Refusal to comply would mean war.

General Taylor countered that he would answer the next morning. He kept his word, but it was not to Ampudia's liking. Taylor said he was under orders to occupy this ground and he could not, as a soldier, disobey the directives of his commander in chief, President James K. Polk.

Ampudia wasted no time in sending patrols across the river. Taylor responded by sending out patrols of his own to keep an eye on them. During the third week in April, a clash between Mexican lancers under Anastasio Torrejón and sixty-five American cavalrymen under Captain Seth Thornton at Rancho Carricitos resulted in an American defeat. Sixteen Americans were killed and the rest, several of them wounded, were captured and marched back to Matamoros.

Taylor reported to President Polk that the war had begun and called for volunteers from Texas and Louisiana to come join him. Meanwhile, more Mexican patrols crossed the Rio Grande, aiming to cut the American supply line.

Anxious about the situation and needing absolutely to protect his lifeline from the coast, Taylor decided to move his army back down the trail to Point Isabel. He left Major Jacob Brown and the 7th Infantry to garrison Fort Texas while he and the rest of the army returned to the bustling supply base that had grown up on the site of the formerly sleepy port. If Major Brown became besieged, he should signal by firing his 18-pounders.

Taylor moved out on at 4:00 A.M. on May 1. Forced marches brought the general and his army to the coast the next day, without having seen any of the enemy along the way.

On the morning of May 3, the men at Point Isabel heard a distant thunder competing with the crashing breakers of the coast; it was the 18-pounders from Fort Texas. Major Brown was signaling that he was besieged. The faint roar continued all day. Major Brown was holding his own for the time being, but the men knew that they would soon be marching again, upstream this time, to the relief of Fort Texas.

However, they did not march as soon as they expected. Taylor knew he must perfect his defenses at Point Isabel and was waiting for reinforcements before turning west again. Besides, he had confidence in Major Brown and in the solid fort his engineers had designed. The American cannon at Fort Texas continued to sound all day on the fourth and for the next three days. It was on the afternoon of May 7 that Taylor ordered his army to step off for the relief of Fort Texas. Lieutenant Thomas J. Wood was with them again, having returned from his long sick leave on April 9.

Taylor's army made seven miles before going into bivouac. The next morning, they had not gone far when they saw the Mexicans arrayed for battle across the road a mile ahead of them. Behind the enemy was a stand of tall mesquite trees that gave this place its name, Palo Alto ("Tall Trees"). Where the Americans stopped there was only spiny, sharp-pointed grass, standing as high as the men's shoulders.

Taylor ordered his men to go fill their canteens from some of the many water-filled depressions that dotted the landscape and marked where the Rio Grande had once flowed. Then he began to deploy for battle. He had brought some extra muscle with him from Point Isabel — two 18-pounders under the supervision of Lieutenant Wood. As Wood recalled it, "I had been detailed by General Taylor to bring up the heavy guns from Point Isabel, and it had been found necessary to use oxen for that purpose, four yoke to a gun, and it was with great difficulty that we brought our ox guns into action."[5]

Wood and the other West Pointers advised Taylor to place his 18-pounders in the center of the line and to load them with canister. At the same time, two infantry regiments and Major Samuel Ringgold's battery of light artillery (called "flying artillery" for its mobility) deployed on the right and two more infantry regiments and a battery of field artillery went into position on the left. Two squadrons of dragoons protected the train of 270 wagons.

A brief period of waiting followed. Then came the order to advance. The Mexican guns opened fire. For the young West Pointers, this introduction into hostile fire must have been unnerving at first, but they soon saw that they were still out of range of the enemy guns and that there was no danger. The enemy's balls fell short, and though they rolled toward the American ranks, the path they took through the high grass was easily seen and the men simply stepped out of their way. The wind was in the Americans' favor and blew the cannon smoke back into the faces of the Mexicans.

When the Americans came into range, they unlimbered their own guns and began returning fire. At the end of an hour, eight hundred of General Torrejón's lancers charged down around the American right flank in an attempt to turn it and to get to the supply wagons behind. The 5th Infantry moved out to blunt the Mexican charge while Lieutenant Randolph Ridgely's two-gun section of Ringgold's flying battery moved up and began blasting them. The

Mexicans fell back, but they were brave and tried at least twice more to cut their way to the wagons before they fell back for good. The American right and center crept forward. General Mariano Arista adjusted his lines accordingly.

When the Mexican left fell back, Taylor threw his dragoons into action. Captain Charles May's horsemen charged forward, were met with a devastating fire from the Mexican fieldpieces, and had to retire. American light artillery responded to the Mexican gunners, who recoiled before they rallied and advanced with infantry support. They were stopped by the Americans' blazing cannon.

As the sun began to sink low in the sky and the tall grass burned, the battle raged on. In the hazy gloom, a ball from one of the Mexican fieldpieces ripped through Major Ringgold's upper legs. Thomas J. Wood remembered that Ringgold "was moving immediately in the rear of my [artillery] section with his light battery when a cannon ball passing directly over my guns struck him, killing his horse and mortally wounding the major." In 1902, Wood inaccurately remembered that Ringgold was the first man he ever saw killed in action. Ringgold did die of his wounds, but not until several days later, in Point Isabel.[6]

The sun was lower now. The Mexican cavalry made two late and unsuccessful attempts to turn the American left flank. The American cannon and musket fire from the infantrymen reversed each charge. About 7:00 P.M., the Mexicans withdrew and the Battle of Palo Alto ended.

Lieutenant Wood's role in his first battle had been an important one. He had skillfully delivered the heavy guns to the scene and stayed to help man them when the fighting started. He had been under enemy fire and he had not quailed. Cadmus M. Wilcox wrote in his history of the Mexican War, "The two 18-pounders under Lieutenants [William H.] Churchill and Thomas J. Wood, the latter of the topographical engineers, were well served; their superior weight and greater range overmatched any guns of the Mexican and were a complete surprise to them." That opinion of Wood's performance endured into the twentieth century. The West Point Association of Graduates in 1904 called Wood's conduct "admirable."[7]

The next morning, May 9, the Americans found that the Mexicans had fallen back during the night. Beyond Palo Alto was a heavy mass of chaparral. The road leading through it was a good place for an ambush, but the army had no choice; they had to get through to Fort Texas. A scouting party of three hundred men found the Mexicans drawn up for battle three miles ahead at a place called Resaca de la Palma, another series of depressions where the Rio Grande had once flowed. The road ran between them, and General Arista's cannon were trained on it. The Mexicans had strengthened their position with a barricade of dead trees and chaparral. The scouts advanced until they drew enemy fire, and then reported their findings back to Taylor.

General Taylor ordered his officers to ready their troops to move forward. The wagon train was parked and a battery of light artillery plus the two 18-pounders were detailed to defend it. The rest of the army advanced across the gruesome battlefield of the day before to where the scouting party had drawn fire. Taylor ordered Lieutenant Randolph Ridgely, Ringgold's successor, to shove his light battery straight up the road while the infantry advanced as best they could through the thorny underbrush and palm trees that hemmed the road. Three hundred feet in front of the Mexican line, Ridgely's guns stopped and began pumping rounds into the enemy. The Mexican gun crews responded in kind. On the left of the road the 5th U.S. Infantry painfully crept forward through the undergrowth while the 4th tried to do the same on the right.

The Mexican artillery crews did little damage to the infantry creeping up on their flanks, but they were really punishing Ridgely's fieldpieces. To quiet the enemy guns, General Taylor ordered Captain Charles May's dragoons to dash forward and capture them — simple as that.

Ridgely's battery threw a few more salvos at the Mexicans (and thus distracted the enemy and drew the fire that might otherwise have been poured down on the dragoons) and then May's horsemen charged, sabers drawn, and rode completely through the enemy position. Their frightened horses had galloped out of control and did not respond to the men sawing at the reins. The Mexican gunners scattered and then quickly regrouped, while May and his men tried to turn their mounts. Thomas J. Wood, who probably did not see the charge but heard about it, called it a "very brilliant cavalry charge."[8]

General Taylor, who was watching, did not consider it brilliant. He was unhappy with the result of May's charge. "Take those guns and by God keep them!" he yelled.[9]

As the horse soldiers got turned, the 5th Infantry burst from the chaparral on the American left. The combined infantry and cavalry attack crashed into the Mexican gun crews and their infantry support. Furious hand-to-hand fighting ensued. Bayonets and sabers flashed. This was the pivotal moment of the battle. The Americans seized nine enemy guns and turned them, blasting the Mexicans with their own ammunition. The Mexican center began to sag. In a moment it collapsed, their flanks crumbled, and suddenly the entire Mexican line was running away with the Americans hot on their heels, all the way to the Rio Grande.

The Battle of Resaca de la Palma was over. The Americans had lost thirty-three dead and eighty-nine wounded. The number of Mexican casualties is disputed. The number of enemy killed, wounded, and missing may have been as high at twelve hundred. One of the captured was General R. D. de la Vega, who was made prisoner during Captain Charles May's comic-heroic charge. For May, it was a fortunate, though thoroughly unintended, outcome, and he was promoted to lieutenant colonel for it.

Any jubilation that the Americans felt over their two victories over the Mexicans was dampened that afternoon when they reached Fort Texas. There they learned that Major Brown had been wounded in the leg by enemy artillery fire on May 6. He lingered for several days, only to die on the morning of May 9, just before the arrival of the army that had been coming to his relief. The soldiers honored their fallen major when they retired the name Fort Texas and rechristened the battered earthen works Fort Brown.

General Taylor became a national hero on account of his victories at Palo Alto and Resaca de la Palma. He was promoted to major general, but the glitter of braid and gold stars did not tempt him any more than it had before. He remained the same plain and essentially decent man. He moved his army across the Rio Grande to Matamoros and warned his soldiers that there would be no pillaging among the citizens of the town.

The daily life of the town was disrupted as little as possible. The civil and religious authorities were permitted to go about their business as usual. Naturally, it was impossible for the American army not to inconvenience the citizens of Matamoros, entirely. The hospital for the American wounded was established in the town and filled the narrow streets with putrid odors.

The soldiers bivouacked on the outskirts of the town near the four tents where Taylor and his staff made their headquarters. The men drilled and performed picket duty, and the dragoons patrolled the country to the south where the Mexican army had gone. The men drew their rations of beans and weevily bread, which they supplemented by fresh shrimp seined from the Rio Grande and (against orders) Mexican cattle, which they obtained in the time-proven method of occupying armies.

Taylor had won his battles with an army of regulars. Now great numbers of one-year volunteers from the states began to reach Matamoros. He kept some troops at Fort Brown across the river and shuffled others to the upstream villages of Reynosa and Mier, but the bulk of the greenhorns settled into camps around Taylor's headquarters. Eventually, there were twenty thousand men in Taylor's army. With such a large percentage of them being poorly trained one-year men, there was bound to be an increase in the number of ugly incidents. The men fought among themselves, and they were abusive toward the Mexicans. Taking a few head of cattle and some fence posts for campfires was one thing, but with the arrival of the volunteers there were incidents of outright stealing and even a few murders. The volunteers' officers, who were elected by the troops, had little control. Taylor tried to impose discipline on the bored men in camp, knowing all along that the real remedy was to go into action.

Taylor had been ordered to carry the war into the Mexican interior. Not wanting to advance south through the desolate lands described by his scouts, Taylor decided to move upstream by means of a small fleet of paddle wheelers.

The Mexican War, 1846–1848 (map by the author).

By the end of the first week in July, a sufficient number of steamboats had been gathered, and the army began to evacuate Matamoros. Their destination was Camargo, 250 miles up the Rio Grande near the mouth of the San Juan River. By water, the trip took about a week, but not all of the soldiers traveled by boat. Some regiments marched up the south bank of the Rio Grande. Lieutenant Thomas J. Wood was one of these overlanders; he marched out on July 6 with some companies of the 7th U.S. Infantry led by Captain Dixon S. Miles. The 150-mile land route from Matamoros to Camargo was far more difficult than the river route. Some of the low-lying land was swampy from recent rains, the mosquitoes were a torment, and the summer heat was murderous. Many fell sick; one corporal actually died of sunstroke. For six days, Miles' detachment of the 7th struggled over this unfriendly line of march, but their agonies were cut short when the steamboat *Enterprise* picked them up at Reynosa. Other regiments and parts of regiments marched the entire distance.

Camargo became notorious as a "yawning graveyard." It was heavily overlaid with mud from recent floods that became a suffocating dust when it dried. There were intermittent heavy rains and days of blinding sun when the temperatures climbed to 120°. The air was filled with stinging insects and the ground was alive with tarantulas and biting ants. Then there was the river. The San Juan became an open sewer, as well as the main source of water used by the volunteers and regulars. Debilitating sickness began to rage among the camps. One-third of Taylor's army was brought down by diseases; fifteen hundred of them died.[10]

Still more regiments continued to arrive at Camargo. As they did, Thomas J. Wood and other members of Taylor's staff directed them to their assigned campsites. Wood's other duties were of more importance than directing traffic. While Taylor contemplated his next move, Captain James Duncan and Lieutenant Wood, along with an escort of Texas Rangers, went out a reconnaissance mission to spy out the country and select the best route. Based on their report, Taylor decided upon a Mier–Cerralvo–Marin advance on Monterrey.

Beginning September 5, Taylor's army pushed off from Camargo for the campaign against Monterrey. General Anastasio Torrejón and a thousand Mexican dragoons were keeping a close watch on them but made no serious attempt to impede their march. On September 19, Taylor's men were at Walnut Springs, only three miles northeast of Monterrey.

The Mexicans had used their time well during the lull after Resaca de la Palma to improve upon Monterrey's natural setting and erect the most formidable works Taylor faced during the entire war. In fact, as one who had mostly fought Indians on the frontiers of the Old Northwest and Florida, he had never faced such a challenge. South of Monterrey were mountains and a river. To the east there were three defensive works commanding the approaches to a bridge into the city. On the west were two steep and heavily defended hills. They protected the road to Saltillo, as well as Monterrey's western neighborhoods. On the north was a bastion called the Black Fort. It was actually a cathedral, never completed and bristling now with eight cannon and the bayonets of four hundred infantrymen. It stood on a wide plain that offered little or no cover to attackers. And since Monterrey was yet another flat-roofed town, its defenders had even been able to make the city center almost impregnable. They had converted the rooftops into gun platforms, snipers' nests, and small, square forts for infantry. On top of all this, the Mexican soldiers, who were commanded by General Pedro de Ampudia, outnumbered Taylor's small army two to one.

One would like to know what Lieutenant Wood thought as he, an engineer, looked at Monterrey's defenses. Sadly, very few of Wood's papers seem to have survived, even into the generation that succeeded him. In 1935, his oldest son, George H. Wood, wrote to Professor A. M. Stickles, "Unfortunately, I have no papers of my father's very far back." He gave no suggestion as to where Stickles might find the papers he needed for his research into the life of Simon Bolivar Buckner. The natural presumption is that the elder Wood's papers and letters had been lost or destroyed. As he was then a shavetail, Thomas J. Wood's reports were considered of little importance, he seems to have had no steady girl to whom to write, none of the letters to his family are known to exist, and he did not write a late-life autobiography as did his friend U. S. Grant. Wood's entire remarks about the sight he saw before him on September 9, 1846, consist of one sentence in an address he gave at the centennial of the U.S. Military Academy in 1902, when he was one of the last surviving West Point graduates who had fought in the war. Of the defenses of Monterrey,

Wood said, "The city had been very strongly fortified by the Mexicans and their position was most formidable."[11]

Monterrey was a sight to see, and as General Taylor looked one of the Mexicans' new British 12-pounders barked from inside the Black Fort and threw a ball at the Americans. The ball bounced and rolled right toward the little knot of officers around Taylor. Some say that it stopped practically at the toe of Taylor's boots, while others claim that the ball bounded over the general's head. In any case, the ball missed the general by mere inches. Those who recounted the incident might have disagreed on the cannonball's trajectory, but they all agreed on Taylor's reaction to it: The general was unperturbed. He simply ordered his staff to set up the headquarters tents under some shade trees a bit farther back while he considered the challenge of attacking a fortified position.

The engineers' reconnaissance reports were discouraging. The defenses were too elaborate and Taylor's army too small to pierce through to the heart of the city in one attempt. The general decided on a two-phase assault. On the first day, Taylor would divide his forces. Two thousand men led by his fellow Kentuckian General William J. Worth would attack Federación, the first of the two well-defended hills west of Monterrey. Meanwhile, Taylor would make a demonstration against the Black Fort from the north and the east with the divisions of General David E. Twiggs and General William O. Butler. Phase Two would begin on the following day, when Worth would take the second hill, Independencia, and then his and Taylor's forces would converge on the Mexicans from the west and from the northeast and crush them.

Worth's advance began on the afternoon of September 20. He and his men moved seven miles, swatting aside a Mexican patrol en route, and settled down in the rain to wait for the next morning's assault. That same night, Taylor eased an artillery battery closer to the Black Fort. The gunners were supported by the 1st Kentucky Volunteers, led by Colonel Stephen Ormsby.

On September 21, Worth threw forward the Texas Rangers, the 5th and 7th U.S. Infantry, and a battery of artillery. They took the first of the two hills as planned, but Taylor, on the east, was not so successful. Colonel John Garland's men — the 1st and 3rd U.S. Infantry plus a battalion of volunteers — plunged forward and were caught in a withering fire. Taylor ordered the 4th Infantry into action. They charged only to be forced back, one-third of them killed or wounded, according to the best estimate of U. S. Grant. A third charge involving fragments of the battered 1st Infantry and volunteer troops from Tennessee and Ohio finally broke a hole in the Mexican resistance on the east, and the Americans gained a frail lodgment on the edge of Monterrey.

Before dawn the next day, General Worth roused his men for their assault on Independencia, the second of the two hills. It was still raining as the Americans advanced toward the Mexican lines just below the crest. They pushed the enemy back to the center of their defense, a fort called the Bishop's Palace. A 12-pounder began to chew up the walls of the fort while the infantry charged forward. The Mexican defenders, caught in a lethal fire outside, began to scale those same battered walls, seeking safety inside. There was no safety inside, for the Americans followed them, bayoneting the enemy gun crews and forcing all who were not killed, wounded, or captured to abandon the fort altogether and race down the far side of the hill. Independencia was won.

Taylor's columns on the east merely traded some fire with the Mexicans on September 22, nothing more. Since they were not heavily engaged, they had the opportunity to watch the spectacle of Worth's troops advancing up the side of Independencia in the rain. They marked the distant division's progress by the puffs of smoke from the muzzles of their muskets. Worth's victory benefited his audience, the soldiers on the east. The Mexican general Ampudia pulled his troops away from the Black Fort, back into the city's interior defenses. Here would be the third day's fight.

On September 23, the Mexicans in Monterrey's center were in a good position to keep the Americans back. Crouching behind sandbags on the flat roofs of the buildings lining the main streets, they made a poor target, and from their positions of relative safety they poured blasts of canister and a sleet of whistling, ricocheting lead slugs on the Americans below.

Taylor's men crept forward from the north and the east while General Worth's victorious soldiers from the previous day's fight on the west applied pressure from that direction. These latter soldiers came through the buildings, room to room and house to house, digging their way through the soft walls unseen, until they were within a block of the plaza. Beyond here, accounts of the final hours of September 23 are a contradictory mess. Some claim that, near dusk, a white flag, then another, appeared among the Mexicans. The plaza was filled with civilians, the city's citizens who had been driven into the center by the fighting in their streets. The rifle fire sputtered to a close and the fighting for control of Monterrey came to an end, aside from an American mortar firing from the cemetery. Others claim that the house-to-house fighting continued until nightfall and resumed in the morning.

The answer to this dilemma seems to be that the situation differed from one street to the next. General Worth kept his division in place near the plaza through the night. The scrappy Texas Rangers fought longer on the twenty-third than did the other units and eagerly resumed killing Mexicans in the morning. Conversely, the fighting did end for General Taylor's troops on the twenty-third, for "Old Rough and Ready" pulled back his troops from the perimeter of the plaza. Taylor was feeling cautious. Urban warfare was a new experience for him, and he wanted a chance to confer with General Worth about how to coordinate the final assault.

Accounts also differ as to exactly when the Mexicans sued for peace. However, it appears that sometime before midnight the Mexican decided to negotiate a surrender. Early the next morning, September 24, General Ampudia formally opened communications with General Taylor. Commissioners were appointed to represent each side, and they drew up a document of surrender that included among its provisions an eight-week armistice and permission for the Mexicans to march out of Monterrey with their weapons and one artillery battery. The terms were considered by some to be overly generous, but the Americans got something in return: they could avoid the terrible loss of life that would inevitably result in a fight for Monterrey's plaza, the last enemy stronghold.

Finally, the number of American casualties is not agreed upon. Some say that the number of killed, wounded, and missing amounted to fewer than 550 over the three days of fighting. Others just as confidently put the tally at just shy of one thousand.

The one fact that seems indisputable is that the Battle for Monterrey was an impressive American victory. General Worth's message of congratulations to his division said that their victories at Federación and Independencia and their subsequent generosity to their foes "bear comparison with the proudest achievements that grace the annals of their country."[12]

In Orders No. 123, General Taylor congratulated his Army of Occupation on "another signal victory." He added, "Superior to us in numbers, strongly fortified, and with an immense preponderance of artillery, they have been driven from point to point until forced to sue for terms of capitulation. Such terms have been granted as were considered due to the gallant defense of the town and the liberal policy of our own government."[13]

If Taylor sounded a bit defensive at the explanation of why he granted terms to Ampudia, he had reason to. President Polk in Washington was livid that a truce had been granted the Mexicans. The war was already dragging on too long. He sent word to Taylor that the eight-week truce must be canceled at once, but by the time the president's order reached Taylor seven weeks had passed, so there was no great loss of face for the general.

President Polk had experienced a small change of heart regarding General Taylor. Polk, a Democrat, knew that he was witnessing the rise of a competitor. The talk of putting Taylor forward as the Whig Party presidential candidate in 1848 was on everyone's lips and in all of the papers. Taylor was more popular than ever before, following the victory at Monterrey. Polk could not diminish Taylor, but he could divide the Whigs by offering up to them a second hero. Consequently, he sent General Winfield Scott to invade Mexico from the Gulf Coast and bring pressure to bear against Mexico City. Taylor would be left with only about seven thousand men, most of them volunteers. Scott ordered Taylor to draw his troops back from the Saltillo area and to concentrate around Monterrey.

Taylor could tell when he was being undercut by a treacherous administration and a general with political aspirations, and it stirred in him a certain defiance. He could not prevent Scott from cannibalizing his army, but neither did he have to fester in Monterrey. Deciding that Scott's order was a mere suggestion, he led about forty-six hundred of his remaining troops to Saltillo and then proceeded another eighteen miles south to a hacienda called Agua Nueva.

Farther south, General Antonio López de Santa Anna, the new president of Mexico, learned by a captured dispatch what was going on. Scott had stripped Taylor's army and was planning to invade Santa Anna's country from Veracruz. He perceived an opportunity. Ignoring Scott for the moment, he could race north and win a quick victory against the reduced force of "Old Rough and Ready." Santa Anna felt confident, and reasonably so, considering his numerical advantage of three to one.

Learning that the Mexican army was on its way, General Taylor dispatched scouting parties to ride out and locate them. One group was a company of Texas Rangers under Ben McCulloch. Another was led by Lieutenant Colonel Charles May, whose wild cavalry charge at Resaca de la Palma had won him a promotion and made him a near legend. He looked the part, with his long dark hair and beard. May was ordered to take four hundred men and a section of artillery toward San Luis Potosí. One of May's four hundred was Lieutenant Thomas J. Wood. Wood believed that the chance for promotion would be greater for a horse soldier than for a staff officer, so at his own request, he had transferred from Taylor's staff to the 2nd Dragoons on October 19. Since then, he had spent long hours in the saddle on scouting expeditions and on escort duty, but this mission to locate the Mexicans as a prelude to battle offered more chance for glory than any since he had joined the mounted arm.

McCulloch's and May's reconnaissance parties rode out of Agua Nueva on February 20 and traveled together until they reached a fork in the road about four miles out. There they separated.

May's men rode another twenty-five miles to a ranch called La Hedionda. They saw no sign of the enemy until they reached the ranch, where they observed the smoke of signal fires rising from the tops of the surrounding hills. Whoever it was they were signaling must be nearby. May scanned the valley through his spyglass and saw a column of dust in the east. It was perhaps ten miles out.

May ordered Lieutenant Wood and a dozen dragoons to ride in that direction and try to lure the enemy into an attack. Two men were sent to the ridge crest north of the ranch to make visual contact with the distant riders. The rest of the command were ordered to barricade the hacienda's buildings and place the fieldpieces.

By nightfall, Lieutenant Wood still had not returned, and the two spies sent to the ridgetop had not reported back — gunshots from that direction indicated that they had run into trouble (it later turned out that they had been captured). When an unsuspecting vaquero appeared at the hacienda, the rough Americans jumped out and took him captive. He was no patriot. He readily confided that Santa Anna was at La Encarnación with his army.

May had all the intelligence he needed, and dreading the possibility of being captured, he decided to ride back immediately to General Taylor with his information. Wood's patrol was left to its own devices. For all May knew, they were already Santa Anna's prisoners.

May and his men reached Taylor's camp at dawn on February 21 and, barely escaping injury by the musket fire of the camp's jumpy pickets, made their way to the general's headquarters. The morning was chilly and they found Taylor warming himself by a fire. He was a little perturbed by the rifle fire that had alarmed the camp. He looked up at May and said, "Doggone them pickets, I knew it was you that was coming."[14]

At about the same time that May arrived, two other groups of riders cantered into camp. One was Lieutenant Wood and his men. Wood had nothing to report except that his party had failed to make contact with the enemy, had missed La Hedionda in the dark, and had ridden directly back to headquarters. The other group was led by Lieutenant Fielding Alston of McCulloch's Texas Rangers. Alston reported that McCulloch had stayed behind to gather more information. He had actually seen the Mexicans at Encarnación, and they were about to move north. In fact, the Mexicans were nearer than anyone supposed. As May, Taylor, and Alston finished their reports to Taylor, forward elements of José Vincente Miñon's cavalry came into sight.

Taylor hurriedly prepared his army to fall back to La Angostura, a narrow pass in the hills five miles south of Buena Vista. The only road north ran through it. The enemy would have to come this way and this was the place to make a stand, but Taylor would not design the defense himself. For that, he turned to General John E. Wool.

Having given Wool his assignment, Taylor rode to Saltillo to help Major William B. Warren's garrison prepare the defenses there. Taylor took with him some artillery, Jefferson Davis' Mississippi regiment, and Lieutenant Colonel May's dragoons.

Taylor returned to La Angostura in time to receive from Santa Anna a demand for surrender, about noon on February 22. Santa Anna's appeal was flowery; Taylor's reply was blunt. As Thomas J. Wood recollected it, Taylor listened to the interpreter read Santa Anna's message and then "the old man, with his characteristic readiness and brusqueness, said: 'Tell him to go to hell.'" Santa Anna launched a small attack that lasted until dark, but it amounted to little. The real fight would come in the morning.[15]

General Wool had deployed his men to take best advantage of the broken country at La Angostura. Taylor later praised the line as one "of remarkable strength." The steep ridge on the west of the road (the American right flank) was occupied by the Captain Braxton Bragg's artillery. In the center of the road, Wool positioned Captain John Washington's artillery, supported by the 1st Illinois Volunteers. On the east of the road there were a series of ridges separated by deep ravines and overlooking the road. The jumbled ridges and ravines angled away from the road toward the southeast, as if the land had been raked by the claws of a gigantic paw. Along the crest of one of the broadest ridges, facing the road, Wool placed in line: the 2nd Illinois Volunteers reinforced by a company of Texas Rangers, the 2nd Kentucky Volunteers, and John Paul Jones O'Brien's artillery. The 1st Kentucky Cavalry and Archibald Yell's Arkansas Cavalry were on the left flank and slightly to the rear. Wool intended for the 2nd and 3rd Indiana Volunteers, the batteries of Captain Thomas W. Sherman and Captain Braxton Bragg, two squadrons of dragoons, and Colonel Jefferson Davis' Mississippi Rifles to be held in reserve.[16]

Taylor was satisfied with Wool's disposition of the troops, but he still felt uneasy about the defenses at Saltillo, especially since there were rumors that some of Santa Anna's cavalry was swinging around in that direction. So Taylor rode back that same night, taking with him those dragoons and Davis' Mississippians who had been held in reserve. Taylor was not at La Angostura when the battle began at dawn on the twenty-third.

In the dim light of the overcast morning, Santa Anna threw one of his divisions straight down the road toward Colonel Washington's artillery, which quickly blunted the force of the Mexican charge. At the same time, two Mexican divisions plus an artillery battery hit the American left flank. It was something of a surprise; the terrain was so rough in that direction that an attack was not expected, especially one that involved artillery pieces. The canister shot from those guns was soon ripping apart the left flank. Benjamin F. Scribner of the 3rd Indiana said that they "raked our flank with terrible effect ... the battery on our left galled us exceedingly."[17]

Lieutenant John Paul Jones O'Brien's battery was ordered to answer them. The 2nd Indiana Volunteers moved up alongside in support. Advancing under fire, they moved into position, unlimbered, and began firing back at the Mexicans. The fight on the left flank went on for about three hours before Colonel W. A. Bowles, commanding the 2nd Indiana, ordered his men to retreat. Order dissolved into disorder; the men of the 2nd Indiana fled the field despite the best efforts of their junior officers to rally them and did not stop until they got to Buena Vista. Worse, they took with them some of the Arkansas cavalry, the 2nd Illinois, and Sherman's battery. Lieutenant O'Brien soon discovered that he was fighting all alone. Unsupported by infantry, he ordered his gun crews to move their three pieces back, but the Mexicans' fire was killing his horses and he was able to save only two. The whole left flank was collapsing under the weight of the Mexican attack.

Zachary Taylor, along with the Mississippians and May's dragoons, was returning from Saltillo when he encountered men fleeing the battle. He snagged up all he could, added them to those he had with him, and galloped to the ridges where the Mexicans were still advancing. The Americans flew into the Mexicans, while Captain Bragg's artillery fired and the 2nd Kentucky plowed into their flank. As they moved toward the fight, the Kentuckians had to cross an intervening ravine. In the confusion it appeared to General Taylor that they were disordered and had lost their will to fight. Taylor shouted to his aide-de-camp Lieutenant Colonel Thomas L. Crittenden, "By God, Mr. Crittenden, this will not do—this is not the way for Kentuckians to behave themselves when called upon to make good a battle—it will not answer, sir."[18]

Soon, the Kentuckians were seen emerging from the ravine to advance against the Mexicans. They fired a deadly volley into them. Taylor saw that he had falsely accused the men of the 2nd Kentucky, and he stood up in his stirrups and yelled, "Hurrah for old Kentuck! That's the way to do it, give them hell, damn them!"[19]

Some men of the 1st Illinois joined in the counter-attack beside the 2nd Kentucky. The Mexican assault stalled, and the Americans began to regain some ground. Bragg's and Sherman's artillery were firing canister in both directions: to the front and also into those enemy troops that had swung around and were approaching from the rear. Taylor wrote that, at that same time, the Mississippi Rifles came under severe attack and the 3rd Indiana raced over to support them. The general wrote,

> The action was for a long time warmly sustained at that point—the enemy making several efforts both with infantry and cavalry against our line, and being always repulsed with heavy loss. I had placed all the regular cavalry and Captain Pike's squadron of Arkansas horse under the orders of Brevet Lieutenant-Colonel May, with directions to hold in check the enemy's column ... which was done in conjunction with the Kentucky and Arkansas cavalry....[20]

Anastasio Torrejón's lancers were not part of the action on the ridge. They had made a wide arc around the battle to make their own attack on the supply and baggage trains at Buena Vista. The 2nd Indiana Volunteers had finally ended their retreat there. Encouraged by Captain Lovell Harrison Rousseau and Major Willis A. Gorman (who had been trying to rally them since they abandoned O'Brien's artillery battery), they were ready to fight again. Taylor had realized what Torrejón was up to and had dispatched Lieutenant Colonel May with two fieldpieces of Sherman's artillery to join in the fight in the rear. The Hoosiers were able to repulse the lancers and save the trains before May arrived. Now they combined forces, along with some of Yell's Arkansans and the dragoons, to chase the retreating lancers back to the base of the hills upon which the main battle was raging. They trapped some of the Mexicans in a ravine and poured slaughter down upon them. Others of the enemy made their way through and rejoined the fight on top.

It appeared that the battle was winding down and Taylor recalled that he had

> left the plateau for a moment when I was recalled thither by a very heavy musketry fire. On regaining that position, I discovered that our infantry (Illinois and Second Kentucky) had engaged a greatly superior force of the enemy — evidently his reserve — and that they had been overwhelmed by numbers. The moment was most critical.... Captain Bragg, who had just arrived from the left, was ordered at once into battery. Without any infantry to support him, and at the imminent risk of losing his guns, this officer came rapidly into action, the Mexican line being but a few yards from the muzzle of his pieces. The first discharge of canister caused the enemy to hesitate; the second and third drove him back in disorder and saved the day.[21]

The infantry pressed the retreating Mexicans, the artillery continued to fire into them, and the Battle of Buena Vista came to an end. The Mexicans withdrew during the night, leaving at least five hundred behind; the Americans had lost 723 killed and wounded. Taylor had nearly been one of them; his coat had been pierced with bullet holes as he directed the battle from horseback. Twenty-three Americans were reported as missing.

Lieutenant Colonel May's contribution to the victory was acknowledged in Taylor's report when the general wrote, "The regular cavalry, under Lieutenant Colonel May, with which was associated Captain [Albert] Pike's squadron of Arkansas horse, rendered useful service in holding the enemy in check and in covering the batteries at several points."[22]

May, in his own report, recognized Lieutenant Thomas J. Wood. He wrote, "To my adjutant, Lieutenant Wood, my thanks are particularly due for the prompt manner in which he conveyed my orders and for the energy and zeal he displayed throughout the battle."[23]

It was a fitting climax to Wood's eighteen-month service with General Zachary Taylor.

Lieutenant Colonel May had been leading a mere detachment of the 2nd Dragoons at Buena Vista, a two-regiment squadron. Six weeks earlier, his other companies had followed orders to move to the mouth of the Rio Grande, there to join General Scott. They proceeded with him to Veracruz and fought through the campaign for Mexico City. May's squadron remained with General Taylor in Northern Mexico during the rest of the war. For these men, the fighting was over. Their job in the north was simply to escort supply trains from the coast to Saltillo. They ate dust while their former comrades won honors at Cerro Gordo, Contreras, Churubusco, and Chapultepec.

Lieutenant Thomas J. Wood, though, did get to Mexico City before it was all over. After the surrender of the capital, Wood was transferred to Winfield Scott's command and was assigned to escort U.S. diplomat Nicholas

Trist during the peace negations. The role Wood played was small, but he did at least get the chance to join Simon Bolivar Buckner, U. S. Grant, and other old friends in their enjoyment of one of the great cities of the world

With a population of three hundred thousand, Mexico City was the same size as New York, though much older and much more cultured. The volunteer soldiers, many of whom had never before traveled beyond the limits of their own counties or hometowns, were dazzled by its exotic beauty and its size. Far from home and weary of war, they were determined to enjoy the array of pleasant distractions that Mexico City offered. The soldiers indulged and overindulged their appetites for drinking, gambling, and whoring. They paid seamstresses to make for them new uniforms and wore their new outfits proudly to the bullfights (tickets 50¢). They made excursions out of the city, and they climbed the surrounding mountains.

While the soldiers frolicked, Nicholas Trist went to work in earnest. Only a few days after his preliminary negotiations began with the Mexicans, a letter postmarked Washington, D.C., was put into Trist's hands. Its contents must have made his knees weak — he was being recalled. President Polk was unhappy on a number of points, but he was especially incensed at a $10,000 bribe that Santa Anna had accepted as a down payment for peace talks after Cerro Gordo. The money might have been considered well spent, except that Santa Anna reneged and the peace negotiations never occurred. Polk was convinced that the Mexicans were unreliable and must be completely humbled on the field of battle before an agreement with them could ever be reached. He was ready for General Scott to resume the war.

Flabbergasted though he might be, Trist had a measure of self-confidence that served him well in situations such as this. That, plus the encouragement of the Mexican delegation, gave Trist all the courage he needed to sit down and write President Polk a sixty-five-page letter that boiled down to one idea: he declined to be recalled. He knew that it would take weeks for the letter to reach Washington, even longer for a reply to reach him, and by that time he felt that substantive things would have been decided. Still, time was limited and Trist knew that he must push hard. In that way, President Polk's annoying letter was useful, for it let the Mexicans know what to expect if peace talks broke down.

On November 24, 1847, Trist and the Mexican peace commissioners began their discussions. They continued until the end of the year. At any time, the next letter from Polk might be delivered. Trist upped the pressure and the Mexicans conceded. The terms were simple. Mexico gave up its northern half, and the United States paid Mexico $15 million and assumed its debts to American citizens. Also, the U.S./Mexican boundary would be the Rio Grande from the Gulf to New Mexico (specifically, to 32° north latitude) thence a thousand miles west to the Pacific Ocean. It was called the Treaty of Guadalupe Hidalgo in honor of the Mexico City suburb in which it was signed on February 2, 1848.

President Polk was livid that Trist had refused his recall, but when he saw the treaty and recognized that it gave the United States all that he had wanted he calmed down and duly presented the treaty to the U.S. Senate. The Senate ratified the treaty on March 10, 1848.

The army began to leave Mexico City in June 1848. As the last soldiers marched out, the man who lowered the American flag flying over the city was Thomas J. Wood's friend Simon Bolivar Buckner. Buckner had done well during the war. He had been promoted twice — once for his behavior at Churubusco, where he was wounded, and again for El Camino del Rey — and had gone from second lieutenant to captain.

The soldiers retraced their route to Veracruz on the Gulf, and on August 1, 1848, they sailed away from Mexico, victorious in the first American war fought on foreign soil.

The Mexican War was the most controversial in American history up to that time. The conflict of 1846–1848 tore deeply into American solidarity over an issue that broke along sectional lines: slavery. The nation was suffering the torture of a thousand cuts over the question of slavery, and once opened the wounds never seemed to heal before new ones were inflicted. The Mexican War was a victory and simultaneously was the newest, and one of the deepest, domestic injuries the United States had suffered. Northerners saw the war as a plot cooked up by a slave-owning president to extend the institution of slavery into the West. New England leaders such as the philosophers Ralph Waldo Emerson and Henry David Thoreau and the congressman John Quincy Adams were constant in their accusing criticism, and some Westerners joined their chorus of complaint. Meanwhile, Southern volunteers eagerly flocked to the army for patriotism, for the adventure, and undoubtedly for the very reason that Emerson, Adams and the others suspected.

Thoughtful men saw trouble growing out of the events of 1846–1848, and their fears were validated. Spokesmen for purely sectional interests would continue to saw away at the country's connecting tissues, until, twelve years later, the country was dismembered.

Thomas J. Wood was untroubled by the future. The young professional only saw that the war had been a practical and successful application of the military sciences. The challenges had been met and overcome, and the victor had won great and significant spoils. Even as late as 1902, when he was speaking at West Point, Wood's evaluation of the war was seen in these cheerful and simplistic terms. He said that the Mexican War

> entirely changed the destiny of the United States. Geographically, in the first place, for the great acquisition of territory of the United States through this

war extended from the western frontier of Texas to the Pacific and embraced New Mexico, Colorado, Utah, and California with its grand coast line from Lower California to the Southern boundary of Oregon; indeed such a vast area of territory was acquired that it requires a brilliant imagination to comprehend its dimensions. The Pacific Ocean with all its vast trade was opened up to us, and our more recent acquisitions of territory on both sides of the Pacific were but an after effect of the Mexican war, which gave to us a country that extended from sea to sea. So much for the effects, great as they were, of the Mexican war....[24]

In personal terms, too, the war had been a real satisfaction to Wood. On December 1, 1847, President Polk nominated him to be promoted to second lieutenant in the 2nd Dragoons. Then, on April 12, 1848, while the occupation of Mexico City dragged on, Wood was nominated for promotion to brevet first lieutenant, 2nd Dragoons, for his "gallant and meritorious conduct at the battles [sic] of Buena Vista ... to date from the 23rd of February 1847."[25]

Wood had taken the next steps upward in his chosen profession and wore the proof of it on his shoulder boards, where all the world could see. Other benefits he gained from his many months in Mexico were less visible but were of equal importance, perhaps, to a young officer just learning his profession. Most elementally, he had tested himself under fire and found that his own courage was not lacking. Also, he had seen men die in battle and found himself willing to continue through the gore. He had had the chance to observe the two great generals of the time and to take lessons from each of how a leader should conduct himself. He had seen an army in the field for the first time and had learned the practical lessons of how men should be transported, fed, armed, and disciplined. He had seen how men could be deployed and made to fling themselves against the enemy when every instinct told them to turn and run. Altogether, it had been a most beneficial training ground for a young officer who was just learning his profession but who expected to go far.

CHAPTER 3

The Crisis

He expected to go far, but it was difficult to see how he could after the army returned to the United States in 1848. Service in the peacetime army was crushing to a young professional's ambitions. After the Mexican War ended, Wood spent years rotating among remote Texas posts, first serving under General William S. Harney and then Colonel Philip St. George Cooke.

Wood had more than one chance to escape duty in the West. In 1849, for example, Wood was called to West Point to be an assistant professor until, at his own request, he was released from the lecture hall to return to the West.

Admittedly, duty on the Plains could be frustrating, but it offered greater chances for promotion that any other setting in which the post-war cavalry operated. Wood was always active and faithful to his duties, and he was rewarded with a promotion in December 1851 to first lieutenant (backdated to June 30).

Another respite from duty on the Plains came in 1854 when Wood reported to old, familiar New York City for a year of recruiting duty. Even there, he never failed to watch for opportunities. In March 1855, when the 1st U.S. Cavalry was formed, Lieutenant Wood transferred from the dragoons. He was ordered to raise Company C of the new regiment and report afterward to Fort Leavenworth, Kansas. According to the West Point Association of Graduates, "after recruiting a good part of his company in Kentucky, [he] proceeded to Fort Leavenworth where the new regiment was to rendezvous." If Wood saw his Munfordville family during his recruiting time in Kentucky, there is no record of it.[1]

A new regiment and a new post opened up farther horizons for Wood. Serving again with General Harney, he fought the Brulé Sioux at Blue Water Creek, Nebraska, in 1855 and went on two different expeditions with Albert Sidney Johnston, the Kansas boundary expedition of 1857 and the Utah expedition of 1858.

The most portentous duty that Wood undertook was to tamp down disturbances on the Missouri-Kansas border in 1858. The trouble had its poisonous roots in the Mexican War. The status of the new territories had to be decided — would they be slave or free? Henry Clay crafted a complicated omnibus bill that settled the issue for only a short while. The question, like a rank weed, was hard to kill. It burst into full bloom again in 1854 when Stephen A. Douglas proposed the Kansas-Nebraska Act, which organized the two territories and gave citizens there the right to choose by ballot whether or not they would allow slavery to spread. Nebraska was never really in play (too far north), but Kansas certainly was. Partisan activists from the opposing sides came rushing in.

At first, simply because of proximity, the slaveholding Missourians had the upper hand in taking up claims. They chose the best Kansas land for their chattels to work. The Missouri emigrants were soon followed by wagonloads of settlers from Arkansas and Tennessee, and even from the Deep South. Almost simultaneously, the New England Emigrant Aid Company was formed and antislavery emigrants hurried to Kansas to balance the scale. People who were willing to relocate over a political issue — be it thirty miles or a thousand — were so passionate in their beliefs that they would quickly resort to desperate measures against their neighbors if it became necessary. Neither side had come to lose. It was clear that there was going to be trouble in Kansas.

The first incident of violence occurred at Hickory Creek in November 1855, when a proslavery man shotgunned to death an antislavery man who, he claimed, was about to slug him with a crowbar. Soon, both sides had groups of armed men on the roads and supplies of powder and ball were being laid by in secret locations. More violence inevitably followed: at Lawrence, at Pottawatomie Creek, and in Linn and Miami Counties. In Lawrence, the early proslavery sentiment was turned back by a Northern influx. A Free-State mentality came to prevail with the growing population, and a town lot that had sold for $8 now went for no less than $2,000.

Sentiments were less uniform around Fort Scott, a post begun in 1842 by two companies of dragoons and named for General Winfield Scott. It was finished in 1848 and continued to keep watch over the Santa Fe Trail for another five years. In 1853, the small garrison was ordered to Fort Leavenworth and the fort was auctioned off building by building. Private homes and businesses were set up where troopers had once oiled their saddles and checked the loads in their pistols. However, troops had to return in 1857 and 1858 because of the border troubles.

In his book *Civil War on the Western Border*, Jay Monaghan wrote:

> By April 1858, Fort Scott had become a haven of intrigue. Settlers who had sold goods here to the soldiers now operated stores in the abandoned buildings. Two hotels housed the slave and free factions. At night, partisans rode out to plunder settlers belonging to the opposing faction and returned to make merry in town....

A new leader of the proslavery settlers had appeared in the Fort Scott area recently. Handsome, wealthy Charles A. Hambleton came from Georgia with his brothers.... In Georgia, the proud Hambleton clan was notorious for violence. Charles had been shot three times in a feud and he came to Kansas with an abiding hatred of "abolitionists." His substantial log house with suitable slave quarters and stockaded corral ... became headquarters for proslavery partisans until [James] Montgomery and his followers drove them all from their claims.[2]

It was soon after Montgomery was forcibly exiled that Lieutenant Wood led a mixed detachment of cavalry and infantry (four companies in all) supported by a section of artillery into Fort Scott. What Wood saw there did not alarm him. One document that survives of Wood's time at Fort Scott is a letter dated May 16, 1858, and addressed to Kansas governor J. W. Denver. In it, Wood said that his company had been cooperating with the deputy marshal, but that no arrests had been made. Hambleton and his minions had gone from the area and resettled eighty or ninety miles away across the border in Missouri. Considering that things were peaceful in Fort Scott, and since the troops were needed elsewhere, Wood continued:

> I determined to withdraw all the troops from this place but the section arty.
> This is left as a guard for the public property, land office, etc.
> The foot company marched this morning; and as it could only act as a guard, if here (not being suited to the duty of a proper comitatus), for which this section of artillery is ample. I do not think it necessary to recall the foot company.
> The truth is, I doubt very much whether any guard is required here....
> I will march with the three mounted companies for Fort Leavenworth tomorrow morning.[3]

What Wood did not realize was that he had observed the situation at Fort Scott during the eye of the storm. He misinterpreted the lull as a permanent condition when, in fact, the disturbances of before were only a prologue to the bloodshed that was about to erupt.

Three days after Lieutenant Wood wrote this letter at Fort Scott, a notorious incident known to history as the Marais des Cygnes Massacre occurred only a few miles away. Charles Hambleton gathered a gang of Missourians and rode back into Kansas. Judging from the distance they had to travel, they were probably already on their way while Wood was proclaiming that there was no need for a military presence on the border near Fort Scott.

On May 19, Hambleton and his men were near the area where the Georgian had farmed before the Free Soilers ran him out. They wasted no time but rode to the cabins where Hambleton expected to find twelve men whose names were on an already-prepared enemies list. They captured eleven of the twelve men and prodded them down the road to a gully on Hambleton's old farm, near the Marais des Cygnes. There the eleven men were made to line up, facing away from their captors. Hambleton's men lined up, too, and leveled their weapons at the Kansans' backs. At Hambleton's order, his men fired, and the eleven fell. Four were dead when they hit the ground, six men were wounded, and one who was not hit at all by these Missouri sharpshooters fell down and pretended that he was dead. The uninjured man was a Baptist preacher named B. L. Reed. He later said, "I lay with my face to the ground and prevented respiration. My back was covered with blood, so they thought me dead." It was this minister's wife and others who later came to the scene of the massacre and tended the wounded.[4]

The killers robbed their eleven victims and rode hard for Missouri, separating like an Indian war party to confuse any who might follow.

The massacre was national news. The North was horrified, but it was naturally in Kansas that the consequences were most keenly felt. It was all the excuse that James Montgomery, Jim Lane, and other antislavery partisans needed to commence new raids among the proslavery communities. The violence spread and new bloody chapters of the border conflict were written.

Lieutenant Wood, by his May 16 return to Fort Leavenworth, had barely escaped being caught up in the tragic start of an escalating cycle of murderous raids along the border. It was a lucky bit of timing, for the endless aggravations of trying to deal with guerrilla warfare could have only hurt his career. There is no particular disgrace in that — more experienced officers than Wood saw their best efforts baffled

Thomas J. Wood at the start of the Civil War (Library of Congress).

by the fluid, bloodthirsty gangs that roamed the border for the next ten years. No one was able to stop them until 1865.

In December 1859, Captain Thomas J. Wood left his current post of Fort Washita, Indian Territory, for a leave of absence in Europe. While his exact itinerary is unknown, it is remembered that he watched reviews of the French military at Champ de Mars in Paris and at Longchamps and that he visited Milan, Italy, where he was witness to yet another review and also a sham battle. Two other stops on his tour are always mentioned. The first was his attendance as an invited guest at the coronation of King Charles XV of Norway on August 5, 1860, and the second was Wood's visit to Alexandria, Egypt. His trip to Alexandria was cut short when he was recalled in January 1861. After the election of Abraham Lincoln in November 1860, states had begun breaking away from the Union. With a crisis looming on the horizon, all leaves had been canceled. Wood left the Old World as soon as he was able. His ship arrived at New York City in March.

He reported to Washington, D.C., and was immediately handed a promotion to the rank of major, 1st U.S. Cavalry (commission dated March 16, 1861), but instead of rejoining his regiment he was ordered to Indiana to begin recruiting. He had some success. Only a month later, on April 23, 1861, Governor Oliver P. Morton wrote to Secretary of War Simon Cameron, "Major Wood has mustered three regiments into the service of the U.S. and is still engaged in the work. We will have four regiments mustered in tomorrow."[5]

This was the only good news that Morton had to report. The five thousand rifles that were required to arm the volunteers had not arrived, and there were no uniforms for the recruits to wear or tents to shelter them. There was growing alarm on the Ohio River front; Governor Morton had requested twenty-four cannon for the defense of the river counties and had received no answer.

Morton sent a similar hand-wringing wire on April 24, but Major Wood's work continued to be a silver lining. By May 2, he had mustered six regiments; ultimately, he would muster into the service some forty thousand Indiana troops, according to a memorial tribute given Wood in 1906 by the Society of the Army of the Cumberland. In his remarks before the former Cumberlanders, Orlando A. Somers explained Wood's success by saying, "He won the hearts of the people in Indiana by his sterling true faith."[6]

Secretary of War Cameron took note of the good work going on in Indiana and nominated Wood for a lieutenant colonel's commission on July 18. The Senate approved the promotion on July 31, though as usual, the commission was backdated, this one to May 9. After he spent years of languishing on the frontier in the rank of captain, Wood's leaping advance to lieutenant colonel was dizzying. It appeared that impending war was good for a young professional.

The rewards continued to come to Wood. By a commission dated October 11, 1861, he was promoted to brigadier general of volunteers, and one month later he was promoted to the rank of full colonel in the regular army.

For his promotion to brigadier general Wood had powerful supporters, including Governor Morton and also Richard W. Thompson, provost marshal of Indiana, who cited Wood's military education and zeal for the Union. In a letter to President Lincoln dated October 6, 1861, Thompson said, "There would be peculiar propriety in sending him [Wood] with a Brigade into Kentucky—his native state."[7]

Another of Wood's supporters was General William T. Sherman, the harried commander of Union forces in Kentucky. Sherman had agreed to serve as a subordinate to General Robert Anderson on the condition that he would never be asked to assume command of the Department of the Cumberland. Anderson was the hero of Fort Sumter, and because he was a native Kentuckian it was thought that he would help to hold the Bluegrass State in the Union. Anderson might have done good work in Kentucky, except for the fact that his physical and emotional health were fragile. On October 8, 1861, he requested to be relieved. Sherman was asked to take his place. Sherman did what he had vowed he would not—he accepted the appointment—and immediately began pacing the floor. The remedy to one of his many worries would be the advancement of good officers. That being so, Sherman wired Lincoln on October 9, 1861, to "at least make Wood at Indianapolis and Colonel [Richard W.] Johnson of Johnson's Regiment Brigadiers and send them at once...."[8]

Sherman followed with a second, longer wire to the president on October 10, in which he referenced Wood's good reputation in the regular army. Conditions in Kentucky were such that Sherman needed Wood. Sherman said, "The force now here or expected is entirely inadequate. The Kentuckians, instead of assisting, call from every quarter for protection against local secessionists. I named T.J. Wood at Governor Morton's insistence, because he is a Kentuckian and has been mustering officer at Indianapolis. He should have a brigade of Indiana volunteers.... All the men in Indiana and Ohio are ready to come to Kentucky, but they have no arms and we cannot supply them arms, clothing, or anything. Answer."[9]

Lincoln overlooked his subordinate's rude closing to the communiqué. He was sorry that could not let Sherman have all the satisfaction he wanted for his troubles, but he agreed with part of Sherman's request; he saw to Wood's promotion on October 11 and ordered him to report to General Sherman at the Galt House in Louisville. General Wood arrived on October 16, 1861.

Wood was thirty-eight years old. He had reached a position very near the top of his profession. He stood at the era's average male height of five feet, eight inches, was soldier trim, and stood ramrod straight. His hair was very dark and cut short and he wore a neatly trimmed moustache and imperial. His eyes were almond shaped, looking almost Asian, and his nose and cheekbones were sharp. His whole face appeared to have been made of blades.

If Wood looked as if he was ready to go to war, to meet and overcome any crisis, it was because he was. He was about to begin the adventure of his life.

The new brigadier trained down from Indianapolis in impressive company. Secretary of War Simon Cameron and Adjutant General Lorenzo Thomas had been on a fact-finding tour to St. Louis and were on their way home to Washington when they decided to stop in and visit Sherman. They picked up Wood at Indianapolis, en route. Sherman and James Guthrie, the president of the Louisville & Nashville Railroad, met the party at Jeffersonville. Together, they all went back across the Ohio River to the Galt House for a brief conference; Cameron and Thomas were anxious to continue east and would leave the next morning. With so little time to recite his litany of troubles, Sherman dived right into his presentation.

Sherman's remarks to the secretary of war and the adjutant general, with Thomas J. Wood and James Guthrie and reporters present, became the subject of controversy, and an accurate account was so important to Sherman that he included in his *Memoirs* (1875) the entire statement written by General Wood about the meeting. Wood's recollections, committed to paper in 1866, covered four and one-half pages in the 1990 Library of America edition of Sherman's *Memoirs*. They are excerpted here. Wood wrote:

> On the 11th of October, 1861, the writer, who had been personally on mustering duty in Indiana, was appointed a brigadier-general of volunteers, and ordered to report to General Sherman, then in command of the Department of the Cumberland, with his headquarters in Louisville, having succeeded General Robert Anderson. When the writer was about leaving Indianapolis to proceed to Louisville, Mr. Cameron, returning from his famous visit of inspection to General Fremont's department, at St. Louis, Missouri, arrived at Indianapolis, and announced his intention to visit General Sherman.
>
> The writer was invited to accompany the party to Louisville. Taking the early morning train from Indianapolis to Louisville on the 16th of October, 1861, the party arrived in Jeffersonville, and accompanied it to the Galt House, in Louisville, the hotel at which he was stopping.
>
> During the afternoon General Sherman informed the writer that a council of war was to be held immediately in his private room in the hotel, and desired him to be present at the council.... When General Sherman entered the room he closed the door, and turned the key in the lock....
>
> Mr. Cameron then asked General Sherman what his plans were. To this General Sherman replied that he had no plans; that no sufficient force had been placed at his disposition with which to devise any plan of operations; that, before a commanding general could project a plan of campaign, he must know what amount of force he would have to operate with.
>
> The general added that he had views which he would be happy to submit for the consideration of the Secretary. Mr. Cameron desired to hear General Sherman's views.

General William T. Sherman (Library of Congress).

General Sherman began by giving his opinion of the people of Kentucky, and the then condition of the State. He remarked that he believed a very large majority of the people of Kentucky were thoroughly devoted to the Union, and loyal to the Government, and that the Unionists embraced almost all the older and more substantial men in the State; but, unfortunately, there was no organization nor arms among the Union men … if Federal protection were extended throughout the State to the Union men, a large force could be raised for the service of the Government.[10]

Next, Sherman reviewed the three Confederate commands in the state as to location and size. Beginning in the western end of the state was the force under Lieutenant General Leonidas Polk, at Columbus on the Mississippi and comprising, in Sherman's estimate, ten thousand men. In the center of the Confederate line was Bowling Green, where eighteen thousand men served under General Albert Sidney Johnston. Wood himself had once served under

3. The Crisis

Johnston; he had marched to Utah with him during the Mormon expedition, but the painful reality of former-comrades-turned-enemy went even further than that. One of Johnston's subordinates was General Simon Bolivar Buckner, who first seized Bowling Green and advanced the Rebel line to Bacon Creek in Hart County. Buckner, General Wood's boyhood friend, had renounced his vow to protect and defend the Constitution. He had turned Rebel, and because of him, their mutual hometown of Munfordville and Wood's own family were behind enemy lines.

The third Confederate force, in Eastern Kentucky, was under General Felix Zollicoffer and numbered six thousand men. Though it did not actually plug Cumberland Gap, Zollicoffer's force controlled the legendary mountain pass and the traffic passing through it.

It was Sherman's military opinion that the Rebels intended to sweep north toward the Ohio River. When they did, they would reap another twenty thousand disloyal men, which would put Confederate numbers at approximately fifty-five thousand.

Wood continued in his account of the Galt House meeting:

> To resist an advance of the rebels, General Sherman stated that he did not have at that time in Kentucky more than some twelve to fourteen thousand effective men. The bulk of this force was posted at camp Nolin, on the Louisville & Nashville Railway, fifty miles south of Louisville. A part of it was in Eastern Kentucky, under General George H. Thomas, and a very small force was in the lower valley of Green River.[11]

Next, Sherman began to assess for his guests' information the state of affairs in Kentucky from the offensive point of view. It was his opinion that the Union must go on the attack to crush the rebellion. Then came the comments that destroyed, for a time, the government's confidence in their department commander in Kentucky:

> For the purpose of expelling the rebels from Kentucky, General Sherman said that at least sixty thousand soldiers were necessary....
>
> General Sherman expressed the opinion that, to carry the war to the Gulf of Mexico and destroy all armed opposition to the Government, in the entire Mississippi Valley, at least two hundred thousand troops were absolutely requisite.[12]

Sherman's listeners were astonished, and the newspapermen began to take mental notes. Here was sensational news. Sixty thousand men simply to drive the Rebels from Kentucky! Two hundred thousand to pursue the war to the Gulf of Mexico! It was incredible. Any man who believed that such numbers were going to be necessary to end the rebellion was the victim of an overheated imagination and was possibly insane. Actually insane. Secretary Cameron asked, "Where do you suppose, General Sherman, all this force is to come from?" Sherman replied that that was not his business; his duty was to lead the men after they arrived.[13]

Sherman's estimate of the numbers he would need was so startling that there seemed to be nothing more to say and the meeting soon after broke up. Its aftereffects, however, were felt for weeks. General Sherman had believed that his remarks were off the record. Cameron had assured him that the men of his traveling party were trustworthy, but one of them was a reporter and Sherman's comments were shortly afterward published in the *New York Tribune*. Wood wrote, "All military men were shocked by the gross breach of faith which had been committed."[14]

The administration in Washington, and in fact the country at large, decided on the basis of this newspaper account that Sherman was dangerously unbalanced. Assistant Secretary of War Thomas A. Scott, for example, said, "Sherman's gone in the head; he's luny."[15]

The upshot of the controversy was that Sherman lost his command. In the second week in November, Major General Don Carlos Buell arrived in Louisville to assume command of the department, which was now styled the Department of the Ohio. General Sherman was shuffled off to Missouri in hopes that he would regain his reason in a less strenuous command.

General Buell was forty-three years old, an Ohio-born Hoosier. From Indiana, he won an appointment to West Point, where he graduated thirty-second in the Class of 1841. He had seen service in the Seminole War and with Winfield Scott in the Mexican War. Buell proved his bravery at Churubusco, where he was badly wounded, and was brevetted major before the war was done. He had spent most of the years following as a staff officer. An adjutant's duties suited his reserved, meticulous nature, but now he was returned to field command in the important department that included railroads and rivers whose control was vital to Union victory.

By the time these adjustments were made at headquarters in Louisville, General Thomas J. Wood had taken to the field. Special Orders No. 55 ordered him to "proceed with all possible speed to the camp at Nolin and report to Brigadier General [Alexander McDowell] McCook, commanding for further orders." Wood took the L&N Railroad down to Nolin. There he was assigned command of the all-Indiana 2nd Brigade at Camp Nevin, the Union's most advanced position in Central Kentucky and the staging area for the campaign that would commence in the spring of 1862.[16]

Chapter 4

From Camp Nevin to Nashville

Camp Nevin was begun on October 9, 1861, by Brigadier General Lovell Harrison Rousseau. It was on the farm of Mr. David Nevin, a secessionist whose six hundred acres on the Nolin River near the village of Nolin were perfect for the Federals' needs. There was plentiful water, and exceptional transportation via the Louisville and Nashville Turnpike and the L&N Railroad.

Rousseau rode onto the farm at the head of the three volunteer infantry regiments, one regiment of cavalry, one battery of artillery, and two battalions of U.S. regulars. More regiments were shuffled forward over the next few weeks until there were nearly fourteen thousand men at Camp Nevin. They were designated the 1st Division, Army of the Cumberland, and were divided into four brigades. Brigadier General Thomas J. Wood arrived on or about October 15 to take charge of the 2nd Brigade.

The commander of the 1st Division at Camp Nevin, as of October 12, 1861, was Brigadier General Alexander McDowell McCook, a West Pointer and a veteran of the Apache Campaigns in New Mexico as well as the Battle of 1st Bull Run. He was a proud, portly Buckeye from Ohio and he was now in charge of what he considered "the most important army in the field." With it, McCook boasted, he could "break the Back of this rebellion in three moves."[1]

The appointment of McCook caused some to scratch their heads, for he was not universally admired. Among the other comments made about him over time was the observation by a newspaperman that he was only "an overgrown schoolboy." One wonders what made Sherman think that McCook was capable of such an important early command. The day-to-day demands of the job were daunting. As commanding general, McCook was responsible for the defense of the camp and the health and welfare of fourteen thousand men, not to mention the military training that was the reason for their being there. He had to approve the placement of all those newly arriving regiments and had to make sure that they had everything needed from ammunition to camp kettles to socks. The volume of work was mountainous, and the energy needed to attend to every detail was incredible. A requisition for the 29th Indiana Infantry, which was in Wood's brigade, was typical of the items that consumed McCook's days. Colonel John F. Miller said that his regiment needed five water buckets, ten bearing chains, one set of complete harness for a four-horse "waggon [sic]," one set of complete harness for a six-mule wagon, fifteen rope halters, three sets of wagon bows, and four horses. "I certify on honor the above requisition correct and Just," wrote Colonel Miller, "and absolutely required for the public service, rendered so from the following circumstances: Necessary to complete transportation train for 29th Regt. Ind. Vol." Miller signed the requisition, kicked it up to General Wood, who also signed it and sent it on to General McCook, who signed it, approving the transaction that would allow the 29th Indiana to complete its transportation train.[2]

There were sixteen regiments at Camp Nevin. Each of them had their own immediate needs, which their colonels and brigade commanders had to attend to before they reached the division commander, who had to attend to them all. When one considers the massive complexities and woes of the job of a commanding general, it is a wonder that there were as many good generals as there were. That there were some exceptional ones is barely short of miraculous. McCook was not exceptional, but he was adequate so far as the bivouac at Camp Nevin was concerned. His qualities as a battlefield commander were yet to be seen.

There was another aspect of life in camp with which the general had to be involved, and that was the presence of contrabands. Runaway slaves were migrating to Camp Nevin in great numbers. McCook was especially perplexed by this problem, which was outside the boundaries of his military training. He pleaded to General Sherman for instructions. McCook wrote, "Ten have come into my camp in as many hours, and from what they say there will be a general stampede of slaves from the other side of Green River. They have already become a source of annoyment to me." He asked permission either to summon their masters to come retrieve the runaways at some location outside the camp or to take the slaves back beyond the Green River and return them to their masters there. In the meantime, he said that he had "put the negroes to work. They will be handy with teams and generally useful."[3]

Sherman's reply was prompt: "I have no instructions from the Government on the subject of Negroes. My opinion is that the laws of the State of Kentucky are in full force, and that Negroes must be surrendered on application of masters or agents or delivered over to the sheriff of the county. We have nothing to do with them at all, and you should not let them take refuge in camp. It forms a source of misrepresentation by which Union men are estranged from our cause." In other words, saving the Union had nothing to do with freeing the slaves and local emancipation only confused the issue. In 1861, General Wood, like Sherman and McCook, was opposed to the suggestion of emancipation as a desirable goal.[4]

The volunteers at Camp Nevin agreed with their generals on the question of emancipation. In one letter, William C. Robinson of the 49th Ohio wrote home that many people in Hardin County "have labored under a mistaken idea as to the cause and object of this war. They supposed that it was waged by the North ... for the extermination of slavery." Robinson found that the people quickly became "good Union men" when they learned that they could keep their slaves."[5]

McCook's effort to remove the slaves from camp was not entirely successful. It appears that his putting them to work backfired in the sense that they made themselves too useful to banish completely. In one of only three known wartime images of Camp Nevin — in this case, a Henry Mosler woodcut that appeared in *Harper's Weekly* on December 7, 1861 — a slave family is shown in the foreground, chatting with a soldier who lounges against the wheel of an artillery piece. The slave man is a woodcutter, judging from the axe across his shoulder. The slaves made themselves useful not only in performing camp chores but as guides in military actions as well. They knew the country, and the boys from the North did not. In a November 20 letter from "Redstick," a soldier in the 49th Ohio, reference is made to a black man known only as "John," who became a well-respected guide. Redstick said, "John is a negro and makes a valuable man in the scouting services."[6]

Uninvited, mainly unwanted, serving without pay or any official status, the blacks at Camp Nevin were still ready to pitch in to do what they could to help the men who wore the blue uniforms. They knew before the administration in Washington, the departmental commanders at headquarters, or the field officers at Camp Nevin what the war was ultimately about.

General Thomas J. Wood's 2nd Brigade was camped near the Louisville and Nashville Turnpike on the eastern end of Camp Nevin. It was comprised of the 29th Indiana (Colonel John F. Miller), the 30th Indiana (Colonel Sion S. Bass), the 38th Indiana (Colonel Benjamin F. Scribner), and the 39th Indiana (Colonel Thomas J. Harrison).

The volunteers in these Hoosier regiments found that learning to be soldiers was a hard and time-consuming job. Every day except Sunday was filled with bugle blasts from 6:00 A.M. until after dark, calling the men to sick call, to police their brigade's section of the camp, to eat, and to drill, drill, drill. General Sherman had specifically warned McCook to "push the drill," and he did. William Sumner Dodge, in his *History of the Old Second Division*, observed that Camp Nevin "became a grand school of instruction."[7]

General Wood saw to it that the men of his brigade were active students in the "grand school." Dodge commented on Wood's "very active physical and mental temperament" and said that he was "very energetic in what he undertakes and tenacious in purpose." It was Dodge's opinion that Wood was "one of Kentucky's most chivalrous men." Chivalry did not mean that Wood had drawing room manners, however. The new brigadier was known as a strict disciplinarian. Moreover, Wood affected a "rugged western style," says historian Larry Daniel, and both he and McCook "swore like pirates."[8]

In addition to the drill, the volunteers had to attend to the duties specific to their arm of the service. The cavalrymen, for example, had the added responsibility of caring for their horses and "equipage." The artillerymen, when they were not learning how to fire their fieldpieces, had to load their own shells. Alpheus S. Bloomfield, a gunner in Battery A, 1st Ohio Light Artillery, wrote to his brothers and sisters on October 19, 1861, "We were ordered to load 150 rounds apiece. We spent Tuesday afternoon and part of the night loading shell; put in 30 to 40 ounce balls in some of the shells; some, pieces of thick glass broken up, and for others we took old horse-shoes and cut them into slugs."[9]

Wood's infantrymen had fewer of these extra duties. They did have frequent target practice with their muskets (twenty rounds of ammunition at a time, if they were like the regiments in other brigades), and they had to march and learn the evolutions. They had picket duty and were made to lend a hand in rebuilding the burned L&N Railroad bridge and also a stockade with blockhouses to protect the bridge from future arson. Still, they seemed to have more free time than those in the cavalry or artillery. The camp offered some amusements, but not enough. The boys missed women and liquor and they missed having enough to read. John W. Leonard of the 49th Ohio Infantry wrote to the Hancock *Jeffersonian*, "If you would oblige the soldiers, send them plenty of newspapers. There is a dearth of reading matter in camp, and a newspaper from home is, next to a letter, the most acceptable gift."[10]

Soldiers pleaded for letters from home. They were so desperate to get mail that they even wrote to relatives whom they had never met. Private George P. Ehrman of the 34th Illinois wrote to his cousin B. Swart and had to begin by introducing himself, "I am your Cousin George P. Ehrman, a brother of Henry S. Ehrman and John W. E. I have heard from you through my brother Henry about three years ago…. I am writing this letter to hear from you…. Please write as soon as you receive this letter."[11]

The greatest pleasure of the infantrymen may have been the chance to leave camp and get out among the locals. From them, the boys in blue could buy pies and fresh milk to supplement their diet of hardtack, pork, and coffee. Relations between the soldiers and the local civilians were not always of the best, however. Redstick of the 49th Ohio described how the boys of his regiment stopped a farmer going to market with a wagonload of apples. They talked him into selling them five bushels and then stole the rest. The apple-stealing 49th also played the trick of drying old coffee grounds and then, pretending that it was fresh roasted, selling it to the Kentuckians at 16¢ a pound. "That is one way of skinning a cat," boasted Redstick.[12]

Lyman S. Widney, a trooper in the 34th Illinois, wrote a fanciful account of an excursion his regiment made to a local farm. Widney wrote:

> Early this morning, our regiment was ordered out to surround and capture a large number of natives, discovered in a field near our camp. We quickly obeyed the call, advancing rapidly ... and soon caught sight of them, standing in line behind a rail fence, exceeding us in numbers; but we were undismayed and charged with cold steel, not firing a shot, as they were unarmed, while they were green enough to stand rooted to the ground. Scaling the fence, my comrade seized one by the ear, while another was cut down by me. There was a husky sound as we leaped over them and stalked like grim death through their helpless ranks, without a grain of mercy. All my comrades were equally active and by noon, the work of mutilation was complete, great piles of ears had been removed and the remains cremated, so that where fifteen acres of corn stood in the morning, nothing but roots remained at noon.[13]

Campaigns against cornfields were one thing, but the young soldiers at Camp Nevin were anxious to march out and meet an enemy who could fight back. They knew that the Rebels were near. Some pickets had been killed and some of the cavalrymen had fought skirmishes with enemy patrols. Also, the men could see daily evidence of the Confederates' proximity. Samuel O. Thomas wrote, "Their signal rockets and balloons are visible nightly from our camp. How well their balloon reconnaissances please their warlike palates I know not; but am inclined to think not very well, as our tented fields are visible almost as far as the eye can reach."[14]

Autumn dissolved into winter, and still the order to advance south did not come. While the men waited at Camp Nevin, General Wood was not idle. On November 29, he took a short leave and traveled to Dayton, Ohio, to marry Caroline Greer, the daughter of a well-to-do stove manufacturer. Wood had met Miss Greer earlier in the year, when he was recruiting regiments in Indianapolis.

Neither were things idle at headquarters in Louisville. William T. Sherman's outburst that he would need sixty thousand men to clear the Rebels from Kentucky had cost him dearly; he lost command of the Department of the Cumberland in the second week in November and General Don Carlos Buell was assigned to take his place. The department was renamed the Department of the Ohio and, on December 2, the divisions in Kentucky were reorganized. McCook's command was now called the 2nd Division and Wood's brigade was now the 5th. In it were the 34th Illinois, the 29th Indiana, the 30th Indiana, and the 77th Pennsylvania.

Wood's honeymoon with his new bride was by necessity a short one, for things began moving quickly on the military front now. McCook's division was ordered to push south to Bacon Creek and Munfordville, beginning on December 7. At Munfordville, Wood's 5th Brigade camped on familiar ground; the several regiments pitched their tents in a long semicircle on the farm of George T. Wood, the father of the general. They were near enough to see the elegant brick house where General Wood had grown up. Lyman S. Widney commented in his diary on the appropriate setting of "Camp Wood." He said:

> Our camp here is called Camp Wood, after the father of General Wood, our brigade commander, who lives within sight of our quarters, in the house where General Wood was born [sic] and now has his tent pitched in the old orchard where he spent his youthful days. The farm is whitened with the tents of thousands of soldiers awaiting his command to carry death and destruction into the ranks of his former playmates, friends, and neighbors, now in hostile array, a few miles distant, under General Buckner, whose house and farm are also within the limits of our camp, not two miles from General Wood's. The corn and hay raised by General Buckner last summer are being fed to our mules."[15]

Of all of General Wood's Kentucky family, only his father had remained loyal to the Union. As a reward for his fidelity and in recognition of his abilities, he was appointed to Kentucky's Military Board, a five-man panel whose members also included Governor Beriah Magoffin. The board controlled the state arsenal and was given funds amounting to $75,000 with which to buy additional guns and accoutrements. The board was also authorized to establish powder mills. They were a powerful body of men and their influence increased after General Simon Bolivar Buckner occupied Bowling Green in mid–September 1861. The WPA's *Military History of Kentucky* called their powers "practically unlimited." Speaking of George T. Wood individually, the Society of the Cumberland said of him that "throughout the entire war Col. Wood was a bulwark in the Union line in the state of Kentucky." Colonel George T. Wood had only just returned to his house on the hill. It was unsafe for him, as one of Kentucky's leading Unionists, to remain at Munfordville during the Confederate occupation of the town. Colonel Wood had fled and, according to an item in the *Louisville Daily Democrat*, his house was the first one in Munfordville to be pillaged by the occupying Confederates. The Rebels also stole one of his horses, presumably the only one left in the barn after the colonel quit his home. It was years before Thomas J. Wood could forgive his old friend Simon Bolivar Buckner for the inconvenience he caused Wood's father. That the brick house on the hill was not destroyed during the Confederate occupation was a wonder, but only the furnishings had been bothered; the structure itself had escaped damage. Now Colonel Wood had returned and could look out his back door to see the vast encampment of the men who had redeemed his town and would go on to help redeem the state and the nation. By a fortunate coincidence, they were the brigade commanded by his own son, who after an absence of fifteen years had returned home.[16]

General Wood had the chance to enjoy his camp on the family farm for only two weeks. On December 22, he was ordered to "proceed at once to the camp of instruction near Bardstown, Kentucky, and relieve Brigadier General Dumont in the command of the same. General Wood's assignment is temporary.... The personal staff only (aides de camp) will change station with the general as ordered herein."[17]

In the weeks ahead, Wood was joined at Bardstown by the 40th, 51st, 57th, and 58th Indiana Infantry regiments, the 64th and 65th Ohio Infantry, and the 15th Michigan Infantry, plus three battalions of cavalry. Wood was not at Bardstown long. On January 16, 1862, he was ordered to move to Danville, Kentucky, there to commence a road improvement project to Somerset. This was in support of General George H. Thomas, commanding the 1st Division. Thomas was facing a Confederate threat. General Felix Zollicoffer had moved north in November with four thousand Tennessee and Kentucky Rebels. A good road would enable men and war materiel to reach Thomas, the better to counter Zollicoffer. It was a slow slog for Wood's men. The horrible road had to be widened to a width of sixteen feet and corduroyed. The project was expected to last ten days, but only three days after Wood received his orders Thomas advanced and met Zollicoffer at Mill Springs. The Confederates were defeated on January 19 and Zollicoffer was killed. The immediate threat to Kentucky passed when the leaderless Rebels fell back into Tennessee.

On February 11, General Wood was put in command of the 6th Division, consisting of the 20th Brigade (Colonel Charles G. Harker) and the 21st Brigade (Colonel George D. Wagner). The same day, Wood received orders from General Buell to prepare to shift his division to Bacon Creek, a move that would begin the following morning. "Encamp your division at Bacon Creek," said Buell, "until further orders, and be always ready to move at a moment's notice." A moment at Bacon Creek was about all that Wood was allowed. He had not even gathered his entire division around him before he was ordered to move again. Only two days later, on the thirteenth, General Buell reported, "Wood will have his division at Munfordville tomorrow."[18]

Wood was unable to move as quickly as Buell had expected. The various elements of his division were having transportation problems. On February 14, Wood wrote to army headquarters, "Want of trains is delaying the movement of troops in a most unlooked for, uncontrollable manner. Regiments have been waiting at the depot for nearly twenty-four hours.... Four regiments have gone and the fifth is embarking and will get off, I trust, in a short time." The railroad agent told Wood that it would take another day to get adequate trains for the remaining men, but Wood promised, "Movement will be conducted as rapidly as transportation is ready."[19]

Wood was not the only one facing the complications of moving thousands of men. McCook in Munfordville was having problems of his own. One delay was caused by the difficult task of rebuilding the L&N Railroad bridge over Green River, just south of the town. Another was the weather. A correspondent for *Harper's Weekly* described the situation. He wrote that the Union soldiers

> encamped about and near this village would probably have moved forward ere this were it not for the terrible condition to which this part of the State has been reduced by the almost uninterrupted rains of the last few days. The surface of the ground has been softened to the depth of several feet by the superabundance of water from above, and the roads and camps are almost bottomless. Movements afoot are fraught with indescribable discomfort.... Military exercises had to be suspended during the continuance of the wet spell.[20]

Meanwhile, farther south, the Confederates were moving. Thomas' victory at Mill Springs had cost the Rebels their right flank, and Grant's victory at Fort Henry on the Tennessee River was the first of two heavy blows that were causing their left flank to crumble. If Fort Donelson on the Cumberland also fell to Grant, the left flank would be gone. Confederate general Albert Sidney Johnston saw no choice other than abandoning what remained of his defensive line in Kentucky. Consequently, on February 12 the Confederates began to evacuate Bowling Green. General Buell responded by pushing the Army of the Ohio forward, with General Ormsby Mitchel's 3rd Division leading the way.

By February 20, Wood was with his division in Munfordville. The next day General Buell ordered him to move forward. On or about March 1, Wood crossed over the boundary of his native state and proceeded toward Nashville. General Wood had seen no fighting yet, but that would soon change. The invasion of the South had begun.

Chapter 5

Shiloh and Corinth

It snowed in Nashville on March 6, 1862. Nashville was already in a sour mood, and a snowfall in this Southern city must have only made the mood worse. Its citizens had gone through a considerable panic as the Confederate Army evacuated after the fall of Fort Donelson, leaving them defenseless. Yankee gunboats were expected on the Cumberland River in a matter of hours, and Albert Sidney Johnston's Rebels skedaddled. Nathan Bedford Forrest took charge. He burned the L&N Railroad bridge across the Cumberland and efficiently went about the business of stripping the city of all the foodstuffs, ordnance, and machinery that would be of use to the Confederate war effort. Only when the Yankees appeared on the north bank of the Cumberland did Forrest ride away. The Federals arrived by foot and by steamer and were soon marching through the streets of the city, flying their banners and playing their ugly Yankee songs. And with the bluecoats came this damned Northern weather.

The occupying soldiers were directed to camps around the edges of the city, but they had enough free time to come into this first occupied Southern capital for some sightseeing. They found the stores locked tight and the streets deserted. The citizens remained indoors, although those most strident of Confederates, the women, would sometimes stick their heads out of an upstairs window to spit on the Yankee soldiers on the sidewalk below.

Despite the precipitation, the soldiers enjoyed seeing the capitol building and the home of 1860 presidential candidate John Bell. They visited the grave of President James K. Polk and stared from the sidewalk at his downtown residence, where his widow still lived.

The officers did more than merely gaze upon the home of President Polk's widow. General Buell paid her a respectful visit and took with him a "party of perhaps twenty of the ranking officers in the area." General Thomas J. Wood would certainly have been included in this group. According to Walter T. Durham, the officers "were received politely and spent about an hour with her [Sarah Polk]."[1]

General Buell hoped that the Federal occupation of Nashville would proceed in the same spirit of respect. He knew that there were a good number of loyal Unionists in Nashville and he wanted to build upon that base. He believed that a lenient policy should be followed in governing the city. It would gratify the loyalists and persuade the Southern sympathizers to return to their old flag. That being his attitude, Buell was absolutely opposed to the appointment of a military governor. Buell had made his headquarters at the St. Cloud Hotel, which was to Nashville what the Willard was to Washington and the Galt House to Louisville. From his office in the St. Cloud, Buell wrote to his friend George B. McClellan that the city was "quiet and orderly" and that his soldiers were finding surprising quantities of provisions that Forrest had overlooked, especially bacon. Things were proceeding nicely. Therefore, urged Buell, "use all your persuasion against the appointment of a military governor for Tennessee. It will do incalculable harm. Beg the President to wait."[2]

General Don Carlos Buell (Library of Congress).

It was undoubtedly because of Buell's insistence on a policy of humane treatment for Nashville's citizens that his soldiers behaved themselves while in the city. The Yankees could be guilty of excesses, as any occupying army might be (and would be, before war's end), but even the *Nashville Banner* had to admit in its March 3 edition, "As far as we know, the officers and men of the Federal army have, thus far, deported themselves toward our citizens in the most unexceptionable manner. We feel bound to say this much in justice to them."[3]

As they wandered about, behaving themselves, the soldiers would have noticed some damage that the retreating Rebels themselves had inflicted on the city, such as the burned L&N Railroad bridge. They would also have seen the streets of empty houses whose well-to-do owners had fled, along with the legislature and the army. Some other Nashville homeowners had left their houses because of flood. The poorer section of the town, down near the Cumberland, was inundated by the highest waters since 1847. The *New York Times* said, "The damage done to property all along the river must be immense. In the lower portion of this city hundreds of families have been driven from their homes by the back waters, and much suffering must be the result, as it will be some time yet before they can return."[4]

When Albert Sidney Johnston fell back from Nashville, he concentrated his troops at Corinth, Mississippi, an important railroad town in the northeastern corner of the state. General Henry W. Halleck, commanding the new Department of the Mississippi, wanted to hit the Rebels there. Consequently, he ordered an advance of U. S. Grant's Army of the Tennessee and Don Carlos Buell's Army of the Ohio to Savannah, Tennessee, far enough from Johnston to safely congregate and still close enough to make a quick strike when the armies were in place. Five divisions of the Army of the Ohio began moving south from Nashville on March 15.

General Wood lingered in the Tennessee capital and did not move out until March 29, two weeks behind the rest of the army. His division had been strengthened in Nashville by the addition of the 15th Brigade under Brigadier General Milo Hascall, but shortly after the march toward Savannah began this new brigade was detached by General Buell to advance by way of Lawrenceburg. After April 4, Hascall made a march separate from the two other brigades of the 6th Division, who were moving down the Columbia Pike.

It was an uneventful march for Wood. His two brigades benefited from marching far behind the others, in that the engineers in the vanguard of Buell's long column had time to rebuild the bridges that the Rebels had burned; the 6th Division could cross the rivers without having to ford them. The worst hardship Wood's men faced was the weather, which was damp, as always seemed to be the case when the Federals moved.

On April 6, when the 6th Division was still eighteen miles from Savannah, Wood received an order to hurry forward and leave behind his supply train. Each man was to carry on his person three days' rations and forty rounds of ammunition. Before the march could commence, a second order arrived amending the first and ordering Wood to bring his supply train as well. Wood moved out as soon as the preparations were made only to find the road ahead of him blocked by the wagons of the divisions that had gone before. Wood later reported, "It was impossible to advance more than a mile an hour."[5]

As they struggled along, a third order came urging Wood to hurry and to leave his ammunition train. The enemy had not waited at Corinth. They had moved north, caught Grant's unsuspecting army at a place called Shiloh, and driven the bluecoats back to the Tennessee River.

Wood hurried forward as well as he was able, but the road was congested and considerably cut up and became even worse about midnight when a torrential rain began falling. There was no way to proceed, Wood thought, so he ordered a halt "until the storm had passed and the road had become sufficiently illuminated to permit the onward movement."[6]

The men continued their march at dawn. Reaching Savannah, they were put on boats and carried down to Pittsburg Landing, beginning with Colonel George D. Wagner's 21st Brigade. The operation consumed the morning hours. It was almost 12:00 noon before Wagner's men reached the battlefield. They went into position on the far left flank of the Union line. Wagner later reported, "We advanced in line of battle, driving the enemy before us, until ordered to halt. While holding this position the enemy attacked us with infantry, cavalry, and artillery. The cavalry were soon dispersed by a few volleys from our advanced line with considerable loss to themselves. The infantry retired at the same time." In this slight action, Wagner's brigade suffered four men wounded, all from the 57th Indiana.[7]

Wood had remained at Savannah until the 20th Brigade, under the temporary command of Brigadier General James A. Garfield, boarded the transports. They did not debark at Pittsburg Landing until 1:00 P.M. The artillery and cavalry lagged behind, but Wood accompanied the brigade toward "that part of the field on which the firing seemed to be the hottest," as ordered by General Grant.[8]

As they marched toward the battle line, Garfield's men were encouraged by the wounded and exhausted survivors of the two days' fight, who told them, "We've got 'em on the run, boy! Go for 'em! Give 'em the best you've got in the shop!" Garfield's men, though game, were too late to become engaged. They did come under some artillery fire from the retreating Rebels, but there were no casualties.[9]

The battle was over. That night, in the rain, Wood's two brigades bivouacked in position and sent out their skirmishers and pickets. The men were ready to fight if the battle resumed in the morning, but it did not resume. The Rebels had lost Albert Sidney Johnston on the first day of battle and his successor, P. G. T. Beauregard, chose not to challenge both the Army of the Tennessee and the Army of the Ohio. The Rebels retreated into their defensive works around Corinth.

On the morning of April 8, Colonel Milo Hascall's 15th Brigade came up and rejoined Wood's division. Hascall had expected to fight the Rebels at Lawrenceburg, but in fact his march had been only slightly more exciting that that of Wagner and Garfield. There were only one hundred Rebels in Lawrenceburg, and they fled toward Florence as Hascall approached. The Federals chased them for eight miles, accomplishing nothing more than the capture of six horses and saddles, some bacon, two drums, and about a dozen antiquated rifles and shotguns. They did not kill any of the enemy, so far as they knew.

Hascall's men could hear the sounds of battle as they approached the

Tennessee River, but they did not arrive at Pittsburg Landing until midnight on the seventh, and though they proceeded to Shiloh as quickly as they could, they were hours too late to join even in the pursuit.

In his report of the battle, General Buell remarked that Wood's division was "entitled to the highest praise for the untiring energy with which they pressed forward night and day to share the danger of their comrades." General Wood, in his report, merely reported the facts of the march and of the final minutes of the battle in which his brigades played a slight role. He was more effusive in his congratulatory message to his troops. Wood cited the stoicism of the men during the march and said, "Although it was not the good fortune of the division to arrive on the field of battle until just before the enemy was driven from his last stand ... all are cheered by the consciousness of having made an extraordinary march, bearing the fatigue and privations incident thereto ... with fortitude and cheerfulness."[10]

When men died in battle, there was a form to fill out at the company level to account for their effects, including such things as forage caps, shirts, socks, blankets, knapsacks, canteens, shoes, rifles, and cartridge boxes. All except the weapons and accoutrements were sent to the deceased's next of kin. The inventory was certified and signed by the captain commanding the company. After the Battle of Shiloh, there were 1,754 such forms to fill out in the Federal army. Mostly they came from Grant's Army of the Tennessee. Only 241 men died in the Army of the Ohio, but they were just as dead and their families grieved just as deeply.

There were over eighteen hundred wounded in Buell's army. Even more grew sick in the days to come because of the gore and the lack of sanitation, a condition that worsened with the heavy spring rains. Diseases like typhoid and dysentery took hold in the soggy camps and began to carry away soldiers who had survived Rebel bullets and bayonets. Those who fell ill joined their wounded comrades in primitive field hospitals at Pittsburg Landing and at Savannah. Others were sent by river packets to military hospitals at St. Louis and Evansville, and still others were sent home.

Wood's men had escaped the carnage of battle but not the suffering that followed. As General Buell explained in his report:

> The circumstances attending and following the battle of Shiloh subjected my troops to the greatest discomfort for some ten days after that event. Rains and use rendered the roads almost impassable, so that the wagons and baggage that had been left behind on the forced march which was made to reach the battle field on the 6th and 7th of April arrived very slowly. The troops, therefore, had not only to live in the open in miry camps and frequent cold, drenching rains, but to carry their provisions some 2 miles from the river to the camps over roads so muddy as to be difficult even for horses.[11]

Then there was the work. The able-bodied were pressed into service as burial parties. They braved the gagging stench to gather up the dead to bury (and to rebury when rains uncovered the graves), and they piled up dead horses to burn. The reality of camp life was so gruesome that those moments when they were called to drop their shovels and grab up their rifles to repel a Rebel sortie must have been welcome. There was one such alarm on the morning of April 10, and the Federal soldiers believed that they were about to come under general attack, an impression that was stiffened when some of the soldiers returning from outpost duty emptied their loaded rifles by firing them into the mud. Captain John W. Tuttle (3rd Kentucky Infantry) remembered, "The long roll sounded all along our lines and our whole army came out in battle array. We advanced about half a mile and stood to arms nearly all day.... We threw out skirmishers and also brought a small force of cavalry from one of our wings and sent them out upon our front."[12]

There were consequences for the man who had caused the panic. Tuttle continued, "The most complete avalanche of oaths the writer ever heard was that day uttered by General Wood and hurled and showered upon the Captain who had allowed his men to fire off their guns upon our front. It was a masterpiece of profanity, faultlessly rendered. Our much beloved little division commander had no equal in that line in the army and perhaps none in the navy."[13]

On April 12, General Henry W. Halleck came to Shiloh to personally lead the advance on Corinth. Shiloh had been a hiccup in Halleck's master plan. Corinth was still the object of the armies gathered on the Tennessee River. The Mississippi town was central to conquest of the Deep South; there the Memphis & Charleston Railroad and the Mobile & Ohio Railroad converged and from there supplies flowed south, west, and east to distant Confederate strongholds.

As miserable as the camp at Shiloh was, Halleck was determined to stay there until everything was in place. That included bringing another army onto the scene, the Army of the Mississippi under General John Pope. On the advance, Pope would be on the left flank. General Buell would be in the center, and the Army of the Tennessee would advance on the right. It would be commanded by General George H. Thomas, not by Grant, who was in the corner for having been caught by surprise at Shiloh.

No matter how loudly the Grant partisans might protest, Halleck believed Grant to be guilty of a great transgression in placing his army on the Rebel side of the Tennessee River before Buell's Army of the Ohio came up. In addition, Grant had not even been in camp when the Rebels attacked on April 6. He had been at his comfortable headquarters in Savannah.

Grant was not to be left behind at Pittsburg Landing, however. He was to participate in the move against Corinth as Halleck's second in command. Perhaps Halleck thought Grant might learn something; at least, he could do no harm. The armies stepped off on April 29, leaving behind a camp where, as Wood said, his men had suffered "every variety of discomfort that absence of its baggage and transportation in the most inclement weather could produce."[14]

On the first day of the march, Wood's division (accompanied by a section of artillery and a squadron of horse soldiers) marched only three and one-half miles, and even that modest advance was well above the average for the Corinth Campaign. Halleck was a deliberate man and drove his one hundred thousand men less than a mile a day, though the march was largely uncontested. There were glimpses of the Confederate cavalry, and there were intermittent clashes with them, especially at creeks and marshy places where the engineers worked to lay down bridges and corduroy roads. General Garfield's brigade fought such a skirmish on the sixth. However, as Captain John W. Tuttle said, "We did nothing that could be called fighting.... There were many little skirmishes in our vicinity or hearing [but] they amounted to little or nothing."[15]

One could never tell, though, when a sighting of the enemy or the exchange of gunfire might develop into something more serious and the commanders had to take appropriate action. In his report of the march on Corinth, General Wood told of a typical incident on May 9. He wrote:

> During the forenoon of the day the brigade [Wagner's] completed the corduroy track already commenced through the bottom of Chambers Creek, repaired the old bridge, built an entirely new and very substantial one, and commenced to lay down an additional corduroy track. While so employed the outposts and vedettes of the squadron of cavalry which was protecting the labors of the brigade, and which were posted beyond Seven Mile Creek, were attacked and driven in. The reports received from the outposts indicated that the enemy was advancing in considerable force. In consequence I ordered Colonel Wagner to post two regiments in line of battle on a strong ridge about 300 yards in rear of Seven Mile Creek, on either side of the road, with the section of artillery disposed between them so as to sweep the passage over the creek and through its quaggy bottom. A third regiment was posted 300 paces in rear of the other two, and the fourth left to continue the work.... Skirmishers were deployed in the thick underwood of the creek bottom and vedettes posted in advance of the creek. The enemy, apparently satisfied with the demonstration he had already made, attempted no farther advance....[16]

Not entirely satisfied that the enemy had gone, Wood ordered Wagner to continue this arrangement of his troops for another twenty-four hours. There was no further trouble and the road building at Seven Mile Creek went on undisturbed for another week. During that time, if the troops were not on outpost duty or helping to lay the corduroy, they received "several lessons ... in the division drill." The men could not be too prepared.[17]

May 21 was another day of alarms. It appeared that there was going to be a real fight. Wood received intelligence from enemy deserters that their infantry, perhaps as many as seventy thousand men under General Braxton Bragg, was massing in front of his center. Wood's men were dug in behind strong fieldworks, but a charge by seventy thousand men would be hard to repulse. The information of an impending attack seemed to be confirmed that afternoon when there was a push against Wood's right flank. The Federals drove the Rebels off and a tense quiet descended. The men waited for a general attack on their center that never came. Wood wrote, "Why the grand attack was not made on the center can never be certainly known, but it is reasonable to conjecture that it was the failure of the movement against the right of our general position." In fact, the Rebels never had any intention of making a "grand attack." The event on May 21 was merely another delaying action. General Beauregard did not intend to make a stout defense of Corinth; he was making plans to evacuate the city. By these persistent rumors and little demonstrations he was simply buying time.[18]

Beauregard threw another scare into the Yankees in the wee hours of May 29. Captain John W. Tuttle recalled:

> We saw beautiful rockets ascending from several points along the rebel line. We did not know what it meant but thought it indicated some general concerted movement of their forces. We thought it highly probable we would be attacked about daylight, if not before, and therefore stood to arms in considerable suspense during the remainder of the night. All remained quiet however until some time after breakfast when a general and rather heavy cannonading was opened by both armies. This was kept up until sometime in the afternoon when it suddenly ceased altogether. There seemed to be something awful and ominous in the silence that ensued.[19]

The men were anxious for nothing; the attack that Tuttle feared did not occur. Early on the morning of May 30, Wood's men heard loud explosions from the direction of Corinth. Looking up, they could see columns of smoke rising from the town. Shortly after, the outposts of General William "Bull" Nelson's 4th Division (which was so advanced as to be within sight of the town) reported back that the Rebels were gone. The news filtered back through the divisions farther behind. The explosions were set off by the last enemy troops to leave Corinth in order to destroy what they could not carry away. And now the enemy was gone and Corinth was won. The campaign had cost General Buell's army only 150 killed and wounded; eleven of the wounded were out of Wood's division.

Halleck congratulated his troops that their bloodless victory was "as brilliant and important as any recorded in history." Wood essentially agreed and celebrated the conquest-by-maneuver of the place where the Confederates had planned to "fight the great battle for the control of the Mississippi Valley."[20]

To some of the volunteer officers, this was just a lot of West Point hogwash. Brigadier General James A. Garfield called the campaign a "disgrace upon

Generalship" and added, "I am nearly disheartened at the way in which the war is conducted here.... If the Republic goes down in blood and ruins, let its obituary be written thus: 'Died of West Point.'" He had grown disgusted with his own division commander, General Wood, and described him as "a very narrow, impetuous, proslavery man in whose prudence and patriotism and brains I have but very little confidence, and a shamefully rough, blasphemous man, quite destitute of fine or manly feelings."[21]

Halleck, Wood, and the other professionals in the officers' corps might have been surprised that they were not held in higher esteem by some of their juniors, but it would not have touched them at their core. They were West Pointers. They knew who they were and they knew what they knew and Corinth was theirs.

Chapter 6

The North Alabama Campaign

General Pope's Army of the Mississippi and Nelson's and Crittenden's divisions of Buell's army followed the Rebels who were retreating from Corinth to near Booneville. When it became clear that the enemy could not be caught and would not turn and fight, Halleck called off the pursuit. Satisfied with having chased the Rebels away, Halleck now turned to planning his next campaign. He wanted General Buell to follow the Memphis & Charleston Railroad across North Alabama toward Chattanooga. Chattanooga was another railroad town. In addition, it controlled a mountain pass into Georgia and was a port on the Tennessee River. Certainly, it was a valuable prize; General Buell had no qualms about that. What he did question was the route by which he was to approach that prize. He would be passing through a barren country and would have to depend upon a long and fragile supply line.

Buell suggested that an advance against Chattanooga through Tennessee made more sense than a march across North Alabama, but Halleck thought otherwise. Halleck commanded the department, so his opinion was the one that counted. North Alabama it was.

Since General Ormsby Mitchel's detached division was already at Huntsville, Alabama, Buell stepped off from Corinth with just four of his divisions, those of Alexander McDowell McCook, Thomas L. Crittenden, William Nelson, and Thomas J. Wood. Wood moved out on June 2, with orders in his pocket that read: "one brigade ... will halt, to furnish working parties and guards at the first bridges [nine miles from Corinth]. The other two brigades will proceed at once to Bear Creek, to commence work there."[1]

Wood was to remain in position until Nelson's division came up. When it did, on June 5, 1862, Wood was ordered to "move forward toward Decatur, leaving a brigade to work at the Bear Creek Bridge until relieved.... In your advance upon Bear Creek, you will repair the wagon road and railroad and will post a brigade at Tuscumbia."[2]

If Wood's men had thought after the Corinth Campaign that their days as a construction gang were over, the North Alabama Campaign cured them of that notion. A few lucky ones stood guard while many others labored with picks and shovels. General Wood later remarked:

> The work was found to be much heavier than originally expected, and much delay occurred in the completion of it for want of locomotives and cars.... It was not an agreeable duty, and the great separation of my forces necessary to carry on the different parts of the work at the same time made it a very dangerous one, as it exposed us to attack by the enemy when we were very much scattered.[3]

The danger was more theoretical than real. There was an occasional exchange of gunfire with Rebel patrols, but for the most part the enemy found it unnecessary to attack the work parties. It was much safer for them to hit the Memphis & Charleston in isolated stretches and to attack the lightly guarded railroads that intersected with it from the North. Only days after the campaign began, Rebels hit the Duck River Bridge at Columbia, Tennessee, and the Elk River Bridge near Pulaski, not to mention various tunnels, culverts, and trestles. It was exactly as General Buell had feared. The rations situation became increasingly dire. Between June 5 and June 8, General Wood's men lived on crackers while waiting for the commissary train to come up. Wagons had to haul supplies to the army from distant railroad breaks and they could not keep up with the demand.

On June 8, the repairs on the Bear Creek railroad bridge were completed and Hascall's 15th Brigade marched for Tuscumbia. They entered on June 16. There some of the men worked on a damaged railroad trestle while others were sent ahead to Town Creek to rebuild a downed railroad bridge. Those who stayed in Tuscumbia were the lucky ones. Captain John W. Tuttle found it to be a "beautiful little city ... the streets well laid off and the sidewalks shaded by comely and thrifty young catalpas." In addition, it had "one of the finest springs in the world."[4]

While he was still at Tuscumbia, Wood's responsibilities increased. Orders arrived from Buell's headquarters near Florence saying, "It will be necessary to establish a temporary hospital in Tuscumbia and it will be done under your direction ... when your division moves to Decatur the hospital at Tuscumbia is to be broken up and the men moved on to Decatur." Before Wood moved on to Decatur, the old worry asserted itself. He asked headquarters, "Whence will I draw supplies after I advance beyond Tuscumbia?"[5]

The answer came back:

> Your orders are to proceed with your division to Decatur, repairing the railroad as you go and drawing your supplies from Florence via Tuscumbia. If you hear of a force of the enemy in your vicinity you are to move upon and drive it off unless it proves to be too large to attack. The entire regiment of the Third Ohio Cavalry is ordered to your division. General [William S.] Smith is directed to send some of the Engineers and Mechanics along to aid in all the repairs and to see to it himself.[6]

It looked so simple on paper: draw your supplies from Florence via Tuscumbia. Wood prepared to move out, but there was an interruption. On June 22, a rumor reached General Buell of ten thousand Rebels who were said to be advancing "toward this line at different points…. [The reports] have been so positive and frequent that I have deemed it proper not to expose Wood's division alone scattered along the road." That very day, Wood began crossing the Tennessee River to the north-bank city of Florence. Now the river was between him and the Rebels.[7]

The 6th Division remained in the vicinity of Tuscumbia/Florence for another week. The strike force of ten thousand Rebels turned out to be nothing more than some cavalry patrols, and so Wood moved out for Decatur in the last week of June. Captain Tuttle remembered that they moved along a white sand road, which reflected the summer sun so brightly that it blinded them.

In Decatur on July 4, there was a break in the routine. The Federals celebrated Independence Day by firing "thirteen guns at sunrise, thirty-four guns at noon, and thirteen at sunset, and by having brigade review and dress parade…. We were nominally relieved of all duty, except guard duty, but were really kept very busy all day preparing for and participating in the celebration."[8]

The men needed something to celebrate, for the North Alabama Campaign was falling apart. Already, Buell had been forced to dismember his army because of enemy raids along the Nashville & Decatur and the Nashville & Chattanooga. McCook's division and Crittenden's division were in Battle Creek, Tennessee, to suppress the Rebels' acts of vandalism. They were not successful. Sufficient rations were not reaching the men in Alabama. For two days after the Independence Day celebration, the men of the 3rd Kentucky Infantry had nothing at all to eat. When they were detailed across the Tennessee River from Decatur on some routine duty, they used it as an opportunity to go out foraging. They were hungry and they did what they had to do, even though foraging was against Buell's orders.

During the week of July 9 to 16, Buell's army received not an ounce of rations. It had appeared on July 12 that the flow of supplies could resume along the Nashville & Chattanooga. On that day, repairs were completed on the Elk River Bridge. But on July 13, Nathan Bedford Forrest destroyed a portion of the railroad and the bridge at Murfreesboro. The railroad was down again. The men's hopes were dashed and their stomachs grumbled.

A shortage of rations did not mean that the men were excused from their duties. On July 10, Colonel Abel D. Streight of the 51st Indiana Infantry (Harker's brigade) learned that forty loyal Alabama men were anxious to come enlist, if they could only get through the Rebel cavalry that blocked their way. Small groups of men had been making their way into the Federal lines all along, but a band of forty was sizable. They needed a protective escort and Streight was ordered to go out and get them. Before a rescue party could be dispatched, the Alabamians on their own got inside Federal lines. They were duly mustered in and reported that there were several hundred more who wanted to volunteer. The trouble was that they were stranded about twenty-five miles out. General Wood ordered Streight to lead a rescue expedition to go out for them

Streight rode out of camp on the morning of July 12 with his command, including sixteen men of Company D, 1st Ohio Cavalry. They headed toward Devil's Gap, with the cavalrymen scouting out front, too far out in front, as it turned out. Contrary to orders, they did not ride back with intelligence of what lay ahead. Instead, Captain Stephen C. Writer stopped at the Menter home and ordered the women to put a meal on the table. There had been no rations to reach Decatur for three days, and Writer and his men were hungry.

While they ate, Writer's horse soldiers were attacked by a mixed force of seventy-five to one hundred Rebel cavalry and guerrillas. Writer did not make a stand. He retreated and returned, not to Streight but to Decatur, with twelve of his men.

Not knowing what had happened, Streight continued blind to within a couple of miles of Menter's farm. There, to Streight's surprise, he caught sight of Writer's men spurring their horses away in the direction of Decatur. The precipitous withdrawal of the cavalry was a small disaster. It weakened Streight, emboldened the guerrillas, and discouraged the locals. Nevertheless, Streight stayed out for another three days and did manage to quickly enlist 150 volunteers before he returned to Wood's camp on the Tennessee.

Captain Writer later explained that he and his sixteen men had tried to defend the farm. They took up a defensive position in the barnyard as the much larger enemy force spread out to envelop both of their flanks. Realizing that their situation was untenable, the Federals gave up the fight and rode back to Decatur. They were fired upon en route. Writer took a bullet but stayed in the saddle. He and his men rode into Decatur about midnight. He reported that he had lost "3 horses ... 2 full horse equipments, 2 carbines, 3 sabers, and 4 pistols." In addition, two of his men were missing. He believed that he had killed two Rebels and wounded two more.[9]

Colonel Streight, in his report of the expedition, mocked Writer's cavalrymen and criticized their withdrawal, "which seems to have been accomplished very precipitously, especially when taking into consideration the fact that the enemy did not pursue him but a few yards."[10]

Regarding the citizenry of North Alabama, Streight had this to say:

> Mostly poor, though many of them are, or rather were, in comfortable circumstances. They outnumber nearly three to one the secessionists ... but situated as they are, surrounded by a most relentless foe, mostly unarmed and destitute of ammunition, they are persecuted in every conceivable way.... Their horses and

cattle are driven off in vast numbers. Every public road is patrolled by guerrilla bands.... They cannot hold out much longer.[11]

Streight volunteered to set up a rallying point thirty miles south of Decatur with his own regiment and believed that, with the people protected in this way, he could raise at least two full regiments "of as good and true men as ever defended the flag." He concluded, "Never did people stand in greater need of protection."[12]

Nothing came of Streight's offer to open a recruiting center south of the Tennessee River. Buell could not even feed the men he already had, and the situation was growing worse. About a week after he destroyed the Murfreesboro railroad bridge, Nathan Bedford Forrest struck again. He dropped the bridge at Mill Springs. Buell dispatched Nelson's division to Murfreesboro and beyond to McMinnville. The 6th Division pressed on toward Huntsville, where Buell ordered two of Wood's brigades (the 15th and the 21st) north to Shelbyville and Decherd. General Wood went with them. The 20th Brigade, commanded once more by Harker, went on to Stevenson, Alabama.

There the advance on Chattanooga came to an end. On July 28, the Murfreesboro bridge was repaired and trains headed south to Buell's army. A trainload of supplies arrived at Stevenson on July 29 and a second train pulled in on July 30. It began to look as if the campaign could continue, but it had taken so long that winning Chattanooga would not be so easily done now. The same day that the second Union train came to Stevenson, Buell received the disheartening news that the leading elements of the Confederate army had begun arriving in Chattanooga. The Army of the Mississippi was led by General Braxton Bragg, who had succeeded Beauregard. The Confederates had taken a long railroad trip from Tupelo to Mobile and from there to Montgomery, Atlanta, and Chattanooga. Nevertheless, they beat Buell to Chattanooga. Now there would have to be a fight for the mountain town.

However, the point was moot after August 12. On that day, John Hunt Morgan hit Gallatin on the L&N Railroad. Morgan's Raiders destroyed tracks and bridges and plugged the Big South Tunnel with tons of debris. With the L&N Railroad down, supplies could not get through to Nashville, and if supplies could not get through to Nashville, there was nothing to send down the Nashville & Chattanooga and the Nashville & Decatur to Buell. Buell's army was unsupplied and an unsupplied army could not campaign.

General Wood found that the supply situation in Tennessee was an improvement over that in Alabama. Though his men were still on half rations, the foraging was much better. Buell had a fairly strict policy against individual foraging, but separated from the commanding general's immediate observation, Wood apparently gave his men more freedom to fill their haversacks from civilian smokehouses and rootcellars. He also seized control of all the gristmills near Decherd and put his men to grinding corn. When Wood was later asked, "What proportion of the other half rations was procured ... in the country to help out the short supply?" Wood replied, "I can answer generally a very considerable portion.... I can say generally that the troops of my command lived very well when they were on half rations. Certainly there was no suffering."[13]

Wood reached Southern Tennessee by forced marches. On July 14, he arrived at Shelbyville, the northwest corner of the slightly askew geographical box in which he was ordered to operate. The northeast corner was Manchester, the southwest corner was Fayetteville, and the southeast corner was Winchester/Decherd. In this area were the important Duck River and Elk River bridges. After July 14, Wood was almost constantly on the move, routinely making rides of thirty miles between one point and the other, responding to rumored Confederate advances and checking on the work and well-being of his widely deployed troops.

From July 17 until mid–August, Wood made Decherd his headquarters. While he was there, on August 1, he learned from General Buell that Bragg's Rebels were apparently on the move from Chattanooga. Buell said, "The enemy have crossed two or three regiments of infantry certainly at Chattanooga and are working on the Anderson Road. Their talk is of Nashville and Kentucky. Be prepared at any hour to march and fight. Keep three days' rations cooked. Nelson is moving forward."[14]

At this moment, Wood's brigades were scattered among the towns of Decherd, Mooresville, Wartrace, Manchester, and Shelbyville and there was a detachment at the Duck River Bridge. Wagner was ordered to concentrate his brigade at Tullahoma, beginning on August 3, and Wood was ordered to select the best location for a supply depot: Elk River, Decherd, or Estill Springs. When the selection was made, he should prepare to defend it. Wood chose Decherd as the best site. His subsequent orders show by what means the Federal army got some of its heavy work done and also the prevailing attitude about slavery and slave owners. Wood was ordered to

> detail from your command suitable parties for the impressments of negroes to be found in the vicinity of Decherd, for the purpose of working upon the fortifications in and about this place. In impressing care should be taken to equalize the number in all instances, leaving a sufficient number to do the ordinary business of the farm house.
>
> Give instructions that each negro bring his blanket and every squad of six his cooking utensils. Take the name of each negro, giving a proper receipt to owner for the same, so that they can be returned to them as soon as the work is completed.[15]

It fell to a detachment of the 3rd Kentucky Infantry to carry out these orders. Captain Tuttle and some men went out to conscript local blacks. Tuttle remembered:

> We gathered up all we could find, about forty in number and repaired with them to General Wood's headquarters a little after dark. The General was at his supper and we concluded not to disturb him by reporting our "contrabands".... Owing to the darkness none noticed him come out and he got in some of his best swearing before the writer could explain to him that our colored friends were not straggling intruders as he seemed to suppose, but had been brought there in obedience to his orders ... on learning his mistake [he] made a graceful and courteous apology.[16]

The defenses of Decherd were not heavily manned for long. On August 14, Wood was ordered to take both of his brigades and join General William Nelson at McMinnville. Since Wood was required to do railroad repair as he marched, the trip was a slow one, and he did not arrive until August 20. The 6th Division moved out again two days later for Altamont, where Buell decided he would make a stand against Bragg. Wood learned from loyal Tennesseans that Bragg was moving in force. He had begun crossing the Tennessee River "as early as the 16th of August ... by the 20th there were four divisions across."[17]

There were no Rebels at Altamont and waiting there proved to be unfeasible. The site was barren of forage and water, and Wood returned to McMinnville on the twenty-sixth, accompanying General Thomas' 1st Division. General Nelson's 4th Division went, too.

It was a confusing time. Rumors abounded about Bragg's strength and destination and there was disagreement among Buell's division commanders about where they should turn to make a stand against the Confederates. General Thomas thought that McMinnville was the place. Wood thought Bragg could be whipped at Sparta. Others thought that Murfreesboro was preferable.

To try to get a clearer picture of what was going on behind enemy lines, Wood relied on spies. They were called "scouts" in the vernacular of that time. He did not always believe what they told him. At McMinnville on August 29, a scout by the name of Thatcher reported to Wood's headquarters:

> This person represented himself as having passed some time in Chattanooga, and as having left there only a short time before. He stated the enemy's force generally to be somewhere in the neighborhood of 60,000 men. He said that there were four divisions at Chattanooga, and that they had about 15,000 men in each division. He went into the minutiae, giving names of commanders of divisions and commanders of corps, strengths of regiments, and strengths of companies.

Wood thought that Thatcher's estimate of the size of Bragg's army was too high. He believed the Army of the Mississippi in the Sequatchie Valley could not number more than forty-five thousand men. This did not include Edmund Kirby Smith's army at Knoxville, which he calculated to be at not more than fifteen thousand men.[18]

The same day as Thatcher's visit, Wood accompanied the 3rd Kentucky Infantry on a successful foraging expedition. According to Captain Tuttle, they brought in "a considerable quantity of corn ... about thirty head of cattle, several head of sheep, nine barrels of peach brandy and a chest of medicines."[19]

The next day, August 30, Wood was ordered to fall back to Murfreesboro. En route, his cavalry had a run-in with some Confederate cavalry and gave them a chase of three miles before giving it up. A more serious encounter occurred the following day. Nathan Bedford Forrest had been active near Murfreesboro for the past several days and was discovered to still be near. Wood ordered Colonel Edward P. Fyffe to lead the 26th Ohio Infantry, the 58th Indiana Infantry, the four-gun 8th Indiana Battery, and a small force of cavalry to cut off Forrest, who was "within 2 miles of this camp, making his way northward." Fyffe was in temporary command of the 15th Brigade because of the illness of General Hascall, who was so incapacitated as to be bedridden.[20]

Fyffe marched surreptitiously through the woods (with the help of a local guide) to the Murfreesboro and McMinnville Road. His men emerged from the trees six miles from camp. In some fields across the way Fyffe saw Forrest's cavalry. Fyffe's mixed force hurried in the direction of the enemy while Forrest formed his men in line of battle. Fyffe ordered Lieutenant Estep and the 8th Indiana Battery to unlimber on a hill to the left and to open fire. Companies A and F of the 26th Ohio were ordered to move to the base of the hill and also to open fire. The rest of the infantry took position immediately behind the two forward companies. The Rebel center gave way under the combined artillery and small arms fire. Their two flanks moved off in different directions. Estep's artillerymen redirected the fire of their pieces by section, two guns each, to pour rounds into the retreating enemy flanks. Each section was supported by companies of the 58th Indiana while the 26th Ohio continued to hold the Union center. Fyffe was content to fight Forrest long range.

"In a very short time," Fyffe wrote, "the enemy were entirely dispersed in every direction, so much so that it was with great difficulty I could determine on which road it would be most profitable to pursue him." Fyffe determined to follow on the Murfreesboro road, but it grew dark and the chase was aborted. It was just as well, perhaps. If one chased Nathan Bedford Forrest too closely, one might have the bad luck to catch him. Colonel Fyffe returned to camp, having killed an estimated eighteen or twenty of the enemy.[21]

During the first week of September, General Buell abandoned control of the surrounding country to the Rebels and ordered the Army of the Ohio to rendezvous in Nashville. The 6th Division arrived in the city on September 6, but General Wood, for one, had already decided that Nashville would not be the scene of a climactic battle between Buell and Bragg. Nashville was not Bragg's objective. Wood believed that Bragg was heading for Kentucky. His prophecy proved to be correct. At Buell's headquarters, the very day of Wood's arrival, reliable news came that Polk's wing of Bragg's army was across the

Cumberland River at Carthage. In response, Buell sent Wood on to Gallatin. If Bragg made a move on Bowling Green, Wood would be in a position to counter him. Once again, Wood employed a spy to gather information for him. At Gallatin, he met with a loyal citizen named Bumpus, who lived in the vicinity. Wood told Bumpus that he wanted "correct information of the position, movement, designs, and strength of the enemy." It was a dangerous mission for the Tennessee man, who was known to favor the Union and was watched by his neighbors because of it. That danger being a factor, Wood promised Bumpus $1,000 if he brought back reliable intelligence and if it was later verified to be true. Bumpus left Wood on September 8 and returned on the afternoon of September 10, after Wood had moved forward to Mitchellville, en route to Bowling Green. The spy had "ridden 150 miles in less than 48 hours." He brought all the information Wood had requested, including the news that Bragg's destination was Glasgow, not Bowling Green. General Buell needed to hear it. Fearing to commit the intelligence to paper, the general provided the hard-riding Mr. Bumpus with a fresh mount and sent him on to Buell in Nashville.[22]

On September 10, the day Bumpus found General Wood, the Kentuckian received orders to send his wagons on to Bowling Green but to keep the men in camp until September 12. General Crittenden's and Rousseau's divisions received the same orders.

Though it was not the Confederates' target, Bowling Green must be made secure. It was a central point on the L&N Railroad, the site of an important railroad bridge, and the depository of 1 million badly needed rations. That being so, Wood wanted the glory of being the first to occupy Bowling Green for his own division, and he refused to wait until September 12 to move. Unfortunately, Rousseau's division was in front of him. The professional's disdain for the volunteer officer broke its bounds. Wood sent a dispatch to Rousseau "to move forward and *get out of my way*" and informed General Buell, "I will go to Bowling Green tonight [italics added for emphasis]."[23]

Rousseau was not a man to be intimidated by arrogant talk and does not seem to have gotten out of Wood's way. Both generals arrived in Bowling Green on September 11. It may be a clue as to who reached town first that Rousseau took command in Bowling Green while Wood moved on through and camped his division one mile north. Rousseau began repairing the city's fortifications and reported on September 13, "I am foraging for grain, etc., for the stock, and have ordered beef instead of bacon while in camp here, and will send train at daylight in the morning to Franklin for $17,000 worth of flour with guard of 300 men. Have ordered the seizure of 100 barrels of salt now here."[24]

However, who first set foot in the Warren County seat was only a detail, unimportant compared to the larger point that now two Federal divisions controlled Bowling Green and the divisions of Generals Jacob Ammen, Alexander McDowell McCook, and Thomas L. Crittenden were on the way. General George H. Thomas was left in charge of the defenses at Nashville. He and his 1st Division would come to Kentucky a few days later and join Buell en route to Louisville.

As the Army of the Ohio crossed the Kentucky line, conditions in the Bluegrass State were bad and getting worse. Edmund Kirby Smith had left Knoxville on August 13 and headed straight for Kentucky. He routed Colonel Leonidas Metcalf at Big Hill on August 23 and then a larger force under Brigadier Generals Mahlon Manson and Charles Cruft on August 29 and 30 at Richmond. Kirby Smith's Confederates proceeded to Lexington on September 2 and occupied Frankfort on September 3. There they raised the colors of the 1st Louisiana Cavalry over the state capitol.

With Edmund Kirby Smith in control of Lexington and Braxton Bragg approaching Glasgow, the Rebels were in a position to envelop Louisville, Kentucky's largest city and the Army of the Ohio's primary supply base, and to arrive there well before Buell. If Louisville was forfeited, Kentucky would be lost, and as President Lincoln had said, that would be the same as losing the game. Yet General Buell seemed to be in no particular hurry.

CHAPTER 7

The Contest for Kentucky

The pressure on Buell to advance from Bowling Green increased after September 14, 1862. On that day, a messenger from Munfordville arrived at headquarters to report that Colonel John T. Wilder was under attack and needed reinforcements.

Munfordville was a transportation hub. It was on the Green River, the Louisville and Nashville Turnpike, and the L&N Railroad. The L&N bridge over the Green River had been one of the engineering wonders of the country before the Rebels destroyed it in late 1861. A temporary span had been built to replace it. Knowing the importance of the town, the Federal authorities had kept a garrison there through 1862, and when Bragg began pushing for Kentucky, Colonel John T. Wilder of the 17th Indiana was sent to take charge of the Munfordville defenses. He expanded and improved the works that had been erected by General McCook's men in early 1862. To man those works, Wilder had his own regiment, as well as the 89th Indiana, the 67th Indiana, two companies of the 74th Indiana, one company of the 18th U.S Infantry, one company of cavalry, one battery of the 13th Indiana Artillery, the Louisville Provost Guard, and sixty completely unarmed men of the 33rd Kentucky Infantry.

On September 13, 1862, Colonel John Scott, a cavalryman serving under Edmund Kirby Smith, caught sight of Wilder's defenses. Scott had been sent west by Smith to try to make contact with General Bragg, and here was this tempting prize, an isolated Federal outpost occupying an important location overlooking the Green River Bridge. Scott broke the L&N north of Munfordville and sent word to Brigadier General James M. Chalmers at Cave City to hurry north and help take an easy prize.

Chalmers was a brigadier in General Leonidas Polk's wing of Bragg's army. The other wing was led by General William J. Hardee. Hardee and Polk had occupied Glasgow on September 11 and Polk had sent Chalmers' men on ahead to Cave City, another L&N Railroad town. At Cave City the next day,

74

Chalmers' brigade had torn up some of the L&N Railroad, seized the telegrapher's office, and captured quantities of clothing, boots, and salt. They were enjoying their plunder when Colonel Scott summoned. Chalmers moved out.

At 3:00 A.M. on September 14, Scott attacked Colonel Wilder. The Hoosier proved surprisingly tough. After the battle had been going on for three hours, General Chalmers' brigade came into line and threw themselves against Wilder's two flanks. Still, the defenders of Munfordville held tight. After three more hours of fighting, Chalmers decided to try a bluff. He sent into the Federal works a demand for surrender. He complimented Wilder on the gallantry of his defense but said that "to avoid further bloodshed I demand an unconditional surrender of your forces." Wilder was confident. He and his men had provisions for several days. They had held their own in the fight so far, reinforcements were coming in from Louisville, and he had sent runners to Bowling Green requesting reinforcements; Buell might arrive at any moment. Wilder declined to surrender. "If you wish to avoid further bloodshed, keep out of the range of my guns," he said.[1]

Chalmers was stumped. This scrappy Hoosier would not surrender and he could not be whipped by the forces outside his works. Reluctantly Chalmers returned to Cave City and, even more reluctantly, reported to General Bragg of the situation at Munfordville. Bragg had a difficult personality under the best of circumstances. He demanded a great deal of his officers and men, not the least of which was the obedience of orders, and he had not ordered an attack on Munfordville. Now an attack had been made and repulsed. Bragg could not begin his campaign for Kentucky with a defeat. The knowledge that they had tried and failed at the very start would poison the spirits of his men. The cranky general had no choice now except to continue a fight he had not sought and did not want. He moved his army to Munfordville to finish the fight that Chalmers had begun but could not win.

The artillerymen of the Army of the Mississippi lobbed a few balls into the Federal works when they arrived on the morning of September 16. Hardee deployed his long gray lines south of the Yankees while Polk's wing crossed Green River and went into position north of Wilder's position. There was a bit of skirmishing and then Bragg demanded that Wilder surrender. Fighting some cavalrymen and a few regiments of Mississippi infantry was one thing, but if Bragg was really out there with his entire army, that was something else again. At the same time, Wilder did not want to fall for a trick; what if he surrendered only to discover later that the whole Army of the Mississippi had *not* really been outside his walls? Knowing that Simon Bolivar Buckner was a division commander in Hardee's wing, Wilder asked to see him. Buckner was an honorable man and his reputation for veracity was known in both armies. So, Wilder asked Buckner straight out if the situation was so hopeless that he should capitulate.

Buckner told Wilder that he could not advise him on the matter. He could only show him the Confederate troops arrayed for battle south of his works so that he could decide for himself. Wilder counted forty-six pieces of artillery ready to blast him out of his position and hordes of butternut infantrymen ready to clean up with their bayonets. He knew that there was a like number on the north. "Well, it seems to me, General Buckner, that I ought to surrender," he said. He secured the right of his men to be paroled and carry out four days' rations, and on September 17 they marched out of Munfordville in the direction of Bowling Green.[2]

As they marched south, a bitter thought of condemnation must have sounded in Wilder's mind. As he later said, "I supposed ... that General Buell's army would come to relieve me before Bragg could get there." He had sent civilian messengers racing to Bowling Green for help. What had happened?[3]

Buell's long list of reasons for not marching to the relief of Munfordville might have surprised Wilder. In a statement before the commission that was later appointed to investigate his actions of 1862, Buell gave several answers for lingering in Bowling Green from September 11 to September 16.

One of Buell's reasons was the fact that Wilder was not under his command. Rather, he was in General Horatio G. Wright's Department of the Ohio, established August 19, 1862, and a separate entity from the Army of the Ohio. Buell considered that it was Wright's responsibility, not his own, to reinforce or relieve Wilder. Indeed, A. G. Craddock, one of Wilder's civilian scouts, testified that when he told Buell at his Bowling Green headquarters of Wilder's plight Buell's only response was, "Colonel Wilder had better evacuate that post."[4]

If Craddock's testimony before the Buell Commission was accurate, then Buell either was equivocating or was the victim of a poor memory, for the general testified before the commission that he did not get the idea from any of the scouts' reports that Wilder was in actual danger.

Buell offered another reason for not marching to Munfordville: that it was a position that favored the enemy and that "must have made the result at least doubtful; and even a very serious check in the exhausted condition of our supplies would have been disastrous."[5]

Buell went on that he "could not have reached Munfordville in less than four days," even if he had left Bowling Green immediately upon receiving Wilder's scouts' reports, and that the idea of sending forward either Wood's or Rousseau's division ("even if the necessity of it had been known") was unreasonable, for it "would have been thrown into the midst of the whole rebel force; a folly which it appears the enemy actually anticipated, and prepared to reap the fruit of."[6]

In this cornucopia of excuses, Buell had one more to add, which some historians have decided was the actual reason behind the general's reluctance to move: he wanted to force Bragg deeper into the state so that he could not double back around the Federal flank to attack Bowling Green or, more seriously, Nashville. If Buell moved too soon, Bragg would have that chance.

Buell offered too many excuses. Reading what he had to say from a distance of a century and a half, Buell sounds defensive and dishonest, trying too hard to justify a controversial decision.

And it *was* controversial. He said that he did not know of any of his senior officers who believed that a move should be made to relieve Wilder at Munfordville, but once again he was not being forthright or his memory was playing him false, for there were some officers who thought that a march to Munfordville was exactly the right thing to do. Among them was the Munfordville native General Thomas J. Wood. On a personal level, he must have been concerned about the well-being of his aging father, Colonel George T. Wood. He may well have been at his home on the hill as the Confederates moved into Munfordville, for his journeys to Frankfort were not so frequent now. The power of the Kentucky Military Board was "virtually annulled" after General Jeremiah T. Boyle became the military commandant in Kentucky on June 1, 1862. In any case, the Rebels would have known of Colonel Wood's sentiments and his past services to the Union cause.[7]

On a professional level, General Wood must have seen this as his chance to hit the Rebels at last. All that the Army of the Ohio had done was march since leaving Shiloh in the spring, and Wood's division had only been lightly engaged there. Waiting ahead at Munfordville was an opportunity to save Wilder and hit Bragg before his junction with Edmund Kirby Smith. Wood did not deny that a rapid march from Bowling Green would be hard, even hazardous, but he later insisted, "It could have been done." Unlike General Buell, Wood's testimony was not at odds with what others recalled. General McCook said that Wood told him at the time, "We ought to march on to Munfordville."[8]

The opinion of Wood was shared by some officers at brigade level and even some of the soldiers in the ranks. Colonel Abel D. Streight said that his troops "were very anxious to move on and relieve the Munfordville force.... We knew that Munfordville was threatened and while at Bowling Green we heard that Colonel Wilder had succeeded in repelling the enemy. From that time there was clearly indignation among both officers and men. It was because we were not allowed to attack the enemy.... Knowing that Colonel Wilder was threatened, and hearing he was attacked the feeling further increased."[9]

In later years, Buell seems to have realized that the failure to march to the relief of Munfordville was damaging to his reputation. In "East Tennessee and the Campaign of Perryville," his contribution to *Battles and Leaders of the Civil War*, Buell compressed events and made it sound as if he had tried to catch

Bragg at Munfordville. Buell wrote that he "learned that the garrison at Munfordville had been attacked, but the result was not certainly known. Bragg was reported at Glasgow, and on the 16th I marched to give battle to him at that place; but during the day it was ascertained that he had marched the day before for Munfordville, the garrison of which, it was ascertained, had repelled the first attack, and my divisions were directed upon that point."[10]

Buell marched from Bowling Green on September 16. Wood's division left about 3:00 P.M. on the Louisville and Nashville Turnpike and camped that night in the vicinity of Dripping Springs. The next day's march brought the army to Prewitt's Knob, though General Wood's division went a few miles beyond to camp around the ruins of Bell's Tavern, where Henry Clay and other notables once slept. Here the army lingered for three days and here Wilder's paroled Munfordville garrison entered Federal lines. Captain John W. Tuttle called them "quite a mournful spectacle." Seeing them, many of the men wept. Wilder brought definite news of the Rebels: they were arrayed for battle on the south bank of the Green River, they were low on rations, and they numbered between thirty-five and forty thousand. Buell had believed, at his highest estimate, that Bragg had sixty thousand soldiers behind him. Wilder's calculation of Confederate numbers meant that Bragg did not have the numerical advantage that Buell once feared; rather, they were about equal in size to the Army of the Ohio, but they were dug in and ready to fight. Wilder's report did not encourage Buell to hurry forward. He kept his army in place until the twentieth.[11]

The foot soldiers of the Army of the Ohio had no great love for Buell, and on the slow march from Bowling Green their indifference turned to ridicule. A comedic routine was repeated whenever the men stopped. "What's up now?" asked the straight man.

"Nothing," said the other, "only Bragg's got a wagon broke down and old Buell's stopped to wait for him to get started."[12]

On September 20, the army at last pulled on its boots and moved out. There had been some skirmishing and the men moved cautiously until they received word that the enemy had only just left Munfordville. Then, said Captain Tuttle, "we abandoned our cautious, devious, and formal manner of advance and pressed forward with all possible rapidity."[13]

When they drew near, they found Fighting Joe Wheeler's cavalry guarding the Green River ford. The 3rd Kentucky Infantry flew into them "and engaged them until our division formed in order of battle and advanced upon them." It turned into quite a little skirmish, lasting about forty minutes, complete with an exchange of artillery fire. When the weight of the enemy became too great, Wheeler fell back and Wood's division crossed the Green River and went into camp. Thus it was that General Wood had the honor of engaging the retreating Confederates before a hometown audience.[14]

One of the Confederates who died in the fight at the Green River ford was a lieutenant colonel named Brown. The next day, Wheeler requested of General Buell that Brown's brothers be allowed to pass through the Federal lines to retrieve the body. Buell declined the request. He directed Wood to reply to Wheeler and give details of Brown's death. Wood's reply to Wheeler showed the peculiar courtesy that often existed between belligerent officers in the War Between the States, particularly if they were both professionals. Wood wrote to Wheeler, "He was killed outright in the handsome cavalry charge executed by your troops yesterday afternoon. His body was taken to a neighboring house and cared for. He will be interred to-day, and doubtless in the vicinity. His watch was taken charge of by an officer of rank in our service, and I will make it a point to have it forwarded to you."[15]

If Wood went to see his father in Munfordville and gazed again on the grave of his mother and the distant eminence of Summerseat Knob, it must have been a short visit, for the army was on the move again the next morning. Now they were seeing the destruction the Rebels had left behind them: a wrecked train and torn-up tracks and a spider's web of shining telegraph wires lying on the ground. It was a summer of drought and every pond that still held water was precious, but the Rebels had filled their canteens and then fouled the ponds with filth and the bloated carcasses of dead livestock.

Passing Bacon Creek, the Federals found more destruction. The Confederates had burned the stockade and the small railroad bridge. The Federals pressed on to Upton, where they bivouacked and inflicted a bit of vandalism of their own. "[We] used an enormous quantity of fencing for fuel," admitted Tuttle.[16]

On September 23, the men passed by the site of old Camp Nevin, where so many of them had spent their first days as soldiers. Here, too, the blockhouse and bridge were burned.

A few miles beyond, Bragg's army turned off the Louisville and Nashville Turnpike and headed toward Hodgenville and Bardstown. The move surprised Buell, who had believed that Bragg would turn to fight at Elizabethtown. Moreover, Bragg had shown by his change in direction that he had no interest in Louisville, the prize for which the armies were contending, or so Buell had thought. At Vinegar Hill, just outside of the railroad town of Sonora, Bragg's rear guard, Wheeler's cavalry, sprang from surprise and fought a skirmish with Union horse soldiers. The fight was brief and resulted in little loss of life. It is notable only because it was the valedictory action of what has come down through history as "The Great Foot Race."

The men passed through West Point on September 24, camped, and resumed the march next morning. The division of General Thomas L. Crittenden was now in the lead and was the first to enter Louisville, to the great jubilation of the citizens and also General William "Bull" Nelson, who had been scrambling to defend the city with whatever rear-echelon troops he could gather. Wood's division did not enter the city until 2:00 A.M. September 26. The last elements of the army came in on the twenty-seventh. The Army of the Ohio would have four days' rest before marching out again on October 1. Those four short days would change everything.

Wood's division was ordered to camp outside of Louisville at Oakland Racetrack, along with the 1st and the 5th Divisions. Only the officers bivouacked in the city, roughing it in the luxurious rooms of the Galt House. General Buell made his headquarters there, and it was there that he began to reorganize his army.

He decided to abandon the division configuration and arrange his army by corps. The I Corps would be given to General Alexander McDowell McCook, the II Corps to General Thomas L. Crittenden, and the III Corps to General William Nelson. Wood's 6th Division would be in General Crittenden's corps. The assignment was a disappointment to Wood, for it was, in effect, a demotion. Both Crittenden and Wood had been with General Taylor in Mexico, both had taken to the field early in Kentucky, and both had been in the Shiloh and Corinth Campaigns as division commanders. Yet Crittenden had won the assignment that made him Wood's superior. Wood, always anxious for promotion, must have felt that he had an equal claim to command of a corps. That he did not receive it was a stinging development, but what was much worse was that he, a West Point professional, was now subordinate to Crittenden, who was a volunteer. Even so, the commanding general had ordered it and the matter seemed settled.

Before the new organization could be effected, however, Buell's proposed arrangement was knocked galley-west. General Jefferson C. Davis had been subordinate to General William Nelson in the days before Buell arrived. They made a poor team, and Davis had taken mortal offense at Nelson's treatment of him. In turn, Davis' conduct was so near to mutiny that Nelson had banished him from the city. Davis left until the morning of September 29, when he returned to confront Nelson. He found him in the lobby of the Galt House. Words were exchanged. Davis threw a wadded-up piece of paper in Nelson's face, and Nelson backhanded Davis before walking away. Davis rushed to his nearby group of friends (which included Indiana governor Oliver P. Morton), was handed a pistol, and rushed back to shoot Nelson dead with a bullet to the chest.

Now Buell had to replace Nelson. It seems that Wood barely knew Nelson, could not have mourned him too deeply, and must have had a glimmer of hope that he would now be elevated to corps command. He was not. Buell did not offer the assignment to him, though he did ask a number of other officers, who turned down the job. Buell finally approached Charles C. Gilbert, a captain who, in these hectic times, had been acting in the role of a major general. Gilbert snatched at the opportunity to command the III Corps and was promptly assigned. Wood would remain as commander of the 6th Division.

At almost the same hour as Nelson's murder, there was another organization upheaval. Colonel J. C. McKibben walked into the Galt House with orders from the War Department for Buell to step aside as commander of the Army of the Ohio. Buell had failed too many times, in the eyes of the Lincoln administration. He had moved too slowly across Alabama; he had failed to reach Chattanooga; he had failed to stop Bragg south of the Cumberland River; he had failed to catch him in Kentucky — it was inevitable that the scale would eventually tip. That it did so on the very morning that Nelson was killed was just a coincidence. The simultaneous murder of a corps commander and a dismissal from command of the army — it must have been the strangest morning of General Buell's life.

General George H. Thomas was to assume command of the Army of the Ohio. Thomas was a Virginian by birth, but he remained loyal to the Constitution he had pledged to protect and defend as a West Point cadet. He was also a man with an admirable sense of duty, and it was plain to him that it was unwise to change commanders at the commencement of a march that would lead to a battle with Braxton Bragg. He politely declined, saying, "General Buell's preparations have been completed to move against the enemy, and I therefore respectfully ask that he may be retained in command. My position is very embarrassing, not being as well informed as I should be as the commander of this army and on the assumption of such a responsibility."[17]

General Halleck replied, "You may consider the order as suspended till I can lay your dispatch before the Government and get information." Later that day, the suspension of the decision to remove Buell as commander of the Army of the Ohio was confirmed by order of the president.[18]

Buell wired Halleck shortly before going to Nelson's funeral on the afternoon of the thirtieth. He said, "Out of sense of public duty I shall continue to discharge the duties of my command to the best of my ability until otherwise ordered." Not knowing quite what to do with Thomas, Buell decided to appoint him as second in command; this he did by Special Orders No. 159.[19]

The army marched out of Louisville on October 1 for their long-delayed match with General Bragg and the Army of the Mississippi.

General Thomas L. Crittenden was an attorney and the son of Senator John J. Crittenden. No one seemed to hold it against him that his brother, George L. Crittenden, decided to go south, where he became a Confederate general. Many Kentucky families were divided. The Union General Crittenden was a lean, bearded man who proved to be popular with the troops, and though he liked his liquor, he was a man of considerable dignity. The photographic portraits of him are the perfect picture of a general, but his looks might be misleading. He was not a professional soldier, after all. The quality of his talents remained to be seen.

Buell's three corps spread out when leaving Louisville. The III Corps under General Gilbert left the City at the Falls by the Shepherdsville Road; the I Corps under General McCook marched out the Shelbyville Road and then the Taylorsville Road. McCook was minus Brigadier General Joshua Sill's division, which had been sent in the direction of Frankfort as a diversion. General Crittenden's II Corps, in the center and with General Thomas accompanying, left Louisville by the Bardstown Road. Since Bragg was in Bardstown, Crittenden's corps was heading directly into a battle, if Bragg would just stand still.

Crittenden's corps marched nine miles to Fern Creek before going into bivouac. They passed through some of the most handsome country in Kentucky. A reporter for the *New York Times* was traveling with the men. He called himself "Curtius" and he wrote, "The country through which we passed today is the wealthiest, the most fertile, and best informed in Kentucky. Broad acres of rich level fields, in a state of high cultivation, stretch on both sides of the road. Fields of ripened corn ... and stacks of grains, show the fertility of the land and the industry of the people. Groves of beech and sugar trees intervene between the fields and present a refreshing appearance."[20]

At Fern Creek, they learned that General Buell had ordered most of the wagons and baggage to remain in Louisville. Unfortunately, the men had already begun their march, and they had not realized that they would spend the night in a camp without rations. "The result," said Curtius, "is that we are here, and many of the regiments are without anything to eat." The march was not yet a full day old and already the general had betrayed them; at least that was how they saw it. The men grumbled and cursed the name of Don Carlos Buell.[21]

On October 2, the hungry men of the II Corps resumed their march. Over the next couple of days, there were occasional brushes with Rebel cavalry, but the most serious encounter was on October 4, at the Nelson County Fairgrounds just outside of Bardstown, where they ran into the Confederate cavalry under Colonel John Wharton. An hour-long fight developed between the horse soldiers, with the Rebels driving back the Yankees. The infantrymen of Wood's division formed a battle line and marched menacingly toward Bardstown. The Union troops moved in without further opposition and bivouacked wherever there was space, even in the streets.

That same day, Buell, Thomas, and Crittenden had a conference in which Buell opined that the Rebels would turn and fight at Perryville. Crittenden

General Thomas L. Crittenden (Library of Congress).

was to follow them there, down the Springfield Pike. The II Corps began moving out at 10:00 A.M. and marched twelve miles to Lynchburg.

There was more skirmishing the next day as the II Corps moved toward Springfield. Fighting Joe Wheeler's cavalrymen would suddenly appear, fire a few rounds in their direction, and slide out of sight again. They were more of an annoyance than a hindrance and the II Corps men spent the night at the fairgrounds in the Washington County seat. It was the misfortune of local merchant E. L. Davison that the camp was near enough to one of his warehouses that the soldiers broke in and discovered fifty barrels of whiskey. They rolled some of the barrels out to the sidewalk, where they bashed in the heads and began filling canteens and tin cups; one man even took off his boots and filled each of them with whiskey. Davison was returning from Louisville, and when still a half mile away he could smell the whiskey. He knew what was happening. He rode directly to General Crittenden's tent to file a complaint, but he got no satisfaction. The merchant rode back to his warehouse to do what he could to stop the pilfering. In a moment, an officer arrived at the head of a large patrol and herded the drunken mob up the street, away from the warehouse doors. The patrol could not keep them all contained, though, and some of the more tactically minded of the drinkers outflanked the patrol and circled back around to where the whiskey was. Davison pleaded with the officer in charge to post a guard over his remaining liquor until he could bring some wagons to haul it away. The officer agreed to do that. Davison and his slaves spent the rest of the night loading whiskey barrels and transporting them to a safer place. The soldiers of the patrol helped them load the wagons. By sunrise, nothing was left behind except those barrels that had been broken open and partially emptied of their contents. Whatever was left in the ruined barrels was offered to the officers passing by when Crittenden's corps resumed its march, next morning. A few hours later, when Davison went into Springfield to see the damage by daylight, he found drunken soldiers lying around the town, their guns and accoutrements scattered about them. One man drank so much of Davison's whiskey that he later died; dozens of others only felt as if they were dying.

Heads pounding in the unnatural October heat, they continued toward Haysville, marching through sycamore-shaded valleys where there were rock-bottomed creek beds, utterly dry. Wood later admitted that there was "a great deal of straggling ... on account of the difficulties of the marches, the difficulty of obtaining water on the road, and other such causes." The thirst of the men was so great that General Thomas ordered the II Corps to go three or four miles beyond Haysville, their intended bivouac for the night, to the Rolling Fork River, where there was still water in this drought-crippled country. The men needed rest, but they needed water more. Wood's division did not reach the camp until three o'clock on the morning of the eighth.[22]

The campsite that General Thomas selected had put the corps a greater distance from Perryville than Buell had intended, a problem that was compounded when General Crittenden began his march the next morning at 7:00, four hours behind schedule. The 4th Division (Brigadier General William S. Smith) moved out first, followed in two hours by the 5th Division (Brigadier General Horatio P. Van Cleve). General Wood and the 6th Division did not break camp until 11:00 A.M. Wood moved slowly and did not begin getting into battle line at Perryville until about 3:00 P.M.

By then, General McCook, six miles away on the left flank, and General Gilbert in the center had been in position for hours and General McCook had come under general attack. Crittenden could hear the sounds of what he thought was a skirmish as he approached his position on the Lebanon Pike. By the time he got his divisions situated, the sound of firing had diminished. The country around Perryville was so knobby that it was particularly vulnerable to acoustic shadows. Crittenden was in one of these shadows and could hear neither cannon fire nor musketry.

Crittenden was not the only one who was fooled by the curious acoustics of Boyle County. The rumor had spread back through the line of approach that a fight had begun, and General Wood rode back to hurry Colonel George D. Wagner's brigade forward. But Wood was not sure of the situation. He asked Wagner, "How is it possible that there is a fight going on when we can scarcely hear any firing at all?"[23]

Not long after the II Corps began arriving in position, Crittenden received a dispatch from General Gilbert that said, "My children are all quiet, and by sunset we will have them in bed and nicely tucked up." The message was so weirdly cute and unworried that Crittenden decided that there was no trouble on the left.[24]

In fact, beyond Gilbert's left there was a tremendous battle raging. Two divisions of McCook's corps, those of General Lovell Harrison Rousseau and General James S. Jackson, were fighting the whole Rebel army. Gilbert could see and hear it, and yet he did not move to help. Crittenden could not see or hear the battle, so, with Gilbert's reassurance and no orders from Buell to do otherwise, he remained in place. Besides, Wheeler's cavalry was demonstrating on his front and for all he knew he might soon be attacked himself. Crittenden waited through the hot, windy afternoon, watching his horse soldiers skirmishing with the butternut cavalry and enduring some ineffective artillery fire from Wheeler's fieldpieces.

Only one brigade of Crittenden's infantry corps saw any action on October 8, Wagner's of Wood's division. On their left, Brigadier General Philip Sheridan's division of Gilbert's corps was attacked by a single Confederate brigade. Wood sent Colonel Wagner's 21st Brigade to reinforce Sheridan. Harker moved up behind, ready to support Wagner. They marched half a mile before Wagner encountered the enemy, only about six hundred yards from Sheridan's line. The Rebels immediately withdrew. Wagner advanced and crowded them until dark, and then the day ended. There were no casualties.

For the second time, Wood's division had missed a battle. They had arrived at Shiloh too late to have any real part in the action, and they had arrived at Perryville too far away from the action to know that on the far left Rousseau and Jackson were fighting what turned out to be Kentucky's bloodiest battle. It was not until that night that they learned that they had missed the fight. They bivouacked that night to the right of the Lebanon Road and comforted themselves with the thought that they would have another chance to draw Secesh blood when the battle resumed the next morning, October 9.

And they did have a splendid chance to resume the battle. Before dawn on the ninth, Colonel Wagner could hear the sound of wheeled vehicles moving in the Rebel lines, and in a few moments, in the gray light of very early morning, he could see a black line of infantry and cavalry moving from Perryville. After a while, a CSA artillery battery unlimbered, but Wagner was quicker and his gunners of the 10th Indiana Battery drove the enemy artillery away. Wagner advanced to the hills on the edge of town and had the 10th Indiana Battery throw a few more rounds at the backs of the retreating Rebels.

The sound of the initial firing caused Colonel Harker's brigade to move a short distance forward to where they could see the town and the Rebels moving through. Harker sent word of what he was seeing back to his superiors. After a while, an aide-de-camp to General Wood came up with orders from General George H. Thomas to fall back. The whole division was being ordered back a few miles, behind Smith and Van Cleve, to serve as the II Corps' reserve during the advance. Fall back in order to prepare to move forward seemed to be the logic. Harker obediently withdrew.

Wagner took the order bitterly. He recalled that he

> pointed down to the town and told the aide-de-camp ... that I had had possession of it from about sunup, and that there had not been a rebel near it, at least in sight, for an hour, and the last I saw of the enemy's cavalry they were retiring from the front of General Smith. At that time they were entirely out of sight.... I remarked to the aide-de-camp that he should go and inform the general of the fact and that I could not consent to march my troops 2 miles to the rear and back again for nothing.

He partially complied, however, and "retired my brigade some half mile to the rear."[25]

The tight leash Thomas held on Wagner's and Harker's brigades in the face of Confederate retreat was a regrettable and preventable mistake. As historian Kenneth Noe wrote, "Thomas ... had made a crucial error, for his orders threw away the last realistic chance to hit the enemy hard in Perryville.... The brigades in question already were in the best position to force Bragg to hold up and fight.... The last critical moment had passed." Noe added that General Wood, whose men had held the high ground behind a retreating enemy, shared the blame for not being aware of the opportunity and because of a "breakdown in communication" in his division.[26]

News that they were about to strike Bragg a blow rippled through the ranks and excited the soldiers, but their enthusiasm dissolved into the habitual disappointment of men who did nothing but march. Captain John W. Tuttle wrote:

> The excitement of the occasion gave me a fine high fever which trebled my strength and made me blood thirsty as a tiger. But we got no fight. We remained in line until 2:00 P.M. without advancing a step.... Our commanders having thoroughly satisfied themselves that the enemy was certainly gone, marched us in triumph into town by the right flank and at route step to the patriotic air, "Go it boots."[27]

Even the length of the march was not up to standard. "Bivouacked about a mile from town near a fine spring," Tuttle added.[28]

The devastation left behind by the Union and Confederate armies was widespread and long lasting. There were over one thousand dead to bury and over five thousand wounded to tend. Citizens in towns as far as fifty miles away saw their homes and churches and schools turned into hospitals to receive the wounded of Perryville. Everywhere around where the armies had fought was a wreckage of equipment, vehicles, and weapons. The fields were littered with scraps of torn uniforms and paper blowing in a hot October wind that carried the stench of decaying piles of amputated arms and legs. And there was considerable material loss to go along with the inconveniences. Squire Henry Bottom, a farmer on whose land much of the hardest fighting occurred, has been given ever since 1862 as the examplar of how a battle affected the ordinary citizens who were unlucky enough to live near where armies fought. The museum at Perryville Battlefield has a display of Mr. Bottom's claim for recompense to the U.S. government for the losses he had suffered on October 8: thirty sheep; two horses; 8,540 pounds of pork; 4,500 pounds of bacon; 320 cords of wood; 3,000 bushels of corn; 50 bushels of oats; and twenty-two tons of hay. And it did not end there. For years afterward, no lumber dealer would buy the timber from Bottom's farm; it was full of shot and shell and would ruin the saw blade of any man who tried to cut it. The cost was staggering, and these were the losses on just one farm.

The people could not have been sad to see the soldiers of both armies leaving. They had their own problems to attend to.

Not that the armies were leaving all that quickly. On October 10, Crittenden's corps marched a modest six miles. Only Harker went farther. Ordered to lead his brigade on a reconnaissance in the direction of Harrodsburg, he exceeded orders somewhat and went all the way to the old town. The men found only seventy head of cattle, two hundred barrels of pork, and a thousand sick or wounded Confederates. The effectives of the Army of the Mississippi were all gone, heading toward Dick's River.

On October 11, Harker's men were on the prowl again, repelling skirmishers as they followed Bragg's retreating column toward Dick's River. Some of Colonel Edward M. McCook's cavalry were riding along. Before the end of the day, the brigade fell back to join the rest of the division, which had not moved from camp near Harrodsburg that day. Harker's men learned that their stationary comrades had had a little scare when some Rebel cavalry skirmished with their pickets; in fact, they went into battle line. But the Rebels were not interested in a stand-up fight and nothing came of the alarm.

Beyond Danville, as Crittenden later reported:

> We skirmished with the rebel cavalry continually, but nothing like a serious engagement. [At Crab Orchard] they made more resistance than at any previous point, so much so as to make it prudent, in my judgment, to send a brigade in advance to drive them along.... I suppose we were delayed only an hour or two at Crab Orchard, and from there on as far as the enemy were pursued by my troops — and they were in advance — we had no serious engagement.[29]

During the pursuit, Crittenden probably kept Wood close by. It was widely believed in the army that Crittenden's appointment had been the result of his father's considerable political influence and that while Thomas L. Crittenden was the public face of the II Corps, it was Wood who was the brains of the operation. Correspondent W. F. G. Shanks, who knew a good many of the Union generals in the West, said shortly after the war that Wood was "ever at [Crittenden's] right hand ... and furnished him with all the military brains, and formed for him all the military character he ever had. It may be impolite to say this now, but it is anticipating history but a short time."[30]

Crittenden was a perfect candidate to fall under the influence of a professional soldier with such ambition and overweening self-confidence as Wood. Crittenden, like many sons of domineering fathers, lacked confidence in himself. His biographer Damon R. Eubank explained Crittenden's personal failings by saying that his "need for his father's approval laid the basis for his failure as a politician and a general. Since Thomas sought the support of others before he acted, he often lacked confidence.... He never trusted his instincts, a tendency that arose perhaps from critical West Pointers like Wood serving under him or perhaps from the aloof Buell never praising his work as a divisional commander."[31]

Eubank added, "It would have been better for Crittenden had he served under Wood rather than become his commander. Wood could have taught [Crittenden] much about being a soldier."[32]

This is not to say that Wood's example was always spotless. He learned on October 12 that he was not exempt from the occasional reprimand from above. On that day, Wood's men captured six Rebel prisoners, and Wood refused to feed them. He sent them back to headquarters hungry, telling them "they must get something to eat where they could find it."[33]

A correction came flying back to him. It read, "The commanding general trusts that you will in the future provide for the wants of prisoners so far as within your power."[34]

The rebuke was unnecessary, for there would only be a couple of more opportunities to snag prisoners. On October 19, the Confederates felled trees in a narrow mountain gap. It took Van Cleve's and Wood's divisions hours to clear the road. They caught up with the Rebels that evening and bumped up hard against Colonel John Wharton's cavalry. The Federals fell back behind a hill and went into camp. If they hoped to fight the next morning, they were fooled, for the Confederates had slipped away. The Confederate strategy for the retreat was working. By continually blocking the road, demonstrating in front of the Yankees and forcing them to deploy for battle, Wheeler and Wharton's cavalry were buying time for the Southern infantry, artillery, and supply trains to escape.

On October 22, the Confederates swept through London, and that is where General Buell stopped and recalled his forward units. Bragg was leaving Kentucky, which is not the quite the same as saying that he was *thrown out* of Kentucky. General Wood later said, "As I did not see a great deal of the enemy's forces while it was in retreat, it is almost impossible to say whether it was conducted in an orderly manner, except from the results and inferences; and, so far as I could judge from the indications along the line of march, my opinion is that it was conducted in an orderly manner, and did not partake in any degree the character of a rout."[35]

Bragg was back in Tennessee, and Buell's old fear returned that he would strike west for Nashville and lay siege to that massive supply depot. The Lincoln administration insisted that Buell should continue the pursuit into East Tennessee. Buell refused. He seems to have had enough of being bullyragged by the men in Washington, but the men in Washington were the ones who had the power, and they exercised it now to end a chapter in the history of the Army of the Ohio. Major General Don Carlos Buell, who had never quite satisfied and who had been living on probation since Louisville, was relieved of command.

Chapter 8

Murfreesboro

General Don Carlos Buell had his supporters, including Generals Crittenden and Wood and Colonel Harker. Damon Eubank explained that Buell's supporters, though not all of them, tended to be Kentuckians, "who liked Buell's conservative approach to restoring the Union." Buell did not favor a scorched-earth policy and neither was he a fire-breathing abolitionist.[1]

Buell also had some influential civilian supporters, including John J. Crittenden (former senator and current member of the U.S. House), Robert Mallory (member of the U.S. House), and Garrett Davis (U.S. senator). James Guthrie, president of the L&N Railroad, was another Buell partisan. Guthrie wrote an impassioned letter in which he argued that Buell had "saved Nashville, then fell back and saved Bowling Green and Southern Kentucky, then fell back and saved Louisville, and brought through all his baggage trains without loss, and now has driven Bragg and Smith out of Kentucky.... No general can now take his place without injury to the service and the cause."[2]

Even in the national press, Buell found some favor. In the November 1, 1862, issue of *Harper's Weekly* there appeared an article that said:

> Take it all in all, it must be admitted that the rebel enterprise in Kentucky has failed. Bragg has not succeeded in the great object he had in view — the capture of Nashville or Louisville. He has not achieved the decisive success which the rebel leaders deemed it essential to achieve before our new levies were in the field. He has not wrested from us and permanently held any single point. He has overrun and plundered the finest region of Kentucky, but this will have no more influence upon the result of the war than the raids of the pirate "290."[3]

None of it mattered. Buell, who was already living on borrowed time because of his earlier disappointments, had disappointed two times too many since leaving Louisville on October 1. He had not destroyed Bragg's army, which he could have done if he had had a better grasp of the Battle of Perryville and thrown in the corps of Gilbert and Crittenden. And he had flatly disobeyed orders to pursue Bragg into East Tennessee, a region that figured largely in President Lincoln's strategic thinking.

This being the case, Buell was removed from command. In his place, Lincoln and Halleck did not turn to George H. Thomas as might have been expected. Thomas had been offered the job only weeks before and had turned it down. His reasons were patriotic and perfectly sound, but the Lincoln administration pridefully ignored him this time in favor of General William S. Rosecrans, a brilliant and eccentric Ohioan.

Rosecrans was forty-two years old. In 1842, he graduated fifth in his West Point class, the same standing that Thomas J. Wood had held in the Class of '45, and like Wood, he had been assigned to the Corps of Engineers. Rosecrans had missed the Mexican War, and eventually growing bored with his unexceptional assignments, he had left the service to enter the coal and kerosene business. Injuries suffered in a fire at his kerosene-refining plant had put him in bed for a year. He went back into the army in 1861 and saw his first action in the mountain counties of Virginia, serving under General George B. McClellan. There was a mutual dislike between the two men, and Rosecrans transferred to the Western Theater. He served under General John Pope in the Corinth Campaign and succeeded him in command of the Union Army of the Mississippi. Rosecrans subsequently fought in the battles of Iuka and Corinth, performing well enough that he was called to succeed General Buell after Perryville.

The men came to know Rosecrans well. He was a bundle of energy and the headquarters office could not contain him. He was often found roaming through the camps, encouraging his men and checking on their welfare. His presence among them made Rosecrans more popular with the troops than the reserved Buell ever was. Spillard Horrall, 42nd Indiana Infantry, said, "There was a dash about the man that took with the soldiers."[4]

More experienced observers saw some troubling characteristics in Rosecrans, primary among them his excitability. W. F. G. Shanks said of Rosecrans, "I have known him ... to grow so excited, vehement, and incoherent as to utterly confound the messenger. In great danger as in small things, this nervousness incapacitated him from the intelligible direction of his officers or effective execution of his plan." When he was excited, which was often, Rosecrans would sputter and stammer.[5]

Now it was the springtime of his command of the Army of the Ohio (soon to be rechristened the XIV Army Corps or, more popularly, the Army of the Cumberland), and the men, the press, and the administration had confidence in him.

General Rosecrans had his work cut out for him. Through the army, there was little uniformity in weapons. As historian Larry J. Daniel pointed out, "Wood's 6th Division was representative of this army as a whole. Of the fourteen regiments, seven had uniform weapons (one Austrian rifles, two Springfields, two Enfields, one Harpers Ferry Rifles, and one .54-caliber rifles), four had a mix of Enfields and Springfields, and the remaining three had a scattering of French, Austrian, Harpers Ferry, and .69-caliber rifles."[6]

In addition, there were shortages of uniforms, brogans, rations, and accoutrements of every sort. The artillery and the cavalry were weak, and the railroads were poorly defended.

A new leader traditionally likes to rearrange things to show those who hired him that he is brimming with ideas and eager to carry them out. One of the earliest and most obvious of the many changes that Rosecrans instituted was to scrap Buell's system of corps and replace it by a configuration of three wings. In this new arrangement, Major General Crittenden's II Corps became the Left Wing and Wood's former 6th Division became the 1st Division. It contained the 1st Brigade (first commanded by General Hascall and, after December 31, by Colonel George P. Buell), the 2nd Brigade (Colonel George D. Wagner), and the 3rd Brigade (Colonel Charles G. Harker). In addition, Wood had three artillery batteries in his command.

The Center Wing was commanded by Major General George H. Thomas, and the Right Wing was commanded by Major General Alexander McDowell McCook.

Rosecrans assumed command in Louisville on October 30, 1862, and began to effect his reforms in Bowling Green. But he did not gather his army closely around him there. Crittenden was sent toward Gallatin on November 7 and began that very day to operate against John Hunt Morgan, the destroyer of railroads. General Crittenden told Wood:

> I have this moment received information that Morgan, with his cavalry, is still in Gallatin. Now, if this is true, I want you to catch him and, although you have marched 20 miles today, you will send a brigade of picked men at 2:00 tomorrow morning [November 8] to Gallatin, so as to reach that point at daylight, with the remainder of your command at 6:00. General Van Cleve will march at 6:00, and will be promptly in supporting distance of you. This is hard on the men, but no chances are now to be lost and I count on you.

Colonel Lewis Zahm's cavalry was to support Wood's picked brigade.[7]

In response to Crittenden's order, Wood sent Harker's brigade. When Harker and Zahm arrived at Gallatin, Morgan was gone, but the Federals followed his trail and captured eighteen men and their mounts. Wood followed slowly behind Harker and was at Gallatin on or about November 8.

A week later, Wood's division was marching again, this time to Lebanon, Tennessee. There Wood found some enemy cavalry, which scooted away on his approach. He destroyed the mill at Lebanon and some wheat and flour and returned to camp.

Despite all that had occurred in the last ten weeks, Wood had not forgotten Mr. Bumpus, the spy he had employed at Gallatin to gather information on September 8. Bumpus had met the conditions of their agreement; his intelligence had proven to be letter perfect, and for that he was owed the $1,000 that Wood had promised. Events had moved so quickly that the spy had never been paid. Wood wrote to Rosecrans at Nashville, explaining the situation to him and citing the accuracy of the information and the speed with which Bumpus had returned with it. Wood asked that Bumpus be paid. "I am not now provided with funds, or I would have it done," Wood said.[8]

Rosecrans wanted verification of the matter, so he wired his predecessor, General Buell, then in Indianapolis. There was a bit of confusion in Buell's reply when the telegrapher rendered the sum of $1,000 as $10,000. Buell thought that even $1,000 was too much to have offered for the information but agreed, "If Wood promised Mr. Bumpus ... it ought to be paid."[9]

Rosecrans had moved his headquarters to Nashville on November 9. The city was grim, filled with poor refugees whose suffering would grow worse as winter approached. The printing presses were closed down. Some of the best private homes had been taken over by the various generals as their headquarters, and others had been turned into hospitals. Schools, asylums, and hotels were also confiscated for government use.

Even the state capitol was not exempt from the usages of war. Curtius of the *New York Times* was in the city and wrote:

> The grand and stately Capitol building, of the purest Tennessee marble ... bears the strong marks of the effects of war ... our cannon point from around the building. Governor Johnson occupies one part of it, and works day and night to restore the civil laws of the states. The halls and vestibules of the tremendous edifice resound to the tramp of the sentinel on duty.... Sick soldiers are here, arms are piled there, knapsacks are jumbled yonder; soiled uniforms, torn garments, rusty weapons, bayonets, ram-rods, hats, caps, swords, and every article in a military line are piled about in indiscriminate confusion.[10]

The city's spacious warehouses had been confiscated by the government and were being filled up with quartermaster and commissary stores as fast as the L&N Railroad and the Cumberland River steamers could deliver them. They could not deliver them very fast. The Cumberland River was still low from the continuing drought, and paddle wheelers could get no closer to Nashville than Harpeth Shoals. There the cargoes had to be off-loaded and reloaded onto wagons, which began a rough overland journey to Nashville.

The L&N Railroad was giving a higher priority to private freight than military cargoes and, in any case, was only partially operational. The Big South Tunnel, which Morgan had collapsed back in August, would remain closed for weeks to come. In addition, there were several bridges down between the Kentucky line and Nashville. McCook's men were working to repair the railroad. In the meantime, freight had to be taken from the boxcars at Mitchellville and had to complete the journey into Nashville by wagon. The creaking wagon trains from Harpeth Shoals and Mitchellville were subject to attack by Confederate guerrillas or cavalrymen.

Rosecrans felt that he was making progress, but to Washington it was all taking too much time. The president and General Halleck wanted Rosecrans to move quickly against Bragg, who was not far away in Murfreesboro. Rosecrans insisted that he must have the time to prepare. "If the Government which ordered me here confides in my judgment, it may rely on my continuing to do what I have been trying to do — that is, my whole duty. If my superiors have lost confidence in me, they had better at once put someone in my place and let the future test the propriety of the change."[11]

Meanwhile, the enemy cavalry threatened Federal operations through all Middle Tennessee. Morgan was on was the east and north into Kentucky, Forrest was on the west, and Wheeler was making a hobby of attacking Union foraging parties on the south and west. They were a bloody nuisance, but in their aggressiveness they made a strategic error. By late December, Morgan and Forrest were too far away to support Bragg, and a shortage of cavalry meant a shortage of intelligence. Rosecrans' supply pinch had eased somewhat, and he now had about five weeks' worth of rations laid by in Nashville, and the continuing flow of supplies was more-or-less ensured. Big South Tunnel had re-opened on November 25, and Rosecrans' attention to protection of the L&N was paying off. Curtius wrote in his dispatch from Nashville, "The Louisville & Nashville Railroad is better and more thoroughly guarded than ever before. Every bridge, trestle, switch and tunnel is most vigilantly guarded."[12]

All these factors being true, now was the last best chance of 1862 to really hurt the Confederates. So, on Christmas night, Rosecrans announced that the three wings of his army would be moving out the next morning to surprise General Bragg in Murfreesboro.

That very day, Harker's brigade of Wood's division was attacked while out foraging for corn. Their wagons were full and they were making their way back to Nashville when they were hit by a mixed force of six hundred infantry and cavalry. The caravan and its defenders got back to the capital city, but the action had cost Harker one killed and two wounded of the 51st Indiana. It is plain from Wood's report of the attack on Harker's foragers that he was not part of Rosecrans' Christmas night council of war, for the report ends with a series of questions he would like to have answered "if we should move tomorrow." Wood asked to be informed "what amount of baggage it is expected we will take. If all is not taken, which I presume will hardly be done, what arrangements will be made with the remainder? Will it be ordered to follow, or sent to Nashville.... Further, is it expected any forage will be taken?"[13]

Wood must have received satisfactory answers to his questions. He moved out as part of Crittenden's Left Wing on the morning of December 26. The Left Wing was on the left, moving right down the Murfreesboro Pike. Brigadier

General John M. Palmer's 2nd Division was in the advance, followed by Wood's. Major General George H. Thomas' Center Wing was on the Federal right, and McCook's Right Wing was in the center.

Approaching LaVergne, about halfway to Murfreesboro, Palmer and Wood ran into some enemy patrols. "The country occupied by these bodies of hostile troops affords ground peculiarly favorable for a small force to retard the advance of a larger one," Wood later recalled. Thick woods separated wide cultivated fields, neither one suitable for maneuvers by large bodies of troops, and the rolling terrain allowed the enemy to conceal themselves until they were ready to be seen.[14]

General William S. Rosecrans (Library of Congress).

The enemy troops near LaVergne hindered the progress of the Federals so that they arrived at their intended campsite after sunset. The dark of night prevented a thorough reconnaissance. "To guard effectually against surprise, a regiment from each brigade was thrown forward as a grand guard, and the front and flanks of the division covered with a continuous line of skirmishers," remembered Wood.[15]

The first day's march had inevitably caused some disarray. Crittenden's wing had the most direct approach to Murfreesboro, while the route of both Thomas and McCook was more of an arc and took longer to cover. As a result, they had not kept pace with Crittenden, and the Left Wing was held in place through the morning of the second day. Wood's and Palmer's men stood in battle line, taking a few artillery rounds, until about 11:00 A.M., when the order came down for them to move out, Hascall's brigade of Wood's division in the lead. Wagner's and Harker's brigades were sent out on either side of the road as flankers.

At LaVergne, Wood found the Rebels "strongly posted in the houses and on the wooded heights in our rear, whence he was enabled to oppose our advance by a direct and cross fire of musketry." Responding to an order from Crittenden to "drive the enemy vigorously," Hascall's brigade hurried across an open field, gouged the enemy out of the houses, and sustained twenty casualties in the doing.[16]

The retiring enemy took up new positions throughout the day's march to pester the Federals. A heavy rain that began in the afternoon added to an already-miserable day, but the troops made five miles beyond LaVergne before stopping for the night at Stewart's Creek. A single bridge crossed the deep and steep-banked creek, and the enemy had set it on fire just moments before the skirmishers came into view. The wet wood did not burn well, so no great harm was done before the skirmishers and the men of the 3rd Kentucky Infantry braved enemy rifle fire to rush forward and put it out. As they saved the bridge, a cavalry attack burst upon the left flank. The 100th Illinois got behind the attackers and cut them off and took seventy-five prisoners, twelve horses, and a quantity of weapons and accoutrements.

The Rebels had failed to have much effect in slowing down Palmer and Wood, and once again, the Left Wing had outpaced the Center and Right Wings. Because it was a Sunday (a day of rest that the devout Catholic Rosecrans liked to honor and keep holy, when possible) and also to give McCook and Thomas time to come up, Crittenden's men remained in their muddy camp on the twenty-eighth and did not move out again until the morning of December 29. They moved with slight opposition to within two and one-half miles of Murfreesboro and there found the enemy in force and arrayed for battle. It was something of a surprise. The Federals had mistakenly believed that the Rebels would leave Murfreesboro. Instead, the enemy was standing there in the fading light of day, ready to fight. Wood responded by putting his division in battle formation and reported to General Crittenden what was in front of him. He did not know that General Palmer had reported to Rosecrans that the Rebels were falling back.

In a while Crittenden relayed orders from Rosecrans for Wood to send a brigade across Stones River to occupy Murfreesboro. Rosecrans based his order on Palmer's report, but by now Palmer had realized his error, and both he and Wood rode to Left Wing headquarters and asked Crittenden to ignore the order. Crittenden refused. The two division commanders ordered their men forward and then tried once again to persuade Crittenden to take the responsible action of canceling an order that was based on faulty intelligence. Their insistence was having an effect, and while Crittenden still refused to cancel the order, he did agree to consult with Rosecrans; in the meantime, the advance across Stones River was suspended for one hour.

Based on this updated and corrected report of the situation on Crittenden's front, Rosecrans canceled his earlier order to occupy Murfreesboro. Unfortunately, Colonel Harker's brigade of Wood's division was already across Stones

River and pushing back the enemy's pickets. Three regiments, the 51st Indiana, the 13th Michigan, and the 73rd Indiana, made up the front line. They advanced to a cornfield on a hillside and there ran into stiffer resistance, infantry fire from Confederates in the cornrows. When the Federal pressure became too great, the Rebels fell back to a new position around one of their batteries on top of the hill. The Federals advanced up the hill, "although the whole ridge seemed to issue forth a continuous flame of fire," in the words of Colonel Abel D. Streight. The enemy fell back and the Federals seemed about to take the enemy artillery. At that moment, they received orders to advance no farther. They lay down in line, and when two regiments of graycoats rushed forward they let them get to within thirty paces before they surprised them with a fire so deadly "that they hardly waited to reply, but broke and fled again." Streight continued, "We remained in our position without further molestation until about 10 o'clock at night, when I was notified that orders had been given to retire to the opposite bank of the river." They had done their duty and now they retired in good order, back across Stones River for a well-deserved rest. In his later report, Colonel Charles Harker said, "Too much praise cannot be accorded to the brave officers and men of this brigade for their bravery and skill in driving a concealed enemy from a strong position after nightfall, and holding their ground in the face of an enemy three times their numbers. Though little was accomplished by this feat, it ... augured well for the more severe work which awaited them."[17]

Wood expected the "severe work" to begin the next day, but Tuesday, December 30, passed in relative quiet. When nothing developed except some sporadic fire between his skirmishers and those of the enemy, he knew that it was simply a delay of the inevitable. Wood ordered that three days' rations be issued to his waiting men and, late in the day, the distribution of twenty more cartridges per man. He wrote, "Commanders were directed to instruct their men to be exceedingly vigilant, and report any indication of a movement in the front by the enemy. The artillery horses were kept attached to the pieces."[18]

That night, with McCook and Thomas finally in position, Rosecrans perfected his plans. His line ran from the southwest to the northeast. McCook was on the far right, Thomas (badly weakened by the absence of three divisions who were on detached duty) held the center, and Crittenden was on the far left. The plan was for Crittenden to cross Stones River and hit General Bragg's right. Van Cleve's division would step off first, followed by Wood's. As they drove the enemy back, Palmer's division of Crittenden's wing and Thomas' shorthanded wing would join in the attack and push back the enemy center. As Rosecrans imagined it, the attack would pivot on McCook. His job was to hold the enemy in place, preventing those in his front from going to reinforce those whom Crittenden and Thomas were driving. Rosecrans thought that if McCook could hold fast for three hours, that would do the trick. By then, presumably, the enemy would be so shattered that all resistance would disappear and the Federals could march into Murfreesboro for a comfortable winter's stay.

During the night, Wood sent scouts from Wagner's brigade up into the trees to keep watch on the CSA lines. After midnight, Wood received word from them that there was movement on his front; the graybacks seemed to be moving to their left, massing in front of McCook. Wood sent the intelligence to Crittenden, satisfied that the necessary action would be taken.

General Wood was sick on the morning of December 31. Nevertheless, he was up shortly after 5:00 A.M., rousing his men for an early breakfast and getting them in line. Van Cleve's division was to cross Stones River first, and when he was across, Wood's division would advance. Harker was to move first with his brigade, followed by Hascall and Wagner. The order to advance would not come for a little while, so Wood rode out through the fog to examine the ground that his men would be crossing.

While they waited, they could hear some firing from the distant right flank, but there had been shooting practically ever since the Army of the Cumberland left Nashville; this commotion on the right was not intense and did not indicate, as Wood said, "that the troops were seriously engaged." Harker commenced his advance about eight o'clock. He had not gone far when he was ordered to stop. Something was wrong. Why stop now, when Van Cleve's division was already across the river? As his brigade stood waiting for further orders, Rosecrans himself rode up and gave Harker, and also Hascall, "direct instructions to proceed immediately to the support of the right wing of our army [McCook's wing], which was yielding to the overwhelming force of the enemy at that point."[19]

What Rosecrans did not know was that General Bragg had developed the same plan of attack: to attack his enemies' right flank. The only difference was that the Southern boys went to work first and they wrecked the unprepared McCook. The extreme right flank was gone and now only General Philip Sheridan's division of McCook's wing was holding back the attacking Confederates, practically single-handedly. Van Cleve's division was recalled from the far side of the river and sent to shore up the right. Wood was ordered to pull Harker's and Hascall's brigades out of line, pass them behind Wagner's, and send them toward the right, also. As the move began, Wood attempted one of his few recorded jests. He said to Crittenden, "Goodbye, General. We'll all meet at the hatter's, as one coon said to another when the dogs were after them." It was a poor effort, but then again, the situation did not lend itself to humor.[20]

When the 1st and 3rd Brigades marched off to reinforce the right flank, Colonel Wagner's 2nd Brigade was left behind to hold secure the left flank of the Army of the Cumberland. To close the gap left by the withdrawal of Harker and Hascall, Wagner had to slide left toward the river. This sector was important not only because it was the left flank but also because it controlled both a Stones River ford and the pike back to Nashville—an escape route, should that become necessary. Wagner's move to the left closed one gap but opened another, which was soon filled by Colonel William B. Hazen's brigade of Brigadier General John M. Palmer's division.

Harker and Hascall did not go far before they ran into a maelstrom of panic. As Harker recalled, "On approaching the right, much confusion was visible; troops marching in every directions; stragglers to be seen in great numbers, and teamsters in great consternation endeavoring to drive their teams they knew not whither." The confusion slowed down Hascall's and Harker's men and made them even more vulnerable to the shells falling among them, but they struggled through the chaos to get into position. Harker's brigade ended up beyond Van Cleve, on the extreme end of the Federal right, and, though heavily engaged on its own front, was out of the fight for the left flank that involved Wood's division of Crittenden's wing.[21]

The section of the line that Hascall reached was behind a patch of woods called the Round Forest. Here was the worst of the fighting in Crittenden's wing. Though Hascall's was essentially a reserve position, he found plenty to do in helping to repulse CSA general James Chalmers' Mississippi brigade and General Daniel Donelson's Tennessee brigade. Hascall recalled, "I was moving my command from point to point, ready to support any troops that most needed it [and after about one hour] the onslaught of the enemy seemed to be in a great measure checked, and we had a reasonable probability of maintaining this line. During all this time my men were exposed to a severe fire of shot and shell from a battery on the other side of the river, and several were killed."[22]

On Palmer's request, Hascall sent the 3rd Kentucky Infantry forward as reinforcements. Within minutes, a bullet hit Lieutenant Colonel Samuel McKee of the regiment above the right eye and tumbled him from his horse. The regiment fought on and was soon decimated. Hascall led his other three regiments to Palmer and took position between Colonel William B. Hazen's left and Colonel Wagner's right.

Hascall said, "Seeing the importance of the position, I told my men it must be held, even if it cost the last man we had." He sent the 26th Ohio into line beside the 3rd Kentucky and summoned Lieutenant George Estep's 8th Indiana Battery just before the Rebels attacked. After an hour of fighting, Hascall's men sent them back into the trees.[23]

Hascall was the senior commander in this section of the line, and he did not hesitate to exercise his authority, even over the brigades of Colonel William B. Hazen and Colonel William Grose, who were actually in Palmer's division. He relieved the 3rd Kentucky, "which was nearly annihilated and out of ammunition," and plugged the hole with the 58th Indiana. He also brought up the 6th Ohio (Grose's brigade) and the 97th Ohio.[24]

Hascall finished his arrangement of the line not a minute too soon, for the Rebels shortly charged again. "As soon as they [Brigadier General Daniel W. Adams' brigade followed by that of Brigadier General John K. Jackson] came in sight, the Sixth and Twenty-sixth Ohio and Estep's battery opened on them and did splendid execution," Hascall remembered. "But on they came till within one hundred yards of our line when Colonel Buell of the Fifty-eighth Indiana ... ordered his men to fire. The effect was indescribable. The enemy fell back in windrows and went staggering back from the effects of this unexpected volley."[25]

Colonel Wagner rightly claimed some credit for helping to repulse Adams' brigade. Wagner later reported that when he discovered the Louisianans emerging from the trees only about three hundred yards from his position he ordered the 15th and 57th Indiana Volunteers to charge them "at a double quick." The charge was a notable success, with the Hoosiers "killing, wounding, and capturing nearly one entire regiment, and driving two others in utter rout from the field.... Captain Cox's battery gave them the last shot they had in their locker, thereby making the rout complete."[26]

The Rebels may have been routed, but they were not done. General John K. Jackson's brigade attacked behind Adams,' pushed back Wagner's two Indiana regiments and headed for Hazen at the Round Forest. They came under heavy artillery fire. Captain Cox had secured some more ammunition for his artillery and Estep's four-gun battery had moved up. Their combined canister fire, plus the murderous rifle fire of Wagner's infantry brigade (augmented by the 26th Ohio of Hascall's brigade), broke up the butternut attack and sent them scrambling back to the shelter of the woods.

A late day attack by Colonel J. B. Palmer's and Brigadier General William Preston's brigades on Hazen's position did not change the result of the first day's fighting. The setting sun put an end to the battle. It had been the first one since the beginning of the Rebellion in which Wood's division played a real role. The men had acquitted themselves well. William Sumner Dodge in his contemporary *History of the Old Second Division* confirmed what Hascall and Wood both claimed in their reports of December 31. Dodge wrote of the battle of December 31 that Wood's division "was the only one in the entire army that lost no ground and no artillery, though twice fiercely attacked after the assault had ceased on every other part of the field."[27]

General Wood's conduct and skillful handling of his troops since leaving Nashville was commented upon by another contemporary writer. William D. Bickham wrote: "The general estimate of the army, touching division commanders, placed General Wood in the very front rank — and his dispositions on the day of his advance from Lavergne and until his wound compelled him to relinquish his command, justified that verdict."[28]

The 1st Division had lost 1,126 men killed and wounded that day; Wood was one of the latter. About 10:00 A.M., in one of the fierce morning fights, Wood was struck on the inside of the left heel by a bullet. The wound was serious, but Wood refused to leave the field. He stayed in the saddle until seven o'clock that evening, hours after the fighting ended. That night, after attending a council of war in Rosecrans' headquarters, Wood "was ordered by the commanding general of the corps to repair that night, by ambulance, with an escort to this city [Nashville]. It was with extreme regret I found myself in a condition to make it necessary, on account of my injury, to leave the division I had formed and so long commanded." He turned command over to Brigadier General Milo Hascall, who, in turn, relinquished command of the 1st Brigade to Colonel George P. Buell. Wood's wound gave him trouble. An amputation of his left foot was recommended, a surgery that Wood refused. There was a lot of war left to fight and he still had work to do. His work at Murfreesboro, however, was at an end.[29]

CHAPTER 9

Winter Quarters at Murfreesboro

The 1st Division of the Left Wing began the new year of 1863 by retiring about five hundred yards from the position they held during the battle of December 31. Harker's brigade had rejoined the division by order of General Rosecrans shortly before midnight, and Wood was in an ambulance on his way back to a Nashville hospital. The capable General Milo Hascall was left in temporary command.

Wood's men had reason to send him off with their best wishes, for he had seen to their well-being. While the men of other divisions wandered the field hacking steaks off dead horses, Wood's men were able to eat from the three days' rations he had caused to be distributed among them on December 30, the day before the battle.

Even General Crittenden was treated to a horse steak that night. He had been on the left flank all day, and for one whose promotion was considered by many to be strictly political he had done just fine. Bickham wrote of his demeanor on the battlefield, "Crittenden was perfectly calm, but an unusual stateliness in his deportment seemed to indicate that he was gravely conscious of the glories and horrors of a great battle." He had seen terrible things during the day, but the thought of eating a horse steak seemed to unnerve him a little, once he knew what he had done. And as a good Kentuckian, he seemed more than a little embarrassed about it. He explained, "Next morning I found that the steak had been cut from a horse that had been killed. I didn't know this at the time I ate it."[1]

It was a bitter night, so cold that wounded men froze to the ground. In spite of Rosecrans' order that no fires be kindled, Federal cavalrymen rode among the men with torches and lit small fires so that they could boil a pot of coffee and at least take the chill off of the horsemeat. The sight of the fires in his rear threw Rosecrans into a small panic. He told General McCook, "They have got entirely in our rear and are forming a line of battle by torchlight." Rosecrans hurriedly ordered his generals to prepare to fight. Crittenden saw the fires for what they were and he mollified the commanding general. In his article about Stones River for *Battles and Leaders of the Civil War*, Crittenden remembered, "I sent Rosecrans word that as the men were cold and were not being disturbed by the enemy, and as it would take all night to put out the fires, we had better leave them."[2]

General Braxton Bragg had no intention of launching an attack that night. He was convinced that he had already won a tremendous victory. Reports were coming to him of wagons heading up the road toward Nashville; obviously, Rosecrans was retreating. Bragg wired Richmond, "The enemy has yielded his strong position and is falling back." He promised to smash them on the road.[3]

What Bragg's scouts thought was a retreat was not that at all. What they were hearing was the evacuation of the Federal wounded. General Wood's ambulance was one of the caravan.

Bragg and his scouts were not the only ones who misinterpreted the sight and sound of the long exodus headed north on the road to Nashville. William Bickham wrote that as homeowners along the turnpike saw the wagons, ambulances, and walking wounded passing by, a rumor took hold that the Yankees had suffered a cataclysmic defeat. Their jubilation could not be contained. "The wife of one Rebel officer climbed to the roof of her house, which overlooked the pike, and clapped her hands and shouted in glee, 'They are beaten back!'"[4]

Bragg was cured of his premature optimism on New Year's Day when he looked across Stones River and saw Rosecrans still in place. Each commanding general came to the realization that the other was not going to leave; battle plans would have to be drawn up for the continuation of the fight. While they worked at headquarters, the day passed in relative tranquility for most of the men on the field. The exception was on the left flank, Crittenden's wing.

General Bragg decided to send General Leonidas Polk splashing across Stones River to see if a hard jab would encourage the Federals to leave. Polk got into the Round Forest, which had been relinquished when Crittenden adjusted his lines the night before, but could make no further progress. Wagner's brigade, aided by some well-served artillery, upset Polk's — and Bragg's — plans. It was going to take something more to send the Yankees back to Nashville.

Rosecrans, too, tried a move on New Year's Day. In an echo of the battle plan of December 31, Rosecrans sent Van Cleve's division (but not Van Cleve, who had been wounded in the first day's battle) across Stones River to take possession of a tactically important hill. They began to entrench. The short winter's day ended with a chill in the air that was more than just frost. The sense of expectation was almost tangible.

In the early hours of January 2, the enemy opened up from their forward position in the Round Forest with a ferocious artillery barrage on the Left Wing's main position, and more particularly on that of Colonel Harker. Caught by surprise, the Federal infantry hugged the frosty ground while the gun crews went to work. On this morning, the Confederates belied their reputation as notably poor artillerymen; their fire was so effective that Estep's 8th Indiana Battery was forced to retire. Near the end of the duel between the big guns, a terrible mistake was made. Captain James Stokes and his Board of Trade Battery, posted behind Harker's infantrymen, mistook them for the enemy and began dropping shells among them. Captain Cullen Bradley rode back to stop them, had his horse shot from beneath him, and continued on foot to where Stokes' men were firing. He managed to make them realize their mistake, and the fire from the rear ended. Stokes had inflicted five of the twelve casualties suffered in Harker's brigade.

Bickham recalled, "While this was going on, an infantry demonstration was made upon Wagner's skirmishers, but the enemy were easily driven back." In his report, Harker acknowledged that the repulse was accomplished with reinforcements from General Cruft's brigade of Palmer's division. The whole affair was over in forty minutes.[5]

The occupation of that hill on the east side of Stones River worried Bragg. It commanded the ford and gave the Federal artillerists a platform from which to fire long-range shells into the Confederate lines. It was an intolerable situation; the Yankees would have to be driven away. The assignment of dislodging the bluecoats from the hill was handed to General John C. Breckinridge, commander of the 1st Division of Lieutenant General William J. Hardee's corps. Breckinridge was an aristocrat from Lexington, Kentucky, and a pre-war friend of Thomas L. Crittenden, whose men he was now ordered to attack. Breckinridge's vehement arguments against the attack did not move Bragg, and the former U.S. vice president went off to do his duty. Kentuckian was about to fight Kentuckian, and neither Breckinridge nor Crittenden was going to pull his punches.

The afternoon was sleety, and the gathering Confederates shivered in line for three hours before the signal came at 4:00 P.M. to advance on the Federals. The spearhead of the attack was the storied Orphan Brigade, Kentuckians whose mother state had never seceded. They lost their general, Roger W. Hanson, in the charge, but on they came until they threw Van Cleve's Yankees back up the hill, over the top, and down the far side.

Across the way, Crittenden had watched Breckinridge's four brigades forming up and knew what was coming. He calmly ordered Captain John Mendenhall, his artillery chief, to begin assembling guns. He rounded up at least forty-five of them and began to deploy them to rake the Confederates, if and when they came into range. Now there was no "if" to it—the Rebels were coming over the hill behind the routed Yankees—and Crittenden said to Mendenhall, "Now, Mendenhall, you must cover my men with your cannon."[6]

The effect of forty-five guns spewing double loads of canister into the massed Rebel infantry was as predictable as it was devastating. The Rebels retreated as quickly as they could, and the Federals came back to occupy the disputed hill.

This was Bragg's last roll of the dice. The Battle of Stones River was over. The Confederates remained in place through the daylight hours of January 3 but slipped away late that night. As usual, Fighting Joe Wheeler's cavalry was left behind to intimidate any Yankee patrols that might come forward. Rosecrans was feeling cautious after the trial the Army of the Cumberland had just passed through and did not move into Murfreesboro until January 5.

Thomas J. Wood returned to duty on February 15, though not immediately to his division. Shortly after his recovery from his Stones River wound, he accepted an interim assignment as commandant of the Post of Nashville. He replaced General R. B. Mitchell. It was light duty, and Wood took the opportunity for the first time since the war began to go to Dayton, Ohio, and his wife of thirteen months, Caroline. She evidently returned with him to Tennessee, and together they traveled to Murfreesboro for a tour of the Stones River battlefield. Colonel John Beatty (3rd Ohio Infantry) recorded in his diary on March 14, 1863, "The weather is remarkably fine today. I saw Mrs. And Major General McCook and Mrs. And Major General [sic] Wood going out to the battlefield this morning."[7]

There was speculation that Wood was going to be replaced as commander of the 1st Division by General John Brannan, but it was not so. Wood remained in charge of the Post of Nashville until the second week in May, when Special Field Orders No. 135 relieved him. General J. D. Cox assumed command, and Wood rejoined his division.

Wood returned to his field command, asserts Larry J. Daniel, because of the insistence of his men. The general remained popular. He was "ranked high for skill and enterprise [and] regarded as second to none in experience and cultural intellect." Furthermore, the Kentuckian enjoyed "a peculiar reputation in the army for his vigor and his vigilance, and his precision in regulating guard duty."[8]

W. F. G. Shanks said that Wood was "a capatious officer" but called him "a decided, brave, and energetic one."[9]

Wood was a strict disciplinarian who was also capable of paying tender attention to the most obscure private. John J. Hight, chaplain of the 58th Indiana, was present one day when General Wood noticed a trooper named Zingu Parks passing by. In addition to his remarkable name, Parks stood out because of his young age; he was only thirteen or fourteen years old. Wood called out to him and asked, "My son, what brought you into the service?"

"Two dollars," answered Private Parks.[10]

On the subject of Wood's strict discipline, Hight told another story. A soldier of the 58th Indiana named Richard Hembree deserted near Haysville, Kentucky, on or about October 7, 1862, and stayed on the loose until May 11, 1863, when he was arrested. He was court-martialed, convicted, and sentenced to die by firing squad. The men of his regiment were upset. "It is safe to say that no event occurred during our entire service up to this time, that stirred the sympathies and feelings of the men so much as did this announcement," said Hight. Hembree had a wife and five children.[11]

Colonel George P. Buell and Lieutenant Colonel James T. Embree got an appointment with General Rosecrans to try to obtain a reprieve or commutation. The meeting failed in its purpose. Embree, who was a lawyer in civilian life, went back for a second chance to argue Hembree's case. At the end, Rosecrans said, "Colonel Embree, you go back to your regiment, get up a paper embodying all that you plead on behalf of the prisoner, and have the same signed by all the officers of your regiment. Bring the paper to me, and I will see what can be done."[12]

This Embree did. He collected all the required names and returned to Rosecrans with the petition on the morning before the execution, which was scheduled to take place between noon and 3:00 P.M. Now began a tense wait. By noon there was still no word from headquarters, but at one o'clock Rosecrans summoned the officers of the regiment to his office "to hear the result of the petition. General Wood disapproved of the commutation of the sentence, but approved of the plea for an extension of the time." General Crittenden leaned toward a commutation. Faced with a split decision, General Rosecrans agreed to delay the execution until Lincoln's decision could be obtained. Wood himself informed the prisoner Hembree of the decision.[13]

To the lengthy written appeal that was sent to the president Wood appended a note dated June 22, 1863, that said in part, "I approve this application so far as granting the respite to the prisoner goes, but I cannot approve the application for a remission of his sentence. The man was absent from his Regiment for more than seven months and did not return until he was arrested.... Justice to the individual is often mercy to the many." Rosecrans' enclosed endorsement, like Wood's, argued for execution, saying, "It is better for the service that a sufficient number of executions should take place in each Corps to show that the law will most probably be enforced."[14]

The petition and its accompanying endorsements went through channels to Judge Advocate General Joseph Holt, who presented it to the president. On July 18, 1863, the president put his decision in the case of Richard Hembree in writing. He wrote one word: "Pardon."[15]

A complete view of General Thomas J. Wood at this time would have to include his free use of profanity, his hubris, and his driving ambition. Certainly, that was one part of the picture. The rest of the portrait showed an officer who was intelligent, capable in camp and brave in battle; who was far-seeing in his attention to the needs of his men, fair in his assignment of picket and other duties; and who, though a firm believer in military justice, was willing to let a death sentence be appealed to a higher authority. It is little wonder that General Rosecrans felt confident in recommending him for promotion to major general "in the interest of the service and the name of the Army of the Cumberland."[16]

Rosecrans was not the only one who believed that Wood was overdue for promotion to major general. There was a coordinated effort from Wood's friends in the month of April, when a flurry of recommendations arrived on the desks of those who were in a position to advance Wood's career. The citizens of Dayton took a rather circuitous path toward winning a promotion for Wood when they wrote to Ohio governor David Tod, but most of the others made their arguments to Secretary of War Edwin M. Stanton. Wood's fellow officers from the old Camp Nevin days, Generals Lovell H. Rousseau and Richard W. Johnson, wrote to Stanton. So did his more recent acquaintances, those who had fought alongside him at Stones River. His brigade commanders Milo Hascall, Charles G. Harker, George D. Wagner, and George P. Buell all petitioned Stanton for Wood's promotion, as did the artillery officer Cullen Bradley and the defender of Munfordville John T. Wilder. John M. Palmer wrote to Stanton and pointed out that there was no brigadier general in the army older than the Kentuckian. Wood's friends used such adjectives as "energetic," "gallant," "high-minded," and "modest" when pleading their case to Stanton. In June, James Speed of Louisville belatedly added his voice to the chorus when he wrote directly to his friend President Lincoln on Wood's behalf.

It was not to be. The recommendations were ignored and Wood remained a brigadier. It pained him more than his bullet-torn foot. Time might finally heal both his foot and his spirit, but for the time being there was nothing else for a professional to do. He reconciled himself to commanding a division under Thomas L. Crittenden.

After the Battle of Stones River, the Army of the Cumberland was reorganized. The changes to the army were authorized by General Orders No. 9 on January 9, 1863, and were implemented by General Rosecrans on February 2. General George H. Thomas' Center Wing was now the XIV Corps, McCook's Right Wing was the XX Corps, and Crittenden's Left Wing was the XXI Corps. Wood's command was still the 1st Division and contained three brigades. The 1st Brigade was commanded by Colonel George P. Buell, successor to General Milo Hascall, who had been transferred to the Army of the Ohio.

The 2nd Brigade was under Brigadier General George D. Wagner, and the 3rd Brigade was led by Colonel Charles G. Harker. Three artillery batteries were attached to the division, all under Captain Cullen Bradley.

When Wood returned to the field, his division was still trying to make good the losses of the Stones River Campaign. The 1st Division of the former Left Wing had lost six wagons, one ambulance, forty-six sets of harness, four draft horses, fifty-six artillery horses, three cavalry horses, and forty-five mules. Of far greater importance, of course, were the human losses. Hascall had lost 343 killed and wounded out of his 1st Brigade, Wagner had lost 329 killed and wounded out of the 2nd Brigade, and Harker's 3rd Brigade had paid the butcher 454 killed and wounded. These were big numbers and to repair the damages would take some time.

Of course, this was only one division of one corps. All of the divisions of all three corps had suffered, and restoring his army to full strength was what occupied General Rosecrans in winter quarters at Murfreesboro. In mid-January, he began receiving twelve to fourteen thousand new troops, who became a reserve corps under Major General Gordon Granger. That helped ease the pinch as far as enlisted men and non-commissioned officers were concerned. However, the decimation of the officers' corps (the Battle of Stones River had cost 549 killed or wounded from the rank of second lieutenant on up, and sixty-six more were dismissed) remained a problem and Rosecrans had to scramble to fill the vacancies. One of the new officers who showed up in the Murfreesboro camp must have been an unpleasant sight to General Wood. Brigadier General James A. Garfield, who developed such a negative opinion of Wood on the Corinth Campaign in 1862, arrived in camp and became Rosecrans' chief of staff.

Rosecrans' persistent telegraphic call for officers became an annoyance to General in Chief Henry W. Halleck, who told him, "I cannot take good generals away from armies in the field, and bad ones you do not want.... You already have your share of the best officers."[17]

The calls from Murfreesboro for more officers were only one irritation that caused an increasingly tense relationship between Rosecrans and Halleck. Rosecrans wanted more cavalry and more weapons, too. He was calling for two thousand carbines and repeating rifles. Halleck lectured his dissatisfied subordinate, "You have already more than your share of the best arms. Everything has been done, and is now being done, for you that is possible by the Government. Your complaints are without reason. You cannot expect to have all the best arms. The Government cannot give them. Your cavalry is as well armed as that of Grant or Curtis."[18]

Rosecrans seized on the reference to his "complaints." He replied to Halleck the next day, "I do not complain. I point out the way to victory."[19]

The spat over tone was a distraction from more important matters, but

9. Winter Quarters at Murfreesboro

neither man was yet willing to let it go. Halleck waited only one day before responding to Rosecrans:

> Your recent telegrams have been couched in terms implying a censure upon the Government for not properly supplying you with cavalry and cavalry arms.... Yours is not the only nor the largest army in the field, and you are not the only general who is urgently calling for more cavalry and cavalry arms.... Everything has been done and will be done for your army which the Government can do without injustice to other troops. You cannot expect the best of arms or of anything else, to the exclusion of others, who need them as much as you do.[20]

Ten days later, on February 13, Rosecrans made a new request. He wanted money to pay the soldiers in his department through December 31. Some of them had not been paid since August, and Rosecrans calculated that it would take $1,700,000 to make the payroll for the Army of the Cumberland. He had inquired about this on February 3, in the middle of his fuss fight, and had received no reply.

He did not like the reply that Halleck sent him now. "Old Brains" said that there was only enough money to pay the Army of the Cumberland through the end of October. "To pay your army to the end of December would leave others unpaid for September and October," he explained. Rosecrans was beginning to appear like a headstrong child who wanted all of the cookies for himself, and he was not nearly done.[21]

In mid–April, Rosecrans returned to the subject of horses. "I have been urgent in asking for horses since October last. We have 3,500 dismounted cavalry," he said. He wanted permission to take horses from the civilian population. In his reply, Halleck told Rosecrans that the Quartermaster General had been ordered to send all the horses they could get to Murfreesboro and that he had the authority to impress horses only in enemy territory.[22]

This never-ending conversation-by-wire with Rosecrans was an aggravation to Halleck, and it was becoming the talk of the War Department. Three days after the horse telegram, Halleck wired a long rebuke to the general, which said, in part:

> My attention has frequently been called to the enormous expense to the Government of your telegrams, as much or perhaps more than that of all the other generals in the field.... The truth is, you report again and again the same thing by telegraph, at a very great expense to the Government, without the slightest necessity. For example, you have telegraphed at least a dozen, and, perhaps, twenty times in the last few months that you require more cavalry. The Government is fully aware of your wants, and has been doing all in its power to supply them. It certainly was not necessary to remind it every day and every hour of its duty.[23]

Rosecrans could not take the correction without answering back: "If I have used the telegraph freely, it has been through an anxious desire to do my duty, and to insure that by no fault of mine should things go unattended to, which, in my experience has shown may be the cause even with the most able and zealous officers, without reminders."[24]

Considering that that was his attitude, it is small wonder that Rosecrans' behavior did not improve. Four days after Halleck's chastisement, the unrepentant general sent three telegrams to Washington: he needed horses. Halleck wearily replied that the government had already sent him over thirty thousand horses and, no, he could not requisition horses among loyal citizens; it was illegal: "I do not precisely understand why you so often urge me to give you authority to violate the law. If you wish to violate the law, you certainly should not throw upon me the responsibility of your illegal act."[25]

And so it went. Whether his hectoring of General Halleck had any effect or whether his needs would have been met without it, Rosecrans was slowly building up the strength of his army in the number of effectives, the tons of stockpiled supplies at Nashville, and the massive new fortification in Murfreesboro called Fortress Rosecrans. It helped that steamers could again unload at Nashville. The Cumberland River was running full because of the winter rains. Even better, the railroad between Nashville and Murfreesboro was operational. The first train pulled into Murfreesboro on February 10. Lyman Widney of the 34th Illinois wrote in his diary, "The shrill whistle evoked hearty cheers from all quarters of our camp. It conveyed to us the agreeable and indisputable intelligence that we are linked again with home and friends by an iron roadway over which may come plentiful rations, letters, newspapers, tobacco, whisky, and numerous other so-called luxuries which soldiers love so well and miss so much when the wagons are overtaxed in carrying only the necessaries of life."[26]

Rosecrans fretted and feuded with Halleck, but overall it was an amiable camp. Even the officers found time to have fun. Crittenden played chess and Philip Sheridan of McCook's XX Corps liked to play tenpins. Sometimes Rosecrans would join in. As for the men, Chaplain John J. Hight remembered, "The camp was full of life. There was a great deal of joy and hilarity prevalent, and much amusement indulged in. But it was not all frivolity and profitless pastime that occupied the men.... Many of them employed the time in learning to read and write." The men of the 34th Illinois built a church. Men passed the time playing cards, writing letters home, and reading the Bible and religious tracts. Novels were wildly popular. Private Luke Lyman, one of the U.S. Regulars in camp, wrote, "Reading novels is the mania in camp and sitting in groups are men, some listening while others are reading there [sic] latest romance." In addition, men in all of the different divisions took an interest in beautifying their sections of the larger camps. Lyman wrote, "We have our camps decorated with evergreens which look beautiful.... Most all of our camps have been decorated with cedars, even large trees by the hundreds being cut down and hauled into camps so that you may stroll into what appears a beautiful cedar grove."[27]

Of course, there were the official duties to attend to, the drilling, the picket and guard duty, the foraging, and the mandatory attendance of the occasional execution. Not all of the cases concluded with the happy ending of the Richard Hembree case. Many deserters came in before April 1, in acceptance of President Lincoln's proclamation of amnesty. Some did not. When the incorrigibles were caught and convicted, they were taken before the firing squad. In addition, there were hangings of at least two Confederate spies.

To keep the men sharp in camp, there were frequent afternoon inspections by the commanding general and the men also put on reviews for him. It was reported in the *Louisville Daily Journal* that after one review Rosecrans "rode alone between the ranks, talking to the men and inquiring into their individual wants.... Finally the General stopped in front of an Irishman, apparently well pleased with his soldierly appearance. 'Well, Pat,' says the General, 'and what do you want?' 'A furlo, please your honor,' answered Pat. 'You'll do, Pat!' said the General, as he rode away laughing."[28]

This kind of easy jocularity made the men love Rosecrans. He was often among them and was genuinely interested in their welfare, and they knew that when he fought with General in Chief Halleck and Secretary of War Stanton he was fighting for *them*. This is not to say that Rosecrans did not keep them busy, for he did, especially on the fortifications, which had become one of his obsessions. William Sumner Dodge, in his contemporary *History of the Old Second Division*, described the impressive result of all this pick and shovel work. He wrote, "North, south, east, and west these works present their fronts, some twenty in number and from their strength and extent they seem to scorn the idea that they can ever be stormed or reduced. They are all of earth, and present tufted slopes, which in summer give them a very beautiful appearance.... These were all mounted with guns of heavy calibre, and it is the opinion of able military men that the town is invincible to assault."[29]

By far, the largest of the fortifications was Fortress Rosecrans, two hundred acres surrounded by fourteen thousand feet of serpentine earthworks. The walls jutted out with diamond-shaped lunettes and inside were four redoubts. One of them was called Redoubt T. J. Wood. Fortress Rosecrans was designed not only for defense but also to be a supply depot. The Nashville & Chattanooga Railroad pierced its walls, as did the Nashville Turnpike and Stones River.

While the men worked, they talked. One day, Major H. F. Kalfus of the 15th Kentucky Infantry began to speak his piece about an issue that was agitating the minds of many of the volunteers. As of January 1, the Emancipation Proclamation was in effect. There was a great deal of uncomfortable speculation that blacks would soon be serving in the army alongside whites. Major Kalfus said, "I am willing for negroes to be employed for such work as this, but when guns are put in their hands we [pointing to his men and speaking for all to hear] are all going home." His remarks were overheard by someone from General Beatty's headquarters. The major was arrested and "dishonorably dismissed [from] the service for using mutinous language in the presence of his men."[30]

Kalfus had spoken the views of many of the western men, from both north and south of the Ohio River, including General Wood. Wood had enough political shrewdness to keep his views to himself, and after the example was made of Major Kalfus others began to see the wisdom in tamping down their criticism of the new policy of the Federal government. It did not, however, put an end to their disapproval of it, and more than a few men made their feelings plain by deserting. The January 29 edition of the *Maysville* (Kentucky) *Dollar Weekly Bulletin* ran an item that said, "There are here in our midst many returned Federal soldiers — deserters, technically — who declare they left without leave and will not return ... they will not fight for abolition."[31]

The *Boston* (Massachusetts) *Press* ran an article in a similar vein. It said, "Kentucky has given over forty regiments to the Union armies and they have borne the brunt of battle shoulder to shoulder with the bravest, but under the effect of the radical programme they are dwindling away by resignations and desertions, from full regiments to mere companies." The Boston paper gave the example of the 26th Kentucky Infantry, which was down from regimental strength to 120 men.[32]

Naturally, there were rumors constantly floating around camp to titillate the men. Forrest was coming; Wheeler was coming; General Longstreet was coming from the Army of Northern Virginia to join Bragg; Bragg was advancing. The *Louisville Daily Journal* ran a small article on April 30 about the rumor carried into camp by a Confederate deserter that "General Breckinridge had shot and killed General Bragg two or three days ago in a personal altercation." The rumor was "credited by many, as it is known that an unfriendly feeling has existed between the two parties since the battle of Stones River, if not previously."[33]

There was whispering among the men that the Army of the Cumberland was about to advance. The anticipation was understandable. Other armies were already in motion. In the West, Grant was maneuvering against Vicksburg and in May he got below Vicksburg and crossed to the east side of the Mississippi River. In the East, the Army of the Potomac had fought a battle with General Lee at Chancellorsville. It could not be long before the Army of the Cumberland began its campaign of 1863. The signs were abundant that a move was nigh. As Widney observed, "Rosecrans is pushing detachments forward at various points to feel the enemy's force and positions. These movements provoke considerable skirmishing."[34]

One such excursion took place on April 20 involving four thousand infantry under General Joseph J. Reynolds and six hundred cavalry under Colonel John T. Wilder. Widney said, "They destroyed almost the entire railroad from Manchester to McMinnville, a cotton mill, two other mills at McMinnville, a small mill at Liberty, captured a large amount of supplies, 180 prisoners, over six hundred animals, and returned with a loss of only one man wounded."[35]

The sorties never developed into anything larger, though, and as spring advanced toward summer the men began to feel restless. "It does not appear to us that we are helping much to put down the rebellion," said Widney. "Here we are digging away in one spot apparently with the purpose of remaining here in security until the end of the war."[36]

To the authorities in Washington, it also appeared that the Army of the Cumberland was awfully slow in advancing against Bragg in Tullahoma. This concern became something like alarm after the third week in May, when Bragg sent General Breckinridge (his rumored murderer) and fifty-two hundred men to General Joseph E. Johnston. Johnston had been appointed by President Jefferson Davis to oversee the efforts of the Army of Tennessee under Bragg and the Army of Mississippi under General John C. Pemberton. Pemberton was trying to defend Vicksburg. Breckinridge and his men were shuffled off to Mississippi to reinforce Pemberton (and they would have except that General Johnston stopped them in Jackson).

Now was the perfect time for Rosecrans to attack. Bragg was weakened, and an attack would perhaps lead to his destruction. Certainly, it would prevent him from sending more troops for the succor of Vicksburg. Even President Lincoln became involved in the effort to pry Rosecrans away from Murfreesboro. He wrote the reluctant Rosecrans, "I would not push you to any rashness, but I am very anxious that you do your utmost short of rashness, to keep Bragg from getting off to help Johnston against Grant."[37]

Rosecrans answered, "Dispatch received. I will attend to it." Yet he did not move.[38]

What he did do was poll his generals. There were five questions they were asked to answer, but it really boiled down to only two: "Do you think an advance likely to prevent additional reinforcements being sent against General Grant by the enemy in our front?" and "Do you think an immediate advance advisable?"[39]

General Wood answered Rosecrans' survey on June 9. To the question about reinforcements moving from Bragg to Vicksburg, Wood said, "In the first place, I do not think the enemy had evinced much disposition to re-enforce Johnston in Mississippi from his army in Middle Tennessee. My opinion is that the re-enforcements have been drawn from elsewhere." It was a surprisingly inaccurate beginning. The rest was speculative but safe. He said, "Should we advance, one of two events would almost certainly ensue: First, the enemy would not consider himself strong enough to fight us; in which case he would rapidly withdraw his entire army from Middle Tennessee ... or, secondly, he would be strong enough to accept the proffered battle; in which case, owing

Thomas J. Wood's Civil War, 1861–1865 (map by the author).

to his advantage of position, we should probably be defeated." In other words, if the Army of the Cumberland advanced, either Bragg would fall back or he would stand and defeat them.[40]

To the question regarding the wisdom of an immediate advance, Wood's answer was terse and to the point: "I answer, unhesitatingly, no."[41]

In his subsequent message to Halleck, Rosecrans fairly crowed about the results of his poll, especially as regarded the third question. Rosecrans said, "To the third question, not one yes; seventeen no."[42]

Halleck remained unconvinced of the wisdom of keeping the Army of the Cumberland stationary. He quoted to Rosecrans a military maxim, "Councils of war never fight," and said, "The prolonged inactivity of so large an army in the field is causing much complaint and dissatisfaction, not only in Washington, but throughout the country."[43]

Rosecrans refused to be bullied, not by Lincoln, not by Halleck, not by public opinion "throughout the country." And though Rosecrans would not admit it, the fact was that by the time of the exchange above he had already begun to feel that the condition of his army was such that an advance could soon be contemplated. In the first week in June, the soldiers noticed a change. Work on the Murfreesboro fortifications ended and "an active course of drill commenced." Their excitement quickened; perhaps this time the rumors of an advance were true.[44]

They were. Two weeks later, the six-months-long encampment at Murfreesboro came to an end and the offensive of 1863 began for the Army of the Cumberland.

CHAPTER 10

Tullahoma and Beyond

General Thomas J. Wood's division of the XXI Corps moved out of Murfreesboro on the Bradyville Pike at 7:00 A.M. on June 24. It was with the easternmost of the advancing Federal columns. In the center was General George H. Thomas and the XIV Corps. Farther west was General Alexander McDowell McCook's XX Corps. The Reserve Corps under General Gordon Granger and the newly refurbished cavalry under Major General David S. Stanley were on the far right flank.

Along with fresh uniforms and footwear, new guns, abundant ammunition, and sufficient rations, the army had gotten new flags while at Murfreesboro. The corps flags were red and fringed around the edges. In the center of the field was an eagle behind a shield and in the shield was the numerical designation of the corps. The division flag was the same, except that the designation of the division was indicated by the number of stars; one star, in the case of Wood's division. The flags were bright and beautiful and would have made quite a sight, flapping in the spring breeze, if it had not been a rainy day when the march began.

The rain matched Wood's mood. He remained unconvinced that the timing of the move against Bragg was wise. As late as June 17, Wood had argued to Brigadier General James A. Garfield, Rosecrans' chief of staff, that it was reckless to commence a campaign at the same time that the Union armies were moving in the East and in the West. If Hooker failed in Virginia and Grant failed in Mississippi, the Army of the Cumberland would be the hope of the nation and it must be kept intact. Furthermore, victory was not assured for the Army of the Cumberland. If all three Federal armies failed, it would be a disaster from which the country might not recover. Wood advocated that the army continue its preparations to move but remain in place until the results were known of the two Union campaigns that were already begun.

The commanding general would not be dissuaded. Now that he had finally decided to move, Rosecrans wanted to move fast, and he ordered the troops to travel light. To follow orders, Wood had his staff calculate closely how few wagons would be required to meet the needs of his men; they figured that "six wagons per regiment for the weaker regiments and seven for the stronger would fulfill the conditions of the problem." Some of these were loaded with twelve days' rations for the men and six days' forage for the animals, and others with ammunition and baggage. The men carried three days' rations on their person, and a herd of beef cattle sufficient to supply meat for six days was to be driven on the hoof.[1]

Wood remembered, "Shortly after the movement was commenced, the rain began to descend, and continued all day, and increased much in violence as the day declined." At the junction of the Bradyville Pike and the Cripple Creek Road, General John M. Palmer's division was passing and Wood's column was forced to stand waiting in the rain until they passed. Nevertheless, the division arrived at its assigned destination of Donald's Church at 2:00 P.M.[2]

The next morning, only four miles out from camp, Wood's division ran into the tail of Palmer's wagon train. Progress was so slow that Wood finally ordered his men to encamp. They loitered all afternoon and into the night while Wood fumed. He had an aide check to see whether the road was clear a couple of hours after midnight, but Palmer's wagons were still inching along, blocking the road. Wood complained to General Crittenden about the delay. The reply from headquarters did not bring him much satisfaction. "The general is using every possible exertion to clear the road for your command. He has no disposition whatever to move without our entire command, but should it become necessary to do so, he will give you timely notice, so that you may arrange for the security of your train, etc., and move up, say, with two-thirds of your infantry." The complaint had no positive result on the twenty-sixth and it was midday on the twenty-seventh — forty-eight hours after the start of the unscheduled halt in the road — before Wood could begin to advance again.[3]

Beyond Wood's campsite, the road turned sharply upward. The continuing rain made it a hard ascent. Man and beast struggled uphill on the slick road for eleven hours, until 1:00 A.M. on the twenty-eighth. To make the climb easier, Harker ordered his wagon cargoes to be reduced by half. He posted a guard to keep watch over the half that was left on the roadside while other men took hold of a long rope and helped the mules muscle the train to the top. General Wood wrote, "It has scarcely ever been my ill-fortune in eighteen years of active service (during which I have marched many thousands of miles) to have to pass over so bad a road." The men had a day to rest after they reached the summit. They moved again at 5:00 A.M. on June 30.[4]

Beginning on July 1, Rosecrans ordered that the wagons be reduced in number, hoping that this would free the marching men to make a quick advance on Tullahoma. Wood recalled, "Under this order I allowed one wagon for my own and each brigade headquarters, and one wagon to each regiment for the transportation, of subsistence for the officers, and the indispensable necessary cooking utensils for the officers and men. The ammunition and ambulance trains were, of course, to accompany the troops. The intrenching tools were to be carried after the fashion of the Roman armies, by the men."[5]

Before the march could resume, word came to Rosecrans' headquarters that the determination of the enemy to fight for control of Middle Tennessee had been overestimated; Bragg was evacuating Tullahoma. Speed was everything now. Wood was ordered to take his division and some cavalry down the Hillsboro Road to Pelham to try to catch at least part of the enemy column, sever it, and prevent it from getting over the Cumberland Plateau. Wood marched at about 6:00 P.M. and arrived at Hillsboro three hours later.

They encountered none of the enemy until the morning of the second. Moving toward Pelham, they began running into enemy cavalrymen, skirmished with them, and pushed them back to the Elk River bridge, which the graybacks set afire as they retreated. As the Federals tried to douse the flames, a band of two hundred of Nathan Bedford Forrest's cavalrymen attacked them. Wood's skirmishers responded and shooed them away. The bridge was saved but too late to be of use in any further pursuit. The enemy had slipped the noose. Wood was ordered that afternoon to move back toward Hillsboro, which he did.

The next morning Wood was ordered to take his division back to Pelham, over the same mushy road his weary men had marched just the afternoon before. They arrived about 3:00 P.M. Later, some CSA deserters came into Wood's camp, and the general learned from them when and by what route Hardee's and Polk's corps had escaped. He made a special inquiry about the three brigades commanded by his former friend General Simon Bolivar Buckner. The answer he received was unsatisfying. "By what road Buckner's command crossed I could not learn," Wood said. In spite of their disappointing ignorance on the question of Buckner, Wood paid them a backhanded compliment, saying, "Some of the deserters were quite intelligent, far more so than I had ever before met from the rebel army."[6]

Wood said, "It has not been the good fortune of my division during this brief campaigning to render any distinguished service or participate in any important action, but it affords me much satisfaction to bear testimony to the untiring zeal and energy displayed by the men and officers of all grades on a most laborious march." He cited their "promptness" and "light-hearted cheerfulness."[7]

Wood might have ended his report on this positive note, but he decided to take his fellow officers to task for their "criminal neglect" in not obeying orders to limit the number of trains on the march. He reminded headquarters that he had limited his regiments to no more than seven wagons at the outset and that he had left the others safe within the fortifications at Murfreesboro, and he condemned the "neglect of other commanders in this army to conform to this order of preparation." Their disobedience led to "the consequent embarrassment of the movements on the march, and the retardation of the concentration of the troops at Manchester." The perturbed Wood lectured, "My military studies and experience have long since taught me that celerity is the soul of military movements. They have further taught me that the most happily conceived combinations may be thwarted by sumptuous baggage trains, which cripple all efficiency of movement, and whose cargoes only serve to enervate the morale of the army."[8]

The little sermon about the obligation to obey a commander's orders and the importance of "celerity" was in perfect keeping with General Wood's sense of self. He was a master of the science of war, and it was his duty to school those who were his inferiors.

General Rosecrans had won a great and bloodless victory in the Tullahoma Campaign. Middle Tennessee was entirely in Federal control and at the cost of only six hundred men. Rosecrans was proud of what his army had done.

Official Washington had a different attitude. In his message to Rosecrans, Secretary of War Edwin M. Stanton glossed over the redemption of Middle Tennessee and hurried on to a masked complaint: "You and your noble army now have the chance to give the finishing blow to the rebellion. Will you neglect the chance?"[9]

The faint praise stemmed in part from a simple matter of timing. Rosecrans won Middle Tennessee in the first week in July. That same week, Grant won Vicksburg and General George Gordon Meade defeated Robert E. Lee at Gettysburg and sent him, crippled, back toward Virginia. These were pivotal events, and they made the success of the Middle Tennessee Campaign easy to overlook.

Rosecrans replied to Stanton with hurt feelings: "You do not appear to observe the fact that this noble army has driven the rebels from Middle Tennessee of which my dispatches advised you. I beg in behalf of this army that the War Department may not overlook so great an event because it is not written in letters of blood."[10]

Former senator John J. Crittenden was dying. Certainly, this was on the mind of his son General Thomas L. Crittenden during the Tullahoma Campaign. As a man of duty, he remained with his corps until the successful conclusion. However, when the Rebels were maneuvered out of Middle Tennessee, General Crittenden prepared to take a leave of absence to be at his father's side. Crittenden was still with his corps as late as July 7, when he ordered his generals to fire a salute in celebration of Grant's victory at Vicksburg, but shortly after that he left for Kentucky. (Senator Crittenden died about two weeks later on July 26, 1863.)

Before he left the Federal camp, General Crittenden made a decision that was innocent in its origin but calamitous in its results. He chose as his temporary successor General John M. Palmer. For the second time in ten months, Wood the professional had been passed over in favor of a volunteer. The first time was in Louisville in September when General Buell chose Crittenden to command his II Corps. Now that appointee had chosen as temporary head of the XXI Corps General John M. Palmer, a man against whom Wood already held a grudge because of his clumsy handling of his troops on the march to Tullahoma.

If Wood vented his feelings in a letter to his wife or his father, it has not come to light. But his feelings of bitter resentment were perfectly revealed in his actions of the next few weeks. It was an unbecoming fit of pique that, in its worst moment, threatened the very existence of the Army of the Cumberland and its prospects in the Western Theater.

A six weeks' stay at Tullahoma was long enough for Rosecrans to repair the bridges and railroads and to gather supplies for his coming march on Chattanooga. It was also long enough to annoy General Halleck, who picked up his badgering of Rosecrans not too long after Stanton's insulting wire. On July 24, Halleck sent dispatches to Rosecrans that said in part, "You must move forward immediately," and, "The patience of the authorities has been completely exhausted, and if I had not repeatedly promised to urge you forward, and begged for delay, you would have been removed from command." Then Halleck really tried to put the spurs to Rosecrans: "It has been said that you are as inactive as was General Buell, and the pressure for your removal has been almost as great as it was in his case."[11]

Rosecrans answered that he was anxious, too; unfortunately, there were obstacles before him that the men in faraway Washington did not understand.

The telegraphic back-and-forth continued over the next few days, during which Rosecrans fell back on an old tactic — offer to resign and dare the government to take him up on it. He said, "As my ambition is something like your own — to discharge my duty to God and country — I say to you frankly that whenever the Government can replace me by a commander in whom they have more confidence, they ought to do so, and take responsibility for the result."[12]

On August 4, Halleck tried to end the sparring with Rosecrans. In a two-sentence telegram he said, "Your forces must move forward without further delay. You will daily report the movement of each corps till you cross the Tennessee River."[13]

That was it, a direct order. But Rosecrans ignored it, and for another twelve days Halleck had to direct his wires to Rosecrans at Tullahoma.

While the men at the top quarreled, the division and brigade commanders went about the business of gathering the rations and forage mandated by Rosecrans for the move on Chattanooga. Wood was able to report from his camp at Hillsboro, "In accordance with a dispatch from department headquarters, under date of August 6, directing ten days' forage and rations to be put in the hands of the troops and packed ready for movement, I have caused the subsistence for that period to be issued to the troops, and prepared for a sudden movement." The forage was more difficult to come by than the rations. Wood admitted, "I have only been able to get grain enough to issue to the brigades the full allowance for ten days for their horses and half the allowance for their mules."[14]

For the move, he had "one wagon for every 75 company officers and enlisted men, one wagon to the field and staff of the regiments, one to the medical department, and one to the quartermaster's department. The above allotment of transportation leaves forty-nine wagons to be used as a division supply train."[15]

It was not all work, though. On August 11, Colonel Harker hosted a dinner party featuring oysters, chicken, Catawba wine, and pastries, among other treats. General Wood attended and spent an enjoyable evening conversing with one of his new regimental commanders, Colonel Emerson Opdyke of the 125th Ohio. The 125th had been transferred to Harker's brigade just before the march toward Tullahoma began. Wood was probably glad for the chance to get to know Opdyke better; he had taken note of him on the march and had remarked one day to General George D. Wagner, "Colonel Opdyke is one of the most promising young officers in the service."[16]

The night of Harker's dinner party, Wood and Opdyke sat across the table from one another. Opdyke had not known Wood before, except by his reputation for profanity and haughty brusqueness. Aside from a few remarks that had passed between them in the course of duty, the two men had never spoken, but as Opdyke told his wife, he found that Wood was a "delightful conversationalist." Wood spoke to Opdyke of his pre-war tour of Europe and of his admiration for the Russians, whose noble class "were the most accomplished and the most clever people in the world." He went on to talk with authority about the state of diplomacy between the crowned heads of Europe. Wood's up-to-date grasp of international relations across the Atlantic was remarkable, considering that he had just finished a campaign and was about to commence another.[17]

The commencement of that new campaign was on August 16. Crittenden had returned to the field on or before August 6 and was apparently unaware of the deep offense he had caused Wood over the temporary appointment of Palmer as head of the XXI Corps. Wood, however, had not forgotten, and he showed his displeasure with Crittenden by simply failing to communicate with him regarding his plans, or even to acknowledge receipt of orders, during the busy hours just before the march began. Crittenden sent him a dispatch complaining about the silence ensuing from 1st Division headquarters: "The general commanding is disappointed at not having received anything further from you in answer to the orders sent you this morning and the letter of inquiry as to the road you will probably take, the location of your headquarters tonight, etc. Your clerk is probably at fault." Wood's refusal to communicate with Crittenden became a cause of repeated complaint in the days ahead.[18]

Once again, Crittenden's corps was to be on the left flank of the Federal advance (and Wood's division would be Crittenden's right). Thomas' corps would be in the center, followed by Granger's Reserve, and McCook's corps would proceed on the right flank. Both flanks would be screened by cavalry. The target in their sights was Chattanooga.

Wood was ordered to Therman and told to be in place there by August 19. He sent Wagner's 2nd Brigade ahead and followed with the 1st and 3rd Brigades. The whole division was over the ridge and in the Sequatchie Valley by the eighteenth and was at Therman by the designated date.

In his report, Wood proudly pointed out that he had been able to exceed orders for the required ten days' supply amount of rations and forage. He reported that he had "twenty-five days' subsistence for the men and sixteen days' grain for the animals." He had made room for the surplus by using "the wagons originally assigned to my division for the transportation of regimental and staff baggage."[19]

"I do not mention this fact in a spirit of egotism," Wood insisted, "but simply to show what can be accomplished by intelligence, good judgment, energy, and a willingness to make some sacrifice of personal comfort by commanders."[20]

On the twentieth, in an attempt to stir up confusion in Bragg's thinking, Colonel John T. Wilder was ordered to lead his mounted infantry (the famous "Lightning Brigade) on a demonstration directly against Chattanooga. Bragg would be misled into thinking that the Federals were going to cross the Tennessee River farther up than was their actual intention and perhaps would even believe that a linkup was planned with General Ambrose Burnside, who was expected to soon occupy Knoxville with the Army of the Ohio. Orders were for each of Crittenden's division commanders to select one brigade to go along in support of Wilder. Wood detached the capable George D. Wagner and the 2nd Brigade to accompany Wilder; meanwhile he and his two remaining brigades would remain at Therman. They stayed there two weeks, during which time Chaplain John J. Hight of the 58th Indiana was invited to deliver a sermon at division headquarters. Hight pointed out that this was a first for the 1st Division. General Wood attended and his sanctity impressed Hight. The chaplain wrote, "There is a great change in General Wood, so far as spiritual matters are concerned, and I hope he will yet become a sincere Christian man."[21]

Whether or not he would become a sincere Christian was an open question, but even if he tended to boast, curse, and hold grudges against his superiors, he did at least demonstrate some of the Christian virtues in his concern for his men. On August 26, three days after Hight's sermon, Captain John W. Tuttle of the 3rd Kentucky Infantry was thrown by a rearing horse. When the 1st and 3rd Brigades moved out from Therman for Jasper on September 1, Wood ordered that Tuttle be moved by ambulance. Tuttle wrote, "Travelled just in front of General Wood and Staff. He rode up twice during the day and inquired how I stood it." As events would soon prove, Wood was not so solicitous about the feelings of his immediate superior.[22]

The two brigades arrived at Jasper and the next afternoon, September 2, were ordered by General Crittenden to begin crossing the Tennessee River at Shellmound. "Send your train under efficient officers to the vicinity of Bridgeport, where it will cross as soon as the way is open," said Crittenden. Two hours later, deciding that his first order might lead to confusion, the general sent a clarifying order. Wood was instructed to keep with him his artillery and his ammunition train; only the supply and baggage train were to go to Bridgeport.[23]

Wood wanted to alter the orders. At the moment he was ordered to prepare to cross the Tennessee, he was in the process of distributing rations, and he would prefer to cross in the morning. "Let me hear at once," he told Crittenden. Then, a bit later, when Wood discovered that the way was clear and the ferry was available, he did not comply with his own suggested change. The 1st Brigade began crossing that night, and the 3rd crossed the next morning. Having reached the far bank without incident, he threw back at Crittenden a little jab that combined equal parts of complaint and passive aggression and a bit of lecture: "As myself and every officer in my command are here without baggage (the order to send the baggage train by Bridgeport was obeyed strictly and to the letter), I would urge that General Crittenden take steps to have a free road for it and hasten it to us as quickly as possible. We cannot move into the interior without it."[24]

On September 5, having waited for two days for the baggage train to arrive from Bridgeport, Wood was ordered to take his 1st and 3rd Brigades "to the junction of the Nashville & Chattanooga Railroad with the Trenton & Chattanooga Railroad, for the purpose of observing and threatening the enemy posted on the spur of Lookout Mountain."[25]

All of Rosecrans' corps were now across the Tennessee River. While Crittenden continued eastward, General McCook was moving far to the south. He would turn sharply east at Valley Head and proceed through Winston Gap and Dougherty's Gap. General Thomas was headed south as well. He would turn eastward at Trenton and enter the valley of Chickamauga Creek through Stevens' Gap. This plan would put the distance between Rosecrans' left and right flanks at more than thirty miles, a dangerous situation if Rosecrans had been operating against an opponent who wanted to fight. Bragg, however, showed no such inclination. Instead, he appeared to be trying to escape, and Rosecrans' plan would catch him behind, before, and in the middle. On the map, the movements looked like the articulated talons of a great hawk reaching out to seize a scared gray mouse.

As they advanced on September 6, Wood's brigades began to encounter bands of enemy soldiers. When the Federals reached the designated railroad junction at Wauhatchie, they were about seven miles from Chattanooga and about two miles from the enemy's works. Wood did not like the looks of his situation. He believed that enemy observers on the mountain peaks had watched his approach and had calculated his exact strength and that there was a superior force ahead, preparing to attack him. He deployed his two brigades in the wide valley as best he could and sent word to XXI Corps headquarters, "So far from being able to make much of a demonstration.... I may be in danger of attack, and would therefore urge that some part of the force with General Crittenden be put in supporting distance of me."[26]

Crittenden refused the suggestion. He told Wood that if he was attacked he should fall back. Not satisfied with that answer, General Wood, on his own volition and without informing Crittenden, gave up his position and retraced his steps two miles to what he considered more defensible ground. The defiant move was just the latest of a growing list of unpleasant surprises from the 1st Division commander.

On the morning of September 6, General Rosecrans had received another carping wire from General Halleck. In this one, he complained that he was getting no information about what was occurring on Rosecrans' front. Rosecrans was too busy to fight with the general in chief just now, so he sent him a straightforward telegram telling what he knew. But, apparently feeling that he himself needed more intelligence, Rosecrans sent Crittenden a dispatch saying that "it will be safe to send forward a part of General Wood's force to feel the enemy at the point of Lookout Mountain."[27]

Wood refused to send a reconnaissance forward. He may have believed at first that the order came from Crittenden, which would have made Wood more likely to balk than if it came from Rosecrans. In any event, Wood did not send forth a reconnaissance. Hours later, when two staff officers came to prod him to carry out the order, Wood exploded, telling the staff officers that "they did not have 'one-tenth' of [his] experience, nor military education." It was a shocking performance and the two staff officers hurried to Crittenden to report Wood's recalcitrant attitude.[28]

It was now after midnight. Crittenden must have been getting weary of this extended and petty back-and-forth with Wood, but he tried once more. He informed Wood that the order had come from Rosecrans and must be obeyed. He also informed Rosecrans of Wood's refusal to carry out the order. Shortly after 3:00 A.M., when Crittenden received a reply from army headquarters, he forwarded a copy to Wood. It arrived shortly before 8:00 A.M. and said, "The general commanding directs that you order General Wood to make a reconnaissance in force, as was intended by the order sent." In case Wood somehow failed to grasp his duty, Crittenden once more added his own order to make the reconnaissance.[29]

Later that same morning and again that afternoon, Wood tried to make a strong defense of his inaction. In the morning dispatch, to Crittenden's headquarters, he pretended that his previous day's move toward the enemy's position was a "very vigorous forced reconnaissance of the enemy's position" and asserted that he "felt him pretty strongly." As to his abandoning of his position and his failure to carry out the ordered reconnaissance, Wood wrote, "I cannot believe General Rosecrans desires such a blind adherence to the mere letter of his order for the general disposition of his forces as naturally jeopardizes the safety of the most salient portion of it, and certainly cripples the force and vigor and accuracy of its reconnaissances."[30]

Crittenden forwarded this to Rosecrans, with the observation that Wood "is evidently opposed to what he terms a 'blind obedience to orders,' although he is well aware by the language employed to him ... that the order was confirmed by the general commanding the army." Further, "He perhaps may question my judgment of the practicability of making such movements, but when he is informed that it is approved.... I take it to be unmilitary to term such a 'blind obedience to orders,' and I think that he has neglected his duty in delaying a reconnaissance the order for which he acknowledges to have received at 7.45 this a.m."[31]

Wood reluctantly ordered Colonel Harker's 3rd Brigade to go out on the controversial reconnaissance and then sent a second written defense of his actions. Wood's account of the last twenty-four hours, which he sent to army headquarters at 6:00 P.M., was imaginative, if not altogether convincing. He said that Crittenden's order had fixed no hour for the reconnaissance to begin; that there had been no delay in sending out the reconnaissance because he began preparing for it as soon as the order arrived; and, in fact, that he had already thought of sending Colonel Harker's brigade on just such a reconnaissance. "In regard to what General Crittenden terms my 'falling back' on the Trenton road," he said, "I will remark that the term 'falling back' is utterly erroneous, and in no fair or military sense is applicable to, descriptive of, the movement I made. I simply shifted my position to the rear."[32]

Wood took great umbrage at the charge that he had neglected his duty. He wrote:

> Now, I state most unhesitatingly and distinctly that I neglected no duty in carrying out the order to make the reconnaissance, and further that the reconnaissance

was not delayed a moment beyond what was absolutely necessary to insure its success and the safety of the troops making it, as also of the troops held in position to protect the reconnoitering party, in case it should meet with a reverse. I do not think it necessary to make a statement of facts to establish the correctness of this declaration, but will simply add that the brilliant success of the reconnaissance shows it was well arranged and splendidly executed.[33]

The tone of Wood's defense of his actions is clear by the preceding examples. It went on for five and one-half pages in the *Official Records*, and he wrote another one that was over two pages in length on the following day. Crittenden had a little more to say, as well, but only a little compared to the blizzard of words that Wood dumped on army headquarters. In the end, Rosecrans essentially told both men to cut it out and attend to their duties. No official action was taken against either officer. The episode grew out of Wood's disdain for volunteers, his smoldering ire at having been passed over for temporary command of the XXI Corps, and his prideful inability to let go of even an imagined insult. The events of September 6 and 7 were of little military importance and would attract only passing notice except that they reveal so clearly the trend of General Wood's thinking. In a few weeks, Wood's continuing petulance would lead to an action on his part that was of great and dire importance indeed.

Harker's reconnaissance, once it was allowed to go forward, turned out to be "very satisfactory," in Crittenden's words. The men traveled light, carrying only canteens and rifles, and returned to camp before nightfall with just the kind of intelligence that was needed. Craig Julian Mannville said of Harker's effort, "The reconnaissance gave army troop numbers, disposition and future plans of the Confederate forces that proved to be influential in Rosecrans' future plans." Wood further damaged his veracity during this difficult period when he said, "I do not believe that military annals offer an instance of a more daring reconnaissance made by so small a force against an intrenched position, strongly garrisoned, attended with so little loss."[34]

Despite his effusive praise, Wood let both Harker and his superiors down when he submitted his own unaccountability-poor report of the reconnaissance. Rosecrans had to call on him for a more complete version of what Harker had learned, "telling where [he] first met the enemy, and in what force, and how near to Chattanooga he pushed the reconnaissance, as it is important that the general commanding the department should know the position, strength, and probable intentions of the enemy in that direction."[35]

Wood planned to send out a second reconnaissance on the morning of September 9 to investigate "some mysterious indications on the part of the enemy." He wanted to confirm his belief that the Rebels were evacuating Chattanooga. Crittenden tentatively denied permission for the reconnaissance until he could hear from General Rosecrans, but before that a report arrived from

General Wagner (still on detached duty with Colonel Wilder) that stated definitely that the Confederates were moving south. Rosecrans ordered Wood to move his division immediately to Chattanooga and to be "prepared for a vigorous pursuit of the enemy." Wood recalled that "this agreeable order was joyfully obeyed."[36]

It was not Rosecrans' intention, however, that Wood's men would be the first to plant the national colors in the captured city; that honor was given to Colonel S. D. Atkins' 92nd Illinois, a regiment in Wilder's 1st Brigade of Reynolds' 4th Division in General Thomas' corps. To be sure that his wishes were carried out, Rosecrans put the order in writing and handed it to Atkins.

Wood's capacity for pettiness seems to have had no boundaries, even on this morning when the Army of the Cumberland's prospects took such a fortunate turn. Peter Cozzens, in his splendid book *This Terrible Sound: The Battle of Chickamauga*, wrote that, as Atkins hurried his mounted regiment forward from Rosecrans' headquarters, "the long column of infantry dutifully yielded the road to the Illinoisans; all, that is, except the division of Tom Wood. Equally anxious to get into Chattanooga first, Wood had no intention of ceding the way. Atkins triumphantly waved his orders from headquarters in Wood's face. Wood read them, swore at them, but in the end let Atkins pass."[37]

The Kentuckian was not out of tricks, though. Atkins' men rode on, pushed some Rebel skirmishers out of the way, and were about to enter Chattanooga when a courier came riding up and said that General Wood wanted to see him; it was an order. "A suspicious Atkins ordered his men forward before riding to see the general. 'Did you send for me?' Atkins asked. 'Yes, Colonel. I wanted to say to you, that if you have any difficulty I will reinforce you,' Wood stammered lamely." It was a transparent effort to delay Atkins, and an unsuccessful one. Atkins' men had been sent ahead and were already approaching the city limits. An irritated Atkins left Wood and rode hard to catch up with his regiment.[38]

Incredibly, Wood tried once more to cheat Atkins of the honor that Rosecrans had reserved for him. Quoting Cozzens again, "Just after Atkins sent a detail into town with his regimental flag, Wood rode up with General Wagner and his brigade colors. He ordered Atkins to march straight for Rossville and stay clear of Chattanooga. Too late, Atkins replied, pointing to the colors of the 92nd Illinois floating above the Crutchfield house." On the morning of September 9, Atkins had had to maneuver against General Wood more skillfully than he had against the Confederates, but in both cases he had prevailed. It was the banner of the 92nd Illinois that announced that the Federals now controlled Chattanooga.[39]

Chattanooga, incorporated in 1839, was a town of about twenty-five hundred citizens, a raw town more like the frontier than the Old South. The area had been in the United States for less than thirty years; until then it had been the Cherokee Nation. The Trail of Tears in 1838 had ended native occupation and a new town had rapidly grown. It was more important than it was beautiful. Chattanooga was at or near the junction of several major railroads and some smaller spur lines, was a port on the Tennessee River, and controlled the pass into Georgia. The most impressive building in town was the Crutchfield House, the three-story hotel from whose roof the U.S. flag now flew.

As ordered, General Wood took command of the town, and, as if determined to squeeze in as much bad behavior as possible before September 9 turned into September 10, he neglected to communicate with Crittenden. The night hours passed with no intelligence from Wood. Finally, at 11:30, the corps commander ordered Wood to send to headquarters news of what he had learned: "The general commanding directs you to report at once what information (if any) you have received since you were put in command of this post concerning the road or roads taken by the enemy in his retreat; also whether you have received any report from your provost-marshal of prisoners, deserters, etc." He must have information, explained Crittenden, "before he can issue orders for the morrow's pursuit."[40]

Wood's official report of this phase of the Chickamauga Campaign was obviously written with an intention to deceive. Wood was less than truthful about the incident with Colonel Atkins, saying that he had led him pass on the road and, not mentioning that he had afterward summoned Atkins, saying instead that he had overtaken the colonel, whose progress was stopped dead by enemy skirmishers. In Wood's version of events, he threw the 26th Ohio Infantry against the Rebels, drove them away, and it was this intervention that had allowed the 92nd Illinois to proceed. Moreover, Wood did not credit the 92nd Illinois as the first regiment to fly its colors above Chattanooga but rather the 97th Ohio of the 2nd Brigade of his own division. Wood asserted that the banner of the 97th had "been brought across the river by a few men in a small boat early in the morning." Likewise, in the matter of his failure to communicate with Crittenden, Wood was not candid. His report stated that he began interviewing "the most intelligent and reliable citizens" of Chattanooga soon after arriving and that he informed Crittenden of what he had learned: "that a portion of the enemy's troops had retreated by the Cove road, and that the remainder with the baggage and material of war, had retreated by the Rossville and La Fayette road." Buckner, incidentally, had retreated toward Ringgold.[41]

Early on the morning of September 10, Wood was ordered to leave one brigade behind to secure Chattanooga and to lead the other two "in pursuit of the enemy, marching via Rossville, Ringgold, and Dalton.... Generals Palmer and Van Cleve will be in the advance and you will follow them closely." The designated hour of departure was 6:00 A.M.[42]

As was becoming his habit, Wood wanted to amend the order. He replied, "As the order to march was not received till near 6 o'clock, and some preparation in the way of rations has to be made, it will be impossible to march, but it will be done as soon thereafter as practicable. Don't reply. I will be on Palmer's heels very soon." Very soon was four hours later, at 10:00 A.M. The brigade Wood chose to leave behind was Wagner's 2nd.[43]

By all accounts, they were chasing a dispirited Bragg. He had not even tried to defend Chattanooga, had just left it behind and kept on running. His once-proud army had dissolved into a mob and the Federal drive into Georgia was more in the character of a mopping-up operation. The Army of the Cumberland under General William S. Rosecrans had not yet suffered even one serious setback and men and officers alike stepped off from Chattanooga with confidence.

Their expectations of an early end to the war in the West were soon to be shattered amid the farms and forests on the banks of Chickamauga Creek.

CHAPTER 11

Chickamauga: Along La Fayette Road

It soon became apparent to the pursuing Federals that the Confederates were not too distant. Only four hours after leaving Chattanooga, Wood reported to General Crittenden that a strong enemy force was reported to be on his right flank, and a contraband told Wood that Bragg and the bulk of his army were at Lee and Gordon's Mills on Chickamauga Creek. Crittenden ordered a reconnaissance in that direction, and Wood chose Harker for the assignment.

Harker left camp at 5:30 on the morning of September 11, 1863. He and his brigade had gone only a couple of miles when they realized that they were being observed by an enemy scouting party. Harker left his wagon train at "the gap in Missionary Ridge on the Rossville and La Fayette road" and detailed Opdyke's 125th Ohio infantry and four guns to hold the gap open in case the 3rd Brigade was forced to retreat. Beyond the gap, Harker began to run into enemy skirmishers. He wrote in his report, "The skirmishing was light until I had proceeded about three miles from the gap, when it became more spirited, the enemy resisting with dismounted cavalry supporting two pieces of artillery, which opened upon my advance." However, the Rebels and their big guns fell back when pressed, and Harker continued his reconnaissance.[1]

The skirmishing continued through the morning, but Harker pressed forward. A wounded and captured Rebel cavalryman told Harker that he was being opposed by two brigades and confirmed that the enemy was waiting in force at Lee and Gordon's Mills. Harker said, "As this man was in a dying condition, I attached much importance to his information.... My movements were therefore made with great caution, in order to prevent a sudden encounter with a superior force."[2]

In the afternoon, when about two miles from Lee and Gordon's Mills, a citizen told Harker that a butternut brigade had just left that morning. From that Harker inferred that there was no significant force of CSA infantry in his front. He sent a dispatch rider to General Wood with the information he had gathered and told the general that he expected to go two miles farther before returning. The skirmishing continued, but Harker reached the mills about 4:30. He had found that there was nothing before him that he could not handle, and he sent word to Wood that "if we are to pursue the enemy by this route it will be unwise to fall back, as I can hold this position until reinforced."[3]

Wood authorized Harker to remain at the mills and joined him there with the other brigade about ten o'clock that night. Opdyke was ordered to move forward as well and arrived at the camp on Chickamauga Creek in the small hours of September 12. Across the creek and extending for some distance were the campfires of the Confederates.

The men and officers in camp at Lee and Gordon's Mills did not know that the day before General Thomas ran into a world of trouble farther south. Thomas' 2nd Division, as according to Rosecrans' master plan, had emerged from Stevens' Gap into McLemore's Cove. Major General James S. Negley, the 2nd Division's commander, suddenly became aware that Major General Patrick Cleburne at the head of a division of five thousand men and Major General Thomas C. Hindman with a corps of fifteen thousand men were moving toward him from the front and the left, respectively. The cove was full of Rebels and he was isolated; Thomas' other divisions were not up. Negley began to fall back into the gap where his flanks would be protected by the terrain. The great Buddha-like Thomas, now enlightened, sent word back to Rosecrans that the Rebels were not running. They were massing to fight the Federals, who were spread thin over a front of nearly forty miles and in peril of being whipped in detail.

Rosecrans received the message about 4:00 A.M. on the twelfth. At first, he refused to believe it, but by midday he was convinced of the truth of Thomas' report. Rosecrans ordered General Gordon Granger to bring the reserve forward. "We are concentrating the army to support General Thomas and fight a general battle," he said. Granger should leave his wagons to bring up the rear, to travel light, and to move by the most direct route. "If all reports are true, we have not a moment to lose," said Rosecrans. He also instructed Thomas to order McCook, whose corps was the southernmost of the three, to begin moving north. The distance was long and communication was slow and McCook did not get the order until after midnight, meaning the very early morning of September 13.[4]

Wood's division enjoyed a rest on the thirteenth. That night, Crittenden was ordered to move with Palmer's and Van Cleve's divisions and report to "a position on Missionary Ridge, with a view of facilitating the concentration with the other corps of the army." The 1st Division would stay in position and was expected to make as stout a defense as possible at the mills. If heavily attacked, the men were to fall back to Rossville. Wood carefully planned for the defense of his position on Chickamauga Creek. "I took advantage of the creek, a very strong defensible feature in the position," he said, "and barricaded my entire front and flanks strongly. So strengthened, I could have successfully resisted a front attack of a vastly superior force." However, it did not come to that. Wood reported, "With the exception of an occasional firing on my pickets, the enemy left me undisturbed at Gordon's Mills till between 11 a.m. and 12 m. [meridian, or noon] on Friday, the 18th instant." As at Stones River, he had scouts up in the trees to keep an eye on the enemy and he knew that they were moving, but neither he nor any other Federal officer could quite interpret what all the activity on the other side meant.[5]

They began to learn what it meant in the middle of the day on September 18, when Colonel Harker looked to the east, beyond Chickamauga Creek, and saw a dust cloud. A column was moving north. Harker reported, "As the head of the column debouched from the skirt of timber, I perceived something white, which I first mistook for a flag of truce. I therefore sent immediate word to the pickets not to fire. I soon perceived my mistake, and as the column approached, it deployed. When in effective range of my artillery, I directed the battery to open upon the enemy, and he at once gave way and sought refuge in the timber."[6]

After a while, the enemy brought up some artillery of their own and began firing into Colonel George P. Buell's position on Harker's right. Captain Cullen Bradley adjusted his guns to respond to those of the enemy and soon quieted them. Harker continued, "From this time throughout the day, all was comparatively quiet on my front, except an occasional shot from the enemy's sharpshooters."[7]

As they stood ready through the long afternoon, Harker's men could hear artillery fire on the north, in the direction of Rossville. They were hearing the sounds of the main Confederate effort of the day, an attack on Reed's and Alexander's Bridges. If successful, Bragg's Rebels could cross to the Yankee side of Chickamauga Creek.

To seize Reed's Bridge, Bragg sent Brigadier General Bushrod Johnson's division and Nathan Bedford Forrest's cavalry. They clashed there with Colonel Robert H. G. Minty's cavalry brigade. Though Minty was a talented and energetic officer, he could only do so much when the numbers were stacked so heavily against him. The Rebels peeled Minty's defenders away from the bridge and, by late afternoon, were across the Chickamauga. About the time they crossed, Johnson's men were reinforced by the newly arrived division of Major General John Bell Hood, of Longstreet's corps of the Army of Northern Virginia. Longstreet's detached corps had made a torturous journey by rail from Virginia. Hood's division clambered down from the boxcars, lined up, and hurried to the sound of the distant gunfire. They arrived at Reed's Bridge too late to be of any help in the fight, but now they turned south to join Major General William H. T. Walker's corps in the attack on Alexander's Bridge.

Meanwhile, Colonel Minty went looking for General Wood to report what had happened. Wood was just writing a report to General Crittenden when Minty appeared. Later, he recounted the conversation he had with General Wood:

> I found General Wood writing, Colonel Harker sitting near him, and a mounted orderly waiting. As I rode forward, Colonel Harker sprang to his feet and exclaimed: "General, here is Colonel Minty now." General Wood looked up and said: "I was just reporting that you had been cut off and your brigade captured." I replied, "My brigade is safe, General, and is now covering our position." He finished writing, told me that he had added a postscript stating that "Colonel Minty has just come in with his brigade," handed his dispatch to the orderly, with instruction to deliver to General Crittenden ... then, turning to me, the following colloquy took place:
> "Well, Minty, what have you been doing all day?"
> "Fighting pretty sharply, General."
> "What have you been fighting?"
> "Infantry and artillery."
> "Where are they?"
> "Close to your position."
> "What! On this side of the creek?"
> "Yes, sir, on this side of the creek."
> "Well, come along, and we'll drive them across to their own side."[8]

Alexander's Bridge was being defended by Colonel John T Wilder and his "Lightning Brigade," who were well armed with seven-shot Spencer carbines. They were doing well against the attackers in their front, Major General William H. T. Walker's corps. They were unprepared, though, for the threat that suddenly appeared on their left: Johnson, Forrest, and Hood. Outflanked and vastly outnumbered, they had to withdraw. They tore up as much of the bridge as they could and set it on fire, but Walker's corps simply waded the creek. By sundown, the Confederates had a powerful force lodged on the same side of Chickamauga Creek as the Yankees.

Wood made no reference in his report to being at the fight at Alexander's Bridge. It was only after Wilder began to fall back that Wood and Minty found him, retreating but doing what he could against the hordes of graybacks following him. Minty recalled that Wood rode up and asked Wilder, "Well, Wilder, where are they?"

"Ride forward a dozen paces, General, and you will see them."

Wood and Wilder spurred their horses only a few steps forward when a Rebel yell and a blast of musket fire split the air. Wood exclaimed, "By God, they *are* here."[9]

Wood's surprise, if Minty's account is accurate, is at odds with the general's report. Wood wrote that he perceived as early as midday that the attack on Harker and Buell was "only a mask to his real design, that of passing a heavy force across the creek lower down [the Chickamauga flows north], with a view of turning our left and cutting off our communication with Chattanooga."[10]

The Yankees had had a bad day. The Rebels had punished them and had forced a lodgment on the west side of Chickamauga Creek. The game was not lost, but adjustments in the Federal deployment needed to be made, and quickly. As soon as he could, Wood informed Rosecrans of the day's actions on his front and on the left. Rosecrans had spent the last four days drawing his army together to meet Bragg's threat. Now he had a clearer idea of exactly what he needed to do. He sent General George H. Thomas' corps on a night march behind Crittenden to take position at the Kelly farm on the far left flank. Faced with an entire corps, Bragg would have a tougher time of it in the morning when he resumed his offensive on the left. Crittenden remained at Lee and Gordon's Mills (now in the Federal center), and McCook, whose corps had come the farthest and arrived the latest, settled in on the right flank. Rosecrans moved his headquarters from the Gordon mansion to the simple log cabin of the widow Eliza Glenn, where he would be closer to the action he expected to begin the next day.

At mid-morning on the nineteenth, General Crittenden and his officers heard an explosion of musketry and cannon fire from the north. As the intensity of the firing increased, they knew that it was not a mere skirmish. General Thomas' men had engaged with those of Forrest and Breckinridge. Through the morning hours, more and more brigades were sucked into the storm. Shortly before noon, with General Rosecrans' consent, Crittenden sent Major General John M. Palmer's 2nd Division to support Thomas. Before Palmer could engage the enemy, Crittenden received a request from Thomas for yet another division. Crittenden sent Brigadier General Horatio Van Cleve's 3rd Division and, remembering his one remaining division, sent a note to General Wood that with Palmer and Van Cleve gone, "he must look out for his left."[11]

Two tense hours passed. At 3:30 P.M., Wood received an order to move his division north and take position on General Van Cleve's right. Wood was careful to inform Rosecrans that there was an enemy force in his front and that someone should come fill the gap that would exist when he left Lee and Gordon's Mills. "No delay however, had occurred on this account in the movement of my command from Gordon's Mills," said Wood. "My command was put in rapid motion for the scene of the great conflict." General Alexander McDowell McCook sent up Philip Sheridan's division to plug the gap, and Wood moved off toward the farm of the unfortunate Viniard family.[12]

Arriving at a cornfield near the scene of the scene of the fighting, Wood was upset to find that there was no staff officer to direct him to his assigned position on the right of Van Cleve, and he could not see enough of the fighting to know where to go. He explained, "It should be borne in mind that many of the troops were engaged in the woods and that it was next to impossible to gain information by sight of the management of the troops already assigned." Colonel Charles G. Harker called it a "perfect jungle."[13]

General Jefferson C. Davis (the same Davis who shot down General William "Bull" Nelson in the lobby of the Galt House) came over to Wood a moment after the 1st Division arrived. Davis commanded the 1st Division in Alexander McDowell McCook's corps, which was mostly on the right (southern) flank of the Federal line. But brigades, divisions, and corps were becoming intermingled as units were hurled into the developing fight, and Davis was ordered to move north to the Viniard farm. Davis had joined the fight in the woods a half mile from Van Cleve's division on the left, a half-mile gap that isolated his two brigades and allowed the Rebels to swirl around his flanks. Davis had been fighting since about 1:30 P.M. and the news he now had for Wood was not good: both of his brigades were in trouble. The crowd of men retreating through the trees was proof of how hard pressed the Federals were. General Hans C. Heg, commanding the 3rd Brigade of Davis' division, was in a desperate fight. Wood told Colonel Harker to deploy his men in battle line facing east across La Fayette Road and to advance into the woods to Heg's support. The view was so limited by the dense forest of pines and redbuds that as they got into line and prepared to move forward, Harker "cautioned the regimental commanders that our own troops were in our immediate front, and not to allow our men to fire until they had passed our lines."[14]

Scarcely had the order to deploy been uttered when Wood became aware that Heg's entire brigade was giving way. Wood gave Harker a new order to hold his left in place on the road but to advance his right so that his line stood at an angle to the road. This would put Harker's brigade in position to fire into the Rebel flank when it came into view.

The adjustment in Harker's line was carried out, but then it became known that more Rebels had swung around Heg's left and were on the road farther north. Once again, new orders were given: Harker was to refuse his left, making it perpendicular to the road, while the right remained at an oblique. The line was shaped like an obtuse "v" with the point aimed at the enemy. All of this sounds simpler to do than it was. This was 1,391 men adjusting position and under hostile fire the whole time. As Colonel H. C. Dunlap of the 3rd Kentucky Infantry wrote, "Found the foe on every front; fought at every point of the compass; no confusion; changed front ... in good order under fire."[15]

Harker took two regiments and advanced north to meet the Rebels, leaving behind two regiments and Captain Cullen Bradley's artillery facing east to hold that stretch of La Fayette Road. For the rest of the afternoon, Harker would be fighting in General Jefferson C. Davis' sector. "In this position," said Harker, "there was some of the most brilliant fighting that it has ever been my fortune to witness. Though its grandeur surpasses description, its severity may be imagined when I state that every mounted officer in the vicinity of this line except the adjutant of the Third Kentucky was dismounted by the enemy's musketry ... while in the ranks a great many of the enlisted men fell while bravely fighting." Harker's brigade captured 204 prisoners.[16]

Wood did not see this fight. As the general later reported, "I followed his advance nearly half a mile, and finding he was doing well, as well as having perfect confidence in his ability to handle his brigade, I remarked to him that I would leave him and go to look after my other brigade, Colonel Buell commanding.... Leaving Harker's brigade, I returned to where I had ordered Colonel Buell to halt and form his brigade." Wood was a little nervous about Buell, who had been in command of the 1st Brigade just four months.[17]

As Harker had been positioned to help Heg, Buell had been positioned to support Brigadier General William P. Carlin's 2nd Brigade of Davis' division. Like Heg, Carlin was being forced back, his panicky men pushing through Buell's men as they tried to deploy in two lines along La Fayette Road. Buell remembered, "The formation of my command was not yet complete, when everything on my immediate front and left gave way, and hundreds of our own men ran through my ranks crying, 'Fall back! Fall back!' as they themselves were in shameful rout toward the rear." These Rebels were from John Bell Hood's division (presently led by Brigadier General Evander Law), Longstreet's corps, Army of Northern Virginia. They were seasoned fighters, accustomed to victory, and they were close on Carlin's heels. Buell ordered his front line to lie down and let Carlin's men and fieldpieces pass over them. He had little faith that the front line would be able to hold, so he ordered his second line to prepare to make a bayonet charge.[18]

As Carlin's men swept up Buell's front line, those in the second line commenced to charge. They did not get far before they were caught in the rout and were carried back two hundred yards across open ground to a fence where they began to rally. In that small span of two hundred yards, the killing was incredible. The 26th Ohio and the 100th Illinois in the front line lost about half their strength (but not before saving most of the guns of Captain George Estep's battery), and the 58th Indiana and 13th Michigan "fell by scores."[19]

At the fence, Buell's men joined a regiment of Colonel John T. Wilder's brigade and also some of Carlin's survivors. Led by General Wood personally, they counter-attacked. From their position farther up the road, Captain Bradley's 6th Ohio Battery, which had been left behind when Harker advanced into the woods, turned and added their firepower to the counter-attack. Thus reinforced, Buell's brigade shoved Rebels back, took possession of the ground they had just lost moments before, and also reclaimed three of the fieldpieces that had been left behind. It came at some cost. That open two hundred yards became a killing ground for a second time. During the charge, one of Wood's staff, Captain John E. George of the 15th Indiana, was killed while by the general's side. Wood came close to death himself. His mount was shot from beneath him during the charge, and he took the horse of an orderly in order to continue with the men.

The enemy was not done. Buell said, "Again the enemy came forward like an avalanche and forced my men back a short distance." One of General Philip Sheridan's brigades had arrived on the scene just in time to make an ineffectual charge before joining in the retreat, but they did help to draw off Estep's battery, which had lost so many horses in the charge that the pieces had to be rolled to safety by hand. General Wood and General Crittenden were there to help encourage the men and, as Buell remembered, "again my men rallied, and retook the same position they had formerly held. The enemy came forward a third time, but were effectually repulsed., and the sun went down with my command holding the field a short distance in advance of its original position."[20]

The sinking sun found the Federal line on the Viniard farm (from north to south): Harker (who had returned from his own fight to rejoin his division) on the west side of La Fayette Road and supported by Bradley's artillery, Buell's brigade in the center and supported by Estep's artillery, then Phil Sheridan's brigades. They were "in a strong position to resist a night attack," said Wood.[21]

A night attack never came, only some exchange of fire between the pickets. The lack of danger did not mean a lack of misery, however. The men especially suffered from a lack of water. Attacking and counter-attacking in the autumn sun, all the while tearing open the paper tops of black-powder cartridges with their teeth, had left them parched in a way that bringing in the hay or clerking in a store back home would never have done. Wood said, "The men were very thirsty, but the distance to water was so great that but few could hope to get permission to go for it. During the night Colonel Harrison brought to us some 400 canteens of good water. They were distributed among my men as equitably as possible, and proved the cooling drop to the thirsty soldiers." The colonel who performed this "Samaritan deed" for Wood's division was Colonel Thomas J. Harrison of the 39th Indiana Mounted Infantry.[22]

The day's fighting had been neither well directed nor well organized, and it was unimpressive by the standards of the military textbooks. General Daniel H. Hill said in *Battles and Leaders of the Civil War*, "It was dulsatory fighting from right to left, without concert, and inopportune at times. It was the sparring of the amateur boxer, and not the crushing blows of the trained pugilist."[23]

In their first real fight since Stones River, the men of the 1st Division, XXI Corps, had done well. And their generals had done well. At a critical moment, General Crittenden had taken the initiative and, as Larry J. Daniel writes, "started both Palmer's and Van Cleve's divisions to the battlefield on his own responsibility and before Rosecrans gave his approval.... Crittenden received prior approval before starting Wood's division, but the idea came from him, not Rosecrans." Peter Cozzens agrees with Daniel and says in *This Terrible Sound*, "Crittenden probably rode up and down the La Fayette road more than any other general that afternoon. He was turning in his finest performance as a corps commander, displaying an uncanny knack for knowing exactly where his units were needed and following through to ensure they got there."[24]

Wood, too, had turned in a good, if not brilliant, performance. He was with Harker's brigade during the start of their fight, showed faith in his subordinate to exercise command independently at the proper moment, and returned to help direct the fight of his less experienced subordinate Colonel Buell. Wood was in the fight, sometimes in front, at other times directing the action from the rear, but always there. As Buell said in his report, "The whole of this afternoon's fighting was done under the eye of General Wood, who was ever present."[25]

Of the men with the stars on their shoulders, the weakest performance was that of Major General Rosecrans. While the battle raged on the Viniard farm, he sat in the Widow Glenn's farmhouse, only a short distance away, passive and unengaged. He relied on the sounds of battle and Mrs. Glenn's knowledge of the countryside to tell him where the troops were most heavily engaged. When Crittenden developed a plan to use Wood's division to hit the Rebel flank, Rosecrans lacked the imagination or the nerve to approve it. On the night of the nineteenth, General John Palmer told Assistant Secretary of War Charles A. Dana (who was really a spy for Stanton and who had come to Rosecrans' camp a few days earlier to snoop and gather damaging information), "I have no hesitation in saying to you, Mr. Dana, that this battle has been lost because we had no supreme head to the army on the field to direct it." Palmer was premature in asserting that the battle had been lost, but his point was well taken. Rosecrans was content to follow the battle from a relatively safe distance. It was as if the pressure paralyzed him. It was strange behavior for a man who was renowned for his restless energy.[26]

By normal standards, the September 19 fighting at Chickamauga would have been considered a major battle — if the curious Battle of Chickamauga could have been measured by normal standards. September 19 was only a prelude. There was a bigger battle coming the next day. In fact, it would be the day of days for the Army of the Cumberland.

CHAPTER 12

Chickamauga: The Day of Days

Late on the night of September 19, 1863, General Rosecrans held a council of war at his headquarters. It was not a jubilant meeting. The men were too tired, the day's contest had been too hard, and the outcome was still uncertain. The Rebels had been repulsed on the left, but they had not gone away. General George H. Thomas, who had endured everything the Confederates had thrown at him through a long day, kept dozing off and woke up only when he was asked a question to mutter the same advice: "I would strengthen the left."[1]

If Wood attended Rosecrans' late council, he made no mention of it. What he did say was that he received orders before daylight to join Crittenden's corps on the slope where Missionary Ridge angled down to the creek valley. The XXI Corps would be the reserve. Colonel Sidney M. Barnes' brigade (Van Cleve's division) was assigned to Wood, giving him a full-strength division once more. Wood's men roused themselves for the mile-and-a-half march to their assigned position. Once they arrived they were allowed to brew coffee, and they also drew three days' rations, so having their sleep disturbed was not a completely unrewarded aggravation. Barnes held the left of Wood's line, Harker was in the center, and Buell was on the right. Harker said, "Spirits buoyant with the success of the previous day, the command was again ready to go forth, and as we thought, finish the well begun work."[2]

If he could have scanned the whole Federal line, Wood would have seen that it was shaped like a hastily scrawled question mark. Down at Crawfish Springs, protecting the hospital tents, was the dot at the bottom of the question mark, Brigadier General Robert B. Mitchell's cavalry. After an interval, the shank of the question mark began with Major General Philip Sheridan's division of McCook's corps, with his right at the Widow Glenn's, behind the Viniard farm. Next were Major General James S. Negley's division, Brigadier General John M. Brannan's division, and Major General Joseph J. Reynolds' division, all of Thomas' corps. Reynolds' division began the curve at the top of the question mark. Major General John M. Palmer's division of Crittenden's Corps, Brigadier General Richard W. Johnson of McCook's corps, and Brigadier General Absalom Baird of Thomas' corps completed the question mark. The curve at the top of the mark curled around the Kelly Field at the base of Snodgrass Hill. Messing up the neat question mark like carelessly dropped blots of ink were Brigadier General Jefferson C. Davis's division, behind Sheridan, and Wood's and Van Cleve's divisions, held in reserve behind Negley and Brannan.

General Thomas had his men on the left working all night strengthening their breastworks, but he realized that his line did not extend to the critical crossroads of La Fayette Road and Reed's Bridge Road. He asked Rosecrans for another division to anchor his extreme left flank and was promised Negley. Yet when Generals Nathan Bedford Forrest and John C. Breckinridge began moving on Thomas' front on the morning of the twentieth (with Major General Patrick Cleburne's division standing ready to join), Negley still had not arrived. It seems that Rosecrans, still in his strange, inefficient mood from the day before, had neglected to follow through on his promise to Thomas. Orders were quickly issued for Negley to march two miles to the north to join Thomas and for McCook to bring some men north to take Negley's place in the battle line. About thirty minutes later, when the commanding general came to inspect that part of the line, he discovered that Negley had moved to follow orders—had moved too quickly, in fact. McCook had not come up to take his place, but he had moved anyway, creating a wide hole in the line. Rosecrans suspended the order for the time being, although he did detach Negley's reserve brigade to go ahead and join Thomas. He sent orders to Crittenden to send Wood's division forward to relieve Negley and then rode off to confront McCook.

When Rosecrans returned from dressing down McCook, he found that Wood had moved only a short distance from his position in the reserve. Getting him to move at all had been a chore. A number of staff officers had been to see him, including Captain J. P. Willard, an officer on Thomas' staff. When Willard inquired about why he had remained in place, Wood explained, "I am ordered to post my troops on this ridge." No, said the captain, "General Rosecrans promised to send one of the divisions of General Crittenden's corps to relieve General Negley that he might go to the relief of General Thomas' left." Wood refused to move. Other staff officers came to convey the order: move to relieve Negley. Finally, Wood did advance a short distance, to a spot overlooking Negley. And there he stalled once again.[3]

Rosecrans discovered Wood sitting there with his staff on the ridge, and the commanding general erupted. Rosecrans said to Wood, "What is the meaning of this, sir? You have disobeyed my specific orders. By your damnable negligence you are endangering the safety of this entire army, and, by God, I will not tolerate it. Move your division at once, as I have instructed, or the consequences will not be pleasant for yourself."[4]

The fuming Wood ordered his division forward. They immediately came under fire from the enemy's skirmishers, but they pushed on, and about ten o'clock, as Negley pulled out of line, they took position on the right of Brannan: the brigades of Barnes, Harker, and Buell, all facing east. For the hour that they stood in line, they remained under fire from both small arms and artillery. When the Confederate fieldpieces opened up about ten fifteen, Harker ordered Captain Cullen Bradley's battery to respond. Bradley later reported, "I then ordered up the center section, and it opened on the woods in which the enemy were totally concealed from view. I fired some 32 rounds here, and I have every reason to believe that they did good execution, as they were fired very low with 2½-second fuses. Both case and shell were used."[5]

About fifteen minutes after the artillery duel commenced, General Jefferson C. Davis of McCook's corps showed up and moved into a small gap on the right of Wood's division. Simultaneously, General Thomas decided that he needed more help. He wanted General John Brannan's division to come take position on his left flank. Captain Sanford Cobb Kellogg of Thomas' staff was sent to General Rosecrans to ask that Brannan be sent, and Rosecrans agreed. Kellogg went forward to the battle line to give Brannan the order. When he read the order, Brannan was unsure; there was a lot of enemy activity on his front. He conferred with General Joseph J. Reynolds, who was commanding the division on his left, and Reynolds advised that Brannan should obey the order. While Brannan prepared to do so, Reynolds asked Kellogg to make sure that Rosecrans be reminded that his right flank would be in the air, once Brannan pulled out of line. Kellogg hurried off to Rosecrans' headquarters with the news that Brannan was moving and that Reynolds needed support on his right. Rosecrans understood and he dictated an order to his aide Major Frank Bond for immediate delivery to Crittenden, who sent Lieutenant Colonel Lyne Starling to deliver the order to Wood. The order that became the object of much dispute in the weeks, months and years to come was brief but confusing. It said, "The general commanding directs that you close upon Reynolds as fast as possible and support him."[6]

Rosecrans' tendency to become slightly incoherent in his speech in moments of excitement has been mentioned earlier. This was one such moment, and Rosecrans had not chosen his words carefully. The words "close upon" and "support" meant two different things. But there was also a verbal clarification, which was given to the courier to pass on to Wood, that the intent of the order was "to enable Wood to fill the gap left by the withdrawal of Brannan." And the fact of the matter was that Brannan, despite his earlier decision to do so, had not moved out of line. There was no gap for Wood to move into on Reynolds' right; it was still filled with Brannan's division and Wood knew it.

He pointed out the fact to Lieutenant Colonel Starling, who replied, "Then there is no order, for that was the object of it." Then, to Starling's surprise, Wood had a change of heart; he said that the order must be obeyed. Starling saw that the situation did not support Wood's sudden determination to obey the order. The lieutenant colonel asked that Wood wait for ten minutes so that Rosecrans could be informed of the true nature of things at the front, but Wood refused to wait and said that he "was glad the order was in writing, as it was a good thing to have for future reference." He is reported by some to have waved the order at his staff while he crowed, "Gentlemen, I hold the fatal order of the day in my hand and would not part with it for five thousand dollars." Whether or not that final bit of flourish really occurred, it is true that he carefully tucked the order in his pocket.[7]

Rosecrans was nearby. Wood could easily have sought clarification, if he had wanted it. It is significant that Wood did not send to know what it was exactly that Rosecrans intended. Instead, he perceived in the intrinsic confusion of the order an opportunity to humiliate one of the men with whom he had been feuding ever since the end of the Tullahoma Campaign. As historian Mark W. Johnson says, "Wood could not have been more satisfied.... Rosecrans had treated him in a very shabby manner, and Wood knew that the ambiguous order from Army headquarters meant the obnoxious Rosecrans would take the blame for the consequences of Wood's actions."[8]

Wood later recalled that he asked General McCook, who was nearby, to move up a division to plug the hole that his withdrawal would create and McCook agreed. McCook later denied that this exchange ever took place. "There was not only no time to fill the space, but I had no troops to fill it with, unless a small brigade could cover a division's interval," he said. In fact, he was surprised when Wood began pulling out of line.[9]

Wood had gone off ahead of his troops to find Reynolds' exact location. To obey the order, Wood would have to pull his division out of line, march behind Brannan, and take position behind Reynolds. While scouting, Wood ran into General Thomas, who told him that Reynolds did not need any support, but General Absalom Baird did, over on the left. Thomas told Wood to move to that flank and agreed to take responsibility for changing Rosecrans' order. With this understanding, Wood got his division in motion, beginning with Colonel Barnes, who got away with no trouble, then Harker, and finally Buell.

Buell had his doubts about the wisdom of this. Before it was quite time to move, he spoke to General Davis, whose division was on his right. Davis remembered, "Colonel Buell rode up to me and informed me he had orders to move to the left; that the other brigades of his division were leaving, and informed me of his convictions of the close proximity of the enemy to our front, and of his fears of his being attacked as he withdrew his troops. I immediately ordered up my reserve brigade, and as this brigade was getting into position ... the attack commenced on my right."[10]

For several minutes before the 1st Division began pulling out of line the Rebel attack had been massing and, as bad luck would have it, was aimed at the exact spot which Wood was vacating. Even worse, the attackers stepped off just as the hole was created in the Federal line. Eleven thousand men of Lieutenant General James Longstreet's wing, i.e., the divisions of Generals Bushrod Johnson, Joseph B. Kershaw, and McIver Law, supported by Alexander P. Stewart (on the right) and Thomas C. Hindman (on the left), came rushing across Brotherton Field and slammed into Buell's flank. Remembering that fatal moment, the colonel later said, "We had scarcely moved one brigade front when the shock came like an avalanche on my right flank. The attack seemed to have been simultaneous throughout the enemy's lines, for the entire right and part of the center gave way before the overpowering numbers of the foe. My own little brigade seemed as if it were swept from the field." It was not only Buell's brigade that was carried away in the gray tide but the whole right wing of the Army of the Cumberland, McCook's corps and much of Crittenden's. In an instant, thousands of panic-stricken men were running like mad for the rear. When some officers turned and tried to rally them, they kept running and shouted over their shoulders, "We'll see you on the other side of the Ohio."[11]

The men who were in the best position to stem the butternut attack that was pouring through Wood's gap were the Union artillerymen, still posted in the rear of the infantry's front line. Some fled, but Captain George Estep of Buell's brigade tried to make a stand. Remembered Buell, "Captain Estep with all speed moved his battery about 400 yards to the rear, on the crest of a hill, where he opened on the enemy with great effect." Buell gathered the 58th Indiana and "some stragglers of other regiments" made a defensive line in front of the battery, but it was futile. The enemy gained Buell's right flank and "shot down 35 horses of my battery, thus capturing the same.... If my battery commander had done as I saw several other batteries doing, he would have saved his battery, but as long as there was any chance to fight, he fought, and then it was too late to start for Rossville."[12]

Captain Cullen Bradley was somewhat luckier with his battery, which was attached to Harker's brigade. Bradley's artillerymen had limbered their pieces and were moving with, and in the rear of, the infantry brigade when the Rebel attack crashed down upon them. Bradley said, "We had not moved more than a half or three-quarters of a mile when there occurred a perfect stampede — guns, caissons, fragments of regiments all came out in one disordered mass, and the enemy closely pursuing. I was entirely cut off from my brigade." Though he was in the midst of the confused mass of running men, animals, and wheeled vehicles, Bradley lost only two caissons and one wagon. With the rest, he made his way to General Negley, who ordered him to place his guns on the crest of a hill. This Bradley did, and there he stayed until the infantry had all passed; then he moved back to La Fayette Road.[13]

General Crittenden saw the artillery as the last hope of the Federals on this ill-fated noon. At the time of the Rebel penetration, he said, "We will go to the batteries and we will yet drive these fellows back and hold them in check." Alongside Major John Mendenhall, one of the heroes of the last day at Stones River, General Crittenden stayed and fought the Rebels. He had fewer than seventy infantrymen to support the big guns. Thirty minutes into the fight, Lieutenant Henry Cushing, who was in command of the U.S. artillery battery (as opposed to the volunteer batteries), decided that he had had enough horses killed; it was time to get out. Crittenden would not have it. "You are not to retire at all, but hold your position!" he shouted. Crittenden's willpower proved to be all that was holding the artillerymen in at their posts. When the general rode a short distance toward another ridge to try to gather more infantry support for his batteries, the gunners immediately limbered and started moving away. They left behind seventeen fieldpieces.[14]

Crittenden said in his report:

> On reaching the crest of the next hill I found only a small number of men, less than 100, who had been rallied by a captain of the Eighteenth Regulars, as he told me, and whom he kept in line with great difficulty. I remained there for some time, probably a half hour, expecting to meet some officers from the commands which had been posted to my right. After this lapse of time Major Mendenhall informed me that the enemy had turned our own guns upon us from the hill we had just left. I then determined to go immediately to Rossville or Chattanooga, if it was practicable. I could hear nothing of General Rosecrans, nor of Generals McCook, Sheridan, or Davis, and I greatly feared that all had fallen into the hands of the enemy. I should have ridden rapidly to Rossville or Chattanooga to apprise whoever was in command of the actual state of things on our right, but that I feared to add a panic to the great confusion.[15]

The reason that Critttenden could not find any of the generals he named was because they had fled the field, outrunning the slowest of their soldiers and even some of the faster ones. Most of the generals on the right or center of the Federal line at Chickamauga that day had to scramble to justify his actions, but the case of Crittenden was an exception. The court of inquiry that later investigated the debacle at Chickamauga said of Crittenden, "For the disaster which ensued, he is in no way responsible.... It is amply proven that General Crittenden did everything he could, by example and personal exertion, to rally and hold his troops, and to prevent the evils resulting from such a condition of affairs, but without avail." Furthermore, the court did not hold Crittenden censurable for eventually leaving the field when Rosecrans and others were already long gone. Crittenden was, in fact, the last general officer from that sector to leave the field. For a man who, a year ago, had been considered by many to be a mere political appointment, Crittenden had shown steady growth as a commander and had done well — better than many of the West Pointers — on September 20 at Chickamauga.[16]

And what of Wood? When he discovered that the fields behind him were full of those Rebels who had taken advantage of the gap in the line, he understood at once that the Army of the Cumberland was in danger of being cut off from Chattanooga. He was trying to make it to the left where Thomas' flank was still intact, but the Rebels were closing on him fast and firing as they came. There was nothing to do but turn and fight. Barnes' brigade, having gotten away first, was far ahead of the others in the 1st Division (and would finally take position alongside General Absalom Baird on the extreme left flank). Wood had only one brigade and a fraction of another with which to do battle. With Harker's brigade and what was left of Buell's, he formed a battle line, facing south across Dyer Field. It was a dicey situation. Wood was badly outnumbered and he had no artillery, but he acted with audacity. He ordered Colonel Emerson Opdyke and the 125th Ohio to charge. "There was a momentary hesitation in the regiment to go forward," Wood said. "Its gallant colonel immediately rode in front of the center of his regiment, and taking off his hat, called on his men to advance. His regiment gallantly responded by a prompt advance, as men ever will under the inspiration of such leadership." Their object was a split-rail fence from which they could form a serious obstacle to the Confederate advance. The 125th beat the Rebels to the prize and were soon joined by the 64th Ohio on their left and three other regiments on their right: the 65th Ohio, the 3rd Kentucky, and the one remaining regiment of Buell's brigade, the 58th Indiana. The fence having been won, the 125th and the 64th Ohio plunged forward again, this time to a grove of trees. Here they would make their own separate fight.[17]

The men on the far side of the field were only about three hundred yards away and in plain view, but the Federals were seized with indecision. As Wood explained, "His blurred and greasy and dusty uniform so resembled our own when travel-stained, coupled with the fact that it was expected a part of McCook's command would come from that direction (the terrible disaster to his force on the right not then being known to us), that for a few minutes the impression prevailed and the cry ran along the line that the troops in front of us were our own." Wood himself was not sure, and he ordered his men to stop firing. Colonel Harker decided to go forward and investigate. He left his brigade under Wood's direction and approached the men across the field. He got close enough to see their colors, and then they fired on him. He quickly returned to his brigade, the Rebels not far behind. As they drew closer, they opened fire on the Yankee battle line. Wood's men could not hold the enemy back. It looked as if the Rebels were going to gain the right flank. Wood ordered his men to fall back. When they left, the two regiments in the grove of trees had no choice but to fall back as well. Wood's hour-long fight at the fence had given General Brannan time to form a defensive line on a steep-sided ridge farther behind. It was called Horseshoe Ridge and it was the high ground Wood always looked for, a good position to defend. "The abruptness of the declivity on either side of it almost gives to this ridge the quality of a natural parapet.... Here I determined to make an obstinate and stubborn stand," Wood said. As he rode toward Horseshoe Ridge, his horse was shot from beneath him. It was the second horse Wood had lost in two days.[18]

Climbing the ridge to their new position, Wood's division split. Buell and what was left of his brigade moved to the right of General Brannan's division, while Harker's brigade, Wood accompanying, took up position on Brannan's left. Soon after arriving, Harker's brigade was reinforced by a fragment of the 44th Indiana.

Brannan's line on Horseshoe Ridge made a jagged east–west line and faced south. Beyond Brannan's left flank, in a curving line that bent from north to south and faced the eastward points of the compass, were a conglomeration of General George H. Thomas' corps, plus those regiments and brigades that had been shaken loose from their proper commands when the right dissolved. Their line was all that remained of our imaginary question mark; now it resembled a backwards "C." The men there were going to make their stand with Old Pap Thomas on Snodgrass Hill. If Brannan's line failed, the Rebels could attack Thomas from the rear as well as the front. Thomas' headquarters was near the north end of this curving line, not far from Harker's position. Thomas rode over to Harker as the brigade commander deployed his men. He said, "This hill must be held and I trust you to do it." Harker was determined to do just that. "We will hold it or die here," Harker said.[19]

In his report of the battle, Harker explained how the ridge was defended. He said that his men were below and behind the crest of the hill and, when the Rebels advanced, his front line would move to the ridgetop and fire by volleys, then retire as the second line "would move forward and execute the same movement. Thus a continuous volley fire was kept up for some length of time. This system was resumed whenever the rebels made their appearance in force, and repulsed them on every occasion. It had never before been my fortune to witness so grand an example of effective musket firing."[20]

After this first charge failed, Rebel sharpshooters began to pepper the Yankees with annoying potshots. The officers were especially vulnerable. Only Colonel Opdyke remained on horseback; he wanted to be able to look over the heads of his men and see what the Rebels beyond were up to. What they were up to was preparation for more fighting and more fighting after that. All through the afternoon, Wood's division lashed back one Rebel attempt after another.

They made an effective defense but used up a great deal of ammunition.

Wood's ammunition train had been lost in the rout. As early as 1:30, Buell's little command had emptied their cartridge boxes and had taken all they could from the dead and wounded. They fired their last volley into the Rebels when they were only ninety feet away. Luckily, the Rebels were stopped. Buell's men fell back a short distance but remained on the field with bayonets fixed on their empty rifles, ready to do what they could if the Rebels made another breakthrough. Anything could happen, this day.

Harker's men, too, were burning cartridges at a furious rate and the danger of running out of ammunition was growing by the minute. About noon, if the hard-pressed men chanced to look to the north, they noticed a column of dust approaching. Certainly, the knot of officers around General Thomas noticed the ominous dust cloud. Could it be possible that the Rebels had flanked them and that they were now completely enveloped? If it was, they were doomed. Rebel cavalry, suggested one of the officers. Wood disagreed: "Don't you see the dust rising above them ascends in thick misty clouds, not in spiral columns, as it would if the force was cavalry?" If it was not cavalry, what was it? The tension rose. Then, to the tremendous relief of all, they saw the blue-uniformed head of a long column, General James B. Steedman's division of General Gordon Granger's Reserve Corps, coming down the road from Rossville. When Granger rode up, General Thomas greeted him with his usual reserve: "I am very glad to see you, General." Granger had brought the two brigades of Steedman's division, plus a battery of artillery, and ninety-five thousand extra cartridges.[21]

Granger had marched from Rossville to Thomas' relief without orders to do so. Since 10:30 A.M. Granger had been hearing the sounds of battle, growing more agitated as the minutes crept by. After a while, his inactivity became intolerable. "I am going to Thomas, orders or no orders," he said. General James B. Steedman's division started south. En route, they encountered Nathan Bedford Forrest's cavalry. Steedman prepared to bite at the tempting bait, but Granger refused to be distracted from his goal of reaching Thomas. He reeled in Steedman, saying, "They are nothing but rag-a-muffin cavalry," and the blue column marched on. The closer they got, the more destruction they saw: dead bodies (and artillery-blasted parts of bodies), burning farms, and even a field hospital that had been struck by artillery fire.[22]

As Granger and Steedman approached Snodgrass Hill, the enemy was forming for another attack on Brannan's position. His approach caused them to hesitate for a precious moment. Thomas indicated the enemy pressure building on Brannan's right and ordered Granger to send Steedman's division in that direction.

As Steedman's division moved to their new position on Brannan's right, the Rebels launched their attack. Granger's chief of staff, Lieutenant Colonel Joseph S. Fullerton, described what happened:

With ringing cheers they advanced in two lines by double-quick — over open fields, through weeds waist-high, through a little valley, then up the ridge. The enemy opened on them first with artillery, then with a murderous musketry-fire. When well up the ridge the men, almost exhausted, were halted for breath. They lay on the ground two or three minutes, then came the command, "Forward!" Brave, bluff old Steedman, with a regimental flag in his hand, led the way. On went the lines, firing as they ran and bravely receiving a deadly and continuous fire from the enemy on the summit. The Confederates began to break and in another minute were flying down the southern slope of the ridge. In twenty minutes from the beginning of the charge the ridge had been carried.... Of Steedman's two brigades, numbering 3,500, twenty per cent had been killed and wounded in that twenty minutes; and the end was not yet.[23]

Steedman's fellows had done all right alongside the veterans, and as the afternoon wore on they had other chances to prove themselves. By 4:30 or so, Steedman's men were about out of ammunition and Wood's and Brannan's men had used up theirs again. Fullerton and others tell that the next Rebel charge was met by a counter-attack with bayonets. This little-known incident sounds very much like Joshua Lawrence Chamberlain's famous bayonet charge down Little Round Top at Gettysburg on July 2. And, as was the case with Chamberlain's charge, the Rebels could not stand the thought of cold steel; they broke and ran. Fullerton said, "So impetuous was this counter-charge that one regiment with empty muskets and empty cartridge boxes, broke through the enemy's line, which, closing in their rear, carried them off in the undertow."[24]

There was at least one more charge, noticeably weaker than the others, on Horseshoe Ridge before the order to withdraw toward Rossville came. Rosecrans, contemplating the situation from safety at General George D. Wagner's headquarters in Chattanooga, had ordered it. The withdrawal began with those brigades on Snodgrass Hill about 5:00 P.M., but the retreat did not begin from Horseshoe Ridge until about 6:00, beginning with Steedman. Darkness was falling. As the sun dipped below the horizon, there was a memorable event. Colonel George P. Buell described it: "As night closed the scene, the whole rebel army, then almost surrounding us, gave one long and exultant cheer. Our few thousand exhausted men, who, without ammunition, had so long struggled and held the trying position, being by no means disheartened, answered their cheers with bold and defiant shouts." Perhaps the Rebels were cheering at the Federal withdrawal, or perhaps they were saluting their opponents' bravery with a cheer. Maybe they were just glad to have survived the day, when so many of their comrades did not. About 7:00 P.M., Buell's little command followed Harker's off of Horseshoe Ridge and hit the road to Rossville. The Battle of Chickamauga was over.[25]

What is one to make of General Thomas J. Wood's behavior on September 20, 1863? There is not now, and there never has been, a consensus in answer to that question.

There is no debate about the consequences of Wood's withdrawal. The Federal line was penetrated, and the right flank and part of the center shattered, because Wood pulled out of line and created a gap where there had been none before. Some historians point to the fact that General Thomas (who *was* under attack, after all) had been calling for reinforcements all morning long and that, in accommodating him, Rosecrans weakened the center and the right. Certainly that is true. It is also true that Longstreet's Confederates might have broken the Union line anyway—but they would have had to fight for it. Crittenden and McCook were still in line and behind barricades, and their batteries were still intact, and the Rebels would have taken terrible punishment as they charged across Brotherton Field. If they had achieved a breakthrough, they would have earned it. As it was, they did not have to earn it. Wood made it easy for the graybacks by opening the gate, so to speak; the Confederates stampeded through and half of the Federal line vanished as a fighting force.

The real question is, was Wood correct in obeying the order? He has modern supporters in his decision to obey Rosecrans without clarification of the written order. Craig Julian Mannville delves deeply into the question. Mannville concludes that considering all the circumstances, "Brigadier General Thomas John Wood did the right thing.... Blame, if blame must be issued, rests squarely upon Major General William Rosecrans." Glenn Tucker agrees, saying: "The only course open to Wood was immediate compliance. That was emphatically the case in view of the fact that he had been severely, even rudely, censored in the presence of his subordinates earlier in the morning.... [Wood] could scarcely be expected to hesitate over execution of an order an hour or so later." Both Mannville and Tucker believe that the responsibility for the disaster on September 20 must rest with Rosecrans, on the basis of his confusing order and his contemptuous behavior toward Wood on that morning.[26]

There are also those who condemn Wood for his actions. Henry M. Cist, in *The Army of the Cumberland* (1882), said that Wood, as a West Point graduate and a lifelong professional, "knew the full meaning of all technical terms used to describe military movements.... He knew he could not execute the order literally as given, and from the wording of it must have known that there was a mistake about it ... he could support Reynolds, but to do this he was compelled to disobey the first part of the order, which in its spirit and intent was to keep him on the line of battle simply moving his division to the left."[27]

Thus, Cist dismissed ignorance or confusion as an explanation for Wood's behavior. He understood the contradiction in the order and he refused to listen to the verbal qualification. Furthermore, he was not ignorant of the state of the Federal line; he knew Brannan was in place and that there was no gap to be filled. Finally, he was not ignorant of the presence of sizable numbers of the enemy in his front. His brigades had been under skirmish fire for an hour, and in addition, an ill-conceived attack (launched before the Confederate breakthrough) across Brotherton Field by Colonel Frederick Bartleson and the 100th Illinois was hurled back by a surprisingly powerful force of Confederate artillery and infantry.

Whitelaw Reid, writing in 1895, addressed the question of "blind obedience." Reid wrote, "It is a well settled principle of military law that a subordinate has the right to disobey an order manifestly given under a misapprehension of facts, and sure to be disastrous in its consequences. To do so involves a grave responsibility and ... a grave personal risk. But there is another and graver responsibility — the ruin of an army." Wood's contemporary Brigadier General John B. Turchin agreed, saying bluntly, "The idea of implicitly obeying orders by such officers as commanders of divisions without reasoning about them is absurd."[28]

There is more to be said about Wood's acceptance of theory of unquestioning obedience — namely, that he did *not* accept it. He had shown repeatedly that he felt free to interpret orders to suit himself, to argue against orders, and to simply disobey them. Remember that only two weeks earlier Wood had wanted to alter the order to cross the Tennessee River to Shellmound and two days later, on September 6, while approaching Lookout Mountain, Wood had initially disobeyed an order to send out a reconnaissance because he believed that neither Rosecrans nor Crittenden fully understood his situation. At that time, Wood had railed against the theory now in question. He said, "I cannot believe General Rosecrans desires such blind obedience to the mere letter of his order for the general disposition of forces as naturally jeopardizes the safety of the most salient portion of it." Remember, too, that Rosecrans himself did not always expect that of his subordinates. On December 30, 1862, when ordered to send a force across Stones River to occupy Murfreesboro, General Crittenden on his own initiative had ordered that the movement be suspended for one hour. New information revealed that the crossing would be more dangerous than first believed. When Rosecrans appeared on the scene, he readily agreed with his wing commander's decision to alter the order in the face of new facts.[29]

Ignorance, confusion, and the unbending principle of obeying orders have been dismissed as motives for Wood's actions on the morning of September 20. What about panic? One might think that a man who was in a state of near panic would cease to think for himself and gratefully take directions — even foolish ones — from a higher authority. There was plenty of panic to be seen on the field that day. Rosecrans, McCook, Garfield, Davis, and Sheridan were among those who fled, and Crittenden followed a bit later. (To their credit, Garfield and Sheridan did return before nightfall and joined Thomas on Snodgrass Hill.) Negley's story was slightly different. He ended up on the left flank with Thomas. When Negley was ordered to move to higher ground near the modest Snodgrass cabin, he decided to make a separate peace. He abandoned the field and took with him to Rossville seven hundred badly needed infantrymen and as many as fifty artillery pieces and caissons. His behavior was widely interpreted as pure cowardice.

However, there is no evidence that Wood was ever panicky under fire. From the Mexican War Battle of Palo Alto to the second day at Chickamauga, he was notable for his calm demeanor when the bullets were flying, a habit that was hard on his horses.

That leaves one explanation for his determination to obey the fatal order: spite. It has been seen that he was deeply resentful of Crittenden's ascension to corps command and also of Palmer's temporary assignment to command of the corps. In addition, Wood was bitter about his own failure to be promoted to major general after Stones River. He became uncommunicative and nearly insubordinate in his refusal to cooperate on the move toward Chattanooga. On top of all this, he had been reprimanded by Rosecrans over the issue of the Lookout Mountain reconnaissance, a chastisement that still rankled. As late as September 16, at Lee and Gordon's Mills and only three days before the fighting began at Chickamauga, Wood was still devoting hours of time defending his actions in the shadow of Lookout Mountain. He was not a man who could easily let go of a slight. The second reprimand, on the morning of September 20, was even more humiliating. He had been profanely corrected in front of his own staff. The wound to his pride was fresh when he received the fatal order, which he understood to be contradictory and confused in its meaning. Like all clever employees of murky-thinking bosses, he decided to exploit that confusion. He wanted to take a measure of revenge on Rosecrans and he could do it by obeying the written order to the letter. That is why he refused to listen to the verbal qualification and refused to wait ten minutes for the order to be clarified. That is also why he so carefully put the order in his pocket. He knew that Rosecrans' order to pull out of line in the face of enemy fire would be controversial, perhaps the object of one of those perpetual boards of inquiry, and he wanted the order to prove what he had been ordered to do. He could plead that he was just a good soldier obeying the orders of his general, and the written order would be unrefutable confirmation.

What Wood could not anticipate was just how great a disaster would come from his obedience to the order. He knew that the enemy was in his front. He did not know that at the very moment when the 1st Division was making its move Longstreet was going to fling five Confederate divisions at the exact spot in the line that his withdrawal had left open and undefended. Wood must have realized immediately what his petty action had led to. It was a serious, perhaps a career-killing error, and as soon as possible he began what the modern world knows as damage control. He scrambled to throw blame on Rosecrans, McCook, and Negley. And he showed a preternatural grasp of the importance of public opinion when he wrote a defense of his actions that appeared in the *New York Times* on January 10, 1864. It was called "Who Lost the Battle of Chickamauga? Notes on Gen. Rosecrans' Report By Gen. Wood." The defense of his actions became a decades-long effort. As late as 1882, Wood was still submitting to the *New York Times* long explanations of his actions on the morning of September 20. And he kept and treasured that yellowing piece of paper on which the fatal order was scribbled as if it were a piece of gold. In an item for the *New York Times* that appeared on December 25, 1881, Wood wrote, "The original is still in my possession."[30]

One who schemes and strives to attain greatness has to accept the risk that there may be one decision above all others for which he will be remembered. In the national memory, a whole life will be distilled down and explained by a man's actions in a single moment. For Wood, even a century and a half later, that moment was 11:00 A.M. on September 20, 1863. Unfortunately for him, there is little good to be found in that one hour, which came almost exactly at the mid-point of a long life. It was an ugly episode and cannot be forgotten, but it marked a dividing line in his professional career. The redeeming finale of Wood's obedience to the fatal order is the depth of his later realization that his performance on the morning of September 20 was dangerous, small-minded, and unworthy. His pride would never let him openly admit his guilt, but his subsequent actions show that he did grasp the horror of what he had done. After that day Wood was never the same general again. He was better.

Chapter 13

Chattanooga

On the morning of September 21, 1863, Wood's division took up a position along the top of Missionary Ridge, to the left of Rossville Gap and alongside General Palmer's division. Across the way, on the right of Rossville Gap, were two brigades of General Negley's division, while a third brigade was down below to defend the road itself. The artillery was placed and the ammunition for both artillery and infantry had been replenished in the night. The enemy had followed them and there was some firing on their front, including a brief exchange of artillery fire, but there was no general attack. That was fortunate. Crittenden's corps had suffered a 28 percent mortality rate in the fighting at Chickamauga. The tally for the 1st Division showed 1,070 men killed, wounded, or missing. In addition, all of the guns of the 8th Indiana Battery were lost.

Still, Missionary Ridge was a strong position and the Federals might have held it except that Rosecrans ordered them to fall back into Chattanooga. During the day, a fatigue party of Colonel Harker's brigade carved a road down the back side of the ridge and about 10:00 P.M. of the twenty-first, his and Buell's men moved down it into Chattanooga.

The Army of the Cumberland was tired, outnumbered two to one, and low on rations and every kind of supply from winter clothes and blankets to wood and nails. Its commanding general was dazed and dispirited and Bragg's Rebels occupied Lookout Mountain and Missionary Ridge. If Bragg decided to attack, there would be little that the bluecoats could do. Luckily for them, Bragg had a peculiar habit of being flustered by victory. After the capture of Munfordville back in September of the previous year, Bragg's aggressive beginning to the Kentucky Campaign suddenly melted into a campaign of timid thought and defensive maneuvers. Likewise, after the tremendous victory at Chickamauga, Bragg seemed to go slack. Instead of using his infantry and artillery to finish the work he had begun at Chickamauga, he decided upon the passive strategy of investment: he would besiege Chattanooga. The Confederates controlled all the roads into the city except for one steep and winding trail over Walden's Ridge. The tons of daily supplies the Federals required could not get through. They would starve and then they would surrender. That was Bragg's calculation.

He was half-right. The Yankees did starve. They were soon on reduced rations and forced to supplement their skimpy army grub in ways they would never have imagined while still back home. They competed with the horses for grain, and when the horses died they ate the horses — and the horses' offal and hooves. They developed an appreciation of dog meat and rats and even cats. However, in spite of their hunger, the second half of Bragg's prediction would never come true. Chattanooga was not going to be surrendered. Colonel Emerson Opdyke wrote, "We are on short rations, about two thirds, and sometimes less, but I think all feel like living on parched corn for a month, rather than yield this important place, now, and then fight another desperate battle for it in 1864."[1]

The first internal problem of the Army of the Cumberland, that of a dazed and downhearted commander, was solved when Rosecrans was replaced by Major General George H. Thomas.

Rosecrans was not the only one who lost his command over the September 20 debacle at Chickamauga. Generals began falling like the autumn leaves. Generals Crittenden and McCook were relieved on September 28. Some might have argued that Crittenden should have been spared on the basis of his performance with the artillery after the Confederate breakthrough, but he had finally left the field for Chattanooga and that sealed it. Neither Crittenden nor McCook held a field command for the remainder of the war.

James Negley was sent home on a medical leave during the first week in October 1863. He was never given a new assignment, not even a rear-echelon duty. Both Brannan and Wood had been loud and bitter in their attitude toward him. Wood called him a "damned poltroon" and, according to witnesses, spoke of his behavior at Horseshoe Ridge "in very violent and threatening terms." Negley had abandoned the field, taking with him a substantial amount of firepower. It was this failure to stand fast that doomed his military career.[2]

They all had their supporters, but Colonel Opdyke was not among them. He spoke for their legions of detractors when he wrote to his wife that Crittenden was "incompetent" and that Negley and McCook were "cowards." Said Opdyke, "McCook was to close the gap made by Wood's moving to the left. McCook (as usual) failed." As for Negley, he "ran away *without firing a gun*, and was not under fire again" [emphasis Opdyke's].[3]

Before the end of the government's great purge, there was another player in the decision-making process. Ulysses S. Grant, once the unhappy West Point cadet and afterward the humble lieutenant who drove mules in Mexico, was now "Unconditional Surrender" Grant, the conqueror of Fort Donelson, the hero of Vicksburg. More than that, he was now the commander of the Military Department of the Mississippi, which included the Armies of the Ohio, the Tennessee, and the Cumberland. When it came time to pick Rosecrans' successor, Lincoln, Stanton, and Halleck placed the power in Grant's hands. If he wished, he could retain Rosecrans; if he preferred, he could choose General George H. Thomas. Grant disliked both men, but he chose Thomas.

October 19 was Rosecrans' last day with the Army of the Cumberland. He returned from a daylong tour of inspection to find a dispatch from Washington waiting for him. He was relieved of command; Thomas was his successor. Rosecrans was gracious in the end. He said to the embarrassed Thomas, "No one but you can safely take my place now; and for the country's sake you must do it."[4]

The appointment of Thomas pleased a great many observers, including the quotable Emerson Opdyke. He wrote, "We all feel a profound confidence in Thomas, not that he is brilliant, but he is firm, solid, industrious, and possesses an irreproachable character, a pure and unselfish love of country; just such a true nobleman, as that when you look at him, you instantly think of Washington." The comparison of Thomas to Washington was one that was often made.[5]

Naturally, Rosecrans' removal was a major story and was covered by all the newspapers of the country. *Harper's Weekly*, one of the most popular periodicals in America, saw some positive signs in the removal that went beyond the simple fact of Rosecrans' losing his job. *Harper's* said:

> Whatever may have been the faults of General Rosecrans, it is encouraging to see that the President, when satisfied that he ought to be removed, had the courage to remove him, without hesitation or explanation to the public ... there can be no doubt that McClellan's removal ought to have taken place much sooner than it did — as soon, in fact, as that General refused to obey orders from Washington, and to report to the Commander-in-Chief. The President temporized and hesitated until a month of invaluable time was lost — fearing the effect of the removal of a commander who had won great personal popularity. We are all of us learning, however, in these days, and Mr. Lincoln ... now understand[s] that the people, of whatever political party, are more devoted to the country than to any individual, and has not hesitated to remove Rosecrans. It was just this nerve and this courage which were required to insure the success of the North.[6]

Rosecrans could not face the men to tell them good-bye. He left camp at 5:00 A.M. on October 20. As they had done with Sherman in 1861 and others since who had fallen into disfavor or disgrace, the authorities ordered him to Missouri, where he remained for the rest of the war.

With so many officers falling, and in light of the fact that it was Wood's petulant obedience to a foolish order that had led to the Confederate breakthrough on the second day at Chickamauga, it was remarkable that the Kentuckian was retained in command of his division. He might easily have been caught up in the purge of officers who were there that day, but he had not left the field and his afternoon conduct on Horseshoe Ridge was impressive, as was his performance on the first day of fighting along La Fayette Road. Curiously, rather than facing dismissal, he was actually recommended for promotion to major general. Even Rosecrans, perhaps the least likely of patrons, spoke in favor of Wood's promotion. Rosecrans said in a letter to Halleck, "In the battle of the 19th he did his duty in the fight well. In that of the 20th, after the right was shattered, he with two brigades of his division and one of Van Cleve's maintained himself against the rebel attack with firmness, skill, and determination."[7]

The promotion did not come through. The government was not quite ready to reward Wood for his admittedly mixed performance at Chickamauga. Even so, he was better off than Crittenden, Negley, McCook, and others. He would at least remain at the front as a division commander, with another chance to prove himself. That chance would soon come.

In the first days of the Chattanooga siege, Wood took the time to attend to some personal duties. The first was a sad one. His wife Caroline's uncle, Edward King, commanding the 75th Indiana Infantry, was killed at Chickamauga and it fell to Wood to tell her. In a graphic letter dated September 23, Wood wrote:

> It is with great grief that I have to give you the sad intelligence of the death of your Uncle Edward. He was killed in the great battle of Sunday. I met General J.J. Reynolds on Monday, and learned from him the circumstances of his death. At the time he was killed there was a perfect cessation in the fighting. Your uncle walked to the front to look out for movements of the enemy, when he was shot by a sharpshooter. The ball struck him just above the right eye, passed through his brain, and, of course, killed him instantly. General Reynolds had his body brought away in the retreat Sunday night and buried it at Rossville, six miles from Chattanooga. The General told me that he had the body distinctly marked, so that when there is an opportunity the body can be removed.

Reynolds' thoughtfulness was appreciated and, as was the case with many Northern officers who died on Southern battlefields, King's body was later disinterred and taken to home for burial.[8]

The second item that occupied Wood's mind was at once both personal and professional. Incredible as it seems in light of all that had since occurred, Wood was still arguing his case in the matter of the reconnaissance toward Lookout Mountain two weeks earlier. On September 25, he forwarded to army headquarters documents that justified his changing of position and his delay in sending out Harker's reconnaissance party. Asked to reply, General Crittenden sent a two-paragraph note. Reading this brief response, one senses that

General Crittenden, soon to be relieved, was sick of what now seemed such an insignificant dispute. He said, "I did expressly leave this matter to his discretion, and therefore, if he did wrong, I am to blame. I will be entirely satisfied if the communications submitted by General Wood vindicate him at department headquarters for his delay in making the reconnaissance.... General Wood has disclaimed any intention of being disrespectful to me in any of his communications, and I hope this matter is ended."[9]

When Crittenden and McCook were relieved, their two corps were combined into the IV Corps, commanded by Major General Gordon Granger. By Special Orders No. 269, dated October 9, Brigadier General Thomas J. Wood was assigned to command the 3rd Division. He lost the services of his talented brigade commanders, Harker, Wagner, and Buell. In the 3rd Division, the 1st Brigade was commanded by Brigadier General August Willich, a communist émigré from Prussia who had settled in Louisville, Kentucky, and had served with the Army of the Cumberland since the days of Camp Nevin. The 2nd Brigade was commanded by Brigadier General William B. Hazen, a contrary but highly gifted officer in the mold of Wood himself. The 3rd Brigade was led by Brigadier General Samuel Beatty, a Mexican War veteran and the former sheriff of Stark County, Ohio. Like Willich and Hazen, Beatty had experience under fire and had fought in all of the battles of the Army of the Cumberland since Shiloh. The only familiar face from the old 1st Division was Captain Cullen Bradley, who would command Wood's artillery. The 3rd Division had a strength of approximately eighty-eight hundred officers and men and nineteen artillery pieces.

The other divisions in Granger's corps were the 1st, under Brigadier General Charles Cruft, and the 2nd, under Major General Philip Sheridan. Only Sheridan's and Wood's divisions were in Chattanooga, though. Cruft's division was scattered by brigade from Bridgeport, Alabama, to Whitesides, Tennessee. The two remaining divisions were directly in front of Chattanooga, facing Missionary Ridge where the Rebels had dug in to wait. The Federals had to be vigilant. Though the main line of the Army of Tennessee was on Missionary Ridge and Lookout Mountain, there were rifle pits at the base of the heights and enemy pickets on the valley floor. There were occasional bursts of gunfire.

General Wood's men were involved in an alarming incident on the night of September 24, when the Confederate pickets suddenly began firing on Wood's right. The general thought that it was the opening gunfire of a night attack and called out his whole division under arms; within a half hour his pickets were involved in the fight. Wood sent orders to them to hold their ground, which they did for an hour before silence fell. Whether it was a temporary cease-fire or simply a breather Wood could not be sure. He ordered fires to be kept burning through the night in front of his line, but the excitement was over. Though it was a minor incident and only two of Wood's men were wounded, it did show the aggressive mood of the Confederates and reminded the Federals that they needed to keep a sharp eye.

On October 23, three days after Rosecrans left the Army of the Cumberland, U. S. Grant and his staff rode into a rainy Chattanooga to take charge of the Union breakout. Grant was on crutches. He had compounded an earlier injury when his horse fell while crossing Walden's Ridge, and the pouring rain did nothing to improve his mood. He made his way to General Thomas' headquarters and the reception he found there was as cool as the night. The two generals sat on opposite sides of the room and listened to a summary of a two-part plan proposed by General William F. "Baldy" Smith (one of Thomas J. Wood's mates from the West Point Class of '45) to end the shortages in Chattanooga. It was a simple plan, but understanding it requires some background.

In addition to removing ineffective officers, the War Department had been working to remedy the besieged army's remaining problems of manpower and supplies. Secretary of War Stanton developed a bold plan by which two corps—those of General O. O. Howard and of Henry W. Slocum—would be detached from the Army of the Potomac and sent racing to Chattanooga by rail. The whole would be commanded by General Joseph Hooker. Stanton predicted that these reinforcements could leave Virginia and be on hand to reinforce Chattanooga in less than a week. Lincoln and others scoffed at the plan, particularly the optimistic schedule. Stanton was not perturbed by their skepticism. He insisted that it could be done. The two corps began leaving Washington, D.C., on September 27 and began arriving at Bridgeport, Alabama, on September 30. "Within two days, 20,000 troopers had

General George H. Thomas (Library of Congress).

arrived, along with sixty artillery pieces, horses, ammunition, and baggage," and more were on their way. The manpower dilemma was solved and Stanton was vindicated.[10]

These "Potomacs," in turn, helped to solve the food and materiel shortages in Chattanooga. This is where "Baldy" Smith's scheme came in. First, the brigade of General William B. Hazen would leave Chattanooga by night and go down the Tennessee River on a small fleet of fifty pontoon boats toward a landing called Brown's Ferry. Simultaneously, General John B. Turchin would lead a force across the narrow neck of what was locally known as Moccasin Point, a peninsula in a great bend of the river. Turchin's objective was the same as Hazen's, Brown's Ferry. Brown's Ferry was out of range of the Confederate guns on Lookout Mountain and only a short distance from Chattanooga. Once the ferry was captured, the Walden's Ridge route (so rugged that ten thousand animals had died trying to cross it) would become obsolete. Steamboats would come up the Tennessee River from the supply base at Bridgeport to Kelley's Ferry. From there the freight would travel overland five miles to Brown's Ferry, where it would cross a pontoon bridge and proceed on the little road into Chattanooga. Hazen and Turchin were ordered to commence their combined operation on the early morning of October 27.

Hazen's waterborne brigade left Chattanooga about 3:00 A.M. Bruce Catton described the scene these Union boatmen saw on their early morning trip down the Tennessee:

> Confederate picket fires were visible, and now and then some lonely picket could be heard singing to keep himself awake. One Federal noticed a quaint picture: by a little bonfire on the Confederate side two pickets sat astride a long, facing each other, their rifles propped up beside them, and one picket was teaching the other to whistle a little tune. The Federal all his life remembered these two boys ... whistling away, while fifty scows full of soldiers drifted by unheard.

Other pickets more attentive than the whistling boys sensed something moving on the river and peered into the dark, only to decide that it was just driftwood floating down.[11]

Turchin's marching men arrived in position at Brown's Ferry before Hazen's men began to debark at about 5:00 A.M. The Rebels had not expected an attack and the ferry itself was lightly guarded, though there were other soldiers back in the hills. When the Federals were all in place, they attacked the surprised Rebels with such vigor that the prize was won in ten minutes. An hour-long counter-attack by the butternuts did not change the outcome, and the Yankees quickly had a pontoon bridge laid. General Joe Hooker's men completed the linkup the afternoon of the next day and the famous "Cracker Line" was opened. The problem of rations, munitions, and stores was solved. All that remained now was the breakout.

As commander of the Military Department of the Mississippi, Grant was impatient to act, but he ultimately felt that the Federals of Thomas and Hooker could not escape Chattanooga without the help of General William Tecumseh Sherman, now commanding his old army, the Army of the Tennessee. Sherman was summoned and was on his way. Until he arrived, Grant satisfied himself by overseeing the stockpiling of supplies, outfitting the ragged Cumberlanders, and rebuilding their strength with the first good meals they had had in weeks.

The officers found the time for some relaxation during this lull. Brigadier General James H. Wilson recalled:

> During the evenings it was customary for the generals to gather at our headquarters. Upon one of these occasions Thomas, Granger, Wood, Brannan, Smith, and several older regulars were gathered about the fire in Grant's sitting room, all official cares thrown aside and all formality discarded. It was pleasant to hear them calling each other by their nicknames. Even Thomas unbent and told his reminiscences with wit and good feeling. Both Grant and he, though noted for their capacity to "keep silent in seven languages," were interesting if not brilliant conversationalists upon such occasions.[12]

General Sherman arrived on November 14, ahead of his army, which was still on the trail. The distress he felt over the recent death of his son Willie did not completely dampen the pleasure at seeing his friend Grant, and the two shared a bottle the night that "Uncle Billy" rode into headquarters.

The next morning, apparently feeling no worse for the liquor they had consumed, Grant and Sherman and others rode out to examine the ground. Sherman teased Grant, saying in mock surprise, "Why, General Grant, you are besieged."[13]

Grant admitted that it was true, but with Sherman on hand that would soon change. Grant's plan, as it finally evolved, was designed to give his old army the bulk of the glory. Sherman's men would march from Brown's Ferry east, moving well behind Chattanooga, until they reached a position where they could attack Tunnel Hill at the northern end of Missionary Ridge or, in other words, Bragg's extreme right flank. Sherman would launch an attack and move south, simply rolling up the Confederate army along the narrow ridgetop. Meanwhile, Hooker and his Potomacs would attack Lookout Mountain on the Confederate left. Thomas and the Army of the Cumberland would "hold the center and right of our front, to cooperate with Sherman, and attack when the proper time arrived." In other words, the disliked Thomas and his scorned army were relegated to a tertiary role and would stand and watch while others carried the day. If needed, they would be called upon.[14]

Sherman's two corps of the Army of the Tennessee began to arrive at Chattanooga on the night of November 17. Uncle Billy was supposed to have his men in position to attack Tunnel Hill at the northern tip of Missionary Ridge on Saturday, November 21. He did not meet his schedule. Neither did he get into position on Sunday.

That day there was considerable movement observed, "some of it singular and mysterious," along the Rebels' front on Missionary Ridge. It appeared as if they might be leaving. On November 23, General Granger was ordered to send a division to reconnoiter toward Orchard Knob "to disclose the presence of the enemy, if he still remain in the vicinity of his old camps." Granger chose the 3rd Division and sent the orders down to General Wood.[15]

The object, Orchard Knob, was one hundred feet high and rose from the valley floor about midway between the Federal line and the Confederate rifle pits at the base of Missionary Ridge. There had been an enemy outpost there since the beginning of the siege, occupied by the 24th Alabama Infantry. Orchard Knob was a strong position, and the Rebels had improved its flanks by erecting fieldworks on a rugged ridge on its right and by rifle pits on its left. These works on the wings were manned by the 28th Alabama.

Wood did not resist or try to amend the order to test the enemy strength on Orchard Knob. He recalled, "Immediately on receipt of this order, I summoned my brigade commander to my headquarters to give them full and minute explanations in regard to the manner in which I intended to execute the instructions I had received." The men were to take two days' cooked rations and have available a larger than normal issue of one hundred cartridges; up to eighty rounds would be carried by each man and the balance would be packed in wagons at Fort Wood, ready to be delivered if needed. Willich's brigade would move directly against the knob, and Hazen would advance against the enemy rifle pits on the right. Beatty would march behind in reserve.[16]

Granger planned for Wood's division to be supported by General O. O. Howard's XI Corps of Potomacs on the left and by General Philip Sheridan's division on the right. Captain Cullen Bradley's artillery was ordered to direct its fire against the CSA batteries on Howard's front.

At the signal of a long drumroll, the 3rd Division formed on the slope south of Fort Wood, the works at Wood's position in the Federal line. It was a lovely Indian summer day. The rain had stopped and the sun was bright and there was enough breeze to disturb the flags and cool the men as they waited. Two hours passed. At 1:30 P.M., a bugle sounded and the men stepped off under the watching eyes of Grant, Thomas, Hooker and others who had come out to Fort Wood to watch. Beatty's brigade, though assigned to the reserve position, had a partial role to play in the vanguard. The 19th Ohio Infantry of the 3rd Brigade was in front of Willich's brigade as skirmishers. General Wood was not with the other officers on the parapet at the fort named in his honor; he was advancing with the attack, on horseback behind the second line at the juncture of Willich's and Hazen's brigades.

Willich's men, marching through a small woods, were somewhat concealed from the enemy, but Hazen's brigade advanced across an open plain and was under fire within two minutes of the bugle call. The enemy skirmishers were "sharply engaged" and Hazen lost about sixty men in his front regiments. Still, they forced the Rebels back and, said Hazen, "no considerable opposition was felt after, until we reached their first line of rifle-pits, about one-half mile to the rear of their picket line, where the pickets and their reserves endeavored to check our advance." Momentum was with the Federals, though, and they captured the works "in the most handsome manner." Hazen added, "This position was actually carried at the point of the bayonet, the enemy being captured behind their work, by the men leaping over it."[17]

Willich's brigade, moving through the woods, had met with relatively little opposition. They burst from the woods while Hazen's fight was going on and rushed Orchard Knob, "ascended its steep acclivity, crowned its summit, and it was ours." They had lost only four killed and ten wounded.[18]

Over on the right was General Philip Sheridan's 2nd Division of the IV Corps. In the reorganization, he had received two of Wood's old brigades, those of Charles Harker and George D. Wagner. With those talented officers leading Sheridan's attack, it was no surprise that he was able to clear the Rebels out of the way and achieve his goal in the attack. The fighting done, his division began to entrench for the night.

Meanwhile, Howard was having trouble on the left. The Cumberlanders had felt some concern over the abilities of their eastern cousins, and sure enough, they failed to carry their share of the load in the attack on Orchard Knob. August Willich reported, "Some uneasy feeling prevailed among the men concerning General Howard's corps, which had formed to the left of our division, but which did not come up to a line with us, though our division had twice cleared the rifle pits in their front." Wood ordered General Beatty to send two regiments of his reserve, the 79th Indiana and the 86th Indiana, to the left "to take the rifle-pits in flank, driving out the enemy's skirmishers therefrom, and relieve the pressure on the front of the Eleventh Corps." The men of the 19th Ohio and the 9th Kentucky crept quietly through the woods, caught the enemy in flank, and captured the rifle pits. Incredibly, the XI Corps men neglected to take possession of them and the Rebels came back in the night. The next morning, the two regiments from Beatty's brigade again captured the pits, which, said General Granger, "for some reason unknown to me, were not even then occupied by the troops of the Eleventh Corps."[19]

Howard's repeated failure to perform notwithstanding, it had been a beautiful little attack. Wood said, "My division seemed to drink in the inspiration of the scene and when the 'advance' was sounded moved forward in the perfect order of a holiday parade." The Confederates thought that it was a parade, or a review, at least. General Bragg, watching from his headquarters atop Missionary Ridge, thought that was all it was, and the next thing he knew, he had lost his advance outpost. U. S. Grant was almost as flabbergasted as Bragg was. A division of the army Grant disdained had been sent out on a simple reconnaissance and had instead captured an important enemy position with a skill that far outshone Howard's Potomacs. Moreover, they had done in twenty minutes what Grant had expected to take two days. Grant, however, did not change his low opinion of the Cumberlanders. He ever after spoke of Wood's accomplishment in the most understated terms. Charles Dana, though, who rarely had a good word to say about anyone, sent a wire to Stanton that very day that called the action on Orchard Knob "brilliant and successful" and a "spectacle ... of singular magnificence."[20]

After the capture of Orchard Knob, the men of Wood's division began entrenching so that the former Confederate fieldworks faced west toward the dark and looming Missionary Ridge. Bright flashes of light marked the spots from which enemy batteries fired down on them from above. As the men leaned over their picks and shovels, shells dropped all around them, but at such a distance that not a single man was killed and only one was wounded. The men went about their work with the nonchalance of veterans. Not only did they dig rifle pits; they also prepared an epaulement on the top of Orchard Knob able to accommodate a six-gun field battery, which was moved up that night.

It was General George H. Thomas whom Grant and Sherman mocked for being slow, but Sherman was not able to get his men into their assigned position to attack the northern tip of Missionary Ridge until November 24, a week after their arrival. Sherman's strike force, three divisions of the Army of the Tennessee, was supplemented by one brigade from the Army of the Potomac and Jefferson C. Davis' division from the Army of the Cumberland. The weather had grown ugly overnight and the morning was foggy and misting rain. Sherman did not launch his attack until early afternoon. His divisions crept over a mile of open ground and did not begin to ascend the heights until about 4:00 P.M. They met only light resistance. When they reached the hilltop, Sherman made a stunning discovery — he was not on Missionary Ridge at all. He was on a detached hill. A deep swale separated Sherman from his actual objective, which was defended by the division of the great Patrick Cleburne. Cleburne was an Irish-born Arkansan who proved to have such exceptional military talents that he was put forward as the successor of Stonewall Jackson after the Battle of Chancellorsville. Not being a Virginian, Cleburne was rejected by General R. E. Lee. The Irishman remained in the West, and now, across that steep-sided chasm, he was poised to demolish William T. Sherman when he tried to advance.

The hill Sherman now occupied was useless, but there was only an hour of light left, so Sherman had his men entrench. He varnished over the incident in his report, admitting that he was mistaken about the topography but insisting, "The ground we had gained was so important that I could leave nothing to chance, and ordered it to be fortified during the night."[21]

Modern observers have not been eager to agree with Sherman's high opinion of his work on November 24. Bruce Catton, for example, says bluntly, "Far from having reached a good place from which to assault Tunnel Hill, Sherman had reached the worst spot imaginable. In effect, he would have to fight a battle just to get to the place from which he could mount his main attack." Peter Cozzens agrees, saying, "By any objective reckoning, Sherman handled the attack against Bragg's right flank, which was supposed to have been the main effort of the Union arms, with a degree of incompetence that bordered on gross negligence."[22]

Tomorrow would show how well Sherman recovered from the double hardship of a bad approach and a masterful opponent

While Sherman was creeping toward a useless hilltop, General Fighting Joe Hooker was assaulting Lookout Mountain over on the Confederate left. It was rugged and steep and slick with rainfall, and seven thousand Confederates defended it. Those divisions of the Army of the Cumberland that remained near Orchard Knob were enjoying what amounted to a day off and watched from their fieldworks the flashes of light that marked the battle line on the distant hillside. General Wood wrote, "We had ample opportunity to watch with eager interest the brilliant operations — though miles away from us — of General Hooker's command for the possession of Lookout Mountain." It was a thrilling thing, made more suspenseful by the fog and the clouds of black-powder smoke that intermittently hid the attackers so that Wood's men on the valley floor, as well as Bragg's Confederates along Missionary Ridge, would lose sight of how the battle was going. Maybe they would see a flash in the fog from a cannon firing. Otherwise it was just the muffled sounds of battle until an airy gap in the mist opened to present a glimpse of the action before closing again. It was hard going for General Hooker's three divisions, but they outnumbered their opponents, who were scattered in small bodies over the slope, and they kept climbing. The enemy began to surrender, at first only in ones and twos and then in clumps of 161 here, 148 there. A little after 12:00 P.M., the Federals began to reach the crest and the battle started to sputter out. The men on the valley floor could hear cheers from on top of the gloomy mountain, but they did not know for sure who had won until the next morning. Wood said, "When the morning sun of Wednesday had dispelled the mist from the mountain top, and displayed to our view the banner of the free and the brave flying from the topmost peak of Lookout Mountain, loud and long were the joyous shouts with which my division made the welkin ring."[23]

Hooker's successful attack, at such contrast with the comedy of errors over on Tunnel Hill, became famous as "The Battle Above the Clouds," a characterization that Grant later dismissed as "romance" and "poetry." In his report to Halleck that night, Grant seemed a bit unsure of what had happened on

Lookout Mountain and was flatly dishonest in what he reported of Sherman's action. He wrote, "The fight to-day progressed favorably. Sherman carried the end of Missionary Ridge.... Troops from Lookout Valley [Hooker's] carried the point of the mountain and now hold the eastern slope and a point high up."[24]

November 25 was a bright, crisp day, cleansed and freshened by the previous day's rain, but better weather did not mean better luck for Sherman as he resumed his effort to get onto Missionary Ridge. The work was even harder now, for Cleburne had been heavily reinforced during the night, and as Sherman's men descended into the steep-sided gap yawning between them and the end of Missionary Ridge a storm of enemy fire rained down on them. Every Federal advance was thrown back. Sherman reported his lack of progress to Grant, who ordered him to try again. He did, with the same results. Hooker was coming down off Lookout Mountain to hit the southern tip of Missionary Ridge. If the going had not been so slow for Fighting Joe, he might have siphoned opponents from Sherman's front or at least distracted Bragg. As it was, the going *was* slow, and the victors of Lookout Mountain were of little benefit to Sherman.

Finally, after watching eight hours of unsuccessful fighting at Tunnel Hill, Grant decided to help his friend Sherman. In mid-afternoon, Grant went to General Wood, who was standing nearby, and had a little conversation with him. Thirteen years later, in an item for the *New York Times*, Wood recalled that Grant began by saying:

> "General Sherman is meeting with very heavy opposition and we must do something for his relief."
>
> I replied, "It seems he is being roughly handled, and we ought to do all we can to aid him."
>
> Gen. Grant then went on to say, "I think if we advance and take the rifle-pits opposite our front at the base of Missionary Ridge, the movement will so menace Bragg's centre on the crest that he will withdraw force enough from Sherman's front to permit him to carry his point of attack."
>
> To this I simply expressed coincidente of opinion and added my confidence that we could readily carry the rifle-pits at the base of the ridge.[25]

Notice that, in Wood's recollection, Grant mentioned only taking the rifle pits at the base of the ridge. It later became a controversial point, whether Grant intended an attack on the rifle pits alone or anticipated a further attack on the ridgetop itself. In his article, Wood said that his recollection of his brief conversation with Grant "was that an assault on the crest of Missionary Ridge was not intended to be a part of that particular movement, however much Gen. Grant intended that such an assault should be subsequently made." Grant went to Thomas, who went to Granger (the proper lines of command hierarchy being scrupulously observed), who then formally issued the order to Wood:

"We are ordered by Gen. Grant to take the rifle-pits at the foot of the ridge and there halt. Get your division ready to move as soon as you can."[26]

It was between 2:30 and 3:00 P.M. The night before, Wood had had his men's cartridge boxes replenished and rations distributed, and in mid-morning (about six hours earlier) his division had advanced to a fringe of trees between Orchard Knob and the foot of Missionary Ridge. They had the firepower they needed and were in position to make a short jump to the Rebel rifle pits.

Somehow, the order to advance did not reach them. General Grant was watching for the advance to step off, but he could see no movement. He later recalled that he "became impatient at last that there was no indication of any charge being made.... Turning to Thomas to inquire what caused the delay, I was surprised to see Thomas J. Wood, one of the division commanders who was to make the charge, standing talking to him. I spoke to General Wood, asking him why he did not charge as ordered an hour before. He replied very promptly that this was the first he had heard of it, but that he had been ready all day to move at a moment's notice. I told him to make the charge at once." In addition to Wood, Sheridan of Granger's corps and Generals Absalom Baird and Richard M. Johnson of John M. Palmer's XIV Corps were ordered to make ready to advance.[27]

Wood quickly conferred with his brigade commanders, relaying the orders to them and assigning them their positions: Beatty's brigade would be on the left flank, the Prussian Willich in the center, and Hazen on the right. In a moment came the signal that Wood's men in the trees had been waiting for, six cannon fired from Orchard Knob, and the men leapt forward from the trees with a shout. To their left, they could see Baird's division. To their immediate right was the division of Little Phil Sheridan and to the far right was the two-brigade division of Richard M. Johnson. Fifty enemy guns (by Wood's estimation) fired down on his men as they advanced, in plain sight now, but nothing would stop them. The Cumberlanders had adopted a particularly meaningful battle cry for the charge; they chanted, "Chickamauga! Chickamauga!" as they approached the rifle pits. The enemy resistance there was puny, and the Federals won the position so quickly that many prisoners were taken. This was the limit of Grant's order, and it was untenable — the Rebels were shooting right down on top of them. The fire coming from above was too intense; they would have to advance or to go back. As General Wood said, "The intrenchments were no protection against the enemy's artillery on the ridge. To remain would be destruction — to return would be both expensive of life and disgraceful."[28]

Some of the Rebels from the rifle pits were trying to escape, scrambling up the side of Missionary Ridge, and a few of the Federals began to follow. Some of Colonel Beatty's men were among them. Willich's men followed. So did Hazen's. Hazen later recalled that he gave his men a five-minute rest, during which they begged permission to climb the hillside. Finally, the colonel gave the order, and the men began to climb, led by the 23rd Kentucky Infantry, who were on their feet and rushing up the hill practically before the order had cleared Hazen's lips. None of Wood's brigade commanders had received orders to advance, and neither Hazen nor Beatty believed that they had been intended to attack the ridgetop. Willich was alone in his initial interpretation of the order. He said in his report, "I understood since that the order was given to take only the rifle-pits at the foot of the ridge; by what accident I am unable to say, I did not understand it so; I only understood the order to advance."[29]

Grant's orders had made a muddle of things. Baird's 3rd Division of the XIV Corps got two different versions of the order and General Sheridan was so unsure that he started up the mountainside and then briefly halted, deciding that he had better wait until he got clarification of what it was, exactly, that Grant wanted.

The hillside was crisscrossed by little roads, and there were dips in the surface of the ridge where the men could huddle, but mostly they did not stop, even to fire. They just moved forward as best they could over the steep ground. Wood was behind the second line of the advance, as he had been in the attack on Orchard Knob two days before. He had not been ordered to make the charge to the top, but he approved of it and of the initiative his men were showing. In that 1876 *New York Times* article, he wrote:

> The average American citizen, possessing a degree of intelligence unequalled by the average citizen of any other nationality ... when placed in the military service of his country, can be trusted in an emergency, without explicit, or in fact any orders in advance, to do what the occasion requires. As an illustration, the front line of my division, seeming instantaneously and certainly spontaneously, appeared to become inspired, grasped fully the situation, appreciated the greatness of the opportunity — without orders and without casting around to see whether the troops on the right or the left had reached the base of the ridge — bounded over the Confederate barricades, and, with a wild huzza, committed itself in the audacious ascent.[30]

And, Wood admitted, "I was simply one of the boys on that occasion. I was infected with the contagion of the prevailing enthusiasm."[31]

The sight was sublime. In some of the officers observing from Fort Wood or Orchard Knob, it inspired undisguised wonder. General O. O. Howard had just recently come from the East and the Battle of Gettysburg, where men attacking up hills not nearly so formidable as Missionary Ridge had tried and failed. Confederate general William C. Oates had lost in his attempt to ascend Little Round Top and dislodge the Yankees there, and the following day General George Pickett had been flung back with great slaughter from the gentle slope of Cemetery Ridge. And here were these Cumberlanders, climbing with inexorable momentum an almost perpendicular five-hundred-foot mountain wall to assault an entrenched enemy. It was incomparable to anything Howard had seen before. He exclaimed, "Why, this is magnificent! Is this the way you Western troops go into action?"[32]

In another observer, it inspired angry astonishment. General U. S. Grant had no intention of sending the men beyond the rifle pits. Indeed, he seems never to have thought about what the men would do after they captured the enemy position at the foot of Missionary Ridge. He knew, however, that he did not order a charge on the ridgetop, and he demanded to know who did. Peter Cozzens recounts that Grant accused both Thomas and Granger. He turned to General Thomas and said, "Thomas, who ordered those men up that ridge?" Thomas said, "I don't know; I did not."

"Did you order them up, Granger?" Grant asked. "No," said Granger, "they started up without orders. When those fellows get started all hell can't stop them."[33]

What Grant said next is reported variously. One account has him saying, "Well, somebody will suffer if they don't stay there." In another version, he specifically named his old West Point roommate, General Wood, as the "somebody" whose head would be on the block. Thomas' biographer, Benson Bobrick, simply has Grant saying, "Well, it will be investigated."[34]

Now that Grant had raised the question, Granger thought it best to try to find out who, in fact, did give the order to the assault on the ridgetop. He ordered his lieutenant colonel Joseph S. Fullerton to "ride at once to Wood, and then to Sheridan, and ask them if they ordered their men up the ridge, and tell them, if they can take it, to push ahead." Fullerton started away, but Granger stopped him, saying, "It is hot over there, and you may not get through. I shall send Captain Avery to Sheridan, and other officers after both of you."[35]

Fullerton caught up with Wood on the slope and conveyed Granger's question. Wood answered, "I didn't order them up, they started up on their own account and supported, we will take and hold the ridge!" Fullerton's recollection of the brief conversation, which he included in his article for *Battles and Leaders of the Civil War*, may have been cleaned up a bit for his Victorian readers. Another version of the Kentuckian's answer has him saying, "The men started up without orders, and I would like to know who in the hell can stop them," which sounds more like Wood.[36]

The battle had passed out of Grant's control, or Thomas' or any of the officers watching from below. This was the division and brigade commanders and the regimental officers and the men themselves who decided to claw their way up through the poison ivy and the honeysuckle and swarms of minié balls to take the crest of Missionary Ridge. It was as if a moment of telepathy had flashed through the mind of every man — they knew what they were going to do, even if no one issued the order. The whole line was going up en masse, hard-breathing men grunting their battle cry, "Chickamauga!" The mountainside changed color as the minutes passed, a strange blue hue staining the mountain, edging up from the base like rising waters about to engulf the gray top of Missionary Ridge.

The men could not progress in parade-ground lines. The ground was too rough and some men were stronger than others. Colonel William B. Hazen wrote in his report, "Not much regard to lines could be observed, but the strong men, commanders and color bearers, took the lead in each case, forming the apex of a triangular column of men. They advanced slowly but confidently, no amount of fire from the crest checking them."[37]

They were very close now. The Confederates could not depress the tubes of their fieldpieces enough to fire down on the attackers, so they lit the fuses on the shells and simply threw them down. Near the top, the Yankees were slowing down. They were tired and the fire from above was heavy. Wood was afraid of a counter-attack. To intimidate the Rebels, he ordered his men to yell at the top of their lungs to fool the enemy above into thinking that reinforcements were coming. The Rebels lobbed hand grenades at Wood's men and, as they began to pour over the rim, jabbed at them with bayonets. The medical director of the IV Corps, A. J. Phelps, said, "A large proportion of the wounds were severe."[38]

In spite of the danger, the Federals kept going. Hazen insisted that one of his regiments was the first to gain the top. He wrote:

> Lieutenant-Colonel [E. Bassett] Langdon, of the First Ohio, gaining a position where the conformation of the hill gave cover till within 3 yards of the crest, formed several hundred men there, checking the head for that purpose, then giving the command, the column broke over the crest, the enemy fleeing.
>
> These were the first on the hill, and my command moving up with a shout their entire front was handsomely carried.
>
> The troops on my immediate left were still held in check, and those on my right not more than half way up the hill, and were being successfully held back. Hastening my men to the right and left along the ridge, I was enabled to take the enemy in flank and reverse, and, by vigorously using the artillery captured there, I soon relieved my neighbors and carried the crest to within a few hundred yards of Bragg's headquarters, he himself escaping by flight, being at one time near my right encouraging the troops that had checked Sheridan's left.[39]

Hazen's claim was not an undisputed one. It is repeatedly said of the Battle of Missionary Ridge that there were a half-dozen places where the Federals poured over the rim almost simultaneously. Some have claimed that the men of Willich's brigade were first, while others believed that Sheridan's division was the first to gain the crest. Most modern historians, though, have dismissed the claim that it was any other than Hazen's brigade of Wood's division. As Glenn Tucker says, "In later years when the question was raised of who first entered the main Confederate line, Wood assembled such an impressive sheaf of eye-witness testimony, some from other than his own command, that it has been difficult to assign the credit elsewhere."[40]

While Wood was proud to seize the credit for his division having first taken the ridge, he was generous in his attitude to the others who attacked on that November day. In his 1876 article for the *New York Times*, he said that the 3rd Division "was not only the first to gain the crest — it was the first to start to gain it." But he added: "Fortunately, to do justice to one body of troops does not involve the disparagement of any others. It is not intended to deprecate the brilliant and meritorious conduct of the two gallant divisions which came up on the right and left of my division soon after it had crowned the crest, nor to detract in the least from the historic renown which they so worthily earned on that ever memorable occasion."[41]

Men in blue were beginning to fill the narrow ridgetop. The Confederates were as surprised as anyone that the Yankees had done the seemingly impossible, and they, too, experienced a moment of telepathy when every man had the same thought — Missionary Ridge was lost. As the Federals continued to come over the rim onto the blade-like crest, the Rebels offered a mostly symbolic resistance to save face before they threw down their haversacks and even their rifles and ran down the back side of the ridge toward Georgia. Philip Sheridan's division pursued the Rebels. It was much to Little Phil's credit and impressed Grant so much that when he went east in a few weeks to undertake his new duties as the commander of all the Union armies in the field he took Sheridan with him as his cavalry commander. Wood's men ended their day's work at the ridge crest and settled down for a breather around the captured fieldpieces. Wood was among them and so delighted that he made the second (and last, so far as is known) jest of the war. It was as clumsy as the first one at Stones River, but he meant it as a compliment to his men, and they took it that way. As it was reported in the *New York Times*, he said, "Brave men, you were ordered to go forward and take the rebel rifle-pits at the foot of these hills; you did so, and then, by the Eternal, without orders, you pushed forward and took all the enemy's works on top. Here is a fine chance to have you all Court-martialed! and I myself will appear as the principal witness against you." He promised to let them off the hook if they would take a vow to continue the fight against Bragg, Joseph Johnston, and Jefferson Davis, and the devil himself. They laughed and promised and cheered, "Bully for him!" and "Three Cheers for old Wood!" and "the gallant officer rode off the field."[42]

The sun was going down. Wood had gained the high ground, and the view was just fine. Bragg was defeated and Chattanooga was liberated. Chattanooga — Orchard Knob and the Battle of Missionary Ridge — was General Thomas J. Wood's finest professional hour, and in addition, it had a particularly personal significance for him. Almost thirty years later, he told an audience at the Military Order of the Loyal Legion of the United States that the successful assault on Missionary Ridge was "the proudest, most exultant moment of my life."[43]

The guilty stain of Chickamauga was still there, but now it was covered by a shining mantle of victory.

Chapter 14

East Tennessee

Immediately after the battle, the congratulatory messages flew. Thomas wrote to Granger, "Please accept my congratulations on the splendid success of your troops, and convey to them my cordial thanks for the brilliant style in which they carried the enemy's works. Their conduct cannot be too highly appreciated." In passing this on to the victorious soldiers of the IV Corps, General Granger added, "I am constrained to express my own admiration of your noble conduct, and I am proud to tell you that the veteran generals from other fields who witnessed your heroic bearing place your assault and triumph among the most brilliant achievements of the war. Thirty cannon, more than 3,000 prisoners, and several battle flags taken from the enemy are among your trophies. Thanks, soldiers!"[1]

Even Charles A. Dana, Secretary of War Edwin Stanton's spy in camp, was impressed. He sent a long telegram to the secretary on November 26, 1863, and said, "The storming of the ridge by our troops was one of the greatest miracles in military history. No man who climbs the ascent by any of the roads that wind along its front can believe that 18,000 men were moved up its broken and crumbling face unless it was his fortune to witness the deed. It seems as awful as a visible interposition of God." He added, "Neither Grant nor Thomas intended it."[2]

Dana knew the truth of the matter, but Grant later pretended that he had planned for the men to make an assault against the top of Missionary Ridge all along; it was just that he did not intend the assault to occur right then. It was only the immediacy of it that made him ask the generals around him if they had ordered the charge. That was his claim and it was a lie, according to Peter Cozzens, who goes on to say, "In both his report of the battle and his memoirs, he insisted that he had given Thomas express authority to carry the ridge itself, and implied that he fully expected that to be done." The national press began almost immediately to conspire to spin the events in such a way that the newest national hero would be seen in the best light. A reporter for the *New York Times* filed a story that said in part, "It was three o'clock when General Grant pronounced that word [attack], and in five minutes after, the two grand columns moved gradually to the attack. They were ordered to strike the mountain at points about a mile apart, and to make the ascent as rapidly as was consistent with good order." This passage in the reporter's dispatch was wrong in every particular, except for the time of day when the attack began.[3]

Grant and Sherman tried their best to claim credit for the IV Corps' victory. In his *Memoirs*, Sherman said, "The object of General Hooker's and my attacks on the extreme flanks of Bragg's position was, to disturb him to such an extent, that he would naturally detach from his centre as against us, so that Thomas' army could break through. The whole plan succeeded admirably." Sherman also reprinted in his book a message from General Grant written the evening after the assault on Missionary Ridge. Grant wrote Sherman, "No doubt you witnessed the handsome manner in which Thomas' troops carried Missionary Ridge this afternoon, and can feel a just pride, too, in the part taken by the forces under your command in taking first so much of the same range of hills, and then in attracting the attention of so many of the enemy so as to make Thomas' part certain of success."[4]

The two generals were looking at the event backwards, which was the most self-serving point of view. Sherman asserted that his and Hooker's actions on the Confederate flanks were planned from the start to be mere demonstrations and that Thomas' attack on the enemy center was meant to be the main attack. Just the opposite was true. Thomas' role was plainly intended to be secondary to Sherman's attack. Grant intended the lion's share of glory to go to Sherman and only threw Thomas' men forward when it was clear that Sherman was stalled. For his part, Grant's pretense that Sherman was ahead of all the other generals in taking a significant portion of Missionary Ridge was a clear prevarication, considering that Sherman had captured a useless knob that was actually of very little importance. Most modern historians have seen through Grant and Sherman's attempts to reinterpret the tale to their own liking and have agreed that their effort to deprive Thomas and the Army of the Cumberland of credit for the victory at Missionary Ridge did not reflect well on either man.

In his report written immediately after the battle, Wood said, "The assault of Mission Ridge is certainly one of the most remarkable achievements that have ever occurred. Military history would probably be ransacked in vain for a parallel…. In fifty minutes from the time the advance commenced, the first flags were seen flying on the crest of the ridge.[5]

The 3rd Division paid a heavy price in the charge up Missionary Ridge. The casualties had amounted to 1,035, which was a third higher than those of Baird on the Federal left and Johnson on the Federal right and about three hundred fewer than those suffered by Sheridan, who was on Wood's immediate right.

According to Wood's report, his men had captured over one thousand prisoners, over two thousand stands of small arms, twenty-five caissons, and twenty-nine fieldpieces. Those fieldpieces became the subject of a small controversy. Sheridan claimed some of them for his own men, and perhaps with good reason. He complained:

> General Wood, in his report to General Thomas of artillery taken, claims many piece which were the prizes of my division, and when told by me that the report was untruthful, replied "that it was based upon the report of General Hazen, who, perhaps, will in time base his on those of the regiments." But whether Wood, Hazen, regimental or company commanders are responsible, the report is untrue. Eleven of those guns were gleaned from the battlefield and appropriated while I was pushing the enemy on to Chickamauga Station.[6]

Wood, having based his total on those of his brigade commanders, believed that he was correct. He wrote, "In regard to the artillery captured there can be no doubt, since we have all the pieces in possession, horses being captured by some of the batteries. In regard to some of the other items of capture and casualties, there may be errors which more minute reports will correct."[7]

In the end, chief of artillery Brigadier General John M. Brannan credited Wood's division with the capture of twelve (not twenty-nine) fieldpieces. Grant approved. Twenty-five years later, the incident still rankled Sheridan, who had decided that his quarrel was with Hazen, not Wood. In his autobiography Little Phil complained about Hazen having claimed those guns and ridiculed his attempt to buttress his claim by the testimony of witnesses. He wrote, "The doubtful character of testimony dimmed by the lapse of many years has long been conceded, and I am content to let the controversy stand the test of history, based on the conclusions of General Grant." Of course, it is understandable that Sheridan would have evoked the name of the commander of the Military Department of the Mississippi; by then, he had joined Sherman to become the third member in the tight and tiny mutual admiration society around Grant.[8]

The night of November 25, General Wood ordered his men to encamp on the crest of the ridge, but they did not have long to rest. The same night, General Grant decided to send an expedition to move toward Knoxville and the relief of General Ambrose Burnside. Burnside, commander of the Department of the Ohio, was besieged in the East Tennessee city by General James Longstreet, who had been detached by Bragg for that very purpose. In a curious twist, these two antagonists had fought at Fredericksburg, Virginia, in December 1862. On that occasion, Longstreet's corps of the Army of Northern Virginia had slaughtered Burnside's Army of the Potomac as they repeatedly charged the famous stone wall at the base of Marye's Heights. Neither man would have predicted that they would fight another round in East Tennessee only eleven months later.

Tennessee was something of a small obsession with President Lincoln, and through the duration of the Chattanooga siege he had repeatedly reminded Grant that he must not forget Burnside. Grant had not been able to do much for Burnside until Bragg was defeated. Now that that had been accomplished, Grant hurried to meet the president's demands. On November 27, Grant ordered General Granger to lead Sheridan and Wood to Knoxville. Granger passed on the instructions to his division commanders:

> The enclosed instructions will be carried into effect as follows: Sixty rounds of ammunition and ten days' rations per man will be loaded upon the *Paint Rock* as soon as possible. One company of sharpshooters from each division will go upon the steamer as a guard. Two wagons to each brigade — one for tools and one for brigade headquarters — will be taken. Tools for building bridges, repairing roads, such as augurs, saws, axes, picks, spades, etc.; also one battery to each division, and two days' forage for each animal will be carried. You will march as early as practicable tomorrow morning. One medical wagon to each brigade will be taken.[9]

Granger did march with his relief column on the twenty-eighth, but Grant was nevertheless annoyed at what he considered more Army of the Cumberland dawdling. Grant tried to encourage Granger to pick up the pace, explaining to him by dispatch the importance of the assignment and the need for speed and saying, "This important task is now entrusted to you."[10]

However, Grant had little confidence that Granger would respond with the appropriate vigor. The same day that he wrote Granger, Grant wrote to Sherman in the field. Uncle Billy had been following Bragg's retreating army and tearing up railroad. Grant wrote Sherman, "Granger is now on his way to Burnside's relief, but I have lost all faith in his energy and capacity to manage an expedition of the importance of this one. I am inclined to think, therefore, that I shall have to send you.... Push as rapidly as you can to the Hiwassee and determine for yourself what force to take with you from that point.... In plain words, you will assume command of all the forces now moving up the Tennessee." Sherman decided to take two divisions each of the XI Corps and the XV Corps. He and Granger did not travel along the same route and seem not to have conferred until each was near Morgantown.[11]

There was plenty of time to confer at Morgantown, for the bridge over the Little Tennessee River was down and there would be an unavoidable wait while the engineers jury-rigged a replacement. In the meantime, the division commanders were ordered to grind corn. Granger told Wood to "use every effort to procure corn and wheat, and to grind all you possibly can. We have three small mills running, but cannot supply much. Johnson's mill ... has three run of stone, and can grind all the grain you can get there." The bridge would be finished that night, said Granger, and Wood should be prepared to cross the river at daylight. Then, he tucked in an interesting bit of intelligence: "Longstreet ... assaulted Burnside on Sunday and was badly whipped."[12]

The next day, December 6, the IV Corps camped between Maryville and the Little Tennessee River. Granger went into Maryville to confer again with Sherman and was ordered to move on to Knoxville. It was a twelve-mile march and Granger did not move until the next morning. Granger's column began to reach the mountain town on the afternoon of the seventh, only a few hours after Sherman.

What the men found at Knoxville must have made some of them laugh and made others curse. Burnside's men in Knoxville were in no distress at all and Longstreet's Rebels were gone. The siege imposed upon the Yankees by General Longstreet must have been one of the most porous investments in history, the inevitable consequence of an imperfect knowledge of the terrain.

The jumbled topography and the serpentine rivers of this region had scared away more than one Union general. Neither Buell nor Rosecrans had shown any interest in moving into the mountainous maze of East Tennessee, and even Sherman griped to Grant, "Recollect that East Tennessee is my horror. That any military man should send a force into East Tennessee puzzles me. Burnside is there and must be relieved, but when relieved I want to get out, and he should come out too."[13]

Longstreet, too, was very aware of the difficulties of campaigning in East Tennessee. Before leaving Chattanooga, he had asked for good maps, but there were no good maps. So it was that Longstreet sealed off the Holston River, thinking that he had closed the French Broad River. By that, he believed, he had gained control over all upstream access to Knoxville. He had not. The French Broad was wide open and loyal Unionists upstream were soon floating cargoes of food down to the besieged Federals. The loyalists were drawing from an immensely fertile agricultural region. Wilma Dykeman, in her study of the French Broad River, observed, "The valley of East Tennessee was the second richest grain producer in the whole Confederacy, superseded only by the valley of Virginia, and ... the fields along the French Broad, from Newport to Knoxville, yielded an abundant share of wheat and corn. In addition, it provided hay for army mules and horses, and beef and bacon for men."[14]

The tonnage of food was not quite sufficient, but it was enough that Burnside's army could not be starved into surrender. Estimates were that Burnside had enough food stored inside to feed his twelve thousand troops for another two weeks, even if no more was sneaked in.

The Army of the Ohio had survived the so-called siege and had defeated Longstreet in battle and now the Confederate chieftain was nowhere to be seen. He and his army were said to be retreating in the direction of Virginia.

When General Sherman arrived on December 7, General Burnside treated him to a day of entertainments that included a tour of Fort Sanders and a sumptuous turkey dinner at his headquarters, a comfortable Knoxville mansion. During the sightseeing and the meal, Burnside explained to Sherman how the Army of the Ohio had fared during the siege and in the battle that concluded it.

The main point in the Federal defensive line, Fort Sanders, was protected by fifty-one artillery pieces. The parapet of the fort was steep and twenty feet high. At the foot of the parapet was a moat twelve feet wide and nine feet deep. If those deadly statistics were not daunting enough, there was still more. Two of the creeks flowing through Knoxville had been dammed and the slack water had flooded some of the approaches to the fort. Trees had been cut down and telegraph wire had been strung between the stumps at ankle and knee height to create an entangling steel web. Abatis and chevaux-de-frise bristled between Longstreet's men and the fort. In addition, on the heights around the plateau where Knoxville sat were well-manned earthworks.

Nevertheless, at 6:30 A.M. on November 29 Longstreet had attacked, beginning with a fierce artillery barrage. After twenty minutes, the sound of cannon was joined by musket fire, and then came a line of Rebel infantry advancing at a run toward Fort Sanders. Many fell at the telegraph-wire entanglements, but the rest pushed on and in a matter of minutes were at the ditch at the base of the parapet. They were stymied by the width and depth of the moat and they could not climb the sides of the parapet, which were slick with frost. The Federals raked them on each side with triple-canister from Fort Sanders' artillery, and those Yankees on top of the wall who were not firing down with their rifles were lighting the fuses on shells and dropping them among the bunched-up Rebels in the moat. The attackers had bought no scaling ladders. They were trapped in the trench, and they died by the score. The attack failed, and when the defeated butternuts fell back they left behind one thousand dead. In the moat the bodies of dead Rebels were layered ten deep.

Burnside offered a truce so that Longstreet could remove his dead. While the corpses were being carried away, Longstreet learned that Bragg had been defeated at Lookout Mountain and at Missionary Ridge and was falling back in considerable confusion to Northern Georgia. Bragg advised Longstreet to abandon the Knoxville front, which he began to do on the night of December 3, slipping away toward the east. Burnside ordered an immediate pursuit.

In his *Memoirs*, Sherman wrote, "I offered to join in the pursuit, though in fact my men were worn out and suffering in that cold season and climate." Burnside said that he only needed General Granger and his two divisions. With those, "he would be able to push Longstreet out of East Tennessee, and he hoped to capture much of his artillery and trains."[15]

Sherman continued, "Granger was present at our conversation, and most unreasonably, I thought, remonstrated against being left; complaining bitterly of what he thought was hard treatment to his men and himself. I know that his language and manner at that time produced on my mind a bad impression, and it was one of the causes which led me to relieve him as a corps commander in the campaign of the next spring."[16]

Whether he liked it or not, Granger was ordered to stay, and Uncle Billy Sherman returned to Chattanooga, happy to turn his back on the region that was his "horror."

General Longstreet spent the winter evading the maneuvering Yankees in East Tennessee and survived to lead his corps back to Virginia. Wood's division had little to do with chasing him. Instead, the 3rd Division operated against guerrillas and protected gristmills from arson. They rotated among Rutledge, Loudon, Powder Springs, and Strawberry Plains, where (shades of the North Alabama Campaign) they rebuilt the railroad bridge.

The men were inadequately provisioned to endure a Tennessee mountain winter, and the weather was brutal. Temperatures began to fall and on New Year's Day the mercury dropped below zero and hovered there. The temporary bridge at Knoxville was down. No flour was coming in and the men were made to go on reduced rations. An officer at Knoxville complained to Wood, "We should have at [least] three-fourths rations (300,000) per week, but not half that comes." Both the commissary and the quartermaster were scrambling to overcome shortages. To ensure that his officers did not pull rank in order to draw more food than the enlisted men, Wood ordered the commissary to limit officers' share to half rations. That was a fair act, and typical of Wood's concern for the men in the ranks, but it did little to solve the overarching problem of food shortages and did nothing to solve the lack of winter uniforms. Two weeks after their arrival, W. W. Blair, the medical director of the 3rd Division, reported, "Having just returned from a personal inspection of the men in this command, I have the honor to report that I feel them exceedingly destitute of clothing. The entire outfit of many soldiers consists of a blouse, worn as a shirt, a pair of pants, well worn, a pair of shoes, and, in some instances, not even those, an oil or woolen blanket, and a hat or cap.... I find the men attached with rheumatism, with diarrhea, and with fever of a typhoid character." He predicted that, without steps to correct these shortages, the division's efficiency would be seriously impaired. Even as poor as they were, Wood's men were better off than Sheridan's, who did not even have shoes.[17]

The prosperity of his men, relative to shoe leather, was of little comfort to Wood. He sent Blair's report to IV Corps headquarters and enclosed a long letter of his own protesting the Valley Forge conditions under which his men labored. "It is very evident from Surgeon Blair's report," said Wood, "that, if the command be left much longer in its present exposed, unprotected, and unprovided condition, the ordinary military commanders will be relieved soon of the further care of very many of the men, as they will have been placed by

Generals Rheumatism, Diarrhea, Pneumonia, and Typhoid Fever beyond the reach of further human care."[18]

Wood continued:

> For reasons not necessary to be given in detail here, but which are well known to the higher commanders, the troops of the Fourth Army Corps — at least the Second and Third Divisions — have not been supplied with clothing since the march from Middle Tennessee in August last. Clothing was beginning to arrive at Chattanooga when we marched from there on the 28th ultimo, but we were not allowed to remain long enough to derive any advantage from this supply. After fighting a great battle, we were hurried off to the relief of the beleaguered garrison of Knoxville. We came cheerfully and with alacrity, not only as a matter of duty, but as a work of love. But the siege being raised (the enemy having retreated), and it being apparent that further active operations in this field for some time to come are impossible, we ask now that immediate and effective measures be taken to supply our wants. The men are not only destitute of clothing, but men and officers are suffering for want of sufficient protection in tents, and both are suffering from want of variety in the rations....
>
> We supposed we should be allowed to return to our supplies as soon as the siege should be raised, and I know of no other effectual remedy but to allow us to return to them at once.[19]

The men were not allowed to return. They were kept on duty in East Tennessee, without winter clothing or tents. The supply situation did not begin to improve until the first of February.

Wood's effective leadership and paternal concern for the well-being of his men was impressive to those who were getting to know him for the first time. The story of his role at Chickamauga followed the Kentuckian — he would never be able to escape it completely — but his fellow officers may have been surprised at the better qualities of the man they saw before them. Brigadier General Jacob D. Cox was one who had the chance to observe him in East Tennessee. In his *Military Reminiscences of the Civil War*, Cox admitted that General Wood was still under a cloud but found him to be a man whose "intelligence and activity were very marked." Cox continued, "His courage was of the cool indomitable character most highly prized in divisions of a great army ... he was a noticeable man in any assemblage of officers. A fluent talker, attentive to polite forms of speech as well as of conduct, he was liked and respected throughout the army."[20]

Others who had known Wood longer and who retained their high opinion of him were determined in their effort to advance him to corps command. As had happened after Stones River, and to a lesser extent after Chickamauga, Wood's friends were petitioning the government in Washington for his promotion to major general. One of them was Governor Thomas E. Bramlette of Kentucky. Before returning to civilian life and politics, he had been the colonel of the 3rd Kentucky Infantry and served in Wood's division. Governor Bramlette wrote to Secretary of War Stanton that Wood was "to my certain knowledge a very superior officer. I served under his Command and know from personal observation his merits as a commander. I solicit for him the promotion which his gallant services claim." Bramlette wrote the same day to President Lincoln, once again citing his service with Wood and saying that he had "nobly earned the right to promotion."[21]

Major General Gordon Granger joined the chorus singing Wood's praises in a letter from Blain's Crossroads, East Tennessee, to President Lincoln dated (incorrectly) January 4, 1863. Granger mentioned Wood's performances at Chickamauga and at Chattanooga and said to Lincoln, "I feel justified in saying that had you been present and witnessed his heroic conduct on those occasions you would have nominated him as Major General on the spot." He expressed the hope that "prompt and full justice will be done him at your hands."[22]

If Wood knew of the recommendations of Bramlette and Granger—and it would be difficult to believe that he was not aware of the efforts being made on his behalf—he was disappointed. No promotion was offered. So far, the new year of 1864 was proving to be a disappointment in every way. The men were suffering, the duties unfulfilling, and the golden hope of promotion had once again turned to lead.

Thomas J. Wood was a professional. Since his teenage years, he had imagined no other life for himself. No matter how onerous the duty, no matter how many times his final promotion was denied, he would remain in the service. This was not necessarily the case with the volunteers in the ranks, and their three-year enlistments were about to expire. They had rushed to the recruiting office in 1861 to fight for Union, but as a consequence of President Lincoln's proclamation they had been called upon for the past year to fight for emancipation, as well. An inevitable corollary to emancipation was the unwelcome possibility of serving alongside black men in uniform.

It has been seen how Major H. F. Kalfus, 15th Kentucky Infantry, was dishonorably dismissed from the service at Fortress Rosecrans for expressing his disapproval of the notion of black soldiers. Since then, harsh feelings over the issue had not moderated, and they were not restricted to men from the Border States. A Pennsylvania soldier quoted in Bell I. Wiley's *Life of Billy Yank* wrote home that he was tired of war and had not known the issue was going to be the freeing of slaves; if he had, he "would not have mingled with the dirty job." There were many in the blue uniform who agreed with him. Men had known that the day of decision was coming. Now it was here, and they had to decide if they would go home or continue to starve, freeze, and risk death in the name of emancipation.[23]

General Wood had reconciled himself to the inevitability of both emancipation and black enlistment. Whether his acceptance of what was now official policy represented a genuine change of attitude or was a calculation to remain in good favor (with a greater possibility of promotion) is unclear. However, he was vocal in his support, if one of his contemporaries is to be believed. Looking back on that time, Colonel Abel D. Streight wrote to President Lincoln:

> I have talked with [Wood] publicly and privately, and I may say frequently and intimately on the subject since the fall of Sixty One. He was at that time a slave holder, and I am an anti-slavery man, hence the subject was often discussed by us, and I assure you, Mr. President, that in my opinion you have had no more hearty, consistent supporter, and co-worker in this army than him. He has to my knowledge written several able articles for publication in the Kentucky papers, urging the people of that state to abolish slavery and to give their united support to the Government in crushing the rebellion. And when the policy to employ negroes as soldiers was announced, General Wood gave it his hearty cooperation.
>
> I have frequently heard him express the wish that there might be a more general co-operation in enlisting Negroes, to the end that a much larger army of them might be speedily put in the field.[24]

The Lincoln administration knew that the men in the ranks were grappling with the same issues of race that Wood had already decided for himself. The government could not spare all of the three-year men whose enlistments were about to expire and who were questioning whether or not they should sign up for another stretch. So, as an allurement, the government began in late 1863 to offer both a bounty of $402 and a thirty-day furlough to go home. As a visible sign of their patriotism, the veteran volunteers were authorized to wear a tricolor chevron on their lower sleeves. Furthermore, if three-fourths of a regiment signed up, then the regiment would continue with its individual status and original number. If not, it would be consolidated with another regiment and receive a different numerical designation. It was a clever and attractive offer that appealed at once to homesickness, greed, personal vanity, and unit pride.

The plan met with considerable success. A great many men overcame their racial prejudice in the face of such generous inducements. Many units veteranized almost to the last man. The camps began to seem empty as the men took their promised furloughs, and it was just as well. There was little active campaigning in the winter. In addition, the absence of thousands of men eased the continuing problems of inadequate shelter and insufficient rations. The veterans could eat their mothers' home-cooked meals for a while and save the government the expense and transport of rations for their men in the field.

Thomas J. Wood returned north during this time as well. The trip really had a double purpose. The first was strictly personal. Caroline Greer Wood gave birth to their first son, William, on January 11, 1864, in Dayton. Their hopes for this child's future were crushed when he died soon after. (There would be two other sons, both born after the war.)

Caroline Wood must have been surprised at the change in the man she had not seen for nearly a year. He was still rail-thin, but gone was the nappy dresser with the coal-black hair. He had grown a beard that extended to the second button of his officer's blouse. It was streaked with gray and the hair of his head had turned almost white. His knee-high boots and worn kepi gave him a more rugged look, as if he had just returned from hard campaigning, which, in fact, he had. Mrs. Wood may have noticed, too, a slight evolution in her husband's attitude. Wood was still a proud man, and he would fight to protect his reputation as a division commander, but his fierce vanity and extreme touchiness had given way in large part to a more mature outlook, a change that was revealed in his testimony before a court of inquiry examining the cases of Generals Alexander McDowell McCook, James Negley, and Thomas L. Crittenden at the Battle of Chickamauga. To appear as a witness was the second reason General Wood had returned north.

The testimony was given in Louisville on February 6, 1864. Wood's comments in each man's case were brief. Regarding McCook, he repeated that McCook had told him he would move into the position in line that would be vacant when Wood went to support Reynolds. He added that he had observed "no want of activity or energy on his part to get his troops into position."[25]

In the case of General Thomas L. Crittenden, Wood said, "He conducted himself during the whole of the time that I saw him properly, both as a soldier and general officer, in my judgment and opinion."[26]

The most anticipated remarks may have been in respect to General Negley, whose behavior Wood had spoken of immediately after the battle in "violent and threatening terms" and whom he had called a "damned poltroon." However, now, five months later, there were no fireworks of any sort. Wood said in the calmest language that he had looked toward Horseshoe Ridge and had seen troops there and was informed that they were Negley's:

> The enemy advanced in very heavy force and we soon became very heavily engaged.... As it was very evident the enemy's force was very superior to the two brigades then with me, I looked to the rear of my then position and toward the position of the troops as already described, with a view of obtaining their assistance in repelling this serious attack, as it was evident that the object of the attack was to get in rear of our main line of battle. I could not see any troops there as they appeared to have withdrawn. The position I was then in was an open one in the valley, and not at all favorable for a small force to repel the attack of a larger one. For the purpose of securing stronger ground I retired my command to the spur which I have already described as having been occupied above. When I reached that position, I found no troops there.

That was the thrust of his comments, no rancor and no condemnation. Simply this: Negley was there, and then Negley was not there. Wood let the court draw its own conclusions.[27]

In the end, the three generals who were the objects of inquiry were cleared of any culpability for the near disaster on September 20. Though Wood was not on trial, he came in for such a heavy share of criticism that it almost seemed he was one of the defendants. Rosecrans insisted repeatedly that Wood had misinterpreted the fatal order. Worse, the court strayed from a simple declaration of their findings in the Negley case to make critical comments of Wood. The court said:

> It appears in the evidence that Brigadier General Wood on one or more occasions at the headquarters of the Army of the Cumberland and in the presence of the commander of that army and a portion of his staff, indulged in severe reflections upon the conduct of Major General Negley, applying to him coarse and offensive epithets. When placed upon the stand before the Court, he failed entirely to substantiate any charge as ground of accusation against him.
>
> The Court deem it their duty to express their marked condemnation of such conduct, leading to vexatious and unprofitable investigation prejudicial to the service.[28]

The court adjourned, and Wood returned to Tennessee. The man who had once bristled at the least criticism accepted the court's reproach without complaint or comment, but if he thought that Chickamauga was put behind him with the reprimand, he was mistakenly optimistic. He and Rosecrans continued to snipe at each other for years over who was to blame for the Confederate breakthrough at Chickamauga and for the rest of Wood's life, like a malaria victim who suffers a yearly recurrence of the fever, he found that Chickamauga was always there, waiting to flare up. There was no getting rid of it.

CHAPTER 15

The Atlanta Campaign

As the weather warmed, Wood's men became more active. On March 24, 1864, for example, Wood informed headquarters, "I will move my camp this afternoon to the vicinity of Powder Spring Gap, for the purpose of keeping on the move, but chiefly to arrange for an excursion into Clinch Valley, opening communication with General [T. T.] Garrard at Cumberland Gap, etc. I will support the movement in that direction with infantry. I will also send some infantry and cavalry up this valley toward Bean's Station." The supply situation still had not been completely resolved. Wood continued, "The cavalry, though coming directly from the railroad, is without any rations; says it has had nothing to eat today. It has a very provident commissariat."[1]

The small maneuvers in the Tennessee mountains were doing nothing to end the war. The 3rd Division was really just marking time until the call came from General Sherman to rendezvous for the beginning of the campaign against Atlanta. In the meantime, the largely pointless marching and riding in East Tennessee would have to suffice. Anyway, the men who had veteranized would not return from their furloughs until the middle of May.

Sherman's summons came during the first week in April. Wood's division was ordered "by easy marches" to Knoxville, thence to Cleveland, thence to Dechard. This was a familiar camp; Wood had camped there during the retrograde from North Alabama in 1862. Chaplain John J. Hight noticed how Decherd had changed because of the hardships of war. He said, "The high fence built by General Wood, to check the advance of rebel cavalry, has been burned. Indeed, most of the fencing in these parts has showed the same fate. Dead mules and horses may be seen by the hundreds. No effort has been made to bury them. The stench is very oppressive in camp. Otherwise, our camp is very pleasant."[2]

From Dechard the division proceeded to Blue Springs and then to Catoosa Springs, Georgia, via Red Clay and Salem Church. They arrived at Catoosa Springs on May 4. A tabulation made of the strength of Wood's 3rd Division at this time showed that he had 9,036 men (counting both artillery and infantry), plus 240 horses and twelve guns. His 1st Brigade was commanded by Brigadier General August Willich. Brigadier General William B. Hazen commanded the 2nd Brigade, and Brigadier General Samuel Beatty commanded the 3rd Brigade. The artillery was commanded by Captain Cullen Bradley. In addition to Wood's division, the two others in the IV Corps were the 1st Division commanded by Major General David S. Stanley and the 2nd Division under Brigadier General John Newton.

A change at the very top of the IV Corps had been made; Major General O. O. Howard now commanded in place of General Gordon Granger. Howard, a West Pointer, was the man who had done so poorly in supporting Wood's attack at Orchard Knob. He had come from the Eastern Theater, where he had fought in the notable battles of the Army of the Potomac. He had not done very well in those battles, either, though he was a personally brave man and had lost his right arm at the Battle of Seven Pines in 1862. Howard was a "Christian Soldier," one of those moral contortionists of a type more commonly found in the Southern armies (Stonewall Jackson was the preeminent example), who spouted Bible verses and practically in the same breath sent thousands of men into battle to kill their fellow man or to be killed. Howard's men called him "Old Prayerbook."

General Howard answered to Sherman, who commanded the Military Department of the Mississippi, but affairs that high in the ether made little difference to the men in the ranks. Of much greater interest to them were their regimental, brigade, and division commanders. Of course, they took pride in serving under the "Rock of Chickamauga," General George H. Thomas, in the Army of the Cumberland.

Besides the Army of the Cumberland, there were two other armies in Sherman's M.D.M.: the Army of the Ohio, commanded by General John M. Schofield; and the Army of the Tennessee, under General James B. McPherson.

The Federals would face a new opponent in 1864. After Missionary Ridge, Braxton Bragg had retreated to Dalton, about twenty-five miles south of Chattanooga. While there, he was relieved. On December 27, 1863, General Joseph E. Johnston assumed command of the Army of Tennessee. Bragg was not humiliated in the change, though; he went to Richmond to become military advisor to President Jefferson Davis. Johnston was genuinely concerned about the welfare of his fifty-five thousand men. He gave his entire army a furlough, one-third at a time. He proclaimed an amnesty for those who were absent without leave. He worked hard to feed and clothe the men in every camp, all of which he personally visited, and was wildly popular as a result. Knowing that activity was another cure for low morale, Johnston also put his men to work fortifying his position around Dalton.

Johnston's position at Dalton was protected in its front by a rugged mountain wall called Rocky Face Ridge. The weak spot was a pass with the unlovely name of Buzzard's Roost Gap. It was so heavily defended as to be practically impregnable. However, a Federal reconnaissance had found that Snake Creek Gap, farther south, was not defended at all. If two of Sherman's armies demonstrated against Buzzard's Roost Gap, then the third could make a quick move against Snake Creek Gap. The Federals would be between the Army of Tennessee and Atlanta and could cut Johnston's railroad supply line, leaving him with no choices but to fight or fly.

Thomas developed the plan for the Snake Creek Gap operation. His Army of the Cumberland was sixty thousand strong and was the presumed choice for the quick strike south. Sherman approved of Thomas' plan. In fact, he liked it so well that he later claimed it as his own, though he made a significant change that showed that the old prejudice against Thomas had not gone east with Grant—Sherman assigned the flanking move to General James B. McPherson and the Army of the Tennessee. McPherson's army, which once had been Grant's and later Sherman's, was smaller, but Sherman told the disappointed Thomas that "the Army of the Tennessee are better marchers than the Army of the Cumberland." Thomas and Schofield were assigned to assault Buzzard's Roost Gap.[3]

May 5 and 6 were spent preparing for the move south. According to the journal of the Atlanta Campaign that was kept by Colonel Joseph S. Fullerton (Assistant Adjutant General, IV Corps), General Thomas ordered his division commanders "to march toward the enemy with as little transportation as possible. Ordered corps, division, and brigade headquarters to move, when orders came, with one wagon each; division to take only enough wagons to carry two days' rations and forage; to take ammunition wagons and wagons with tools.... General Wood [said] that he will require eighty-five [wagons]." The rest of the train would be parked at Salem Church.[4]

The Atlanta Campaign opened at 4:30 A.M. on May 7. Schofield's Army of the Ohio was on the left flank, Thomas was in the center, and McPherson was on the right, poised to move swiftly south. The assignment of Howard's corps was to demonstrate against Tunnel Hill, with Stanley's and Newton's divisions in advance and Wood's in reserve. They discovered that they faced light opposition, only artillery and cavalry. The three divisions made good progress and occupied Tunnel Hill by midday. Here they stopped, although skirmishing continued until sundown. In all of the IV Corps, there were fewer than a half-dozen casualties, though several men were felled by sunstroke.

The IV Corps eased forward through the fog the next morning toward Buzzard's Roost Gap. They skirmished along the way, but once again, the weight of the Federals was too much for the defending Rebels. Colonel Emerson Opdyke's 125th Ohio (now in Harker's 3rd Brigade, 2nd Division, IV Corps) actually gained the top of the narrow ridge and shoved the Rebels back nearly a mile. Later that day, the men learned that McPherson had seized Snake Creek Gap. The plan seemed to be working.

The skirmishing continued on the ninth, while they waited for good news from McPherson. When the news did come, late that night, it was not good. McPherson had cautiously sent only two divisions forward from Snake Creek Gap and found that Rebels occupied works at the important railroad town of Resaca in division strength. McPherson recoiled. He pulled back into the pass and dug in. Sherman, with Thomas in agreement, decided to send all except the IV Corps racing south to reinforce McPherson. They pulled out on May 11. Johnston realized the danger he was in and abandoned Dalton to Howard's corps in order to defend Resaca. He entrenched before the reinforcing Yankees arrived and dared them to attack.

After the IV Corps arrived at Resaca on May 14 and took its place on the left of the Federal line, Sherman accepted Johnston's challenge and ordered an attack. About 1:00 P.M., Wood pushed forward his skirmishers, Stanley advancing simultaneously and Newton shortly afterward.

Wood's 1st and 2nd Brigades advanced in two lines, with the East Fork of Big Camp Creek between them, while the 3rd Brigade was behind in reserve. The way was challenging, a succession of heavily wooded steep ridges, and Willich's brigade, which was on the right of Hazen's, had to cross marshy ground approaching the creek and then the creek itself. The line had not advanced far when the 1st Brigade fell behind.

Hazen's 2nd Brigade hit the Rebels' first defensive line, carried it, and proceeded toward the second line, 250 yards behind and across an open field. About halfway across the clearing, they seized an enemy battery on a small hill, and there they stopped. According to General Wood, "It was problematical whether this line could be carried by even the most determined enemy, such was its natural and artificial strength." Hazen barricaded his position and deployed his sharpshooters, who shot down all the artillerymen and horses they could see. Through the afternoon, this stalemate pertained, while behind the line, engineers cleared a road to the rear to allow the ammunition train to come forward. One of Hooker's brigades was sent to the far left to help throw back an attempt by the Rebels to turn that flank. The sun was going down. Hooker's whole corps moved over to join his detached brigade during the night. Willich came up on Hazen's right, Beatty's brigade stayed in reserve, and the first day of fighting at Resaca ended.[5]

Wood reported that, on the morning of the fifteenth, "an intimation was received from Major-General Howard … that an attack was to be made on the extreme right of the enemy's position by the Twentieth [Hooker's] Corps, accompanied by an order to observe closely its effect on the enemy's center.… Whatever may have been on the enemy's extreme right no material effect therefrom was perceivable in his center."[6]

Though he could see no change in either the enemy's strength or deployment in front of Hazen and Willich, Wood decided to test the center of the butternut line. He sent the 1st and 2nd Brigades forward into a fire so suddenly heavy that Willich and Hazen were quickly withdrawn. Hazen said that the losses in his brigade were 120 men in thirty seconds. Sporadic fire from enemy sharpshooters followed the attempted advance; one of them brought down Brigadier General Willich with a wound that was not mortal but serious enough that he was unable to hold a field command for the rest of the war. Colonel William H. Gibson took Willich's place as commander of the 1st Brigade.

In mid-morning, a sheet of flame erupted along the length of the Confederate line. The Confederate infantry was firing on the Federals to cover the start of their army's withdrawal, and the firing continued all day. Lieutenant Colonel Fullerton wrote in his journal, "There was scarcely any cessation of fire along our whole line, in fact, from daylight until dark." By the morning of the sixteenth, the Confederate trenches at Resaca were empty, the bridges across the Oostanaula River were burning, and General Johnston's army was on its way to Adairsville.[7]

The Federals followed, skirmishing through the day with the Confederate rear guard. The IV Corps camped at Calhoun that night and continued the next morning along the tracks of the Western & Atlantic Railroad. They advanced in a two-division front, Newton's on the left of the railroad and Wood's abreast on the right. Again, there was heavy skirmishing. Howard said, "During this day's march the resistance was unusually great." The enemy rear guard formed in three lines several hundred yards apart, and as the Federals approached, the first line would fire, then pass through to the rear, where they re-formed. The second line would fire, then pass through to the rear, and so on in sequence. The Federals advanced through steady musketry. The Rebels were orderly in their retreat and deadly. There was no doubt that the Rebels knew how to fight; it was rumored that they steeled themselves for battle by drinking whiskey seasoned with a big dose of gunpowder. Even the country was their ally. Lieutenant Colonel Fullerton wrote, "The country along the road was rolling, and covered with dense woods and undergrowth with occasional cultivated fields. It was admirably suited for the movements of the enemy's rear guard, he being able to make a stand every few hundred yards."[8]

The Federal pursuit continued south through Adairsville, Kingston, and Cassville. There was daily skirmishing and some loss of life, but the Rebels would not stand and fight. On the night of June 19, the Army of Tennessee crossed the Etowah River. They fell back to a strong defensive position at Allatoona, where there was a gap through which the Western &Atlantic Railroad passed. Sherman had no appetite for making an attack there. He decided instead to abandon the railroad and try to flank Johnston on the west. Such a maneuver required that tons of supplies of every description be carried along, so for the next three days, while the men enjoyed a rest, Sherman loaded wagons with twenty days' worth of rations, forage, and ammunition. He also sent all the "sick, wounded, and worthless" to the rear, along with the surplus baggage. On Monday, May 23, the Federals crossed the Etowah River and struck for Dallas. Wood's division led the IV Corps. The going was rough, because the men were made to march in the woods adjoining the road and leave the road to the enormous wagon train.[9]

Hooker's corps was in front of Howard's, so it was Fighting Joe's men who first discovered that Johnston had divined Sherman's plan and had left Allatoona Pass to move west to counter the Yankees. Hooker ran into the enemy late on May 25 at a place called New Hope Church, tangled with them there, and soon sent back a request for assistance. Howard sent Newton's division forward to Hooker's right. Darkness put an end to the developing battle. The next morning the Rebels were still in place. Howard ordered a few regiments out of Stanley's division to fill an interval between Newton and Hooker, while the rest of the division was held in reserve. Wood's division took its place on Hooker's flank, bridging Brown's Mill Creek and driving back enemy pickets as it moved into position. The Kentuckian called his maneuver "very brilliant and successful." The bluecoats entrenched and brought their batteries forward, and the two sides traded fire throughout the day. Howard said that the firing was "constant and cost us many men."[10]

It was out of character, but the Rebels were still there behind their works on May 27. Some artillery fire was ordered to probe their strength and, as Wood said, "rendered it evident that a direct front attack would be of most doubtful success, and would certainly cost a great sacrifice of life. Hence, it was determined to attempt to find the extreme right of the enemy's position, turn it, and attack him in flank." General Howard was given the assignment to locate and shatter the Confederate flank. He sent Wood's division and that of General Richard W. Johnson (Palmer's corps) to march far to the east, passing behind the XXIII Corps, to turn south when it was believed they were at the enemy's flank, then go forward and attack. After they had marched south for about a mile "through dense forests and the thickest jungle" and still had encountered no enemy, Howard and Wood decided that they had gone too far east and bypassed the enemy's right flank. They wheeled and marched another mile and a half, then realigned and marched toward the southeast to try to find the Rebel flank. The day was muggy and overcast, so the men could not direct their movements by the sun. Hazen said, "We could keep our direction only by compass." About 2:30, after a day of zigzagging, Howard and Wood believed that they had finally located the hard-to-find flank. They had. The Rebels were preparing their fieldworks even as the Yankees emerged from the woods to where they could see what was before them. This would be no surprise; this would be an attack against a barricaded position.[11]

Almost nothing that has been written about the Battle of Pickett's Mill gives an accurate impression of the difficulty of the terrain. Between Wood's line and that of the enemy was a precipitous ravine eighty feet deep. The bottom was so narrow that a long-legged man could step from one incline to the other. Another, less common name for the battle, the Battle of Allatoona Hills, is more descriptive of what the men faced, for they really were fighting in the foothills of the Appalachians.

It took two hours for Wood to array his men according to orders and for Johnson's division to come up and form on Wood's left. At 4:30, Wood signaled the advance. He had been instructed to advance in six parallel lines. Hazen's brigade made the first two lines. Gibson's 1st Brigade was next, and finally was the 3rd Brigade, now led by Colonel Frederick Kneffler, commanding in place of Brigadier General Beatty, who had been sick since May 23. Hazen's men moved southeast through the jungle, their lines forced into disarray by the trees, and down into the ravine, where they stopped to regroup before surging up the opposite hillside. They ran immediately into devastating enemy fire in their front and on both flanks. The men behind those barricades were the division of General Patrick Cleburne, who had stopped Sherman dead in his tracks at Missionary Ridge and had fought a brilliant rearguard action afterward. If anyone had saved the Army of Tennessee after Chattanooga, it was Cleburne. And now here he was at Pickett's Mill, slaughtering the Yankees with musketry and canister fire. Hazen called the charge of his brigade "one of the most desperate engagements of my experience."[12]

The bluecoats pushed on to within thirty feet of Cleburne's barricades. The men knelt and fired from behind the trees. Johnson's division on the left was giving them no support at all. Hazen's brigade was carrying the battle alone. Ambrose Bierce, who was on Hazen's staff, remembered that "the uproar was deafening.... In the steady, unvarying roar of small-arms the frequent shock of the cannon was rather felt than heard, but the gusts of grape which they blew into the populous woods were audible enough, screaming among the trees and cracking against their stems and branches. We, of course, had no artillery to reply." The fury of the Confederate defense was fierce, but the enfilading fire on Hazen's left was even worse. Wood said, "It was from this fire that the supporting and covering divisions should have protected the assault column, but it failed to do so. Under such a fire, no troops could maintain the vantage ground which had been gained, and the leading brigade ... was compelled to fall back a short distance to secure its flanks, which were crumbling away." Hazen's men — there were five hundred fewer of them now — continued to fire back until their cartridge boxes were empty; they had nearly used up their sixty rounds. He sent back requests for support. None came. The Rebels brought up a fresh brigade and hit both of Hazen's flanks and bent them back. Hazen had to withdraw. As he did, he met Gibson's men coming forward. Hazen's part of the fight had lasted forty minutes and he was bitter about the lack of support. When asked where his brigade was, he answered, "Brigade, hell, I have none." That was an excusable exaggeration, considering the shock of seeing so many of his men shot down. Brigadier General Hazen remained proud of his men and later pointed out that this was his brigade's "first and only unsuccessful effort during the war."[13]

Gibson's men moved forward toward the enemy's works, helped by a knowledge of the ground that Hazen's men had gained. They got no closer than one hundred feet before converging fire from the Rebels' flanks forced them to retire. Like Hazen's brigade before it, Gibson's fired at the enemy until their cartridges were expended. Now it was the 3rd Brigade's turn, but they were not ordered to make an assault on the enemy works, just to relieve the 1st Brigade and maintain their position. "The purpose of holding the ground was to cover bringing off the dead and wounded," said Wood. It was a difficult task in that terrain and in the fading, smoke-filtered light. Kneffler's brigade stayed in line and sustained one more counter-attack. It took nerve to stand their ground. The enemy charged, giving the "demonic" Rebel yell, and Kneffler's men were low on ammunition. They let the enemy get close, then fired a deadly blast into them which broke up the charge and allowed Kneffler and his men to make their withdrawal. The Rebels made no attempt to follow and the Battle of Pickett's Mill sputtered out.[14]

Wood said, "It may be truly said of it that it was the best sustained and altogether the fiercest and most vigorous assault that was made on the enemy's intrenched positions during the entire campaign" and commented that the 3rd Division had made the attack with no artillery support at all. By 2:00 A.M., the dead and wounded men who could be found in that dense tangle of Georgia brush had been removed from the field. The division had sacrificed fourteen hundred men killed, wounded, or missing (only one hundred men were lost out of Johnson's division). More than a third of the 3rd Division casualties were from Hazen's brigade. This hard-fighting general resented that his men did not get the credit they deserved and complained in his autobiography that the Battle of Pickett's Mill "is scarcely noticed in any of the reports of the Union commanders, and is ignored by Sherman in his memoirs."[15]

Ambrose Bierce agreed entirely. He said that Hazen's brigade was a "wreck" after the fight and moaned that Cleburne's Rebels had "destroyed us." Almost as hurtful as memories of the battle was the ingratitude of the commanding generals, who later saw fit to ignore the sacrifice Hazen's men had made. In his essay "The Crime at Pickett's Mill," Bierce complained, "Buried in the official reports of the victors there are indeed imperfect accounts of the engagement.... It is ignored by General Sherman in his memoirs, yet Sherman ordered it [and] General Howard ... dismissed it in a single sentence; yet General Howard planned it."[16]

The survivors of the fight on May 27 remained in camp behind their own breastworks until June 6, locked in a virtual stalemate with General Joe Johnston's determined Confederates.

Most of the reports from this period repeat some variation of the phrase "nothing of consequence." There was a sameness to every day, with no particular landmarks of military glory or cravenness to distinguish one day from the next. The Union armies basically kept their positions, shifting their lines a bit to the left and probing the enemy's lines for weakness. There was daily skirmishing but no progress to speak of. Wood did try a ruse on June 3 to lure the Confederates into an attack. Lieutenant Colonel Fullerton said that the Kentuckian "hid his pickets and skirmishers and struck tents to deceive the enemy and to try and induce him to attack us. The ruse did not succeed, although every appearance was that General Wood had withdrawn from his position."[17]

The gradual Federal shift to the left presented enough of a threat to the Rebels that they moved out of their works at New Hope Church on the night of June 4. The whole next day Howard's corps remained in camp and rested. They marched on the following day, but no serious pursuit occurred until June 14, when the IV Corps and the XIV Corps advanced three-fourths of a mile and pushed the enemy out of his barricades at Pine Mountain. They fell back into their works between Kennesaw Mountain and Lost Mountain. The next morning, Schofield's Army of the Ohio on the Federal right flank and McPherson's Army of the Tennessee on the left pushed the enemy. At 2:00 P.M., Thomas was ordered to pitch in: Hooker on the right, Howard in the center, and Palmer on the left. They advanced a mile through strong opposition to a hill beyond which they could make no progress. In Howard's corps, Newton's division led the attack and suffered most of the casualties. Lieutenant Colonel Fullerton said that night, "The hill that our main line is now on is on the line of ridges that connects Lost Mountain and Kennesaw, and from which the waters flow toward the Chattahoochee." They brought up artillery in the night.[18]

The next day, that artillery was used so effectively that every observer commented on it. It also inflicted upon the Rebels a notable casualty. General Howard wrote, "Here it was that my batteries, opening fire under the direct instruction of Sherman, drove back the enemy from his exposed intrenchments on Pine Top. It was at this time that General [Leonidas] Polk was killed." That night the enemy fell back across Mud Creek toward his fieldworks at Kennesaw Mountain. Wood's division led the IV Corps pursuit the next morning, skirmishing as they advanced. Two more days of unprofitable maneuvering and skirmishing followed. General Thomas thought that he could successfully attack them on the morning of June 19 and ordered his Cumberlanders to launch an assault, but the enemy had already forfeited his lines and had withdrawn into his Kennesaw Mountain barricades. A two-week stalemate followed.[19]

The day before the stalemate began, Sherman off-loaded a wagonful of complaints about the Army of the Cumberland in a letter to his friend Grant. Ignoring Rocky Face Ridge, Resaca, and especially Pickett's Mill, Sherman said, "My chief source of trouble is the Army of the Cumberland, which is dreadfully slow. A fresh furrow in a plowed field will stop the whole column, and all begin to entrench. I have again and again tried to impress on Thomas that we must assail and not defend; we are on the offensive, and yet it seems the whole Army of the Cumberland is so habituated to be on the defensive that, from its commander down to its lowest private, I cannot get it out of their heads."[20]

As had happened after the Battle of Pickett's Mill, the days between June 19 and June 27 were punctuated by frequent skirmishes and artillery duels. Johnston had Sherman at a dead standstill and Uncle Billy finally grew tired of it. He decided that a frontal attack was the answer to his dilemma. McPherson would strike from the north, General Thomas would strike simultaneously a mile to the south, and Schofield would demonstrate against the Confederate left flank farther south. Sherman said in his memoirs that the entire Union battle line was ten miles long.

The attack began at 9:00 A.M. and continued through the day. In the end, it was clear that the experiment with frontal assault had been a flat failure. The total number of Federal casualties amounted to three thousand men killed, wounded, or missing; two-thirds of that number were men from the Army of the Cumberland. General Howard mourned Sherman's reckless expenditure of brave men's lives. In his article about the Atlanta Campaign for *Battles and Leaders of the Civil War*, Howard wrote, "We realized now, as never before, the futility of direct assaults upon intrenched lines already well prepared and well manned."[21]

Wood's only role in the Battle of Kennesaw Mountain had been to hold his division ready to move up in support in order to exploit any success the Cumberlanders might have. "Unfortunately," wrote Wood, "the attack was not successful and as a consequence no part of my division was engaged." The Federals returned to their lines, and the Confederates settled back into their works, and the usual game of probing and skirmishing resumed. A truce was called so that the dead could be buried. The bodies putrefied so quickly in the steamy Georgia heat that the men of the burial parties could not handle them. Instead, the men bent their bayonets into hooks and grappled the softening bodies into their graves. When the men were not on burial details, they were fighting the Rebels across the way. Wood wrote, "Constant skirmishing wore away the second week in front of Kenesaw [sic] Mountain and brought us to Saturday night July 2. On that night the enemy evacuated his position around Kenesaw Mountain, being the eighth strong line of works abandoned, and retreated south of Marietta."[22]

Stanley, Newton, and Wood (in that order) gave chase to the retreating Rebels beginning at 5:00 A.M. on July 3. Later that day, they came too close to the enemy's works at Smyrna and all three divisions had to go into line of battle. Howard remembered that, when Sherman came up on the fourth,

> he could not believe at first that Johnston would make another stand north of the river. "Howard," he said to me, "you are mistaken; there is no force in your front; they are laughing at you!" We were in a thinnish grove of tall trees, in front of a farm-house. "Well, General," I replied, "let us see." I called Stanley, whose division held the front. "General, double your skirmishers and press them." At once it was done. The lines sped forward ... but a sheet of lead instantly came from the hidden works in the edge of the wood beyond us, and several unseen batteries hurled their shot across our lines, some of them reaching our grove and forcing us to retire. Sherman, as he rode away, said that I had been correct in my report.[23]

Johnston was undoubtedly hoping for a repeat of the costly Union assault on Kennesaw Mountain. Sherman had learned a hard lesson at Kennesaw, however, and here at Smyrna he was not going to send his men in to be slaughtered. He had General Thomas demonstrate in Johnston's front while McPherson sneaked around the Confederate flank, but by the time McPherson's men got into position Johnston had figured out the Federal plan and he was gone. The Confederates fell back toward their pre-prepared works at the Chattahoochee River.

By 10:00 A.M. on July 5, Howard's three divisions had advanced five miles and were one mile from the Chattahoochee. At Vining's Station, a stop on the Western & Atlantic Railroad, the Federals captured the stationmaster and learned from him that the enemy was slipping across the river at Pace's Ferry and had been crossing for hours. The Federals hurried forward. A quarter mile beyond Vining's Station, they ran into a heavy line of graycoat skirmishers behind a barricade of rails and crossties. The Yankees drove them away, but at some risk, for friendly artillery rounds from behind were falling among them. At 12:30, said Fullerton, "Hazen's brigade ... drove the enemy across the Chattahoochee, and so hard was he pressed that he could not burn the pontoon bridge over which he crossed, but cut it loose on one side so that it swung across and now he's on the other side of the river."[24]

The enemy established a strong defensive position on the other bank of the river, including sharpshooters and artillery. Wood went into position at a ridge one half mile short of the river crossing, Newton behind and to the left, Stanley on the left flank of Newton. Thomas ordered Howard to try to cross in the morning, and Howard picked Wood. He was ordered to make the attempt at 5:00 A.M. with artillery support.

When morning came, Wood found that the Rebel line was too strong and he could not cross. Later, when Sherman, Thomas, and Howard came forward to examine the position, they decided not to make another attempt to cross the Chattahoochee. The Union troops barricaded in position. They remained there until July 9. During this three-day sojourn, when they were not busy on the firing line, the men and officers liked to go to a nearby hill to enjoy the view. From the top, they could see Atlanta ten miles in the distance.

Since leaving Marietta, Sherman's three columns had shifted from their original configuration. Now McPherson's Army of the Tennessee was on the left flank, Schofield's Army of the Ohio was in the center, and Thomas' Army of the Cumberland was on the right flank. They annoyed the enemy with infantry and artillery fire. Simultaneously, Sherman kept cavalry patrols out, scouting for a place where the armies could cross. They found it near Roswell, where Sope Creek (sometimes given as "Soap Creek") flowed into the Chattahoochee, a crossing place where the Rebels evidently did not anticipate a push. General Schofield quietly brought up his artillery and pontoon boats and plunged forward on July 8. The Rebels were caught completely off-guard, so much so that they fired only a few rifle shots and one artillery round before fleeing. The division of Brigadier General Milo Hascall worked the boats to get the men across, where they established a mile-deep *tete-de-pont* (bridgehead). Stanley's and Wood's divisions supported Schofield, while Newton was sent to support the crossing of General Kenner Garrard's cavalry division (of Hooker's corps). On July 12, the three divisions of IV Corps were reunited. Wood and Stanley crossed the Chattahoochee at Power's Ferry, and Newton crossed the next morning. General Howard said, "There was great animation and manifest joy on our side ... we now firmly believed that the end of the campaign was sure."[25]

The Chattahoochee River was both a physical and a psychic boundary. It was the last topographical feature that the Rebels could use to their advantage in keeping the Federals away from Atlanta. Beyond the river, it was a straight and easy march to the endangered city. In the mind of Jefferson Davis, measuring from his Richmond office the alarming amount of ground that had been lost since the first week in May, the Chattahoochee marked Johnston's last chance to prove that he was going to give the Federals a serious contest for Atlanta. Now he had failed to give battle at the last, best place to stop Sherman, and Davis was furious. Soon, at the Confederate War Department in Richmond, new orders were being drafted for immediate dispatch to the defending army near Atlanta.

Howard's corps spent the next three days in position on the south bank of the Chattahoochee. Wood's men built barricades, while Newton and Stanley's men were detailed to build a trestle bridge a short distance downstream at Pace's Ferry. Thomas' army was the pivot point upon which a great wheel turned; as Thomas held the right and advanced on a straight line toward

Atlanta, McPherson on the far left was ordered to swing east to Decatur and turn south to hit the Georgia Railroad. Schofield, in the center, would make a move corresponding with McPherson's.

On July 17, Wood was ordered to move his division down to Pace's Ferry, as well, to protect the bridge builders from enemy skirmishers and to cover the XIV Corps as it crossed. Howard said, "Owing to the rugged nature of the country, the want of roads, and the proximity of the enemy's masses to Pace's Ferry, Wood's movement was an important and delicate one. It was satisfactorily executed, and without an engagement." Wood's division appeared so suddenly from the woods that the Rebels "scampered off in indelicate haste. They were greatly surprised, and some, who were in the river swimming did not have time to put on their clothes," according to Chaplain Hight of the 58th Indiana. Wood allowed the men an hour to get the bridge laid. It was done, and Wood's division returned to Power's Ferry that night.[26]

The next morning, July 18, the corps broke camp and headed south toward Buckhead. The road was better than any other they had found in Georgia, and the march was uneventful, but for a skirmish with the Rebel rear guard near Nancy's Creek.

About this time, advance units of Schofield's Army of the Ohio came across an Atlanta newspaper a day or two old. They carried it back to Schofield. On the front page was an announcement that surprised them all: General Joseph E. Johnston had been dismissed from command and General John Bell Hood elevated to command in his place. A bit later, when General Sherman came over, Schofield showed him the paper. The red-bearded commander sat in the shade of a persimmon tree while he read the notice about Johnston and then, it is said, looked up and asked, "Schofield, do you know Hood? What sort of fellow is he?"[27]

Indeed, Schofield did know Hood; they had been classmates at West Point, and he had tutored Hood in mathematics there. Schofield said to Sherman, "Yes, I know him well, and I will tell you what sort of a man he is. He'll hit you like hell, now, before you know it."[28]

General Johnston's recall broke the heart of the Army of Tennessee. The Confederate fighting men appreciated the way he had shown his concern for them at Dalton, after the stingy and vindictive (and hated) Bragg relinquished command to go to Richmond. They admired the way in which Johnston conducted his retreats, quietly, orderly, and never leaving behind an artillery piece or any other useful item of equipment. They admired the science with which he constructed his barricades and always inflicted more casualties on the Federals than he suffered. And now he was taken from them. Sam Watkins of the 1st Tennessee Infantry, the most famous Confederate chronicler of events in the Western Theater, wrote in his memoirs that the announcement "came like a flash of lightning, staggering and blinding everyone. It was like applying a lighted match to an immense magazine. It was like the successful gambler, flushed with continual winnings, who staked his all and lost. It was like the end of the Southern Confederacy." Watkins reported that some men, hearing the news, threw down their guns and took off their haversacks and just walked away. He added, "I saw, I will say, thousands of men cry like babies — regular, old-fashioned boohoo, boohoo, boohoo."[29]

Lieutenant General John Bell Hood did not look as if he was able to command. He had lost the use of his left arm at Gettysburg on July 2, 1863, and had suffered the amputation of his right leg after being wounded assaulting Wood's men at Chickamauga on September 20. He was a crippled man, but his fighting spirit, buffered by large doses of laudanum, remained undiminished. Schofield had told Sherman that Hood would "hit you like hell, now." And so he did. On July 20, he hit Thomas' column pretty hard. Wood and Stanley had led their divisions east into the interval between Thomas and Schofield and were two miles away when the Rebels struck. They had no part in the Battle of Peachtree Creek. Their fellow division commander, General John Newton, was not so lucky.

The Confederates first slammed into Thomas' left flank — Newton's division — and continued westward into the corps of Fighting Joe Hooker: the divisions of William T. Ward, John W. Geary, and, finally, Alpheus Williams. The fighting was vicious across that broad front. It was after dark before the Federals were able to silence the attacking Confederates. Hood's first try at the Federals had ended in costly defeat.

The other two armies had continued moving toward Decatur, opposed lightly by General Joe Wheeler's cavalry, and while the fighting raged in Thomas' sector they were busy tearing up the Georgia Railroad. Having failed in his attempt to crush the Federal right flank, Hood now decided to try his luck against the left. He believed that McPherson had left his flank in the air, and he sent General B. F. Cheatham to pin down McPherson's front while General William Hardee made a long, looping march to strike hard at the exposed flank. A similar tactic had given General Lee a victory over Joe Hooker at Chancellorsville.

McPherson was conferring with his corps commanders when the attack began. He rode off toward the sound of the guns and ended up within rifle range of a whole host of Confederate infantrymen. Before the young general could gallop away, a Rebel bullet plowed through his body and he fell mortally wounded from his horse.

The Rebels were doing better here, at what came to be called the Battle of Atlanta, than they had done against Newton and Hooker at Peachtree Creek, and McPherson's men were in trouble. Elements of Schofield's army on the near right were ordered forward in support. When Cheatham's Rebels blew a hole through the Federal line, Schofield's capable gunners made deadly use of their artillery, drove the attackers back, and restored the line. This happened late in the battle, about 4:00 P.M. The attack sputtered out. The Federal line had held and Hood was defeated again, defeated badly, for he had gambled almost all he had on this attempt and had lost eight thousand men whom he could not replace. Even the Georgia militia had been sacrificed. Hood's two attacks so far had cost him thirteen thousand men.

The death of McPherson had an unanticipated effect on the leadership in the Army of the Cumberland. To replace him, General Sherman called upon General Howard, who in turn relinquished command of the IV Corps to General David S. Stanley. The Richmond, Virginia, newspapers reported that General Wood had been killed in the Battle of Atlanta. That was wishful thinking on their part — he had not even been engaged. Wood lived, but once again, he had had been passed over. However, providing another example of his growing maturity since the Battle of Chickamauga, he did not react with the same bitterness as he had done earlier on such occasions. This was not the case with General Joseph Hooker, who ranked Howard and believed that he was entitled to command the Army of the Tennessee. When General Sherman gave the nod to Howard instead, Hooker resigned.

To replace General Stanley as head of the 1st Division, Thomas chose Colonel William Grose, who was soon succeeded by Brigadier General Nathan Kimball.

By July 23, the Federals were close enough that they could begin to throw shells into Atlanta. The nightly barrages were so beautiful that Colonel Emerson Opdyke said that he could hardly make himself go to bed. The Confederate gunners inside the city's defenses responded with spirit, even though they were running low on ammunition. During artillery duels, the Federals found that spikes, window weights, files, padlocks, horseshoes, and even pieces of coffee mills were raining down on them.

Atlanta was running out of everything. The Western & Atlantic Railroad was in Sherman's hands. The Georgia Railroad was destroyed by Schofield and the late McPherson. The railroad that connected Atlanta with Montgomery, Alabama, was broken by Major General Lovell Harrison Rousseau in a daring raid through the heart of Alabama. The only lifeline left to Atlanta was the Macon & Western Railroad, which ran south out of Atlanta to Macon before turning in the direction of Savannah. To break it, Sherman sent two different cavalry strikes, one under Brigadier General Edward M. McCook and the other under Brigadier General George Stoneman. Sherman also initiated a cumbersome shift of his infantry forces. The Army of the Tennessee was to leave its position on the left flank, march behind Schofield and Thomas in a wide arc, and end up on the west side of Atlanta, where it would turn south and move down the east bank of the Chattahoochee River toward Ezra Church. Its ultimate destination was Jonesboro and the Macon & Western Railroad. The army had already begun its march to the right flank when Howard joined it as its new commander.

At midday on the twenty-eighth, a new Southern corps commander named Lieutenant General Stephen D. Lee came crashing into Howard's position at Ezra Church. Both Lee and Howard were freshly promoted, and each wanted to prove his worth the first time out. So, a series of determined charges was met by a series of equally determined repulses. When it was all over at the end of the day, there were an estimated three thousand Confederate casualties and six hundred casualties on the Union side. Some observers noted that each charge had less force behind it than the one before. Hood's punches were losing their power. Colonel Emerson Opdyke wrote, "Hood is getting his army knocked to pieces rapidly: their own papers own to a loss of twenty-three thousand in the battles of the 20th and 22nd. I hope Hood may be retained in Command."[30]

On August 1, General Schofield moved to join the Army of the Tennessee on the railroad west of Atlanta and left the Army of the Cumberland on the left flank of the Union line. The XIV Corps moved in the same direction on August 3, weakening the vulnerable left. An attack on Wood's front was anticipated. A reconnaissance was ordered to try to determine the enemy's intentions; if the Secesh flank was found to be weak enough, Wood was authorized to turn the reconnaissance into a full attack. The action never developed into anything more than a heavy skirmish, which cost Wood forty men. In the subsequent days, the division commanders were ordered to do all that they could to create the impression that they were a much larger force than was actually the case. They were told to make the camps as lively as possible and to march their men in areas where the observing Rebels would catch only a glimpse before the men in blue disappeared again in the trees or behind a hill, only to make a circle and march across the Rebels' line of sight for a second, a third, and a fourth time.

Each day that followed was enlivened by sharp skirmishing and demonstrations to support yet another cavalry raid against the Macon & Western Railroad. Sherman had sent Brigadier General Judson Kilpatrick on August 18 to strike the railroad at Jonesboro, but his raid was so ineffective that trains were pulling into Atlanta just one day after Kilpatrick returned to camp on August 22. Of all the cavalry operations launched against the Confederate railroads supplying Atlanta, only that of Major General Lovell Harrison Rousseau had been successful. Sherman came to believe that cavalry alone was not up to the work; he would have to depend on the artillery and infantry to perfect the isolation of Atlanta. That being so, Sherman ordered the IV Corps to move to the west and join the bulk of the army there. Wood wrote, "Silently and quietly the troops drew out from the immediate presence of the enemy undiscovered."[31]

Wood's division reached its assigned position on August 31 and the next morning joined in the work of demolishing the railroad. The men did not labor with their crowbars very long, though, before they were ordered to pick up their rifles again and proceed to Jonesboro. A battle was raging there. Generals William Hardee and Stephen D. Lee were trying to block General Howard from making a lodgment on Atlanta's last link to the outside world. The Federals proved too strong for them, and the Rebel defenses were shattered. The tattered butternut remnants fell back to form another battle line while a courier carried the news of the Jonesboro defeat to Hood.

Even Hood, a man not overburdened with intellect, could realize that, without a single railroad to serve it, the city of Atlanta was lost. Before dark on that very day, the Confederates began evacuating the city. As they left, Atlanta's Rebel defenders set fire to eighty-one boxcar loads of ammunition, which detonated in the night with a colossal explosion, blown to atoms, just like their hopes.

The next morning, September 2, the IV Corps moved out to look for the Rebel works. They found the works at noon. The Confederates had stopped at Lovejoy to make a stand, one last stand that would give Hood another day to complete his evacuation of Atlanta.

The men went into battle formation, with Newton on the right, Wood in the center, and Kimball on the left. There was a delay while the Army of the Tennessee, who would advance with the IV and XIV Corps, got into position. The attack stepped off at 3:30 P.M. Wood and Kimball found the ground in their front to be very difficult ("the most unfavorable that can be conceived," Wood said). It was near the head of a small creek and was marshy and full of gullies. So bad was it that their two divisions did not reach the enemy until 6:00 P.M.[32]

Wood described what happened next:

> Having arrived near the enemy's works, and while the troops were halted to readjust the lines, I became satisfied that the most favorable point for attack in front of my division was in front of my left (or Third) brigade.... Thinking we had arrived at on near the right flank of the enemy's line, I went toward the left to concert with the two brigade commanders next on my left for a simultaneous attack. To reach them I had to pass over an open space which was swept by a sharp fire of musketry from the enemy's works. I crossed this space safely in going over, saw the two brigade commanders, and made the necessary arrangements. As I was retiring across the dangerous space, I was struck down by a rifle shot.[33]

The bullet splintered the bones and shredded the muscles in General Wood's left foot, the same foot that had been so badly wounded at the Battle of Murfreesboro. Though bleeding and surely sick with pain, Wood remained on the field and ordered the attack to commence. The men stepped forward at his command and there was a bit of fighting. They took the first line of CSA defenses but soon ran into heavy artillery fire, and that stopped their forward momentum. Darkness was falling fast and the battle never really developed.

That night Hood's Rebels completed their withdrawal from Atlanta, and the next morning Mayor James Calhoun and municipal office holders came to the Federal lines to surrender their city. Wood's division remained in the field and endured some skirmishing until September 8, when they moved into Atlanta.

In the months of May through September, the 3rd Division of the IV Corps had been under almost constant fire, and the casualties piled up. In the 3rd Division, the killed, wounded, and missing amounted to 2,751, which was more than in any other division of the IV Corps. In comparison, the 1st Division had lost approximately 1,825 men and the 2nd Division had lost 2,622. It had been a campaign unlike any other these Federals of the West had seen or would see again.

In summarizing the Atlanta Campaign, General Wood said:

> If the length of the campaign, commencing on the 3d of May and terminating on the 2d of September, with its ceaseless toil and labor, be considered; if the number and extent of its actual battles and separate conflicts and the great number of days the troops were in the immediate presence of, and under a close fire from, the enemy be remembered; if the vast amount of labor expended in the construction of intrenchments and other necessary works be estimated; if the bold, brilliant, and successful flank movements made in close proximity to a powerful enemy be critically examined, and if the long line of communications over which vast and abundant supplies of every kind for the use of this great army be regarded, it must be admitted that the late campaign stands without a parallel in military history.[34]

Its Deep South sequel, the legendary March to the Sea, was a mere stroll by comparison. Army commander Thomas, corps commander Stanley, and division commander Wood would have no role to play in that. But there was an Upper South sequel to the Atlanta Campaign, as well. And in that sequel, they would be in the very center of the fighting, facing John Bell Hood once again.

Chapter 16

Nashville

After Sherman occupied Atlanta, he spent his time in outfitting and resting his army and transforming the battered town into a supply base and a vast encampment for the exclusive use of the military. To that end, he banished all civilians from the city. It was an unpopular order, one that was vigorously protested by Mayor James Calhoun and others. Their appeals to humanity did not sway the general. He wanted full use of the city, its resources, its buildings, and its railroads, and the citizens were made to leave. Sherman did offer to make the removal of the civilians "as easy and comfortable as possible" but would not rescind his order. He wrote to Calhoun, "You cannot qualify war in any harsher terms that I will. War is cruelty, and you cannot refine it: and those who brought war into our country deserve all the curses and maledictions a people can pour out." While the brokenhearted and hate-filled Southerners prepared to leave, the occupying soldiers enjoyed sightseeing and other pleasures. Barbershops and bakeries opened. The mail caught up with the troops. New uniforms were issued. And every night the regimental bands performed concerts.[1]

Of course, there were thousands of soldiers stationed outside the city, as well. Stanley's IV Corps camped about two miles east of Atlanta near the Georgia Railroad. There had been a shake-up at the top of the Army of the Cumberland. General Thomas had been sent to Tennessee to deal with Nathan Bedford Forrest, who was making mischief along the railroads. In Thomas' absence, General David S. Stanley was commanding the Army of the Cumberland, as well as his own IV Corps.

Mostly the enemy was quiet. Then, on October 2, 1864, word came to Stanley's headquarters to quickly prepare his corps to march to Marietta. Hood had been on the move since September 28, screened by his cavalry and stepping off so rapidly that he had forty thousand men across the Chattahoochee by the end of the day on October 1. He was pushing hard for the north, his obvious target Sherman's lifeline, the Western & Atlantic Railroad.

The IV Corps moved out at 5:00 A.M. on October 3. The men were well rested and well fed and they marched rapidly. They were at Smyrna that night and at Kennesaw Mountain the night after that. They passed by Pine Mountain, Cartersville, and Kingston over the next week. All around them, they could see the harm that Hood was doing, the uprooted railroad tracks and the burned supplies. There were a few clashes between the butternut rear guard and the Federal vanguard, but mostly these were only jabs. General Sherman could not put together the crushing combination that would put General Hood out of business. Hood was controlling the action. He fought when he wanted to fight and disengaged when he wanted to disengage, and he moved so quickly that Sherman could not catch up. His men were trying, though. Some days they marched a staggering twenty miles.

To the Federals, it must have been a peculiar thing to chase Hood over the same route and across the same battlefields that they had won at such a cost of blood and time only a few months earlier. On the fourteenth, they reached Resaca. They were almost back at the starting point, and it looked as if they were going to have another battle there. On the fifteenth, they received a report that the Rebels had turned and were in position to make a fight at Snake Creek Gap. The IV Corps and the XIV Corps deployed for battle and moved forward, only to find that the report was false. The Rebels were gone. The IV Corps pushed on toward Dalton.

The next morning, they received another report that Hood had turned sharply west and was heading toward the Alabama line. This time, the report was true. The long blue column pursued him cross-country, cutting a road through the woods, toward Villanow. It was there that General Wood returned to active field duty.

After the fall of Atlanta, Wood's name was floated once again for promotion to major general. General Sherman recommended it in a dispatch to Halleck. General Stanley recommended all three of his division commanders — Newton, Kimball, and Wood — for promotion to major general but went further in the case of Wood by pointing out that his claim for promotion was the strongest, considering his service with the Army of the Cumberland since its organization and the fact that he had fought in every one of its battles. The testimonials of his superiors had no effect; Wood was not promoted. At the time, he was still recuperating from the wound in his foot and was not even in command of his own division. Since Lovejoy, Colonel P. Sidney Post had commanded the 3rd Division.

That changed on October 17 at Villanow, when Wood called on the headquarters of the IV Corps. He was still on crutches and his wounded foot was wrapped in a buffalo robe in lieu of the boot that he could not fit over the bandages. He had come to say that he was well enough recovered to resume active service.

General Stanley did not quibble with the Kentuckian's self-diagnosis. Glad to get some relief from the double duty of commanding that part of the Army of the Cumberland that was still in Georgia as well the IV Corps, Stanley offered temporary command of the IV Corps to Wood, who accepted.

Wood was with his corps the next morning, his crutches strapped to the saddle, when they moved out toward La Fayette. Beyond there, they turned south and followed General Hood in the direction of Summerville. They had to stop en route to rebuild a bridge and did not reach Summerville until October 19. They learned there that Hood was still twenty-five miles ahead of them. They marched the next morning for Gaylesville, across the Alabama line, and it was there that Sherman ordered an end to this senseless chase. Hood was gone. He had vanished into the wilds of North Alabama, and Sherman had no further interest in him. Uncle Billy was planning his March to the Sea, trying to persuade Grant of the wisdom of it, and as far as he was concerned, Hood was now General Thomas' problem. He told Thomas by wire that he was going to send him the IV Corps, two divisions of the XVI Corps (currently in Missouri), General John Schofield with the XXIII Corps, and James H. Wilson's cavalry. Sherman temporarily moved his headquarters to Kingston to contemplate how he would make Georgia howl, and the men assigned to Thomas moved toward Chattanooga to continue their journey by train.

On October 27, General Stanley resumed command of the IV Corps and General Wood returned to the 3rd Division, and they reached Chattanooga two days later. From there, they did not proceed directly to Nashville. To block Hood, who had not yet crossed the Tennessee River, they turned west and traveled through Bridgeport, Huntsville, and Decatur, Alabama, in a huge convoy of trains. Each brigade required three locomotives and thirty-six cars. On October 31, they detrained at Athens and were ordered to move immediately to Pulaski, Tennessee, and to prepare for a "stubborn defense." They forded the Elk River very early on the morning of November 1 and reached Pulaski at 4:00 P.M. They had outdistanced their wagon train, and General Stanley requested of Thomas, "Please direct the medical purveyor at Nashville to send to Pulaski medical and hospital supplies, such as chloroform, stimulants, opiates, dressings, blankets, etc. The hospital and ambulances, etc. of this corps will not be up for several days. In case of an engagement these supplies will be needed."[2]

The IV Corps may have left their train behind, but they had their digging tools. Beginning the next morning and continuing over the next several days, the 3rd Division was assigned to construct Pulaski's defenses. Looking at the defenses with an engineer's eye, Wood said, "When completed, the works were impregnable; the Fourth Corps could have easily held them against the entire rebel army commanded by General Hood." One feature of the defense was a set of three dams across a small creek, causing one approach to the Federal position to be flooded with ten feet of standing water. The attacking Confederates were going to have a very difficult time of it at Pulaski. The defensive works were even more daunting after Wood's artillery arrived on November 12.[3]

If the IV Corps could delay Hood, they would give General Thomas in Nashville the time to gather his far-flung forces and patch together a defense. Sherman had taken many of the more experienced troops and most of the good cavalry mounts with him for his (largely unopposed) jaunt across Georgia. General Wilson was sending details as far north as Louisville to requisition horses for his cavalry, and Thomas was organizing a hodgepodge consisting of Nashville's non-combatants, the ambulatory wounded, new volunteers, some regiments of the USCT, and units coming in slowly from Missouri (two divisions under General A. J. Smith), Kentucky, and elsewhere.

In the middle of the alarm of November 1864, Wood received a gift from Major General Lovell Harrison Rousseau, who was the commander of the District of Tennessee. Rousseau had been assigned to the defense of Murfreesboro during the present crisis. In civilian life, Rousseau was a lawyer and a sometime officerholder, and in the fall of 1864 he was a candidate for one of Kentucky's U.S. Senate seats. Senators were at that time appointed by the various state legislatures, and while Rousseau was in the field friends like the influential Speed brothers in Louisville were working on his behalf. Rousseau may have been genuinely fond of General Wood, but he was also trying to solicit help from those acquaintances who might have some influence in Kentucky's politics. Wood came from one such family, particularly considering the high profile of his father, so it was not surprising that Rousseau found the time to cultivate Wood's favor with a gift that he knew his fellow Kentuckian would appreciate. Wood acknowledged the present in a letter from Pulaski dated November 19, 1864. He said:

> The *box* came safely to hand this morning, though the train met with an accident yesterday. It would have been a pity for such good stuff to have been lost. I have this morning distributed the bottles as marked.
>
> General Johnson was in my quarters when the box was received and opened and the morning being *some* wet, we wisely concluded an anti-fogmatic would not be out of place, so poured the bourbon and found it *good*.
>
> Accept my thanks for your thoughtful contribution to our comfort.[4]

Wood promised in the conclusion to his letter to "do all I can in your behalf. Let me hear from you giving your views and opinions how we can best operate." He signed it, "Truly Your Friend, Th: J. Wood."[5]

Politics and Kentucky bourbon were only a brief respite from the war. On November 13, General Schofield came to Pulaski (with Brigadier General Jacob D. Cox's 3rd Division of the XXIII Corps) and assumed command of all the forces there. Information was coming into the camp all the time that Hood's Confederates were on the move. Their numbers included ten thousand cavalrymen under Nathan Bedford Forrest. By November 22, it was confirmed; Hood was twenty miles west of Pulaski at Lawrenceburg and had a good turnpike to Columbia. Schofield ordered the 3rd Division of the XXIII Corps and the 2nd Division of the IV Corps to move north to Lynnville to be in position to oppose the advance. The next day, the 1st and 3rd Divisions left their handsome, never-defended works at Pulaski and followed the 2nd Division to Lynnville.

Lynnville was not quite far enough. Wood later recalled, "Information received during the night at Lynnville indicated that the enemy was rapidly advancing on Columbia and would probably reach that place on the 24th. This would have placed him between us and Nashville."[6]

The situation was critical. The Federals must get ahead of Hood or be cut off. Schofield got General Cox's division in motion about midnight. An hour later, the IV Corps began to move. The race to Columbia was on. By late morning, the 2nd Division and Wood's 3rd Division were approaching Columbia, and they could hear firing from that direction — Cox was fighting the head of the Confederate column. When the IV Corps men got a bit closer, Rebel cavalrymen swooped down on them. Wood threw a regiment forward and shoved the horse soldiers back. The corps reached Columbia and deployed for battle. Brigadier General George D. Wagner's 2nd Division was on the right, Wood's 3rd in the center, and Brigadier General Walter Whitaker's 1st (which had been behind with the artillery brigade and the wagon train and was the last to arrive) on the left. The defensive line was thin. Wood said that his division was "now stretched out like a [sic] India rubber string," and there was a worrisome gap between the IV Corps and Cox's division on the far right. The men burrowed in to improve their position as best they could. Then they waited.[7]

Within a couple of days, Schofield determined that his four-division force was inadequate to the task. He had been reinforced by one brigade and two regiments of the XXIII Corps under the command of General Thomas H. Ruger, but even so, the Confederate line was longer than that of the Federals. In addition, the Duck River "could easily be crossed, above or below the town." That being the case, "Orders were given to withdraw to the north side on the night of the 26th, but a heavy storm prevented. The next night the crossing was made, the railroad bridge burned, and the pontoon boats were scuttled. This was an all-night job; the last of the pickets crossing at 5 in the morning." As time-consuming as the crossing had been, it was fortunate that the enemy had not tried to hinder the crossing of the Duck River.[8]

The next day Forrest got his cavalry across to the north bank and clashed with the Union horsemen, forcing them back. Fearing that Hood's infantry would soon follow, Schofield gave orders to retire toward Franklin beginning at 8:00 A.M. on the twenty-ninth. Once more, good timing saved them, but just barely, for a Rebel corps (spearheaded, ominously, by General Patrick Cleburne's division of General B. F. Cheatham's corps) was reported even then to be making their own crossing. Schofield ordered his column to begin moving with all of their wagons, ambulances, and artillery. Colonel P. Sidney Post, commanding the 2nd Brigade of Wood's division, was sent on a reconnaissance to keep watch on the enemy, and he confirmed that the Rebels were across.

Wagner's division took the lead on the march to Franklin, followed by Kimball, Ruger, and Wood, whose division was detailed to guard the train as it crept along in the rear. Cox remained behind to hold the crossing at Columbia. He followed after nightfall.

Hood had hoped that his crossing of the Duck River could be kept quiet. General Forrest had clashed with General James Wilson's cavalry and had driven them far to the north, and Hood thought that Schofield was traveling blind. The crippled Confederate had not counted on Colonel Post, who kept the Federal column well informed through the day about the enemy's movements. The graybacks, reported Post, were headed north in force, moving along a parallel route a few miles to the east.

Wagner's division arrived at Spring Hill shortly after noon. The town garrison — two regiments — was already under attack by Brigadier General Abraham Buford's cavalry. It appeared that the Rebels had won this race. Wagner threw Colonel Emerson Opdyke's brigade into the fight. The Union infantry pushed the Rebel cavalry back, while the rest of the 2nd Division deployed east of the road and parallel to it to keep the route to Nashville open. They made a barricade of fence rails and waited, skirmishing through the afternoon but holding their ground.

At 4:30, Cleburne's division appeared in their front. They were across a wide cornfield, and the afternoon sun was in their faces as they began their advance. The Yankee fieldpieces drove them back. The Federals were gathering, but so were the Confederates. Cleburne was joined by another division and they combined forces to try the Federals again, and again the attackers were repulsed. By now it was getting late and they did not make another try. Instead, they bivouacked in position, well east of the turnpike. Hood had decided to wait until morning to make a new attack. There was no sign that the Federals were going anywhere.

Even so, it would have been prudent for the crippled general to make sure that his men, Cleburne's or Buford's or *somebody's*, made a move beyond the Yankee left to block the turnpike to Nashville. Somehow, incredibly, he did not. The road to Nashville was left wide open. There never has been any sensible answer as to why such a simple precaution was neglected when the stakes were so high. Shelby Foote quotes a Rebel who said, "The most charitable explanation is that the gods of War injected confusion into the heads of our leaders."⁹

The Federals did not pause to question their supernatural good luck or to thank the gods of war. They began to move, with Cox's division in the lead, followed by Wood and Kimball. Wood had missed all of the excitement of the afternoon. As a guard for that enormous train of five hundred wagons, his division had to creep along, and they did not reach Spring Hill until midnight. The men had only a moment to rest. They turned the protection of the train over to Kimball's division, then fell in behind the marching column. Wood said, "It was necessary to move the troops rapidly and silently through Spring Hill to avoid a night attack from an entire corps of four divisions — Cheatham's — which lay encamped within 800 yards of the road. The effect of a night attack on a column en route would have been, beyond doubt, disastrous. The embarrassment of the situation was greatly increased by the presence of the large number of wagons, artillery carriages, etc which had to be protected and quietly withdrawn." Wagner's division remained in position to cover the Federal withdrawal. Only when all the others had cleared the town did Wagner's division leave Spring Hill and the sleeping Confederates behind.¹⁰

The Rebel cavalry were the only men in gray who were still awake, and they made a swipe at the wagon train after it had gone only about two miles from town. This might have been the disaster that General Wood dreaded, but his skirmishers and Kimball's responded with alacrity and threw the Confederates back. The butternut cavalry repeatedly flailed at the trailing brigade (Opdyke's) of Wagner's rear guard, who kept whipping them back. Henry Stone wrote, "So efficiently did his [Opdyke's] admirable brigade do its work, though surrounded by a cloud of the enemy's cavalry, which made frequent dashes at his lines, not a straggler nor a wagon was left behind."¹¹

The column began to reach Franklin about 9:00 A.M. on November 30. An hour later Stanley came in with the IV Corps, and two hours after that the rear guard made it safely to town. The bridges across the Harpeth River were down, and Schofield began digging in while his engineers laid a new deck on the stringers of the railroad bridge and began preparing a bridge for the foot soldiers.

When the railroad bridge was floored, Schofield ordered Wood to cross to the north bank with the wheeled conveyances and some of the artillery. He took position on a hill overlooking the town and the growing Union works. When a report reached Schofield about 1:00 P.M. that the Rebs were crossing the Harpeth River upstream, he ordered Wood to be alert and to protect the wagons. Wilson's cavalry was on the north side of the Harpeth, so Wood was not entirely isolated. Schofield established his headquarters on the north bank of the Harpeth, also, and left General Cox in command of the forces south of the river.

By mid-afternoon, the fieldworks south of Franklin were finished. A bend in the river made it possible for the Yankees to anchor both their right and left flanks on the river. On the right flank was Kimball's division of the IV Corps, in the center was General Thomas H. Ruger's oversized brigade, and on the left was General Cox's own division. Colonel Opdyke's brigade was held in reserve behind the brick home of F. B. Carter. The other two brigades of Wagner's hardworking division were left about two miles south of town to hinder Hood's troops when they showed up, which they did about noon. Wagner's position was not a good one. The country was open, perfectly suitable to flanking movements, and when Wagner saw those long enemy lines appear before him he began almost immediately to think of retiring. He fell back to a position astride the turnpike about one-third of a mile out of town. There he waited.

There was a pause in the action while General Hood pondered what his move should be. He was enraged that the Yankees had been allowed to escape the trap at Spring Hill, blamed his generals for it, and was in no mood for any fancy West Point tactics. He wanted a heads-down slugfest. And he thought that his officers and men needed it. In his opinion, they had grown timid, too accustomed to fighting behind barricades, and they needed to be reacquainted with the discipline needed for a headlong attack. It was exactly the same reasoning that had prompted General Sherman to order a frontal attack against the entrenched Confederates at Kennesaw Mountain. Hood's generals tried to talk him out of it. They could not see the wisdom in attacking the Yankees across open ground, particularly considering that they had no artillery with them. Knowing that artillery was a ponderous burden to a marching army, Hood had ordered that the cannon be left behind. The attack was to be made without the help of the big guns. Cheatham and the others tried to reason with Hood, but they had taken an awful tongue-lashing that morning because of the Spring Hill debacle and they did not object to the simpleminded plan as strongly as they might have on another day. Bold Nathan Bedford Forrest was the most insistent. He pressed Hood for the chance to augment his cavalry with an infantry division and flank the Yankees out of their works. The general would not listen. It was to be a frontal attack.

The attack stepped off a few minutes before four o'clock. Patrick Cleburne's division was in the center of the attack, coming straight up the turnpike. If the Yankees could see him, on horseback amid his men, they would have noticed that his feet in the stirrups were bare; he had given his boots to one of his infantrymen who had no shoes in which to make charge.

Sam Watkins of the 1st Tennessee was one of the advancing Rebels and he recalled, "A sheet of fire was poured into our very faces, and for a moment we halted as if in despair, as the terrible avalanche of shot and shell laid low those brave and gallant heroes, whose bleeding wounds attested that the struggle would be desperate.... The air loaded with death-dealing missiles.... It seemed that the very elements of heaven and earth were in one mighty uproar."[12]

Wagner's men resisted as well as they could, but it was hopeless. Wood watched it from a distance and reported, "Unwilling to abandon their position as long as there was any probability of maintaining it, unfortunately, the gallant commanders remained in front too long, and as a consequence, when they did retire, they were followed so closely by the enemy as to enter the works through the break which had been caused by ... the retiring brigade." The charging Confederates being so close to Wagner's men and even intermingled with them, the Yankees in the trenches hesitated to fire, and that, too, helped the graybacks gain a lodgment in the works.[13]

When he saw the Rebels break the Union center, General Schofield became convinced that the battle was lost; the defenders would soon be trying to cross the river and the Confederates would be right behind them. He deployed Wood's 3rd Division on the north bank: Beatty was upstream from the town, Streight was immediately opposite the town, and Post was a short distance downstream. Schofield should have had more faith in General Cox and in the fighting men in the ranks.

The Rebels had created a hole as wide as a regiment's front in the Union line and even seized two four-gun artillery batteries, only to find that they could not exploit their gain. They had no friction primers for the cannon. Opdyke's brigade of reserves (strengthened by the addition of two regiments, the 12th and 16th Kentucky) charged down on them. Opdyke wrote, "Thank God the 1st Brigade proved irresistible, the breastworks were ours, and several hundred prisoners, and ten rebel battle flags were their trophies." Those Confederates who were not killed or captured fell back out of the trenches, but the battle was not anywhere near over. "On came fresh columns of the enemy and the musketry exceeded anything I ever heard; the powder smoke darkened the sunlight. The 125th Ohio retook two guns and worked them without the expert help of a single artilleryman."[14]

Henry Stone recalled, "General Cox was everywhere present, encouraging and cheering on his men. General Stanley, who, from the fort where he had gone with General Schofield, had seen the opening clash, galloped to the front as soon as possible and did all that a brave man could do until he was painfully wounded." Stanley, the only Union general to be wounded, was shot through the neck and would soon have to relinquish command of the IV Corps.[15]

No one knew exactly how many charges were made as the weak winter sun went down. One estimate puts the number of charges as high as seventeen. Lieutenant Colonel Fullerton thought that there were at least four main assaults and a half-dozen lesser ones. What everyone did agree on was that the Rebels were slaughtered by the thousands, and yet they still tried. The attacks continued even after darkness fell, and each one was repulsed. At the end, the

Confederates were not even aiming; they were simply lying on one side of the barricades and shooting blindly with their muskets into the Yankees huddled in the trench on the other side. About 9:00 P.M., the battle began to wind down. The Rebels had had enough. They had sustained close to seven thousand casualties, including twelve generals, six of whom died of their wounds. One of the dead was General Patrick Cleburne, killed near Mr. Carter's cotton gin. Sam Watkins wrote that Franklin "was the grand coronation of death."[16]

The Federal losses were only about one-third of those of their opponents. That night, just about midnight, the victors of the Battle of Franklin began to withdraw toward Nashville. Their wagons on the north bank had already started north. The Rebels had set fire to some of the houses in town to light the scene, but darkness was the Federals' friend and, according to General George H. Thomas' report, General Wood and some others got a fire engine from the town and extinguished the fires. The Rebels tried no further tricks and offered little resistance to the escaping Federals. As the infantrymen crossed on the pontoon and railroad bridges, Wood's three brigades stayed in position, as Schofield had deployed them, to cover the withdrawal. By 3:00 A.M., the last of the troops had crossed to the north bank. They set fire to the bridges. Wood's division fell in at the tail end of the column and reached Nashville at ten o'clock the next morning, December 1.

Wood assumed command of the IV Corps on December 2 and turned over command of the 3rd Division to General Samuel Beatty. The IV Corps took position just right of the center of General Thomas' line. Wood wrote, "As the condition of the forces was not such as to warrant the commencement of offensive operations immediately, the first duty to be provided for was the safety of Nashville against assault. For this purpose, a line of strong intrenchments, strengthened with an abatis, slashes of timber, and pointed stakes firmly planted in the ground, was constructed along the entire front of the corps." The two-mile line stretched across Granny White and Hillsboro Pikes. To man his works, Wood had slightly over sixteen thousand effectives under his immediate command.[17]

Wood was still on crutches (he would be until May) and still went about with his left foot swaddled in a buffalo robe. He needed a comfortable home in which to make his headquarters. He found it at Belmont, the Italianate mansion of Mrs. Adelicia Acklin. Mrs. Acklin was the widow of Joseph Acklin and a canny businesswoman in her own right. Earlier that same year of 1864, she had arranged a cotton deal that earned her $900,000 in gold. She was obviously not a timid belle, but a houseful of Yankee officers was more than her sensibilities could bear. When General Wood and his twenty-man staff moved in, Mrs. Acklin and her children moved out. She may have gone to the downtown home of her friend Mrs. Sarah C. Polk, the widow of President

James K. Polk. To help guard against outrages on her home, Mrs. Acklin left behind her late husband's niece, Sallie Acklin. Miss Sallie was a great favorite of Wood's staff and their callers. Said one houseguest during this time, "The Federal officers find her irresistible, and her being an ardent rebel only adds to her fascinations."[18]

The Widow Acklin need not have been too worried. General Wood intended no harm to come to the Big House at Belmont. He ordered that some of the fine portraits and other artwork from the mansion be sent to safety. Mrs. Acklin may or may not have gone to Mrs. Polk's, but that is where her *objets d'art* went for safekeeping.

However, Wood's concern did not extend to the property outside of Belmont's walls. His men had personal and military needs, and the plantation was made to supply them. A *New York Times* reporter named Benjamin C. Truman wrote, "Our line of battle just escapes the exquisite grounds of this lady [Mrs. Acklin], although all of her 'nigger huts,' walls and fences have been torn down for breastworks." In addition to the slave quarters and fences, Mrs. Acklin's overseer's brick house was torn down, along with barns, sheds, corncribs, the smokehouse, and the henhouse. The ornamental trees were cut for firewood and the lawns were trampled into miry acres of mud.[19]

The Federals were still working on their barricades when Hood's infantry arrived at Nashville on December 3. Wood rode out to inspect his fieldworks that day and reported, "I have examined the entire line of defense occupied by my command and can report it in a very defensible state now, and in a few hours more I think it will be impregnable. I will keep the men employed till the work is complete." Hood's men threw up works of their own, and both sides settled down to watch each other for a while.[20]

Hood hoped that the Federals would come out of their works to attack him, and that is exactly what General Thomas planned to do. He began on December 7 to inform his officers of his plan of attack for a battle tentatively scheduled to begin on December 10, but an ice storm hit Middle Tennessee at dawn on December 9, continued all that day, through the night, and into the next day. Nashville was locked in a cage of ice. On the tenth, General Thomas inquired of his corps commanders about the condition of the ground between their lines and those of the Confederates. General James Wilson replied that "it was folly to jeopardy the chances of success by moving in such a storm and over ground covered ... by a continuous glare of ice." Wood agreed, saying, "The ground between the enemy's lines and my own is covered with a heavy sleet, which would make the handling of troops very difficult if not impracticable. I am confident troops cannot move with facility." The other generals reported pretty much the same. There was no getting around it; Thomas would have to wait for conditions to improve. Then he would launch his attack.[21]

The Rock of Chickamauga must have known that the delay would cause him trouble with his superiors. Ever since December 2, General Grant, who was stalled in front of Robert E. Lee's trenches at Petersburg, had been ordering him to attack. Modern students of the 1864 campaign in Tennessee have generally agreed that Hood had virtually no chance of carrying the war through Kentucky, but Grant, studying the situation from faraway Virginia, believed that the Confederates were on their way to the Ohio River unless Thomas stopped them, and right then. On December 3, even before General Hood's army moved up, Grant wired Thomas, "You should attack him before he fortifies. Arm and put in the trenches your quartermaster employés, citizens, etc." Three days passed. On December 5, Grant instructed, "Hood should be attacked where he is. Time strengthens him, in all probability, as much as it does you." The next day, the order was imperative: "Attack Hood at once, and wait no longer for a remount of your cavalry. There is a great danger of delay resulting in a campaign back to the Ohio River."[22]

Thomas did not know that Grant's impatience was being nourished by a continuous diet of treacherous complaints about the Federal lack of vigor at Nashville. The complaining wires came from one source, General John M. Schofield. Schofield envied Thomas his command and calculated that the way to get it was to poison Grant's mind against "Old Pap." It was not a difficult task, considering Grant's pre-existing bias against Thomas and the Army of the Cumberland. Wilson and Wood, who had developed a close professional relationship and agreed on most things, tried to warn Thomas that there was a Judas in Jerusalem, but Thomas was reluctant to believe it, and even if he did there was little that he could do. So, Thomas continued to prepare for battle when the time was right, and Schofield continued to scheme his takeover. His perfidious campaign appeared to have been a success when, on December 7, Grant wired General Halleck, "You probably saw my order to Thomas to attack. If he does not do it promptly, I would recommend superseding him by Schofield."[23]

Halleck and his civilian superiors had a somewhat more favorable attitude toward Thomas than did Grant, and they did not make the move to remove him. Grant tried once more to prod Thomas into action on December 8, when he sent a wire to Nashville that was full of mistaken information. Grant said, "It looks to me evident that the enemy are trying to cross the Cumberland River and are scattered. Why not attack at once? By all means avoid the contingency of a foot race to see which, you or Hood, can beat to the Ohio River."[24]

When no word of attack reached Grant's headquarters, he issued an order dated December 9 removing Thomas from command and putting Schofield in his place. A short time later, Thomas announced to his superiors in the East that a major ice storm had hit Nashville and that the attack that he had planned must be postponed. For the moment, this mollified Grant, who wired Thomas, "Receiving your dispatch of 2 pm from General Halleck, before I did the one to me, I telegraphed to suspend the order suspending you until we should hear further."[25]

Thomas called a council of his corps commanders the next day and concluded from their reports that an attack was still infeasible. Men could not stand even on level ground, and it was impossible for horses to keep their footing. Lieutenant Colonel Fullerton wrote in his journal, "The ground is yet covered with a cake of ice, and ... the weather still continues very cold — below the freezing point." Their only comfort was in the knowledge that the Rebs across the way were suffering, too; suffering even more, for they were dressed in rags and were unaccustomed to such frigid weather. Any relief the Rebels got may have come from their enemies across the way, for the same day as Thomas' second meeting with his commanders Wood had to issue an order to his division commanders to clamp down on contact with the graybacks. The order read, "It has been reported that our pickets have been conversing and holding truces with the enemy's pickets. This must be at once prevented, and officers of the pickets who hereafter allow such practices, or who do not prevent the same, will be arrested and tried by courtmartial for correspondence with the enemy." The commerce in Southern tobacco, Northern coffee, and newspapers came to an end and the men went back to waiting. They were in the same situation as their officers — all they could do was hope for the weather to moderate so that the killing could begin.[26]

By December 11, Grant was back in the pulpit, exhorting Thomas to attack. He said, "If you delay attack any longer the mortifying spectacle will be witnessed of a rebel army moving for the Ohio River.... Delay no longer for weather or reinforcements."[27]

There was nothing that Thomas could do. The land was glazed with ice, but when the storm blew itself out on December 12 Thomas called another meeting at his headquarters to determine whether or not an attack was practical. The officers decided that it still was not. However, they also agreed that the time was now short before an attack *could* be made. That afternoon Wood issued an order to his division commanders to make sure their men had adequate clothing and warned them, "The clothing must be drawn today." He also ordered that the men be supplied with sixty rounds of ammunition and three days' rations "counting from tomorrow morning."[28]

On December 13, the wind shifted around to the southwest and a thaw began. By dawn the next morning, the ice had all melted, and at a council of war at General Thomas' headquarters the decision was made to attack the next day, December 15. The commanders were ordered to have everything ready by 6:00 A.M.

December 15 dawned foggy. An invisible army moved with muffled sounds into position. Thomas rode out to be with Wood near the center. On the Federal right, west of Nashville, was James Wilson's cavalry (many of the men dismounted); adjoining him was A. J. Smith; then at the southernmost point of the convex line was Wood, and finally General James B. Steedman on the Union left. Steedman's provisional division from the District of the Etowah was a patchwork of various units and included two small brigades — eight regiments — of black troops. This was the first time that most of the whites in line were going to see African-American soldiers in battle and they would have an answer, at last, to the question that had been in many of their minds since black enlistment began in 1863: would Negro soldiers fight?

The plan was for Steedman to move forward and demonstrate against the Rebel right. Simultaneously, Wilson and Smith would perform a great left wheel, pivoting on Wood. At the right moment, Wood would join the wheel and attack the Confederate salient on Montgomery Hill. On Wood's right (west) flank was Brigadier General Washington L. Elliott, commanding the 2nd Division. Elliott had succeeded General Wagner, who had taken leave after the Battle of Franklin to go home to his sick wife. In the center was General Kimball's 1st Division. On the left (east) was General Beatty's 3rd Division, which had previously been Wood's own.

Schofield's corps was assigned to be the reserve, to linger between Wood and Steedman and be prepared to move as the battle developed to whichever flank needed his help. The ambitious Schofield was unhappy with the secondary assignment, but it was his to do, nevertheless.

At about eight o'clock, while Steedman's men were making a big noise over on the Federal left, Wilson and Smith stepped out to begin their wheel against the Confederate flank. The attack was fully underway by 10:00 A.M. The two right flank generals had momentum and they had a lot of firepower, and they did not have too much difficulty shoving their opponents back. At 1:00 P.M., Wood was ordered to join the attack. He had assigned his old division to spearhead the attack on Montgomery Hill, and Beatty had chosen Colonel P. Sidney Post's brigade to be the point of the spear.

Since October of 1862, Wood had wanted to command a corps. Now he had achieved that ambition, and six thousand men were pushing forward at his command to take Montgomery Hill away from General Alexander P. Stewart's Confederates.

Wood could not sit on horseback and passively watch them from the rear; he was right with them as they climbed the flank of Montgomery Hill, clambering toward the top. Wood wrote, "The enemy had encircled the hill just below its crest with a strong line of intrenchments, and embarrassed the approach of an assaulting force with an abatis and rows of sharpened stakes firmly planted in the ground." Wood had ordered the enemy works to be "well pounded" by artillery fire during the morning, and his infantry was now enjoying the benefits. Wood wrote, "As sweeps the stiff gale over the ocean, driving every object before it, so swept the [third] brigade up the wooded slope, over the enemy entrenchments; and the hill was won.... Our casualties were small compared with the success."[29]

The relatively low number of killed and missing gives weight to Shelby Foote's assertion that Wood was assaulting a position that was no longer the main Rebel line. Foote writes that the taking of Montgomery Hill "was by no means as difficult an undertaking as it appeared to be.... Five days ago, screened by the blinding fall of sleet, Hood had had Stewart withdraw his main line half a mile rearward, from the brow to the reverse slope of Montgomery Hill, leaving no more than a skeleton crew to man the works." Foote says that the grayback defenders only fired a couple of volleys at Colonel Post's assault force before they fell back and continues, "What was won in fact was the crest of the hill and a line of empty trenches, not the new main line resistance, half a mile beyond." However, a writer for the *New York Times* who witnessed the fight wrote that the "First and Second Divisions of the Fourth Corps had the hardest part of the task to perform. They had to move in an exposed position, to the rebel works in their front, and these works were more formidable and stronger than elsewhere." This unnamed correspondent attributed the low number of casualties to the fact that the Rebels were shooting too high on account of having to fire downhill, which is, in fact, a challenge for even experienced shooters.[30]

In any case, Wood had won Montgomery Hill. At about this time, Schofield was ordered to commit his reserve and join the attack to the right of General Smith, and the whole line swept forward. Wood was now facing Stewart's second position, another hill, and he ordered General Elliott's division to take it. Elliott stalled for an hour. Wood lost patience with him and ordered General Kimball to lead his division forward instead. Once again, Wood had softened up the position for his infantry by having two batteries blast the hill with converging fire for half an hour before Kimball's division lurched forward and drove away the Confederate defenders and entered their works. Wood did not complain about Elliott's sluggish behavior in his report. He simply said, "The Second Division of the corps (General Elliott's) followed the movement of General Kimball's division, and entered the enemy's works farther to the right shortly after the main assault had been successful." About the same time, Beatty's division seized the Confederate works a short distance farther left.[31]

Foote points out that General Stewart was at this moment under tremendous pressure from not only Wood but also Smith and Schofield and that by the time Kimball's division overran the salient it was already being abandoned, defended only by Confederate "laggards, or members of the forlorn hope, left behind to cover the main body of defenders." Corps commander Wood did not agonize over the poor quality of his opposition. Instead, he focused upon the gallantry of his men and proudly listed their day's trophies. Wood reported, "The result of the day's operations for the corps was the capture of 10 pieces of artillery, 5 caissons, several stands of colors, a considerable number of small arms, and some 500 prisoners." Wood's corps had lost 350 men killed and wounded. Wood himself was almost one of them. The unnamed *New York Times* reporter wrote, "Wood like to have lost his head to a cannon ball twice."[32]

It had been a fair day's work. However, the work was not quite done. The enemy was everywhere in retreat, and General Thomas wanted to expand upon the day's gains while there was still daylight enough to see. At five o'clock, he ordered Wood to advance another two and a half miles to the Franklin Pike, drive the enemy away from it, and take position astride it. Wood formed his corps in two lines and moved forward, swatting the Rebel skirmishers out of the way and getting to within three-fourths of a mile of the pike before the gathering darkness made it impossible to go farther. They bivouacked in position.

Even then, there was no rest for the generals. Wood wrote, "After having provided for the safety of the corps for the night I repaired to the quarters of the commanding general to receive his orders for the operations of the morrow. These orders were to advance at daylight for the following morning, the 16th, and if the enemy was still in front to attack him; but if he had retreated to pass to the eastward of the Franklin pike, to face southward, and pursue him till found."[33]

The Federals had awakened too many mornings to find the Confederates gone to be sure that they would stand fast, but Hood was not from the same mold as General Joseph E. Johnston. When the Yankees looked out the next morning, the Rebels were still there, though they had shifted their corps around in the night. Now General Stephen D. Lee was on the CSA right, his flank curled around Overton Hill; General Stewart was in the center between Franklin Pike and Granny White Pike; and General B. F. Cheatham was on the enemy left, with his left anchored on Shy's Hill.

Thomas had not shifted his corps from their resting places of the night before. Once again his battle plan called for Wilson, Smith, and Schofield to hit the Confederate left. The main difference was that on this second day Steedman on the Federal left would have a more vigorous role to play. He would not be making a mere demonstration; his assault, with Wood supporting on his right, would be an all-out attack.

The skirmishing began at 6:00 A.M. and the IV Corps began to advance a half hour later. Elliott's division was on the left, Beatty was on the right, and Kimball brought up the rear.

They pushed the Rebels back until they ran into a strong line of skirmishers and began to deploy. When they did, they discovered that there was a half-mile gap between Elliott and General A. J. Smith, so Kimball's division moved from the rear to fill the hole. Moving again, they drove the enemy back three-fourths of a mile, until they came to the enemy works on Overton Hill. Here they halted. Wood said, "Farther advance was impossible without making a direct assault on the enemy's intrenched lines, and the happy moment for the grand effort had not yet arrived." Until the "happy moment" came, he ordered up the artillery to batter the enemy and ordered that the skirmishers keep up a harassing fire to hold the Rebels in their trenches. They could keep it up as long as was necessary; Wood said that their supply of ammunition was "inexhaustible."[34]

About noon, General Wood rode through a chilly December rain over to his left and conferred with General Steedman "and submitted to him some suggestions in regard to the disposition of his command.... General Steedman coincided in opinion with me and promptly and handsomely, though exposed to sharp fire from one of the enemy's batteries, placed his command ... in a position which effectually secured my left from being turned." Just before three o'clock, Wood ordered the assault to begin. Colonel Post's brigade of Beatty's division led, supported by Colonel Abel D. Streight's brigade. Steedman was moving simultaneously on the left and his artillery was trained on the barricades ahead. The assault was vigorous, and the men dashed up the steep embankment to the abatis. There they were met by a "most terrific fire of grape and canister and musketry." Colonel Post was blasted out of his saddle by a round of grapeshot and his horse was killed. Despite the fall of their colonel, Post's men pushed ahead and some of them got into the enemy works. But they could not make a lodgment. Reserve troops (two brigades, according to division commander Beatty) began adding their fire to that of the defenders in the trenches and "poured in a fire before which no troops could live." The bluecoats were driven out with 450 casualties, and Post's wound was so severe that it was feared that he would die. Seeing two of his old brigades retiring, Wood ordered heavy artillery fire to cover them and keep the Confederates back. The simultaneous attempt of Steedman's men was likewise unsuccessful. Looking over the carnage in front of Overton Hill, Wood took special note of something he had never seen before. He wrote, "After the repulse our soldiers, white and colored, lay indiscriminately near the enemy's works at the outer edge of the abatis." Those officers and men who feared in 1863 that African-American soldiers would not fight had received an answer to their doubts.[35]

Undoubtedly, Hood was missing the talents of Patrick Cleburne and the other five generals who had died at the ill-conceived attack at Franklin, but he could take considerable pride in the leadership of General Stephen D. Lee and his successful repulse of Wood and Steedman on the Confederate right. Lee had done well. The story was different on the left. Union generals Wilson, Smith, and Schofield had shattered that flank with the concentrated fire of nearly one hundred fieldpieces. An infantry division rushed forward and punched a hole through the enemy entrenchments, and just as a leak will destroy a dam, the whole line began to crumble. Lee had no idea of the disaster on his left and was startled to find soldiers and officers streaming toward him from that direction, utterly routed.

The Federals were equally surprised. After the repulse at Overton Hill,

Wood had ridden over to General Kimball's section of the line when he heard "an electric shout, which announced that a grand advance was being made by our right and right centre.... I at once ordered the whole corps to advance and assault the enemy's works, but the order was scarcely necessary. All had caught the inspiration.... So general and so combined an attack on all parts of the enemy's line was resistless. It rushed forward like a mighty wave, driving everything before it."[36]

General Lee's gallantry did not fail him even now. Caught in a tidal wave of panicky and running Rebels, he leaned down from the saddle of his horse, grabbed a flag out of the hands of one who would no longer defend it, and shouted to the men around him, "Rally, men, rally! For God's sake, rally! This is the place for brave men to die!"[37]

Most believed that the place for brave men to die was a little farther down the road and they just kept running. The gallant few who did gather around Lee patched together a rear guard south of Overton Hill. General Henry Clayton's division from Overton Hill was still intact and they marched in good order to join Lee, as did another infantry brigade and an artillery battery. Their courage, plus the continuing rain and the fact that night was falling, blunted the enthusiasm of the charging Yankees, who undoubtedly felt that they had done enough this day. Thomas watched the retreating Rebels from the crest of Overton Hill, waved his hat in the air, and cried out, "Oh, what a grand army I have! God bless each member of it!" When he saw the bodies of the black and white soldiers side by side in front of the abatis, he was moved again and said, "The issue is settled; Negroes will fight!"[38]

General Steedman, who had committed the African-American troops in the fight for Overton Hill, was also watching the Rebel retreat and made a remark that captured at once an observation about the bravery of his black soldiers and the racial prejudice of the defeated Confederates. He said, "I wonder what my Democratic friends over there would think of me if they knew I was fighting them with 'nigger troops'?"[39]

Wood's infantry and artillery joined in the pursuit of the fleeing Confederates, clashing periodically with the rear guard and making a few late day captures. The chase did not end until they were within a mile of Brentwood. The IV Corps' total prizes for the day, Wood wrote, "were 14 pieces of artillery, 980 prisoners, 2 stands of colors, and thousands of small arms." The corps had sustained seven hundred killed and wounded.[40]

Nashville had been a stunning victory for the Federals. Some, like Thomas B. Van Horne, have claimed that the battle plan was actually Wood's and had simply been adopted, with a few refinements, by General Thomas. That may be so, but if it was, Wood did not make a grab at the credit. He simply eulogized the past two days in his report by saying, "It may be truthfully remarked that military history scarcely affords a parallel of a more complete victory."[41]

CHAPTER 17

War's End

After the Battle of Nashville, as had happened after the Battle of Missionary Ridge, there arose a dispute over who had captured certain cannon. General Kenner Garrard's 2nd Division (of General A. J. Smith's XVI Corps) claimed credit for the capture of four fieldpieces that the IV Corps also claimed as their own. General Smith put an end to the argument with the finesse of a diplomat, saying:

> The Second Division claims that they captured four more guns on the left, which were afterward taken possession of by the Fourth Corps, but as they were on the Fourth Corps line, and they were unquestionably assisted by that corps in their capture, I am not disposed to question their right to them. I only hope that there may always be the same ardent desire to capture from a disloyal enemy his means and munitions of war; it is certainly a laudable rivalry.[1]

Of more importance than the disputed cannon was the effort to run the Army of Tennessee to ground, if army it could still be called. Sam Watkins doubted that the word still applied to the dispirited men he saw all around him, retreating down the Franklin Pike. Watkins wrote, "The once proud Army of Tennessee degenerated to a mob. We were pinched by hunger and cold. The rains, and sleet, and snow never ceased falling from the winter sky, while the winds pierced the old, ragged grayback Rebel soldier to his very marrow." Escape was all that was left for these Confederates, after Nashville. Along the dreary road, Watkins shared in what must have been the common lament among Hood's soldiers: "Our country is gone, our cause is lost."[2]

The pursuit lasted from the late afternoon of December 16 until December 30, 1864. The first full day set the pattern for those that followed. General James Wilson's cavalry led the way. The IV Corps was up and on the move by 8:00 A.M. They immediately began to see evidence of the low spirits of their enemies. Wood wrote, "The whole line of march of the day bore unmistakable evidence of the signalness of the victory our arms had achieved and the completeness of the rout. The road was strewn with small-arms, accoutrements, and blankets." In addition, they picked up Confederate stragglers and deserters all day long. The Federals hurried forward until they reached the Harpeth River, which was swollen from the rain and, what was worse, was bridgeless. It took the engineers until the morning of the eighteenth to finish a makeshift bridge. The corps moved out at 7:30 A.M. They went into battle line at Spring Hill and then bivouacked there.[3]

The next morning they began moving at about the usual time, in a torrential rain. When they reached Rutherford Creek, they once again found a watercourse that was bank-full and without a bridge. Enemy soldiers posted on the far bank kept the engineers from even laying down a footbridge. They had built works on both sides of the pike and fired on the Federals with musketry and rounds from four cannon. Wood ordered up a battery and General Wilson added a battery of his own, and together they were able to stop most of the firing from the other side, although Confederate sharpshooters remained a deadly annoyance. In the meantime, some of General Elliott's soldiers went upstream to chop down trees that they hoped would be tall enough to fall across the creek and land with their branches on the other bank. The distance was hard to accurately judge. The trees did not quite reach, and the current grabbed them and propelled them downstream as if they were caught in a mill-race.

Throughout the war, soldiers reported that a feeling of physical and emotional ennui settled over them after a battle, even when they were victorious. General Wood seems to have experienced a similar sag in his spirits during this third day of the chase. His blue mood was uncharacteristic but understandable. It was cold and muddy, his foot hurt, and the delays at every creek and river were maddening. He wrote that December 19 was "one of the most dreary, uncomfortable, and inclement days I remember to have passed in nineteen and a half years of active field service." This from a man who as a young lieutenant had marched through the baking hot and pestilential valley of the Rio Grande in 1846 and had led men during the Tullahoma Campaign of 1863 when it rained every day.[4]

The next morning, December 20, General Kimball got a footbridge laid downstream and began to cross his troops about 11:30. General Elliott also had a bridge across, and by 1:30 all three divisions were over the creek and on their way to Columbia. There they came up against the Duck River, which was predictably swollen and bridgeless. Lieutenant Colonel Fullerton caught some of Wood's bad humor and wrote a frustrated entry in his journal, saying, "The corps has already been delayed thirty-four hours waiting for the pontoon train to cross Harpeth River, Rutherford's Creek, and now Duck River. The enemy has, therefore, gained so many hours in his retreat."[5]

On the twenty-first, while Schofield was building a trestle bridge across

Rutherford's Creek so that the artillery and wagons could get across, the men at the Duck River remained in camp. Wood made use of his stationary situation and sent to Nashville a requisition for fifteen thousand pairs of shoes and a like number of pairs of socks, asking that they be delivered as soon as possible "to the nearest point on the railroad, and then forwarded by wagon train. The men are not barefooted, but traveling on the pike in the wet will, in a very few days, ruin their shoes and disable many of our men." While they waited for the new brogans, Wood's men fanned out over the countryside to gather two days' forage for the five hundred draft animals of the train that would soon be there. They managed to collect twelve wagonloads of forage. When they returned to camp, they learned that a mistake had occurred. The pontoon train had moved out on the wrong road, Murfreesboro Pike, instead of Franklin Pike. Those essential pontoons were delayed a few hours longer and did not reach Wood's camp until after midnight.[6]

On the twenty-second, the 51st Indiana gained a foothold on the other side of the Duck River and protected Colonel Abel Streight's brigade of Beatty's division while they laid the pontoon bridge. The corps crossed after nightfall — Beatty's division first, followed by Kimball's and finally Elliott's — and it was midnight before the tail of the infantry column was over the river. A few of the wagons and artillery pieces got across that night, but most did not cross until early the next morning. The going was slow. By 5:00 A.M. on the twenty-third only three batteries were over, and it was the middle of the afternoon before the advance could resume. They had some skirmishing with CSA infantry and Forrest's cavalry, with a particularly sharp brush with the enemy only five miles below Columbia. There they found the enemy positioned on the high ground on either side of a gap through which the pike passed. Wood ordered Kimball forward with two regiments, and a section of artillery was set up. They dislodged the enemy and settled down for the night.

They might have gone farther if they had not had to wait for Wilson's cavalry to get in front. Thomas had indicated that he wanted the IV Corps and Wilson's cavalry to work in closer conjunction. The resulting partnership between Wood's foot soldiers and Wilson's horse soldiers was unwieldy. They were forever getting in each other's way. Still, with "Devil" Forrest's men waiting ahead, it was not really safe to travel otherwise.

At midday on the twenty-fourth, after the cavalry had gotten out front, Wood's men marched. Wilson knew that Wood was feeling out of sorts about the perpetual delays, and he wanted as much as possible to stay out of the road, so that the soldiers could use it without interruption. The weather made it impossible. Wilson sent back a message to Wood saying, "From the nature of the ground I find it impossible to move off of the turnpike, and as the head of my column is constantly skirmishing with the enemy's rear guard, my progress is necessarily slow. I beg, therefore, that you will not become impatient, as I am pushing forward as rapidly as possible." Wood's men slogged on in the mud and made a good afternoon's march of sixteen miles before nightfall. They bivouacked near Lynnville.⁷

The next day, the fourth Christmas Day of the war, the men went ten miles, marching in the rear of the cavalry through Pulaski, where the turnpike ended. Beyond there, the road was "next to impracticable because of the mud." Seeing the condition of the road ahead, Wood reluctantly limited the number of ammunition wagons, lightened their load to only ten boxes each, and ordered that all of his artillery except four batteries be left behind. The pieces he took along were double-teamed, and their caissons were pulled by ten horses. He explained, "Without extra teams to the artillery carriages and lightening of the usual load of an ammunition wagon, it would have been impracticable to get the vehicles along; a vigorous pursuit would have been impossible." The men struggled on through the mush for another six miles, and bivouacked on Richland Creek. They ate the last of their rations in camp that night. Wood had ordered some more, and Thomas had promised to send them forward with all speed, but the muddy road was so cut up that the supply wagons did not catch up to the IV Corps in time for the foodstuffs to be distributed before afternoon of the next day. It had not been a very merry Christmas.⁸

The men broke camp at 6:00 A.M. on the twenty-seventh. They followed the cavalry down to where the Lexington Road angled off toward Florence, Alabama, and this was the road they took. At noon, Wood and his staff found General Wilson at Pinhook Town, and the cavalryman's news was not good. As Fullerton reported it, Wilson said that he was "unable to move farther, as he has not forage for his horses nor rations for his men.... It is impossible to bring rations from Pulaski (or rather, it is impracticable) as the road from that point is nearly impassable. It will take twelve hours to haul a wagon six miles." The chase seemed to be at a practical end, anyway; it was Wilson's opinion that the enemy had crossed the Tennessee River. Wood went into camp that night at Sugar Creek.⁹

The next day, Wood's men continued the march another eleven miles. The road was so bad that they abandoned it in favor of the brushy right-of-way. Fullerton reported that the wagon trains behind were stuck in the mud, strung out over five miles, and that the mules were worn out. During the day, Wilson confirmed his earlier suspicion that the enemy had gotten across the Tennessee River and had destroyed the bridge as they went. This intelligence was kicked back to Thomas, who ordered a halt to the pursuit and ordered the men to remain in camp pending further orders. They were six miles south of Lexington, Alabama, and that is where they stayed, foraging and making small forays against local guerrillas until December 31, when they marched toward Huntsville. They had abandoned the chase, but hard traveling conditions had not abandoned them. They were stopped at the flooded Elk River and spent the first two days of 1865 building a bridge. Two more days of marching followed, and the IV Corps reached Huntsville on January 5. "Thus was closed for the Fourth Corps one of the most remarkable campaigns of the war," said General Wood.[10]

Wood must have been aware that General Thomas had recommended him for promotion to major general on Christmas Day. In a letter to Halleck, Thomas harkened back to November of 1863 in his review of Wood's qualifications and rightful claim to this last promotion. Thomas wrote:

> Brig. Gen. T.J. Wood, commanding Fourth Army Corps, to be promoted to the rank of major general of volunteers, for gallant and meritorious conduct and good generalship displayed in command of the Third Division of the Fourth Corps, and during the present campaign as commander of the Fourth Corps, particularly in the battle of Missionary Ridge, November 25, 1863, throughout the Atlanta Campaign, and at the assault upon the enemy's intrenchments at Lovejoy's Station, Ga., where he received a severe wound. Notwithstanding this wound he retained command of his division and participated in the operations against Hood in his movements upon our communications with Atlanta, and later confronted him in the invasion of Tennessee, took a conspicuous part in the battle of Franklin, November 30, 1864, in which seven desperate assaults of the rebels were repulsed, 5,000 of them killed and wounded, and nearly 1,000 of them, with 5 stands of colors, captured. He has also rendered brilliant and important services during the battle of the 15th and 16th instant before Nashville, and since in the campaign which was then inaugurated and is now in progress.[11]

It was not only his superior officer who advocated on Wood's behalf but at least one subordinate officer as well. Colonel Abel D. Streight wrote to President Lincoln recommending Wood's promotion, citing his "untiring energy and devotion to cause," which he said had "long been a theme of remark with the whole army." Streight continued, "His council, his good judgement, and courage in trying times have been such as to inspire us all with confidence in his superior qualifications to command an army...." Streight did not fail to include the information that Wood was still on crutches from his Lovejoy Station wound.[12]

Neither Thomas' nor Streight's appeals had any immediate effect. It was true that promotions often came slowly for Kentuckians. They were considered Southern, they came from a slave state, and their loyalty was always suspect. It is also true that of the forty-one Union generals from Kentucky, no fewer than fourteen of them became major generals before 1865, so it was by no means an impossibility. One is led to the conclusion that Thomas J. Wood was continually passed over for promotion to major general because of his recalcitrance earlier in the war, especially in the period from late 1862 to late 1863 when he resented serving under General Thomas L. Crittenden, and because of his infamous decision to obey to the extreme Rosecrans' foolish order at Chickamauga on September 20, 1863. The reform in Wood's attitude and his exemplary service since then had not completely erased the dark blot beside his name, and he continued to serve as the oldest brigadier in the Federal army.

When the IV Corps went into camp at Huntsville, General Grant in Virginia had made it plain that he did not "intend that [the] army shall go into winter quarters; it must be ready for active operations in the field."[13]

Those instructions were in exact accord with Wood's thinking. He wanted to start right away and carry the war through to Mobile on the coast. Even before the IV Corps had reached Huntsville, Wood had proposed an audacious plan, based largely on reports of Confederate deserters who informed Wood of the destitute condition of Hood's army, the only army left in the Trans-Appalachian to oppose them. Hood's soldiers were barefoot and living on parched corn. They had no blankets. Of most interest to Wood was the information that about half of Hood's men had deserted; of those who remained, only half were armed. Moreover, the Army of Tennessee had abandoned three-fourths of its artillery. All of that being true, Wood concluded that "the whole country from the Tennessee River to Mobile is open to us. Should we not then improve the present opportunity for bringing Alabama — at present the best State for supplies the rebels have — under our control?"[14]

Wood laid out his plan for the proposed campaign. He wrote:

> I estimate that 40,000 infantry, 10,000 cavalry, and one battery of artillery to each division of infantry, with a reserve battery to each corps, would be an ample force for the expedition. To raise this force the whole country behind us, if necessary, might be almost entirely stripped of troops, as I am confident our offensive movement would abundantly protect the rear.... Starting with a force composed as above, and taking with us hard bread, sugar, coffee, and a double allowance of salt for forty days, one day's salt meat in seven, a small supply of forage for exigencies, driving as many cattle with us as could conveniently be done, and trusting to the country to supply the remainder of the meat ration and forage for daily use, I have no hesitation in saying that we could eat our oysters in Mobile in forty days from the date of departure. The distance to be traversed is about 300 miles, and an average of less than ten miles a day would carry us through in the period assigned.[15]

He recommended that the troops should move by way of Tuscumbia, Tuscaloosa, and Montgomery to reach the Gulf and further recommended that no time be lost in beginning the campaign. "I would say to the commanding general that the success of the expedition would be greatly facilitated by moving before Hood's command could be reorganized, armed, and equipped, and before a force could be concentrated from other quarters to oppose us."[16]

Wood soon had indications that his idea would be acted upon, for within a week he received an order from General Thomas in Nashville saying, "Get your men well clothed and prepared for three months' campaign; take as little transportation as you can possibly get along with, and have the animals in good condition; make up all returns to date; and when you start take nothing but rations, forage, intrenching tools, a few carpentry tools for repairing, and the necessary blanks and stationary."[17]

Before the preparations could begin, however, attention was diverted by the approach of Confederate general Hylan B. Lyon and his large raiding party, who were returning south after a long, destructive ride through Tennessee and Kentucky. General Hood had sent the rebellious Kentuckian into his native state to wreck the L&N Railroad and cut the telegraph wires, thereby denying Thomas his communications to the north. Imagining that he would win a great victory over Thomas in Middle Tennessee and continue his campaign north from there, Hood also wanted Lyon to get control of as many gristmills as possible so that the invading Confederates could be fed when they arrived.

Lyon had performed his part of Hood's campaign with near perfection. He had defeated or successfully eluded every Federal force sent against him, had found good saddle mounts for his men, and had recruited hundreds of volunteers. He was in the process of destroying L&N tracks at Elizabethtown, Glendale, and Nolin when he learned of Hood's defeat at Nashville. His raid no longer had any purpose. Lyon turned south and headed for Alabama. It was reliably reported to Thomas' headquarters on January 6 that Lyon had crossed the Nashville & Chattanooga Railroad between Decherd and Elk River. Wood mobilized his forces and dispatched them to the fords and bridges on the Tennessee River where Lyon was likely to show up. He ordered a gunboat on the Tennessee to patrol from Bridgeport downstream to guard against a Rebel crossing, and he asserted command over General Charles Cruft's command (which was actually in Steedman's provisional division) and dispatched them to the neighborhood of Paint Rock and Larkinsville to watch for Lyon.

Despite the best Federal precautions, Lyon got across the Tennessee River at Gunter's Landing on January 9. His command split up and scattered, but Colonel William J. Palmer and two battalions of the 15th Pennsylvania Cavalry found one band of them, numbering 150 men, on January 13 at Red Hill. Lyon himself was sleeping in a farmhouse about a half mile away. The camp was captured by one of Palmer's battalions, while he went ahead with the other to capture Lyon. They surprised General Lyon, still in his nightclothes, and (quoting from Colonel Palmer's report) he

> surrendered to Sergt. Arthur P. Lyon, while the advance guard was charging the escort, who were camped in a barn lot 100 yards back of the house.... The general begged permission to put on his pantaloons, coat, and boots, which Sergeant Lyon unfortunately granted, and went into the bedroom with him for the purpose. At that moment, the escort fired a volley at the advance guard, when

the sergeant said, 'Come, general, I can't allow you much more time.' The general then suddenly seized a pistol and shot the sergeant, killing him instantly, and made his escape through the back door in the dark.... The escort fled at the same time through the woods.[18]

Lyon and his escort had escaped. Other small bands were not so lucky. Through the morning they were rounded up, until the prisoners finally totaled ninety-five men and 120 horses. This was the last day of the manhunt. Palmer concluded by saying, "I do not think Lyon's command will give much more trouble as an organization." And it did not.[19]

Aside from dealing with the threat of guerrilla attacks on his foraging wagons, contending with Lyon was the only real excitement that occurred during what remained of Wood's command of the IV Corps. The campaign through Alabama from Huntsville to the Gulf never occurred, although General James Wilson was authorized to lead a cavalry raid through Alabama in a few weeks. It was not General Thomas' fault that a campaign through Alabama did not come off. It was the responsibility of Grant. Thomas wrote Sherman that he had intended a campaign against Montgomery and Selma, but Grant took Schofield and the XXIII Corps for the support of Sherman in the Carolinas and General A. J. Smith's command was sent to General Edward R. S. Canby in the Military Division of West Mississippi. That left Thomas with only the IV Corps and some cavalry. He offered to make an attempt on Montgomery with the forces he had available, when the roads became passable, or, as an alternative, to move east through the Tennessee mountains to support Sherman's Campaign of the Carolinas on the left flank.

Neither the spring campaign so confidently advocated by Wood nor the alternative proposed by Thomas ever occurred. Grant had decided that Thomas was too slow — the old complaint — and that it would be better for his remaining forces simply to remain in position, more or less, until war's end.

General Stanley was scheduled to return to duty on January 31. January 30 was Wood's last day to command the IV Corps. He went to visit Colonel Emerson Opdyke that day and stayed an hour. He was in the mood to unburden himself, according to Opdyke, who said:

> He feels deeply the neglect of the Government in not advancing him or any other member of the glorious old 4th Corps for its services have been eminent ever since its first organization and at Franklin and Nashville they were beyond comparison of more importance than those of other Corps, important to the Nation, and yet not one single promotion has been made in it since those battles! Grant and Sherman have everything their own way, and the old 4th has never been a favorite with them, *it is just possible* had it belonged to the Army of [the] Tennessee instead of the Army of the Cumberland our "Status" would have been different![20]

Wood could not know it, but the major source of his unhappiness about his "status" was about to change. The very day that Wood had his long chat with Opdyke, Secretary of War Stanton proposed to President Lincoln the promotion of Wood to major general of volunteers. Wood's name was part of a long list of suggested promotions submitted to the Senate, who sent it to the Committee on Military Affairs on January 6. The promotion was reported favorably out of committee on February 9. The Senate took up the matter on February 14 and resolved to "advise and consent" to the appointment. After years of trying, Wood had won his promotion to major general.[21]

It was undeniably true that Grant and Sherman were biased against the Army of the Cumberland, Thomas, Wood, Opdyke, and others were painfully aware of it. The two Ohioans' misuse of the western army was hurtful to the Union cause and their shabby treatment of General Thomas was undeserved. However, they were not ultimately responsible for promotions, and it was not their fault that Wood had been made to wait until war's end. If he were looking to assign blame for that, he had to look to his own conduct between October 1862 and September 1863.

Now that was forgiven, if not quite forgotten. Horseshoe Ridge, Missionary Ridge, Pickett's Mill, Lovejoy, and the two days at Nashville had proven that there were other, better sides to the man from Munfordville. Major General Thomas J. Wood had reached the heights that had been on the horizon, just beyond his reach, for so long.

With that peculiar awkwardness in timing that marked so much of Wood's life, he commanded a corps in battle before he became a major general and, after he became a major general, never commanded men in battle again. It would be satisfying to describe a great, climactic contest that marked the successful end of the history of the Army of the Cumberland and Wood's long service with it. The fact is that there was no such battle. The war in the West gasped and died when General Joseph Johnston was called upon to take the place of John Bell Hood and took what was left of the Army of Tennessee east to oppose General William Tecumseh Sherman's northward advance through the Carolinas. With no great opponent with which to contend, the Army of the Cumberland simply marked time through long weeks of anticlimax until the war ended in April.

What the corps did during this period was move from point to point on the map. On the same day that General Stanley resumed command of the corps, General Wood's division was ordered to move to Nashville, preparatory to a move by river transports to Eastport, Mississippi. The rest of the corps remained in Huntsville. The 3rd Division arrived in the Tennessee capital on February 2. The wagons, ambulances, and artillery were started overland, but on the fifth new orders were received to have the division return to Huntsville. This they did, arriving back at their familiar camp on February 7. The train and artillery rejoined them there. With no immediate move expected, the corps went back to the old camp routine of drills and inspections, hateful to soldiers who had been in battle and had developed a disdainful attitude toward military spit and polish.

Shortly after returning to Huntsville, Wood took a thirty-day leave of absence. While at home with his wife, he wrote another of his antislavery letters. This one, dated February 12, urged Kentucky to outlaw slavery and was reprinted in the *New York Times*. Kentucky was a slave state, but it was also a loyal state and exempt from the terms of the Emancipation Proclamation. Wood's letter pointed out to his fellow Kentuckians that in other areas where the emancipation did not apply, such as the area around New Orleans and in Tennessee, the seismic tremors had nevertheless been felt and the very foundation of the "Peculiar Institution" had cracked. Furthermore, public sentiment was with the president and slavery would never again be regarded with a tolerant attitude in the United States. Wood asked, "Will she [Kentucky] longer cling to an institution whose very existence jeopardizes all her other interests, and may be used for their destruction? I sincerely pray not. How small is the value of slavery compared with her other vast and varied interest[s]. It is but as a drop of water in the ocean, a grain of sand on the sea shore."[22]

Wood pointed out that in Missouri, Maryland, Tennessee, West Virginia, and Delaware the move was on to abolish slavery. Only Kentucky was proving to be obstinate in holding on to the "Peculiar Institution." If she would only follow the lead of her sister states, the "Commonwealth would enter, with renewed vigor, on a higher, greater career of improvement, prosperity, and civilization, than she has yet known."[23]

Wood's appeal did not have the desired effect, though the truth of what he said was perfectly evident. The corrosive effect of the war on slavery could be seen all around the state. Perhaps as many as three-fourths of Kentucky's slaves had left their masters by 1865. Yet Kentucky did not pass a state law to abolish slavery, waiting instead for the Thirteenth Amendment to accomplish that in December 1865.

Only a few days after Wood's return to his division at Huntsville, the IV Corps was ordered to move by rail to Bulls Gap, East Tennessee. The 1st Division moved out on March 12; the 3rd Division did not begin to leave Huntsville until 8:00 A.M. on the fifteenth. They detrained at Knoxville. From there, Kimball's 1st Division went to Bulls Gap and Wood's moved on to New Market. Elliott's 2nd Division remained in Huntsville for the time being. The two that were sent to East Tennessee were detailed to help string telegraph wires and to guard workers who were repairing the East Tennessee & Virginia Railroad.

Wood felt obligated to remind his soldiers that they were now "in a country inhabited, in a great majority, by loyal people, and the practice heretofore prevailing of using fence rails for fuel must be discontinued, as these people cannot raise crops for their own maintenance if their fences are destroyed.... Parties sent out for wood must cut the wood, and under no circumstances will the fences or buildings of loyal citizens be allowed to be disturbed or destroyed."[24]

East Tennessee was an unpleasant assignment in another way. The government had not provided well for these men who had been ordered to the mountain counties. They were on short rations and on March 23, the day after the fence rail circular, General Wood addressed his troops on the subject of food. He assured them that the railroad, now repaired, would soon be able to deliver full cargoes, and in addition, he expected the paddle wheelers to begin delivering supplies to Knoxville soon. Therefore, the soldiers "must bear this privation with fortitude, and commit no depredations or do unauthorized foraging or other acts unworthy of soldiers. Every effort within his power will be made by the commanding general to have the troops placed on full rations at the earliest date possible."[25]

The promised rations must have arrived soon after, for on April 4, when new orders sent Wood's division to Greeneville, the division was ordered to take along ten days' rations. Two weeks later orders arrived for the IV Corps to concentrate at Nashville. Wood's infantry left from Rogersville, his artillery and wagon train left from Knoxville, and the ambulances left from Chattanooga. The 3rd Division arrived in Nashville on April 27 and moved six miles out on the Murfreesboro Pike, where they had their last wartime bivouac.

General Thomas held a review for the IV Corps on May 9, 1865. The day was bright and the air was clean after a morning shower. The troops formed by division, and when General Thomas came to the parade ground they cheered. Old Pap rode down the line, stopping to speak to each brigade commander, and then went to the reviewing stand that had been erected for the occasion, and twenty thousand men marched past his gaze. As they came up even with the stand, "the guns were brought down to the shoulder and a little nearer officers on horse saluted the colors dropped and each regiment as it past again gave three mighty cheers. General Thomas was very happy and declared it to be the best display he had ever seen." Desiring to see one final charge, Thomas asked that a brigade be selected to demonstrate, and Opdyke's was put forward as the best choice, "the brigade that saved the day at Franklin." Thomas was delighted with the mock charge and called it "first rate." The officers of the Army of the Cumberland were invited to headquarters afterward. There "an entertainment was spread" and "Champagne Ale Beer Brandy and Whiskey flowed freely," according to Opdyke. The officers seem to have been reluctant to say their farewells to those at whose side they had fought for four years, but finally the party ended, the officers went back to their camps, and in the days and weeks ahead the veterans in the ranks began to go home.[26]

Robert E. Lee surrendered on April 9 and Joseph E. Johnston on April 26, 1865. The nation's capital celebrated with a Grand Review a month later. The Army of the Potomac paraded on Pennsylvania Avenue on May 23, and Sherman's Army, a hodgepodge of western troops, marched on the next day. The Army of the Cumberland was not invited to take part. The war was over.

CHAPTER 18

Post-War Duty

Those men of the IV Corps whose enlistments did not expire remained in Nashville, waiting for further orders. On June 7, they were ordered to New Orleans. They traveled by rail to Johnsonville on the Tennessee River and there boarded transports for the trip downriver. This had the familiar feel of a campaign against Hood or Johnston; the men were ordered to take forty rounds of ammunition in their cartridge boxes and three days' rations in their haversacks. Elliott's 2nd Division moved first, followed by Wood's 3rd Division and, finally Kimball's 1st Division. Some reorganization in the regiments was required, since so many men had gone home, and General Stanley ordered, "The detachments of men whose terms of service do not expire ... will be assigned by division commanders to veteran regiments from the same State before the movement commences, if possible." Furthermore, each division was reduced to two brigades. Wood's division consisted of the 1st Brigade under Brigadier General August Willich and the 2nd Brigade under Major General Samuel Beatty.[1]

Before they boarded the trains for Johnsonville, Wood addressed the men whose service had come to an end. As had happened so often before, the general's words were reprinted in the *New York Times*. He said to his departing troops that he could not let them leave "without expressing my warmest thanks and sincere gratitude for the noble conduct which you have ever displayed while under my command. Participation in common dangers, and in privations and hardships, has united us in the bonds of indissoluble friendship." These were not empty words for Wood. For the remainder of his life, his focus would be fixed on the men of the Army of the Cumberland and a celebration of his service with them. He continued, "You have done your duty as good soldiers and patriots, engaged from the highest motives, in the holiest of causes.... Noble soldiers, your work is finished; now rest from your labors.... May your future be as happy as your military life has been glorious! To each of you, individually, and to all, collectively, I bid a kind, a friendly good-by. God bless you."[2]

The IV Corps moved out of Nashville on June 15. The rail trip to Johnsonville took one day and the trip down the Tennessee River, Ohio River, and Mississippi River to New Orleans took another five, counting stops at Paducah, Island No. 10 and Vicksburg. The 2nd Brigade of the 3rd Division, at least, made the waterborne leg of their trip on four steamers whose names are known: the *Jewess*, the *J. H. Baldwin*, the *W. F. Curtis*, and the *Anna*.

Upon arriving at the Crescent City, the IV Corps bivouacked outside the city. Opdyke's brigade of the 2nd Division camped on the old Chalmette plantation, the scene of Andrew Jackson's victory over the British on January 8, 1815. Troops on their way to the Mexican War had camped on the same spongy ground, and one would think that the army would have learned better. The air was filled with mosquitoes and there were frequent showers. The whole atmosphere was damp and unhealthful. The men were allowed to visit the city, however, and see the fine cathedral and the lovely grillwork and Spanish architecture. For the Kentucky troops, one especially interesting site was the celebrated statue of Henry Clay at the intersection of Canal and Royal Streets. There were other pleasures to be found in the city, as well, and the young men of the IV Corps undoubtedly took advantage of them, though they did not detail them in letters home.

The corps was now out of the Department of the Cumberland and instead in the Department of the Southwest (later called the Department of the Gulf), commanded by General Philip H. Sheridan, an assignment that might have been uncomfortable for someone who lacked General Wood's confidence, considering their tiff over the Missionary Ridge cannon. If there was any renewal of their old feud, though, there is no mention of it in the documents. Perhaps there was no incident because the IV Corps was not in New Orleans long. On July 5, Wood's division boarded boats for a trip across the Gulf to the Texas coast, thence up Matagorda Bay and Lavaca Bay to Indianola. Wood ordered General Willich, "Disembark your troops as promptly as you can on your arrival there, and put them into camp at the first place you find wood and water on the Victoria road. Every effort will be made to prevent depredations by the troops."[3]

A new assignment came three weeks later on July 28, when Wood was ordered to report for duty to Major General J. J. Reynolds, commanding the Department of Arkansas and the Indian Territory. That assignment was also a brief one, for on August 6 Wood was on duty in the Central District of Texas, with his headquarters back near the starting point at Victoria. On August 6, he was ordered to move his division to San Antonio, there to "camp your troops with reference to a healthy location. No officer will be allowed to occupy a house, excepting by permission of the owner, and then not at Government expense."[4]

Wood knew the San Antonio area. He had done duty there in the years after the Mexican War, and he was able to advise his brigade commanders as to the best campsites to adhere to his mandate to find a "healthy location." He told General Willich, for instance, to post his brigade about three miles out at San Antonio Springs, except for one regiment, which should be assigned to San Pedro Spring, nearer the town.

Wood's instructions for his duty at San Antonio were lengthy and detailed and give a glimpse of the demands of service in Reconstruction Era Texas. He was told to "afford all necessary and proper aid to the Provisional Governor of Texas, appointed by the President of the United States (General A.J. Hamilton), and to the duly appointed authorities under him." Also, Wood was to "afford all proper and necessary aid to any duly appointed assistant commissioner of the Bureau of Refugees, Freedmen, and Abandoned Lands, and to his assistants or agents." He was to serve as the intermediary between the freedmen and the planters to make sure that the first were not mistreated and to Ensure that that they fulfilled the terms of their voluntary labor contracts. Note the adjective "voluntary"; Wood was told explicitly: "The institution of slavery will in no case be regarded as existing."[5]

In addition, Wood was told, "You will notify all persons concerned that until they comply with the terms of the surrender of E.K. Smith by coming forward to be paroled and to deliver up their arms and public property they are not entitled to the benefits of the President's amnesty proclamation." Also, Wood was to "repress all disorders, outrages, and depredations by guerrillas, jayhawkers, or other marauders, robbers, and disorderly persons, and arrest and bring to trial before a military commission the guilty parties." He was to protect peaceful citizens and to see to it that the troops under his command conducted themselves with honor and good order.[6]

It was an interesting assignment. Wood might have enjoyed the challenge of it, if he had not been appointed on September 8 to command the Central District of Arkansas. Then, with disorienting speed, he was reassigned in November to command the Department of Mississippi, with headquarters at Vicksburg.

During this dizzying cycle of assignment and reassignment, Wood's influential friends were advocating that he be promoted to major general in the regular army. The issue of rank was confusing for professional officers during the Civil War and for years afterward, for they might hold multiple ranks simultaneously. In the case of Wood, he was a major general of volunteers, but that was not all. By a commission granted in September (backdated to March 13, 1865), he was a brevet brigadier general in the regulars, and he also retained his rank of colonel, 2nd U.S. Cavalry. In the effort to win the rank of major general in the regular army, Wood wrote to Adjutant General Lorenzo Thomas, saying, "I feel that my professional honor and pride are touched by not receiving a recognition ... from the Government commensurate with my rank and services.... I feel that a bvt. as Brigadier General in the regular army is not a recognition at all proportional to the rank I hold in the volunteer or provisional army."[7]

Within a few months, Wood did receive a promotion to brevet major general in the regular army, also backdated to March 13, 1865. It became a source of confusion in later years. Many biographical sketches of Wood fail to make any mention whatsoever of this final promotion, and even post-war government documents are inconsistent, referring to Wood at times as brigadier general and at other times as major general. There was no confusion in Wood's mind, however. In retirement, he signed his letters: "Thomas J. Wood, Major General USA."

Wood followed General Henry Slocum as commander of the Department of Mississippi. The challenges were daunting in a state described by a well-traveled Northerner as "far behind the other states in the expressions of loyalty and obedience." He added, "There seems to be more bitterness and discontent manifested [in Mississippi] than in any other sections I have been."[8]

The fractured economy and the powder-keg relations between blacks and whites in Mississippi were elemental issues and would require a long effort to correct, but there was a more immediate and more transient matter that concerned Wood within weeks of his arrival in Vicksburg. His role in the matter of the *Sultana* tribunal was small. It was, however, in his department, where everything was ultimately his responsibility.

On April 27, 1865, the steamboat *Sultana* was heading upstream after a stopover in Vicksburg, where she had her damaged boilers repaired and picked up her human cargo of about 1,880 Union soldiers who had just been released from Confederate prison camps. The *Sultana* was taking them home. A few miles north of Memphis, the *Sultana*'s boilers exploded and killed most of her luckless passengers. The number was initially set at over 1,100, but it may actually have been 1,700 or more. This was a greater loss of life than the *Titanic* disaster forty-seven years later. In fact, it was the most tragic maritime disaster ever and outdistanced many recently fought battles in the death tally.

Such a calamity required that someone be blamed. As commonly happens, it was not anyone at the top of the military hierarchy but a third-level official at whom the accusing finger was pointed. His name was Captain Frederic Speed. Captain Speed was charged with neglect of duty and with assuming unwarranted authority in directing the arrangements for the transportation of the parolees. His military trial was held at Vicksburg between January 9 and June 5, 1866.

During the course of the trial, Captain Speed's defense counsel was able to prove that, in the case of the first charge, there was no criminal neglect. The *Sultana*, though loaded beyond her legal capacity, had blown up because of a shabby repair to her boilers. Said the court, "Terrible as was the disaster to the *Sultana*, there is no evidence that it was caused by the overcrowding of her decks and it is therefore difficult to say upon whom the responsibility for the loss of 1,100 lives should really rest.... Whoever should be regarded as meriting punishment for his connection with the event, it is believed that it is not Captain Speed."[9]

As to the second charge of taking onto himself too much authority, the court found that Captain Speed had consulted with his superior Captain R. R. Hatch, "the officer who possessed exclusive authority in the premises." It was Hatch who had more to do with selecting the *Sultana* in preference to other available boats and approving the boat's manifest of 1,800-plus passengers. Although the overcrowding of the boat had not caused the explosion, it did obviously contribute to the enormity of the disaster and resulted from Hatch's promise of a "full load" to the riverboat captain, J. C. Mason. There is no mystery why Captain Mason desired to cram as many soldiers as possible aboard the *Sultana*; it was a matter of commerce. He was paid $5 by the government for every soul he transported.[10]

The court concluded its report by absolving Speed of both charges and by saying, "It is recommended that ... Captain Speed be publicly exonerated from the charges which have been made against his character as an officer." The findings were approved by General Wood and submitted to Judge Advocate General Joseph Holt, who sent them on to Secretary of War Stanton.[11]

During the six months that the tribunal sat in judgment of Captain Speed, the tense situation in Mississippi continued to simmer outside the courtroom halls. General Wood had been ordered to keep the peace and establish justice in a situation of terrible difficulty. The state was poor and a generation of young white men had been killed or maimed. Hodding Carter writes in his study of the Lower Mississippi River Valley that the purchase of artificial limbs accounted for 20 percent of Mississippi's budget in 1866. As bad or worse were the wounds that could not be so easily seen. The heart had been taken out of these former Confederates. George Washington Cable famously said, "After Shiloh, the South never smiled again." How hard must it have been for the people of Mississippi to smile after ten more Shilohs? A white population whose wealth was gone, whose sense of loss was palpable, and whose way of life had been completely overturned, living in uncomfortable intimacy with a population of former slaves who were poor, uneducated, rootless, and protected by Federal bayonets — it is no wonder that there were sensitive issues threatening to boil up and erupt into conflict: conflict between the Northerner occupiers and the Southerners, between the races, between landowners and their workers, or some combination of all of these.

One such issue involved the presence of black soldiers. A *New York Times* reporter on the scene said, "You do hear very strong expressions against negro soldiers and New Englanders."[12]

The governor of Mississippi, former Confederate general Benjamin G. Humphreys, agreed with the reporter, saying in an interview, "The fact is, they hate nigger soldiers and freedman's bureaus; and until they are removed you cannot expect a healthy current of confidence and good feeling. Everyone is afraid of the negro soldiers — they crowd everybody off the sidewalks, and shoot and kill us, and protect the freedmen in their indolence and acts of crime."[13]

General Wood, though described by the same reporter as "one of the most radical officers in the army," had his own concern about soldiers of the USCT assigned to duty in Mississippi. Governor Humphreys might have exaggerated their misconduct, but Wood knew that Mississippians looked upon black soldiers as a humiliation and he knew, too, that there were incidents of poor discipline among the occupying troops. However, he blamed the situation more on the poor quality of their officers than on the soldiers themselves. He said, "The diffusion of troops at many posts under inexperienced and negligent commanders ... is one of the greatest enemies to efficiency and discipline. Looseness of discipline leads to many useless conflicts with the citizens, and many complaints from the latter of outrages and lawlessness on the part of the troops is the natural consequence."[14]

Major General Thomas J. Wood (collection of the author).

Whoever was to blame, the fact remained that the presence of black troops threatened the peace that Wood was honor-bound to maintain. The general's solution was to order seven of the nine Negro regiments from the state — an order that the War Department revoked. The War Department directed that blacks "be retained in service to work on the levies." Since their presence was mandated, Wood outflanked his superiors by simply keeping the men of the USCT in camp. The officer directing the levy work did not come to conduct them to the work sites and the weeks passed. Wood knew that time was on his side. The black enlistments were due to expire in March, and "in the month of April an order came directing General Wood to muster out the remaining Negro regiments and by the 20th of May, 1866 all Negro troops in Mississippi had been removed. This left one small battalion of regular infantry."[15]

If Wood's restriction of black troops to camp were the entire story, it would not reflect well on his sense of equality, but he also issued an order keeping white soldiers in camp, until they learned the business of soldiering. He directed that they would "remain in their camps and cantonments when not absent on duty, and to receive tactical instructions twice a day of not less than one hour each lesson. These and other regulations of General Wood [such as his decree that prohibited white officers from moonlighting in the cotton trade] brought about an improvement in discipline and a reduction in the number of outrages."[16]

Wood's area of responsibility spilled over into civilian affairs as well. The state legislature did not make his job easier; he said that they had done "many unwise things." For example, the legislature had passed a law forbidding blacks from owning property. Without any hope of ever getting titles to their own farms and expecting mistreatment by the planters for whom they must then work, many blacks migrated to the towns. Fearing trouble from throngs of idle rural migrants, Wood ordered unemployed blacks out of the towns. However, he also encouraged planters to treat their workers fairly. It could be done and sometimes was. The plantation blacks commonly made labor contracts for $15 a month. A planter named Taylor had learned that the key to getting the freedmen to work was to pay them. The *New York Times* reporter wrote, "Mr. Taylor pays his hands $15 a month, gives them a suit of clothes, and gives them all they want to eat and has it cooked for them." General Wood also engaged in what some latter-day pundits mock as social engineering when he encouraged the planters to provide education and religious instruction for the blacks who were working their land. He went so far as to urge blacks "who have families to contract for the year only with planters who will agree in writing to afford them the means of maintaining schools for the education of their children." By December of 1866 Wood was able to express "his thanks to the many planters who have assured him that they will establish during the coming year, plantation schools for the education of the children of their colored laborers, and make arrangements to have religious instruction given to the whole; and he hereby renews his recommendation and request to all planters to pursue the same course."[17]

Wood agreed with the State Bureau of Refugees, Freedmen, and Abandoned Lands that until some literacy among the blacks was achieved they might easily be cheated in their labor contracts. It was not the authorities' role to interfere in the contract-making process, but at the same time they must watch for any attempts on the part of the whites to take advantage; Federal observers "must not relax their vigilance in watching the exercise of authority by the State officials, and should be prompt in reporting all cases that need the interference of higher authority."[18]

Wood realized that economic security and educational opportunities were only two parts of the equation. The freedmen also needed protection and even-handed treatment in the courts, and he had something to say about that, as well. He informed the civil authorities that blacks and whites must be treated equally in the eyes of the law. In his department, courts would not be allowed to prosecute blacks for crimes for which a white person could not likewise be held to account. If it was a crime for blacks, it was also a crime for whites. He advised blacks to take their cases to court and announced that reports of inequitable treatment would be investigated by his officers.

Wood appealed to the "spirit of justice and equity" of the planters in their dealings with the blacks, knowing all the while that he could not have complete confidence that the whites would comply with that hope. Thinking of the need for blacks to protect themselves, he refused Governor Humphreys' request to restrict blacks from carrying guns unless they had a special permit. Entrusting the freedmen with personal firearms may have been Wood's most dramatic expression of his faith in black Mississippians and in his insistence that they have all the same rights enjoyed by whites.[19]

Wood's untiring efforts to create a fair and mutually beneficent society in Reconstruction Mississippi met with some degree of success. He reported to the secretary of war, "I think it is not going too far to say that substantial justice is now administered throughout the state by the local judicial tribunals to all classes of persons, irrespective of race or color, or antecedent political opinions." However, there were signs that the prevailing condition of justice and relative calm between the races was more wide than deep. In the same report, Wood admitted that there had been crimes committed "by the vicious and criminal upon the weak" and that too often they had gone unpunished. Then he added:

> When it is remembered ... what a vast population of slaves was suddenly emancipated by the violence of war and that the late slaves now occupy as freed people the very same soil, in the closest juxtaposition to the formerly dominant class, on which the two races lived in the relation of master and slave, it should not, perhaps be a matter of surprise that so many outrages and crimes occur and go unpunished, but rather a matter of marvel that so few occur.[20]

From the start of Wood's administration, there had been troubling hints of possible retrenchment. Carl Schurz reported to the Senate in December 1865, shortly after Wood's assumption of office, that the whites of Mississippi held deep resentments and seemed anxious to maintain the institution of slavery in everything but name. Three months later, Colonel Samuel Thomas, assistant commissioner of the Freedman's Bureau, made an inspection tour of the state at Wood's request and found that while "the feeling of the people ... seems to be improved toward the colored men, it is hourly growing more hostile toward Northern men and toward the Government.... No one known to represent the Government is treated with respect or decency unless backed by military force.... Lawless and bad men have got into office, who will not execute the laws."[21]

Obviously, the effort to reconstruct Mississippi was going to take much time and a continuing military presence to guarantee that the reforms took root. It was a complicated job, made more so for Wood because of the fact that his responsibilities kept growing. Before his tenure was done, the general was the department head, the assistant commissioner of the Freedman's Bureau, and the acting superintendent of schools for black children. It was a great deal of work for one man to shoulder. At the same time, he had the usual concerns of a general in feeding, clothing, arming, and seeing to the discipline and health of his command. In August 1866, there was such an outbreak of illness among the men of the 15th U.S. Infantry in Vicksburg that Wood had to order the construction of two additional hospitals.

It was perhaps the Gordian complications of the job that made Wood seek another position. Some reports indicated that he was frustrated. Or perhaps it was the desire for a more active position in the West. Wood had served on the frontier in the years after the Mexican War. Now the Comanche and Kiowa were killing and burning in Texas, Cochise's Apaches were raiding in Arizona, and along the Bozeman Trail in Wyoming the Cheyenne and Red Cloud's Sioux were waging a full-blown war. There was plenty of work for a professional soldier in the West, work that was much more tempting than the aggravating job of maintaining peaceful race relations in Mississippi.

Whatever his motivation, Wood resigned his volunteer commission and was mustered out on September 1, 1866. He continued to serve at his post in Vicksburg until January 17, 1867. The people of Mississippi paid him numerous tributes. The Grand Jury of the Criminal Court of Warren County, Mississippi, offered Wood their "highest consideration" and expressed the hope that "the civil judiciary has at least shown itself competent to protect the innocent and punish the guilty." General George H. Thomas praised him, saying," I take pleasure in testifying to the marked ability with which you have administered the affairs of the [renamed] District of Mississippi." But he did not stop there. General Thomas took the opportunity to praise Wood for a lifetime of service. He said, "Always conspicuous for your bravery and gallantry in the field of active operations, your cheerful and hearty cooperation in moments of critical national crises, has cemented feelings of warm personal regard ... permit me to express my sincere wishes that your future career may be marked by that distinguished success which has always characterized your past."[22]

Wood was not soon forgotten in Mississippi. Writing in 1902 after decades of Jim Crow and racial strife, James W. Garner looked back on Wood's military administration in Mississippi in favorable terms, saying that there were "no serious conflicts between the civil and military." In 1906, the *Vicksburg Herald* spoke of Wood's time in Mississippi in complimentary terms, as well. The newspaper editorialized:

In that position which he held all through 1866, duties were devolved upon him which were a severe test of administrative ability and that proved his character as well. Socially, industrially and politically, there prevailed chaos, confusion and uncertainty.... It can readily be seen that such a situation demanded a military ruler who combined with firmness and fairness, sagacious judgment. The chronicles and the surviving memories of the period credit General Wood with proving himself such a commander.[23]

Wood issued a grateful farewell address to the people of Mississippi, to Governor Humphreys and the civil authorities of the state, and to his officers and men. He also included a long paragraph specifically directed to the black people of Mississippi. He said:

The undersigned cannot take leave of these people [Afro-Americans] without expressing his warm commendation of their general good conduct, and their remarkable exhibition of industry, faithfulness, general sobriety and anxious desire for the improvement of their race under particularly trying circumstances. The year just closed has been attended by circumstances well calculated to try the virtue of the colored people. The general failure of the crops, and the consequent honest inability of many planters to pay the wages of labor, attended by an enhanced price of food, might readily have given rise, without much surprise ... to discontent, violence and lawlessness among the colored people; but no such outrages have marked their conduct. On the contrary, they have displayed, in a high degree, a sense of their appreciation and of all the obligations imposed by humanity and the social compact.[24]

In twenty-first-century terms, there might be some insensitive language used in Wood's farewell, but he had taken special notice of a group whom many found easy to mistreat or ignore and the complimentary sentiment behind his words is clear. In nineteenth-century terms, this section of Wood's farewell was a progressive bombshell.

Wood retained his commission in the regular army. He took a short leave of absence and then traveled to Fort McPherson, Nebraska, to assume command of the 2nd Cavalry. He took command of the regiment beginning December 19, 1867. In the weeks following, he discovered that the wound in his left foot had disabled him to such an extent that he was not physically able to hold an active command on the Plains. While he was still in Mississippi, a *New York Times* reporter had bluntly described him as "lamed for life," and a winter on the Plains seems to have convinced him that the amateur's diagnosis held more truth than not. On January 25, 1868, Wood surrendered his command, and on June 9 of that year he was retired from active service with the rank of brevet major general.

For the first time since 1841, Thomas J. Wood was a civilian.

Chapter 19

Dayton

Wood moved into his wife's house at 33 North Main Street in Dayton. It could not properly be called his. He had never lived in it and he did not own it. It appears that it was either bought or built for Caroline Greer Wood by her well-to-do father. The 1870 U.S. Census shows that General Wood owned no real estate. Caroline's father's generosity plus the general's pension kept the Woods in a comfortable lifestyle. The same census shows that they had three female domestic servants and employed a young black man named Isaac Williams as their coach driver. Williams was twenty-four years old and was born in Kentucky; one wonders if he was General Wood's former slave. Williams does not appear as a member of the Wood household after the 1880 census. By that time their address had changed to one door up, to 35 North Main, and within five years they would move one block north to 124 North Main.

When Wood returned to Dayton in 1868, he was the father of an infant son, George Henry Wood, born in Dayton on November 3, 1867. The Woods would have another son, Thomas John Wood, Jr., born January 11, 1875.

Caroline; George; Thomas, Jr.; and a few household servants — General Wood's troops had diminished down to a pitiful few, compared to the days when he commanded divisions.

Some of Wood's fellow officers, such as George H. Thomas and Gordon Granger, died while still in the service, and some like William T. Sherman and Philip H. Sheridan remained in the service until near the end of their lives.

Others found productive ways outside of the military to spend their post-retirement years. Don Carlos Buell made his home in Kentucky and became the president of the Green River Iron Company. He was appointed to be a trustee of the A&M College that would later become the University of Kentucky, and he became the Kentucky State Pension Agent. Williams S. Rosecrans was appointed by President Andrew Johnson to be the U.S. Minister to Mexico and served until the election of U. S. Grant. Grant removed him from office and thus had the personally satisfying experience of dismissing Rosecrans twice from positions of power and honor. Old Rosey bounced back to become a university regent and president of the Safety Powder Company in Los Angeles, California, and to win a congressional seat. He served five years as a Democrat in the U.S. House of Representatives.

One of the old Camp Nevin generals, Lovell H. Rousseau, also won a seat in the U.S. House but resigned to go back into the army. He was named special envoy of the U.S. Government to accept the transfer of Alaska from Russia in 1867. Richard W. Johnson, another Camp Nevin general, taught military science at both the University of Missouri and the University of Minnesota. He was also an unsuccessful gubernatorial candidate in that latter state. The other brigade commander from Camp Nevin, James S. Negley (who had been pilloried by Wood for his performance at Chickamauga), served in the U.S. House of Representatives and became a Gilded Age investor in utilities and railroads.

Major General Thomas L. Crittenden became the Kentucky State Treasurer. David S. Stanley served in the military until forced into retirement by age. Afterward, he superintended the Old Soldiers Home in Washington, D.C. O. O. Howard also remained in uniform for decades after the end of the Civil War and managed to combine humanitarian endeavors with his military service. He was the first commissioner of the Freedman's Bureau, helped found Howard University, and after his retirement helped begin Lincoln Memorial University in Harrogate, Tennessee. Many of these men also wrote of their wartime experiences, either full memoirs or magazine articles or pieces for that great collaboration *Battles and Leaders of the Civil War*.

Wood was not like them. He had an interest in literature and was chairman of the sociological section of the Dayton Literary Union, but he did not write except for an occasional speech and periodic letters to the *New York Times* in defense of his actions at Chickamauga, and he did not pursue a career in business, education, or politics after his retirement from the U.S. Army. For Wood, there was no other career. On those occasions when he did venture into the public eye, it was usually connected in some way to his military career. When he applied for a passport in anticipation of a trip to Europe, he listed his occupation as Officer of the Army of the United States. He attended most reunions of the Society of the Army of the Cumberland, delivering speeches and serving on various committees through the years, and he served as the ersatz host and delivered the keynote address to the graying veterans when the reunion met in Dayton in 1872.

He was the chairman of the effort to erect a Soldiers and Sailors Monument in Dayton and secured passage of a bill in the state legislature to raise the money for the monument through a special tax. The bill became a law in 1881, the monument was built, and a dedication ceremony was held on July 31, 1884. General Rosecrans attended, as did former president Rutherford B. Hayes and throngs of interested citizens and G.A.R. members.

Wood supported the creation of a national military park to mark and preserve the battles of Chickamauga and Chattanooga, subscribed to it, and in 1892 helped lay out the boundaries of Chickamauga Battlefield Park. That same year, he attended a New York City reunion of the West Point Class of 1845. The reunion was small; there were only six old cadets left who graduated in that class.

This was how Wood spent his latter years, serving from the periphery the profession that was lost to him now. He and his family attended services at the Westminster Presbyterian Church and vacationed on Middle Bass Island in Lake Erie, but those were mere distractions. His career — that is, his former career — remained his only true and abiding interest.

There were three campaigns left to Wood after his retirement, each of them, predictably, connected to the military. The first was in response to an 1875 law that reduced his pension. By the new statute, men who had been retired because of disability had to be pensioned at the rank they held at the time their wound was inflicted and not by the rank they had at the time of their retirement. Since his retirement in 1868, Wood had received a major general's annual pension of $5,625; the new law reduced the pension to $4,125, or that of a brigadier general. There were nineteen other officers whose pensions were reduced by the new law.

Wood took his case to the U.S. Court of Claims, where he slightly exaggerated the history of his bodily scars. He claimed that he had been wounded at Stones River, that his horse had been shot from beneath him at Chickamauga, and that he had suffered a serious wound at Lovejoy Station. These were all true. He also claimed that he had been wounded twice on the second day at Chickamauga and that he had taken another wound before Atlanta on July 22, 1864. It might be going too far to say that these last wounds were fabrications, but they were certainly embellishments; if he was wounded at Chickamauga and Atlanta, the wounds were so minor as to escape the notice of anyone else. In addition, the number of wounds or their severity was beside the point, which was simply this: he had not been a major general when he was wounded.

On that basis, his petition to have his former pension restored was denied by the Court of Claims. Never one to quit easily, he appealed to the Supreme Court. The court heard the case of *Thomas J. Wood v. the United States* in 1883. By this time, eight of the affected officers had had their reduced pensions restored, but Wood was not able to join them. The High Court denied his claim on the same basis as had the Court of Claims, namely, that he had been a brigadier general when wounded and was only entitled to a brigadier's pension.

The second campaign waged by Wood in his retirement grew out of his ambition to be appointed to the West Point Board of Visitors in 1895. The Board of Visitors was the group that gave West Point cadets their year-end examinations. To plead his case, Wood collected a group of supporters who wrote to President Grover Cleveland, much in the same way he had solicited men to write in support of his promotion to major general during the Civil War. In this matter of the Board of Visitors, his advocates included Senator John Sherman (General Sherman's brother), Congressman Paul J. Song, and Wood's own son George H. Wood, who was by this time a Dayton attorney. They mentioned to President Cleveland that Thomas Wood, too, was a Democrat, that he was a valued citizen of his community, and that he had shed his blood for his nation. In this campaign, Wood was more successful than in that of 1883. He was named to the Board of Visitors and returned to the bluff above the Hudson to run the cadets through their academic paces in 1895.

The final campaign Wood fought showed that his ambition, though banked, was not extinguished. This time he reached for the highest prize of all: he wanted to be awarded the Medal of Honor. General Wood began the effort by a letter, dated October 25, 1897, to President Cleveland. This was the general's first known typewritten letter. That he had lived into the age of the typewriter was a great relief to those who had to try to read his angular, at times illegible penmanship. In the letter to Cleveland, he said on his own behalf, "Assured that my presence among the assaulting troops [on December 15, 1864, at Montgomery Hill, Nashville] — old soldiers whom I had commanded on so many hard-fought fields, would be most highly prized, I charged with the assaulting brigade — though at the time in command of a corps. My presence with the assaulting brigade was made the more conspicuous by my being attended by an orderly bearing my crutches."[1]

Wood's application slowly worked its way through the channels of official Washington. He did not hear anything from anyone in the military or political hierarchy until May 7, 1900. The decision was disappointing. Wood was denied the Medal of Honor. G. D. Meiklejohn, the assistant secretary of war, explained in a letter to the general, "It is evident that the case does not come within existing law and the regulations prescribed by the President." An accompanying memorandum dated December 24, 1897, referred to the relative ease with which Montgomery Hill was taken and concluded, "There nowhere appears any allusion to General Wood's charging with this brigade. It is also evident that Montgomery's Hill was not well defended, and that a slight effort sufficed for its capture. The Confederate commander [A. P. Stewart] remarked that the fortifications were unfinished." The memorandum called Wood's career "most honorable," before concluding, "Neither the evidence submitted nor the official records describe any incident of service at the battle of Nashville that would make a case for a medal of honor under the present statute and present regulations."[2]

Wood frequently saw his Union friends. He met with them at the Soldiers Home in Dayton and most years at the reunions of the Society of the Cumberland, and occasionally he ran into others unexpectedly, as when he saw General David S. Stanley at the Centennial Exposition in Philadelphia in July 1876. There was one friend from Wood's distant past, though, with whom he had very little contact through the years, Simon Bolivar Buckner. Buckner had been a Confederate and, more than that, had caused Wood's father to be exiled from his own home during the Rebel occupation of Munfordville in 1861. Wood was a long time forgiving him, but forgiveness eventually came. The general's son George H. Wood said that "with the passage of years this feeling [of bitterness] quieted down and his remarks about Buckner became those of an old boyhood friend." As mentioned, Wood was an enthusiastic supporter of Buckner's vice-presidential race in 1896. Verbal messages carried by mutual friends to Wood and Buckner soon led to letters passing back and forth between Dayton and Munfordville, and each man invited the other to visit. There is no evidence, however, that either man ever paid a visit to the home of the other; if it had happened, George H. Wood surely would have mentioned it, for he was his father's companion and confidant.[3]

The only known post-war meeting between the two old men was at West Point, at the 1902 celebration of the Academy's centennial. George H. Wood accompanied his father "as half valet half companion, for his health was not very good and one morning when we were sitting on the porch of the old hotel a carriage drove up and father said, 'By God, it is Bolivar Buckner,' and went down the steps to meet him. The greetings between the two men were most friendly ... and the two men sat down and had a long talk about their days in Kentucky." One thing about the reunion that stuck in George Wood's mind was that Buckner called his father by the unusually informal name of "Tom Wood." It may have been on this occasion that Buckner confided to Wood that the CSA was lost when Chattanooga fell. He said, "You Yanks had got too far into our innards."[4]

Wood was asked to make some remarks at the West Point Centennial as one of the few remaining cadets who had fought in the Mexican War. Mindful that the days were dwindling for the old soldiers, he concluded, "And now, since the graduates of this decade of the forties are not likely to meet with you again, I bid you a last farewell, and with it this benediction, a true heritage of the old Academy which we love so well: When you and I and Benny, and General Jackson, too / Are brought before the final board our course in life to view / May we never 'fess' on any point, but then be told to go / To join the army of the blest and Benny Havens oh."[5]

Since the end of the war, Wood had made frequent mention of his failing health. When he was forty-nine years old and planning his trip to Europe, he complained of his poor condition and said, "If I don't get some relief soon, I can't possibly live long." It was a common refrain in the years to come, but nearly a quarter century later, when the Spanish-American War was declared, he wanted to follow his son George into active service. George H. Wood would go on to serve in both Cuba and the Philippines and reach the rank of captain, but the general's offer of military service was declined and he was made to stay home. The following year, 1899, he made his third voyage to Europe. The evidence is strong that he had far more vigor than he claimed.[6]

Like many who have a touch of hypochondria, Wood was not destined for an early grave. The general lived to see indoor plumbing, electric lights, the phonograph, and automobiles. If he was interested, he could have seen a motion picture. And in 1904, when his Dayton neighbors the bicycle mechanics Wilbur and Orville Wright gave a demonstration of their flying machine at Huffman Prairie on the east side of town, he may have been in the crowd. He would have been quick to grasp the military applications of a flying machine. The world had changed in so many unimaginable ways since his boyhood in Munfordville. He lived so long that his life began to double back on itself. The circle began to close, as his renewed friendship with Simon Bolivar Buckner demonstrated.

Death was bound to catch up eventually, even to one with Wood's vitality. He suffered a decline on Christmas Day 1905 and was bedridden for two months before he died at his home on February 25, 1906. General Wood was the last survivor of the West Point Class of 1845, a fact that he must have known and undoubtedly pleased him. His whole life had been a competition.

The day of his death, George H. Wood telegraphed the War Department, "General Thomas J. Wood died this afternoon. Request permission interment at West Point. Also request detail six non-commissioned officers to act as pall bearers at Dayton. Kindly notify me of post from which the detail is made so that I may communicate with commanding officer as to time of service in Dayton."[7]

On February 27, a delegation of the Society of the Army of the Cumberland traveled to Dayton. One of the mourners, Orlando A. Somers, recalled:

> We went to the home of General Wood and our presence was announced to Captain George Wood, who admitted us to the library. Then Captain Wood summoned another brother [Thomas J. Wood, Jr., come home from his residence in Idaho] and then the noble mother was summoned, and conversation was continued until we remained there until 10 o'clock that night. It is my information that two private soldiers were the only persons, outside of the family relations, who were permitted to view the remains of General Wood. As we went into the room where lay the remains of the dead general, I was profoundly impressed. [He] lay there in the uniform of a Major General, his sword beside him."[8]

A West Point burial was authorized and the pallbearers were detailed from Columbus Barracks. The funeral was held at Wood's Main Street home on

February 28. When it was done, the casket was taken to Union Station, accompanied by an honor guard composed of (among others) four companies of the 3rd U.S. Infantry, the Ohio National Guard, a group from the Military Order of the Loyal Legion of the United States, and another from the Grand Army of the Republic. The remains were put aboard a train bound for West Point. Burial there was on March 1.

Since boyhood, Wood's ambition motivated him to seek the high ground, to scale that hill on the horizon. From the hill where his boyhood home sat overlooking Munfordville he traveled to the bluffs above the Hudson River where the U.S. Military Academy made him into a soldier. He had won honor fighting on the high ground at Buena Vista in 1847 and had gone on to win honors at Horseshoe Ridge, at Orchard Knob, at Missionary Ridge, and at Montgomery Hill and Overton Hill in Nashville. Ambition was sometimes an untrustworthy guide, and Wood could not always see the clear path forward. He made occasional missteps and at least once he lost his way entirely. However, he always regained his bearings, pressed forward, and finally climbed to the heights of his beloved profession.

Now, high above the Hudson, his mortal remains rested where he was always most comfortable, among his fellow professionals, but his spirit had gone on ahead to climb those final heights where the view was unobstructed and encompassed all.

APPENDIX

Wood in Command: An Organizational Chart

At Camp Nevin (Oct.–Dec. 1861)
Army of the Cumberland — Brigadier General Robert Anderson/Brigadier General William T. Sherman
1st Division — Brigadier General Alexander McDowell McCook
    2nd Brigade — Brigadier General Thomas J. Wood: 29th Indiana, 30th Indiana, 38th Indiana, 39th Indiana
After the reorganization of December 2, 1861:
Army of the Ohio — Major General Don Carlos Buell
2nd Division — Brigadier General Alexander McDowell McCook
    5th Brigade — Brigadier General Thomas J. Wood: 29th Indiana, 30th Indiana, 34th Illinois, 77th Pennsylvania

At Shiloh
Army of the Ohio — Major General Don Carlos Buell
6th Division — Brigadier General Thomas J. Wood
    15th Brigade — Colonel Milo Hascall: 17th Indiana, 58th Indiana, 26th Ohio, 3rd Kentucky
    20th Brigade — Colonel Charles G. Harker (temporarily commanded by Brigadier General James A. Garfield): 51st Indiana, 64th Ohio, 65th Ohio, 13th Michigan
    21st Brigade — Colonel George D. Wagner: 24th Kentucky, 15th Indiana, 40th Indiana, 57th Indiana
    Artillery — 5th Ohio Battery, 6th Indiana Battery, 10th Indiana Battery
    Cavalry — 3rd Ohio Cavalry

At Perryville
Army of the Ohio — Major General Don Carlos Buell
II Corps — Major General Thomas L. Crittenden
6th Division — Brigadier General Thomas J. Wood

15th Brigade — Brigadier General Milo Hascall: 3rd Kentucky, 100th Illinois, 17th Indiana, 58th Indiana, 26th Ohio, 8th Indiana Battery
20th Brigade — Colonel Charles G. Harker: 51st Indiana, 73rd Indiana, 13th Michigan, 64th Ohio, 65th Ohio, 6th Ohio Battery
21st Brigade — Colonel George D. Wagner: 15th Indiana, 40th Indiana, 57th Indiana, 97th Ohio, 24th Kentucky, 10th Indiana Battery
1st Cavalry Brigade — Colonel Edward D. McCook: 1st Kentucky, 3rd Kentucky, 2nd Indiana, 7th Pennsylvania (one battalion), Battery M, 4th U.S. Artillery (one section)
Unattached — 1st Michigan Engineers (four companies), 1st Ohio Cavalry (four companies), 3rd Ohio Cavalry (four companies)

At Stones River
Army of the Cumberland — Major General William S. Rosecrans
Left Wing — Major General Thomas L. Crittenden
1st Division — Brigadier General Thomas J. Wood/Brigadier General Milo Hascall
> 1st Brigade — Brigadier General Milo Hascall/Colonel George P. Buell: 3rd Kentucky, 100th Illinois, 26th Ohio, 58th Indiana
> 2nd Brigade — Colonel George D. Wagner: 15th Indiana, 40th Indiana, 57th Indiana, 97th Ohio
> 3rd Brigade — Colonel Charles G. Harker: 51st Indiana, 73rd Indiana, 64th Ohio, 65th Ohio, 13th Michigan
> Artillery — 8th Indiana Battery, 10th Indiana Battery, 6th Ohio Battery

At Chickamauga
Army of the Cumberland — Major General William S. Rosecrans
XXI Corps — Major General Thomas L. Crittenden
1st Division — Brigadier General Thomas J. Wood
> 1st Brigade — Colonel George P. Buell: 13th Michigan, 26th Ohio, 58th Indiana, 100th Illinois
> 2nd Brigade (at Chattanooga) — Brigadier General George D. Wagner: 15th Indiana, 40th Indiana, 51st Indiana, 57th Indiana, 97th Ohio
> 3rd Brigade — Colonel Charles G. Harker: 3rd Kentucky, 73rd Indiana, 64th Ohio, 65th Ohio, 125th Ohio
> Artillery — 8th Indiana Battery, 10th Indiana Battery, 6th Ohio Battery

At Chattanooga
Army of the Cumberland — Major General George H. Thomas
IV Corps — Major General Gordon Granger
3rd Division — Brigadier General Thomas J. Wood
> 1st Brigade — Brigadier General August Willich: 32nd Indiana, 68th Indiana, 25th Illinois, 35th Illinois, 89th Illinois, 15th Ohio, 49th Ohio, 8th Kansas, 15th Wisconsin
> 2nd Brigade — Brigadier General William B. Hazen: 5th Kentucky, 6th

Kentucky, 23rd Kentucky, 6th Indiana, 1st Ohio, 6th Ohio, 41st Ohio, 93rd Ohio, 124th Ohio

3rd Brigade — Brigadier General Samuel Beatty: 9th Kentucky, 17th Kentucky, 79th Indiana, 86th Indiana, 13th Ohio, 19th Ohio, 59th Ohio

Artillery — 6th Ohio Battery; 20th Ohio Battery; Bridge's Illinois Battery; Battery B, Pennsylvania Light Artillery

Atlanta Campaign

Army of the Cumberland — Major General George H. Thomas
IV Corps — Major General O. O. Howard/ Major General David S. Stanley
3rd Division — Brigadier General Thomas J. Wood

1st Brigade — Brigadier General August Willich/Colonel William H. Gibson/Colonel Charles T. Hotchkiss: 32nd Indiana, 25th Illinois, 35th Illinois, 89th Illinois, 15th Ohio, 49th Ohio, 15th Wisconsin

2nd Brigade — Brigadier General William B. Hazen/Colonel P. Sidney Post: 5th Kentucky, 6th Kentucky, 23rd Kentucky, 1st Ohio, 6th Ohio, 41st Ohio, 93rd Ohio, 124th Ohio

3rd Brigade — Brigadier General Samuel Beatty/Colonel Frederick Kneffler: 9th Kentucky, 17th Kentucky, 79th Indiana, 86th Indiana, 13th Ohio, 59th Ohio

Artillery — 6th Ohio Battery, Bridge's Illinois Battery

At Franklin

Army of the Cumberland — Major General George H. Thomas (Major General John M. Schofield in the field)
IV Corps — Major General David Stanley (w)
3rd Division — Brigadier General Thomas J. Wood

1st Brigade — Colonel Abel D. Streight: 89th Illinois, 51st Indiana, 8th Kansas, 15th Ohio, 49th Ohio

2nd Brigade — Colonel P. Sidney Post: 59th Illinois, 41st Ohio, 71st Ohio, 93rd Ohio, 124th Ohio

3rd Brigade — Brigadier General Samuel Beatty: 79th Indiana, 86th Indiana, 17th Kentucky, 13th Ohio (one battalion), 19th Ohio

Artillery — Captain Lyman Bridges: Bridge's Illinois Battery; 1st Kentucky Battery; Battery A, 1st Ohio Light Artillery; Battery G, 1st Ohio Light Artillery; 6th Battery, Ohio Light Artillery; 20th Battery, Ohio Light Artillery; Battery B, Pennsylvania Light Artillery; Battery M, 4th U.S. Light Artillery

At Nashville

Army of the Cumberland — Major General George H. Thomas
IV Corps — Brigadier General Thomas J. Wood

1st Division — Brigadier General Nathan Kimball
2nd Division — Brigadier General Washington Lafayette Elliott
3rd Division — Brigadier General Samuel Beatty
Artillery — Major Wilbur F. Goodspeed

Notes

Introduction

1. George H. Wood, letter to A. M. Stickles, 30 April 1935, Simon Bolivar Buckner File, Collection of the Hart County Historical Society, Munfordville, Kentucky. Hereafter cited as Wood to Stickles, HCHS.
2. Thomas J. Wood, letter to Simon Bolivar Buckner, 7 April 1890, Thomas J. Wood Miscellaneous Papers, Collection of the Filson Historical Society, Louisville, Kentucky.
3. Thomas J. Wood, letter to Simon Bolivar Buckner, 18 November 1896. Hereafter cited as Wood to Buckner, HCHS (first quote); Wood to Stickles, HCHS (second quote).
4. Ibid.

Chapter 1

1. Samuel Haycraft, *Haycraft's History of Elizabethtown, Kentucky* (Elizabethtown, KY: Hardin County Historical Society, 1975), 109.
2. Susan C. Lafferty, *Civil War in Hart County, Kentucky: A Different Perspective* (N.p.: n.p., 2009), 21.
3. Ibid.
4. Wood to Buckner, 2 May 1840, HCHS.
5. Ibid., 29 May 1840 (first quote); 30 June 1840 (second quote), HCHS.
6. Ibid., 29 September, 1840, HCHS.
7. Ibid., 2 January 1841, HCHS.
8. Ibid., 9 March 1841 (first quote); 19 March 1841 (second quote), HCHS.
9. Stephen Ambrose, *Duty, Honor, Country: A History of West Point* (Baltimore: Johns Hopkins University Press, 1999), 125 (first quote); James L. Morrison, *The Best School: West Point 1833–1866* (Kent, OH: Kent State University Press, 1998), 29 (second quote); ibid., 31 (third quote).
10. Morrison, 41.
11. Ambrose, 131.
12. Morrison, 64.
13. Wood to Buckner, 22 August 1841, HCHS.
14. Ibid., 29 August 1841, HCHS.
15. Ibid., 2 July 1843, HCHS.
16. Ibid.
17. Ibid., 19 July 1843, HCHS.
18. Ibid., 1 August 1843, HCHS.
19. Ezra J. Ward, *Generals in Blue* (Baton Rouge: Louisiana State University Press, 1992), 378.
20. Stephen Ambrose, *Crazy Horse and Custer: The Parallel Lives of Two American Warriors* (Garden City, NY: Doubleday, 1975), 90.

Chapter 2

1. Billy Reed, *Famous Kentuckians* (Louisville: Data Courier, 1977), 36.
2. James Longstreet, *From Manassas to Appomattox* (New York: Konecky & Konecky, 1992), 21.
3. Paul Horgan, *Great River: The Rio Grande in North American History, Volume II* (New York: Rinehart, 1954), 611.
4. Ulysses S. Grant, *Personal Memoirs of U.S. Grant* (New York: Library of America, 1990), 63. Hereafter cited as Grant's *Memoirs*.
5. United States Military Academy, "Address by Brigadier-General T. J. Wood, U.S. Army, Retired," *The Centennial of the United States Military Academy at West Point, New York, 1802–1902, Volume I: Addresses and Histories* (Washington, DC: Government Printing Office, 1904), 63. Hereafter cited as U.S. Military Academy, Wood's Address.
6. Ibid., 65.
7. Cadmus Marcellus Wilcox, *History of the Mexican War* (Washington, DC: Church News, 1892), 57 (first quote); Association of Graduates of the United States Military Academy, *Thirty-Fifth Reunion of Graduates of the Association of Graduates of the United States Military Academy* (Saginaw: Sherman & Peters, 1904), 88 (second quote).

8. U.S. Military Academy, Wood's Address, 65.
9. Horgan, 687.
10. Ibid., 714.
11. Wood to Stickles, HCHS (first quote); United States Military Academy, Wood's Address, 66 (second quote).
12. William J. Worth, "General William J. Worth's General Orders after the Battle of Monterey," http://www.history.vt.edu/MxAmWar/Newspapers/Niles/Nilesd1846NovDec.htm#NR71.15November71846GenWilliam, accessed December 10, 2010.
13. General Zachary Taylor's Congratulatory Orders on the Capture of Monterey." http://www.history.vt.edu/MxAmWar/Newspapers/Niles/Nilesd 1846NovDec.htm#NR71.15November71846Gen Zachary, accessed December 9, 2010.
14. John S.D. Eisenhower, *So Far from God: The U.S. War with Mexico, 1846–1848* (Norman: University of Nebraska Press, 2000), 180.
15. U.S. Military Academy, Wood's Address, 67.
16. Zachary Taylor, "Battle of Buena Vista, Official Report," http://www.dmwv.org/mexwar/documents/Bvista.htm, accessed on May 31, 2008. Hereafter cited as Taylor's Buena Vista Report.
17. Benjamin F. Scribner, Papers, Folders 2–4, SC 1322, Collection of the Eugene and Marilyn Glick History Center, Indiana Historical Society, Indianapolis, Indiana.
18. Federal Writers Project, *Military History of Kentucky* (Frankfort: The State Journal Company, 1939), 134.
19. Ibid.
20. Taylor's Buena Vista Report.
21. Ibid.
22. Ibid.
23. A.W. Drury, *History of the City of Dayton and Montgomery County, Ohio* (Chicago: S.J. Clarke, 1909), 120.
24. U.S. Military Academy, Wood's Address, 68.
25. *Senate Executive Journal, 30th Congress, 1st Session*, http://memory.loc.gov/cgi-bini/ampage, accessed May 17, 2010, 380.

Chapter 3

1. Association of Graduates of the United States Military Academy, *Thirty-Fifth Reunion of Graduates of the Association of Graduates of the United States Military Academy* (Saginaw: Sherman & Peters, 1904), 91.
2. Jay Monaghan, *Civil War on the Western Border, 1854–1865* (New York: Bonanza Books, 1955), 102–03.
3. Thomas J. Wood, letter to J. W. Denver, 16 May 1858, "Border Disputes and Warfare," http://territorialkansasonline.org/~imlskto/cgi-bin/index.

pho?SCREEN=border&topic_id=66&search=United%20States.%20Army.
4. Benjamin Floyd Streeter, *The Kaw: The Heart of a Nation* (New York: Farrar & Rinehart, 1941), 71.
5. United States War Department, *The War of the Rebellion: A Compilation of the Official Records of the Union and Confederate Armies*, Series III, Volume I (Washington, DC: Government Printing Office, 1880–1901), 102. Hereafter cited as *OR*.
6. Society of the Army of the Cumberland, *Society of the Army of the Cumberland, Thirty-Fourth Reunion* (Chattanooga: MacGowan-Cooke, 1907), 65.
7. "Richard W. Thompson to Abraham Lincoln, Sunday, October 6, 1861," Abraham Lincoln Papers at the Library of Congress, http://memory.loc.gov/cgi-bin/query/?ammem/mal:@field(DOCID+@lit(d1232400)), accessed December 22, 2010.
8. "William T. Sherman to Abraham Lincoln, Wednesday, October 9, 1861," Abraham Lincoln Papers at the Library of Congress, http://memory.loc.gov/cgi-bin/query/?ammem/mal:@field(DOCID+@lit(d1238500)), accessed June 23, 2010.
9. *OR*, Series I, Volume 4, 300.
10. William T. Sherman, *Memoirs of General W.T. Sherman* (New York: Library of America, 1990), 228–229. Hereafter cited as Sherman's *Memoirs*.
11. Ibid., 230.
12. Ibid., 231.
13. Ibid.
14. Ibid., 232.
15. Alexander K. McClure, *Recollections of Half a Century* (Salem, MA: Salem Press, 1902), 332.
16. *OR*, Series I, Volume 4, 308.

Chapter 4

1. Alexander McDowell McCook, letter to William Dennison, 15 November 1861, Collection of the Ohio Historical Society, Columbus, Ohio.
2. Shelby Foote, *The Civil War, a Narrative: Fort Sumter to Perryville* (New York: Vintage Books, 1986), 728 (first quote); John F. Miller, "Requisition for 29th Regt. Ind. Vol.," collection of the author.
3. *OR*, Series I, Volume 4, 337.
4. Ibid., 347.
5. William C. Robinson, letter to Charlie, 17 October 1861, Collection of the Abraham Lincoln Presidential Library, Springfield, Illinois.
6. "Redstick," letter to the *Fremont Journal*, 22 November 1861, Collection of Bowling Green State University, Bowling Green, Ohio.
7. *OR*, Series I, Volume 4, 307 (first quote); William Sumner Dodge, *History of the Old Second*

Division, Army of the Cumberland (Chicago: Church and Goodman, 1864), 74 (second quote).
  8. Dodge, 568 (first, second, and third quotes); Larry J. Daniel, *Days of Glory: The Army of the Cumberland, 1861–1865* (Baton Rouge: Louisiana State University Press, 2004), 19 (fourth and fifth quotes).
  9. A.S. Bloomfield, letter to his brothers and sisters, 19 October 1861, http://www.crab.state.oh.us/images/stories/September_1861.pdf, accessed December 22, 2010.
  10. John W. Leonard, letter to the Hancock *Jeffersonian*, 20 October 1861, Collection of Bowling Green State University, Bowling Green, Ohio.
  11. George P. Ehrman, letter to B. Swart, 28 October 1861, collection of the author.
  12. "Redstick," letter to the *Fremont Journal*, 29 November 1861, Collection of Bowling Green State University, Bowling Green, Ohio.
  13. Lyman S. Widney, *Campaigning with Uncle Billy*, ed. Robert I. Girardi (Victoria, British Columbia: Trafford, 2008), 19–20.
  14. Samuel O. Thomas, letter to the Hancock *Jeffersonian*, 15 November 1861, Collection of Bowling Green State University, Bowling Green, Ohio.
  15. Widney, 36.
  16. Federal Writers' Project, 168 (first quote); Society of the Army of the Cumberland, *Society of the Army of the Cumberland, Thirty-Fourth Reunion* (Chattanooga: MacGowan-Cooke, 1907), 95 (second quote).
  17. *OR*, Series I, Volume 52, Part I, 201.
  18. *OR*, Series I, Volume 7, 606 (first quote); 611 (second quote).
  19. Ibid., 615.
  20. "Our Army on Green River," *Harper's Weekly*, 1 February 1862.

Chapter 5

  1. Walter T. Durham, *Nashville: The Occupied City, The First Seventeen Months, Feb. 16, 1862 to June 30, 1863* (Nashville: Tennessee Historical Society, 1985), 55–56.
  2. *OR*, Series I, Volume 7, 679.
  3. "The Nashville Papers; Suspended," *The New York Times*, 9 March 1862.
  4. Ibid.
  5. *OR*, Series I, Volume 10, 377.
  6. Ibid.
  7. Ibid., 380–381.
  8. Ibid., 378.
  9. Edward O. Cunningham, *Shiloh and the Western Campaign of 1862*, eds. Gary D. Joiner and Timothy B. Smith (New York: Savas Beatie, 2007), 367.
  10. *OR*, Series I, Volume 10, 296 (first quote); 379 (second quote).
  11. Ibid., 672.
  12. John W. Tuttle, *The Union, the Civil War, and John W. Tuttle: A Kentucky Captain's Account*, eds. Hambleton Tapp and James C. Klotter (Frankfort: Kentucky Historical Society, 1980), 91.
  13. Ibid.
  14. *OR*, Series I, Volume 10, Part I, 705.
  15. Tuttle, 101.
  16. *OR*, Series I, Volume 10, Part I, 706.
  17. Ibid.
  18. Ibid., 708.
  19. Tuttle, 97–98.
  20. Shelby Foote, *The Civil War, a Narrative: Fort Sumter to Perryville* (New York: Vintage Books, 1986), 385 (first quote); *OR*, Series I, Volume 10, Part I, 708 (second quote).
  21. Allan Peskin, *Garfield: A Biography* (Kent, OH: Kent State University Press, 1978), 138–139.

Chapter 6

  1. *OR*, Series I, Volume 10, Part II, 236.
  2. Ibid., 251.
  3. *OR*, Series I, Volume 16, Part I, 164.
  4. Tuttle, 103.
  5. *OR*, Series I, Volume 16, Part II, 29 (first quote); 11 (second quote).
  6. Ibid., 11.
  7. Ibid., 48.
  8. Tuttle, 104.
  9. *OR*, Series I, Volume 16, Part I, 791.
  10. Ibid., 788.
  11. Ibid., 789.
  12. Ibid., 790.
  13. Ibid., 172.
  14. *OR*, Series I, Volume 16, Part II, 241.
  15. Ibid, 291–292.
  16. Tuttle, 109–110. Wood's cursing was so memorable that it became the subject of a soldier's letter to the *New York Tribune* and was afterward brought up in a meeting of the Committee for the Conduct of the War. The committee, having more important matters to attend to than a profane general, took no action. According to Tuttle, the letter was brought to the attention of Wood, who "acknowledged its justice and said he would try to do better" (113).
  17. *OR*, Series I, Volume 16, Part I, 169.
  18. Ibid., 152–153.
  19. Tuttle, 114.
  20. *OR*, Series I, Volume 16, Part I, 904.
  21. Ibid., 905.
  22. Thomas J. Wood, letter to William S. Rosecrans, 11 November 1862, William S. Rosecrans Papers (Collection 663, Box 7), Department of Special Collections, Charles E. Young Research Library, UCLA, Los Angeles, California.
  23. *OR*, Series I, Volume 16, Part II, 502.
  24. Ibid., 513.

Chapter 7

1. *OR*, Series I., Volume 16, Part I, 961.
2. Lowell H. Harrison, *The Civil War in Kentucky* (Lexington: University Press of Kentucky, 1975), 45.
3. *OR*, Series I, Volume 16, Part I, 213.
4. Ibid., 315.
5. Ibid., 48.
6. Ibid., 46.
7. Federal Writers Project, *Military History of Kentucky* (Frankfort: The State Journal Company, 1939), 177.
8. *OR*, Series I, Volume 16, Part I, 151 (first quote); 105 (second quote).
9. Ibid., 148–149.
10. Don Carlos Buell, "East Tennessee and the Campaign of Perryville," *Battles and Leaders of the Civil War: The Tide Shift*, eds. Robert Underwood Johnson and Clarence Clough Buel (Edison, NJ: Castle Books, 1995), 41.
11. Tuttle, 122.
12. Robert E. McDowell, *City of Conflict: Louisville in the Civil War, 1861–1865* (Louisville: Louisville Civil War Roundtable, 1962), 85.
13. Tuttle, 123.
14. Ibid.
15. *OR*, Series I, Volume 16, Part II, 536.
16. Tuttle, 124.
17. *OR*, Series I, Volume 16, Part II, 555.
18. Ibid., 555.
19. Ibid., 559.
20. Curtius, "Department of the Ohio," *The New York Times*, 6 October 1862.
21. Ibid.
22. *OR*, Series I, Volume 16, Part I, 181.
23. Ibid., 237.
24. Ibid., 528.
25. Ibid., 237–238.
26. Kenneth W. Noe, *Perryville: This Grand Havoc of Battle* (Lexington: University Press of Kentucky, 2001), 318–319.
27. Tuttle, 128.
28. Ibid.
29. *OR*, Series I, Volume 16, Part I, 539.
30. W.F.G. Shanks, *Personal Recollections of Distinguished Generals* (New York: Harper & Bros., 1866), 295.
31. Damon R. Eubank, *In the Shadow of the Patriarch: The John J. Crittenden Family in War and Peace* (Macon, GA: Mercer University Press, 2009), 175.
32. Ibid., 51.
33. *OR*, Series I, Volume 16, Part II, 607.
34. Ibid.
35. *OR*, Series I, Volume 16, Part I, 152.

Chapter 8

1. Eubank, 87.
2. *OR*, Series I, Volume 16, Part II, 647.
3. "The Rebel Enterprise in Kentucky," *Harper's Weekly*, 1 November 1862. The number "290" was in reference to the Confederate commerce raider *Alabama*.
4. Spillard Horrall, *History of the 42nd Indiana Volunteers* (Chicago: Spillard Horrall, 1892), 155.
5. Shanks, 17.
6. Larry J. Daniel, *Days of Glory: The Army of the Cumberland, 1861–1865* (Baton Rouge: Louisiana State University Press, 2004), 187.
7. *OR*, Series I, Volume 20, Part II, 18–19.
8. Thomas J. Wood, letter to William S. Rosecrans, 11 November 1862, William S. Rosecrans Papers (Collection 663, Box 7), Department of Special Collections, Charles E. Young Research Library, UCLA, Los Angeles, California.
9. Don Carlos Buell, 14 November 1862, William S. Rosecrans Papers (Collection 663, Box 7), Department of Special Collections, Charles E. Young Research Library, UCLA, Los Angeles, California.
10. Curtius, "Department of the Cumberland," *The New York Times*, 26 December 1862.
11. *OR*, Series I, Volume 20, Part II, 118.
12. Curtius, "Department of the Cumberland," *The New York Times*, 26 December 1862.
13. *OR*, Series I, Volume 20, Part I, 165.
14. Ibid., 457.
15. Ibid., 458.
16. Ibid. (first quote); *OR*, Series I, Volume 20, Part II, 245 (second quote).
17. *OR*, Series I, Volume 20, Part I, 507 (first, second, and third quotes); 501 (second quote).
18. Ibid., 460.
19. Ibid., 460 (first quote); 502 (second quote).
20. Shelby Foote, *The Civil War, a Narrative: Fredericksburg to Meridian* (New York: Vintage Books, 1986), 90.
21. *OR*, Series I, Volume 20, Part I, 502.
22. Ibid., 467.
23. Ibid., 468.
24. Ibid., 468–469.
25. Ibid., 469.
26. Ibid., 493–494.
27. William Sumner Dodge, *History of the Old Second Division, Army of the Cumberland* (Chicago: Church and Goodman, 1864), 568.
28. William D. Bickham, *Rosecrans' Campaign with the Fourteenth Army Corps* (Cincinnati: Moore, Wilstach, Keys and Co., 1863), 333.
29. *OR*, Series I, Volume 20, Part I, 463.

Chapter 9

1. Bickham, 333 (first quote); Thomas L. Crittenden, "The Union Left at Stone's River," *Battles and Leaders of the Civil War: The Tide Shifts*, eds. Robert Underwood Johnson and Clarence Clough Buel (Edison, NJ: Castle Books, 1995), 633 (second quote).
2. Ibid., 634.

3. Shelby Foote, *The Civil War, a Narrative: Fredericksburg to Meridian* (New York: Vintage Books, 1986), 94.
4. Bickham, 304.
5. Ibid., 307.
6. Peter Cozzens, *No Better Place to Die: The Battle of Stones River* (Urbana: University of Illinois Press, 1990), 191. Some accounts say that Mendenhall collected fifty-eight artillery pieces.
7. John Beatty, *The Citizen Soldier* (Cincinnati: Wilstach, Baldwin, 1879), 177.
8. Bickham, 41–42 (first quote); 167 (second quote).
9. Shanks, 295
10. Hight, 458.
11. Ibid., 132.
12. Ibid., 135.
13. Ibid., 136.
14. Ibid., 140.
15. Ibid., 142.
16. *OR*, Series I, Volume 23, Part II, 83.
17. Ibid., 20.
18. Ibid., 31.
19. Ibid., 33.
20. Ibid., 37–38.
21. Ibid., 76.
22. Ibid., 245.
23. Ibid., 255–256.
24. Ibid., 279.
25. Ibid., 285.
26. Widney, 138–139.
27. Mark W. Johnson, *That Body of Brave Men: The U.S. Regular Infantry and the Civil War in the West* (Cambridge, MA: Da Capo Press, 2003), 330–331.
28. Steven L. Wright, ed., *Kentucky Soldiers and Their Regiments in the Civil War: Abstracted from the Pages of Contemporary Newspapers, Volume III* (Utica, KY: McDowell Publications, 2009), 97.
29. Dodge, 451.
30. Horrall, 184.
31. Wright, III, 20.
32. Ibid., 22.
33. Ibid., 71.
34. Widney, 140.
35. Ibid., 141.
36. Ibid., 142.
37. Peter Cozzens, *This Terrible Sound: The Battle of Chickamauga* (Urbana: University of Illinois Press, 1992), 16.
38. Ibid.
39. Ibid.
40. *OR*, Series I, Volume 23, Part II, 406.
41. Ibid.
42. *OR*, Series I, Volume 23, Part I, 8.
43. Ibid.
44. Widney, 144.

Chapter 10

1. *OR*, Series I, Volume 23, Part I, 523.
2. Ibid.

3. *OR*, Series I, Volume 52, Part I, 375.
4. *OR*, Series I, Volume 23, Part I, 524.
5. Ibid., 525.
6. Ibid., 526.
7. Ibid., 527.
8. Ibid.
9. *OR*, Series I, Volume 23, Part II, 518.
10. Ibid.
11. Ibid., 552.
12. Ibid., 585.
13. Ibid., 592.
14. *OR*, Series I, Volume 30, Part III, 41.
15. Ibid.
16. Emerson Opdyke, *To Battle for God and the Right: The Civil War Letterbooks of Emerson Opdyke*, eds. Glenn V. Longacre and John E. Haas (Urbana: University of Illinois Press, 2003), 83.
17. Ibid., 85.
18. *OR*, Series I, Volume 30, Part III, 960.
19. *OR*, Series I, Volume 30, Part I, 626.
20. Ibid.
21. Hight, 170.
22. Tuttle, 142. Wood's genuine concern for the welfare of his men was widely commented on. It made him popular among them. In 1906, Orlando A. Somers told the 34th reunion of the Society of the Army of the Cumberland, "There is not a soldier who marched and fought with General Wood that did not love and respect him.... We all loved and respected him, and no matter whether in the battle or on the march, we always felt the utmost confidence in him" (65–66).
23. *OR*, Series I, Volume 30, Part III, 978.
24. Ibid., 979 (first quote); 981 (second quote).
25. *OR*, Series I, Volume 30, Part I, 626.
26. Ibid., 987.
27. *OR*, Series I, Volume 30, Part III, 391.
28. Eubank, 123.
29. *OR*, Series I, Volume 30, Part III, 414.
30. Ibid., 416.
31. Ibid., 414–415.
32. Ibid., 420.
33. Ibid., 419.
34. *OR*, Series I, Volume 30, Part I, 602 (first quote); Craig Julian Mannville, "The Limits of Obedience: Brigadier General Thomas J. Wood's Performance During the Battle of Chickamauga" (Master's Thesis, U.S. Army Command and General Staff College, Fort Leavenworth, Kansas, 2005), 49 (second quote); *OR*, Series I, Volume 30, Part I, 683 (third quote).
35. *OR*, Series I, Volume 30, Part III, 991.
36. *OR*, Series I, Volume 30, Part I, 628.
37. Peter Cozzens, *This Terrible Sound: The Battle of Chickamauga* (Urbana: University of Illinois Press, 1992), 64.
38. Ibid., 65.
39. Ibid.
40. *OR*, Series I, Volume 30, Part III, 994.
41. *OR*, Series I, Volume 30, Part I, 629.
42. *OR*, Series, I, Volume 30, Part III, 995.
43. Ibid., 996.

Chapter 11

1. *OR*, Series I, Volume 30, Part I, 685.
2. Ibid.
3. Ibid., 684.
4. *OR*, Series I, Volume 30, Part III, 586.
5. *OR*, Series I, Volume 30, Part I, 630.
6. Ibid., 690.
7. Ibid.
8. Charles Eugene Belknap, *History of the Michigan Organizations at Chickamauga, Missionary Ridge, and Chattanooga, 1863* (Lansing: R. Smith, 1899), 278.
9. Ibid.
10. *OR*, Series I, Volume 30, Part I, 631.
11. Ibid., 607.
12. Ibid., 631.
13. Ibid. (first quote); 693 (second quote).
14. Ibid., 656.
15. Ibid., 700.
16. Ibid., 692.
17. Ibid., 632.
18. Ibid., 654.
19. Ibid.
20. Ibid., 655.
21. Ibid., 634.
22. Ibid.
23. Daniel H. Hill, "Chickamauga: The Great Battle of the West," *Battles and Leaders of the Civil War: The Tide Shifts*, eds. Robert Underwood Johnson and Clarence Clough Buel (Edison, NJ: Castle Books, 1995), 650–651.
24. Daniel, 321 (first quote); Cozzens, *Chickamauga*, 200 (second quote).
25. *OR*, Series I, Volume 30, Part I, 655.
26. Daniel, 321.

Chapter 12

1. Daniel, 322.
2. *OR*, Series I, Volume 30, Part I, 693.
3. Ibid., 355.
4. Daniel, 324. There are many versions of what Rosecrans said to Wood on the morning of September 20. They range from the mild to the heated and profane. The least plausible came from Wood himself. In "The Gaps at Chickamauga" (*New York Times*, 19 November 1882), Wood said that Rosecrans asked him why he had not moved and then said to him, "Hurry up and relieve Gen. Negley on the line." This does not fit the mood of the morning, considering that Rosecrans had barked furiously at every subordinate who crossed him that morning. It is almost certain that Rosecrans addressed Wood in language both heated and profane, and that the Kentuckian took grave offense. Wood's subsequent actions give weight to that assertion.
5. *OR*, Series I, Volume 30, Part I, 650.
6. Ibid., 635.
7. Allan Peskin, *Garfield: A Biography* (Kent, OH: Kent State University Press, 1978), 206 (first quote); Daniel, 327 (second quote), Cozzens, *Chickamauga*, 363 (third and fourth quotes).
8. Johnson, 417.
9. Cozzens, *Chickamauga*, 363.
10. *OR*, Series I, Volume, 30, Part I, 952.
11. Ibid., 656 (first quote); Glenn Tucker, *The Battle of Chickamauga* (Jamestown, VA: Eastern Acorn Press, 1969), 34 (second quote).
12. *OR*, Series I, Volume 30, Part I, 656–657.
13. Ibid., 650.
14. Daniel, 330.
15. *OR*, Series I, Volume 30, Part I, 611.
16. Ibid., 996.
17. Ibid., 636.
18. Ibid., 637.
19. Daniel, 332.
20. *OR*, Series I, Volume 30, Part I, 695.
21. Shanks, 68–69 (first quote); Daniel, 333 (second quote).
22. Cozzens, *Chickamauga*, 440 (first quote); 442 (second quote).
23. Joseph S. Fullerton, "The Army of the Cumberland at Chattanooga," *Battles and Leaders of the Civil War: The Tide Shifts*, eds. Robert Underwood Johnson and Clarence Clough Buel (Edison, NJ: Castle Books, 1995), 667.
24. Ibid.
25. *OR*, Series I, Volume 30, Part I, 657.
26. Mannville, 79 (first quote); Tucker, 33 (second quote).
27. Cist, 32.
28. Whitelaw Reid, *Ohio in the War: Her Statesmen, Generals, and Soldiers* (Cincinnati: Robert Clarke & Co., 1895), 350 (first quote); Cozzens, *Chickamauga*, 365 (second quote).
29. *OR*, Series I, Volume 30, Part III, 416.
30. Thomas J. Wood, "Who Lost the Battle of Chickamauga? Notes on Gen. Rosecrans' Report By Gen. Wood," *The New York Times*, 10 January 1864 (first quote); Thomas J. Wood, "Wood at Chickamauga," *The New York Times*, 25 December 1881.

Chapter 13

1. Opdyke, 118.
2. *OR*, Series I, Volume 30, Part I, 1018.
3. Opdyke, 99.
4. Daniel, 354.
5. Opdyke, 119.
6. "The Removal of Rosecrans," *Harper's Weekly*, 31 October 1863.
7. William S. Rosecrans, letter to Henry W. Halleck, 16 October 1863, Thomas J. Wood File, U.S. National Archives, RG-94/9W3/19/33/B/Box821.
8. David Bittle Floyd, *History of the Seventy-Fifth Regiment of Indiana Volunteers* (Philadelphia: Lutheran Publication Society, 1893), 176.

9. *OR*, Series I, Volume 30, Part III, 852.
10. Dan Lee, *The L&N Railroad in the Civil War* (Jefferson, NC: McFarland, 2011), 7.
11. Bruce Catton, *Grant Takes Command* (Boston: Little, Brown, 1969), 52.
12. James H. Wilson, *Under the Old Flag: Recollections of Military Operations in the War for the Union, the Spanish War, the Boxer Rebellion, Etc., Volume I* (New York: D. Appleton, 1912), 280.
13. Sherman, 387.
14. William F. Smith, "Comments on General Grant's 'Chattanooga,'" *Battles and Leaders of the Civil War: The Tide Shifts*, eds. Robert Underwood Johnson and Clarence Clough Buel (Edison, NJ: Castle Books, 1995), 716.
15. *OR*, Series I, Volume 31, Part II, 253.
16. Ibid., 254.
17. Ibid., 280–281.
18. Ibid., 255.
19. Ibid., 263 (first quote); 256 (second quote), 130 (third quote).
20. Ibid., 254 (first quote); 65 (second and third quotes).
21. Ibid., 573.
22. Catton, 77 (first quote); Cozzens, *The Shipwreck of Their Hopes: The Battles for Chattanooga* (Urbana: University of Illinois Press, 1994), 391 (second quote).
23. *OR*, Series I, Volume 31, Part II, 257.
24. Catton, 76 (first quote); Grant, 441 (second quote).
25. Thomas A. Wood, "A Thrilling War Chapter: The Battle of Missionary Ridge. Recollections of Gen. Thomas J. Wood," *The New York Times*, 16 July 1876.
26. Ibid.
27. Grant, 445.
28. Shelby Foote, *The Civil War, a Narrative: Fredericksburg to Meridian* (New York: Vintage Books, 1986), 853 (first quote); *OR*, Series I, Volume 31, Part II, 258 (second quote).
29. *OR*, Series I, Volume 31, Part II, 264.
30. Wood, "A Thrilling War Chapter."
31. Thomas J. Wood, "The Battle of Missionary Ridge," *Sketches of War History, 1861–1865: Papers Read Before the Ohio Commandery*, eds. Robert Hunter and William Henry Chamberlain (The Military Order of the Loyal Legion of the United States) (Cincinnati: Robert Clarke & Co., 1896), 37.
32. Floyd, 235.
33. Cozzens, 282.
34. Ibid. (first quote); Bobrick, 211 (second quote).
35. Joseph S. Fullerton, "The Army of the Cumberland at Chattanooga," *Battles and Leaders of the Civil War: The Tide Shifts*, eds. Robert Underwood Johnson and Clarence Clough Buel (Edison, NJ: Castle Books, 1995), 725.
36. Ibid. (first quote); Society of the Army of the Cumberland, *Society of the Army of the Cumberland, Thirty-Fourth Reunion* (Chattanooga: MacGowan-Cooke, 1907), 98 (second quote).
37. *OR*, Series I, Volume 31, Part II, 282.
38. Ibid., 140.
39. Ibid., 282.
40. Glenn Tucker, *The Battles for Chattanooga* (Jamestown, VA: Eastern Acorn Press, 1987), 42.
41. Wood, "A Thrilling War Chapter."
42. "An Incident of the Capture of Lookout [sic] Mountain," *The New York Times*, 6 December 1863.
43. Wood, "The Battle of Missionary Ridge," 40.

Chapter 14

1. *OR*, Series I, Volume 31, Part II, 138 (first quote); 139 (second quote).
2. Charles A. Dana, telegram to Edwin M. Stanton, 26 November 1862, Abraham Lincoln Papers, Library of Congress.
3. Cozzens, *The Shipwreck of Their Hopes*, 391 (first quote); "General Grant's Army," *The New York Times*, 2 December 1863 (second quote).
4. Sherman's *Memoirs*, 390.
5. *OR*, Series I, Volume 31, Part II, 259.
6. Ibid., 192.
7. Ibid., 252.
8. Philip H. Sheridan, *Personal Memoirs of P.H. Sheridan* (Cambridge, MA: Da Capo Press, 1992), 173.
9. *OR*, Series I, Volume 31, Part II, 139.
10. Ibid., 49.
11. Ibid., 49–50.
12. *OR*, Series I, Volume 31, Part III, 331.
13. Ibid., 297.
14. Wilma Dykeman, *The French Broad* (New York: Rinehart, 1955), 78–79.
15. Sherman's *Memoirs*, 393.
16. Ibid.
17. *OR*, Series I, Volume 32, Part II, 45 (first quote); *OR*, Series I, Volume 31, Part III, 409 (second quote).
18. *OR*, Series I, Volume 31, Part III, 408.
19. Ibid.
20. Jacob D. Cox, *Military Reminiscences of the Civil War, Vol. II* (Teddington, Middlesex, England: Echo Library, 2008), 98.
21. Thomas E. Bramlette, letter to Edwin M. Stanton, 30 November 1863, Thomas J. Wood File, U.S. National Archives, RG-94/9W3/19/33/B/Box821 (first quote); Thomas E. Bramlette, letter to Abraham Lincoln, 30 November 1863, Ibid. (second quote).
22. Gordon Granger, letter to Abraham Lincoln, 4 January 1864, Ibid.
23. Bell Irwin Wiley, *The Life of Billy Yank* (Baton Rouge: Louisiana State University Press, 1978), 281.
24. Abel D. Streight, letter to Abraham Lin-

coln, 31 January 1865, Thomas J. Wood File, U.S. National Archives, RG-94/9W3/19/33/B/Box821.
25. *OR*, Series I, Volume 30, Part I, 944.
26. Ibid., 981.
27. Ibid., 1018 (first and second quotes); 1020 (third quote).
28. Ibid., 1043–1044.

Chapter 15

1. *OR*, Series I, Volume 32, Part III, 136.
2. Ibid., 264 (first quote); Hight, 281 (second quote).
3. Steven Newton, "Snake Creek Gap and the Campaign that Never Happened," *North and South*, August 2009, 63.
4. *OR*, Series I, Volume 38, Part I, 840.
5. Ibid., 374.
6. Ibid., 375.
7. Ibid., 855
8. Ibid., 191 (first quote); 857–858 (second quote).
9. Ibid., 560.
10. Ibid., 377 (first quote); 193 (second quote).
11. Ibid. (first quote); William B. Hazen, *A Narrative of Military Services* (Boston: Ticknor and Co., 1885), 257.
12. Hazen, 423.
13. Ambrose Bierce, "The Crime at Pickett's Mill," www.ambrosebierce.org/pickett.htm (first quote); *OR*, Series I, Volume 38, Part I, 378 (second quote); Daniel, 403 (third quote); *OR*, Series I, Volume 38, Part I, 424 (fourth quote).
14. *OR*, Series I, Volume 38, Part I, 379.
15. Ibid. (first quote); Hazen, 256 (second quote).
16. Bierce, "The Crime at Pickett's Mill."
17. Ibid., 870.
18. Ibid., 878.
19. Howard, 309.
20. *OR*, Series I, Volume 38, Part IV, 507–508.
21. Howard, 311.
22. *OR*, Series I, Volume 38, Part I, 381.
23. Howard, 311–313.
24. *OR*, Series I, Volume 38, Part I, 893.
25. Howard, 313.
26. Hight, 341 (first quote); *OR*, Series I, Volume 38, Part I, 201 (second quote).
27. David Evans, *Sherman's Horsemen: Union Cavalry Operations in the Atlanta Campaign* (Bloomington: Indiana University Press, 1996), 86.
28. Ibid.
29. Sam Watkins, *Company Aytch* (New York: Plume, 1999), 144 (first quote); 150 (second quote).
30. Opdyke, 204.
31. *OR*, Series I, Volume 38, Part I, 383.
32. Ibid., 384.
33. Ibid.
34. Ibid., 384–385.

Chapter 16

1. Brooks D. Simpson and Jean V. Berlin, eds., *Sherman's Civil War: Selected Correspondence of William T. Sherman, 1860–1865* (Chapel Hill: University of North Carolina Press, 1999), 708.
2. *OR*, Series I, Volume 39, Part III, 584.
3. *OR*, Series I, Volume 39, Part I, 606 (first quote); *OR*, Series I, Volume 45, Part I, 120 (second quote).
4. Thomas J. Wood, letter to Lovell Harrison Rousseau, 19 November 1864, John A. McAllister Collection, Collection of the Library Company of Philadelphia, Philadelphia, Pennsylvania.
5. Ibid. Despite the help of Wood, the Speeds, and other influential Kentuckians, Rousseau did not win the Senate seat, which went to L&N president James Guthrie.
6. *OR*, Series I, Volume 45, Part I, 120.
7. Ibid., 1039.
8. Henry Stone, "Repelling Hood's Invasion of Tennessee," *Battles and Leaders of the Civil War: Retreat with Honor*, eds. Robert Underwood Johnson and Clarence Clough Buel (Edison, NJ: Castle Books, 1995), 444.
9. Shelby Foote, *The Civil War, a Narrative: Red River to Appomattox* (New York: Vintage Books, 1986), 660.
10. *OR*, Series I, Volume 45, Part I, 123.
11. Stone, 449.
12. Watkins, 202.
13. *OR*, Series I, Volume 45, Part I, 124.
14. Opdyke, 250.
15. Stone, 452.
16. Watkins, 210.
17. *OR*, Series I, Volume 45, Part I, 127.
18. Walter T. Durham, *Reluctant Partners: Nashville and the Union, July 1, 1863 to June 30, 1865* (Nashville: The Tennessee Historical Society, n.d.), 205.
19. Benjamin C. Truman, "The War in Tennessee," *The New York Times*, 12 December 1864.
20. *OR*, Series I, Volume 45, Part II, 33.
21. Wilson, 467 (first quote); *OR*, Series I, Volume 45, Part II, 132 (second quote).
22. *OR*, Series I, Volume 45, Part II, 17 (first quote), 55 (second quote), 70 (third quote).
23. Ibid., 84.
24. Ibid., 97.
25. Ibid., 115.
26. *OR*, Series I, Volume 45, Part I, 154 (first quote); *OR*, Series I, Volume 45, Part II, 133 (second quote).
27. *OR*, Series I, Volume 45, Part II, 143.
28. Ibid., 156.
29. *OR*, Series I, Volume 45, Part I, 129.
30. Foote, *Red River to Appomattox*, 691–692 (first quote); "The Battle of Friday," *The New York Times*, 19 December 1864.
31. *OR*, Series I, Volume 45, Part I, 129.
32. Foote, *Red River to Appomattox*, 695 (first

quote); OR Series I, Volume 45, Part I, 130 (second quote); "General Thomas' Army," *The New York Times*, 24 December 1864 (third quote).
33. *OR*, Series I, Volume 45, Part I, 130.
34. Ibid., 131.
35. Ibid., 133–134.
36. Ibid., 134.
37. Foote, *Red River to Appomattox*, 703.
38. Bobrick, 297.
39. Stone, 464.
40. *OR*, Series I, Volume 45, Part I, 134.
41. Ibid.

Chapter 17

1. *OR*, Series I, Volume 45, Part I, 436.
2. Watkins, 209–210.
3. *OR*, Series I, Volume 45, Part I, 135.
4. Ibid.
5. Ibid., 160.
6. *OR*, Series I, Volume 45, Part II, 299.
7. Ibid., 331.
8. *OR*, Series I, Volume 45, Part I, 137.
9. Ibid., 165.
10. Ibid., 138.
11. *OR*, Series I, Volume 45, Part II, 343.
12. Abel D. Streight, letter to Abraham Lincoln, 31 January 1865, Thomas J. Wood File, U.S. National Archives, RG-94/9W3/19/33/B/Box821.
13. *OR*, Series I, Volume 45, Part I, 174.
14. *OR*, Series I, Volume 45, Part II, 424.
15. Ibid.
16. Ibid.
17. *OR*, Series I, Volume 45, Part II, 533.
18. *OR*, Series I, Volume 45, Part I, 799.
19. Ibid., 800.
20. Opdyke, 276.
21. *Senate Executive Journal, 38th Congress, 2nd Session*, http://memory.loc.gov/cgi-bini/ampage, accessed May 17, 2010, 167.
22. Thomas J. Wood, "Kentucky and Slavery," *The New York Times*, 12 February 1865.
23. Ibid.
24. *OR*, Series I, Volume 49, Part II, 54.
25. Ibid., 62.
26. Opdyke, 290–291.

Chapter 18

1. *OR*, Series I, Volume 49, Part II, 966.
2. "Major-Gen. T.J. Wood; Farewell Address to His Command," *The New York Times*, 17 June 1865.
3. *OR*, Series I, Volume 48, Part II, 1050–1051.
4. Ibid., 1167–1168.
5. Ibid., 1169–1170.
6. Ibid., 1170.
7. Thomas J. Wood, letter to Lorenzo Thomas, 20 October 1865, Thomas J. Wood File,

U.S. National Archives, RG-94/9W3/19/33/B/Box 821.
8. "Affairs in the South," *The New York Times*, 4 February 1866.
9. *OR*, Series I, Volume 48, Part I, 219. In the December 2011 issue of *Civil War Times*, historians Joseph M. Thatcher and Thomas H. Thatcher write that Robert Louden, a Confederate saboteur, later confessed to placing a bomb disguised as a lump of coal in the coal-bin of the *Sultana* while she was at dock in Memphis. While admitting that it will probably never be possible to prove that a coal-bomb sank the *Sultana*, the Thatchers make the case that such a device could easily have been sneaked aboard the boat and point out that the nature of the April 27 explosion was very much like the earlier sinking of another boat which was known positively to have been sunk by a coal-bomb.
10. Ibid.
11. Ibid., 220.
12. "Affairs in the South," *The New York Times*, 4 February 1866.
13. Ibid.
14. James Wilford Garner, *Reconstruction in Mississippi* (New York: Macmillan, 1902), 114.
15. Ibid., 106–107.
16. Ibid., 107.
17. "Affairs in the South," *The New York Times*, 4 February 1866 (first quote); "Mississippi: Education of the Freedmen — Circular from Gen. Wood," *The New York Times*, 26 December 1866 (second and third quotes).
18. "Affairs in the South," *The New York Times*, 4 February 1866.
19. Ibid.
20. Garner, 108.
21. "The Freedmen — Report of Col. Samuel Thomas," *The New York Times*, 25 February 1866.
22. Association of Graduates of the United States Military Academy, *Thirty-Fifth Reunion of Graduates of the Association of Graduates of the United States Military Academy* (Saginaw: Sherman & Peters, 1904), 123 (first quote); "Gen. T.J. Wood Relieved — Complimentary Note from Gen. Thomas," *The New York Times*, 22 January 1867 (second quote).
23. Garner, 108 (first quote); A.W. Drury, *History of the City of Dayton and Montgomery County, Ohio* (Chicago: S.J. Clarke, 1909), 124 (second quote).
24. "Gen. T.J. Wood Relieved — Complimentary Note from Gen. Thomas," *The New York Times*, 22 January 1867.

Chapter 19

1. Thomas J. Wood, letter to Grover Cleveland, 25 October 1897, Thomas J. Wood File, U.S. National Archives, RG-94/9W3/19/33/B/Box821.
2. G.D. Meiklejohn, letter to Thomas J. Wood,

7 May 1900 (first quote); War Department Memorandum, 24 December 1897 (second and third quotes). Both from the Thomas J. Wood File, U.S. National Archives, RG-94/9W3/19/33/B/Box821.

3. Wood to Stickles, HCHS.

4. Ibid. (first quote); Wood, "The Battle of Missionary Ridge," 40 (second quote).

5. Association of Graduates of the United States Military Academy, *Thirty-Fifth Reunion of Graduates of the Association of Graduates of the United States Military Academy* (Saginaw: Sherman & Peters, 1904), 126.

6. Thomas J. Wood, letter to E.D. Townsend, 8 July 1874. Thomas J. Wood File, U.S. National Archives, RG-94/9W3/19/33/B/Box821.

7. George H. Wood, telegram to U.S. War Department, 25 February 1906, Thomas J. Wood File, U.S. National Archives, RG-94/9W3/19/33/B/Box 821.

8. Society of the Army of the Cumberland, *Society of the Army of the Cumberland, Thirty-Fourth Reunion* (Cincinnati: Robert Clarke & Co., 1907), 66–67.

Select Bibliography

Adams, George Rollie. *General William S. Harney: Prince of Dragoons*. Lincoln: University of Nebraska Press, 2001.

"Affairs in the South." *The New York Times*, February 4, 1866.

Ambrose, Stephen E. *Crazy Horse and Custer: The Parallel Lives of Two American Warriors*. Garden City, NY: Doubleday, 1975.

———. *Duty, Honor, Country: A History of West Point*. Baltimore: Johns Hopkins University Press, 1999.

Association of Graduates of the United States Military Academy. *Thirty-Fifth Reunion of Graduates of the Association of Graduates of the United States Military Academy*. Saginaw: Sherman & Peters, 1904.

"The Battle Friday." *The New York Times*, December 19, 1864.

Bauer, K. Jack. *The Mexican War: 1846–1848*. Lincoln: University of Nebraska Press, 1992.

Beatty, John. *The Citizen Soldier*. Cincinnati: Wilstach, Baldwin, 1879.

Belknap, Charles Eugene. *History of the Michigan Organizations at Chickamauga, Missionary Ridge, and Chattanooga, 1863*. Lansing: R. Smith, 1899.

Bickham, William D. *Rosecrans' Campaign with the Fourteenth Army Corps*. Cincinnati: Moore, Wilstach, Keys and Co., 1863.

Bierce, Ambrose. "The Crime at Pickett's Mill." www.ambrosebierce.org/pickett.htm. Accessed April 7, 2011.

Bloomfield, A. S. Letter to his brothers and sisters, 19 October 1861. http://www.crab.state.oh.us/images/stories/September_1861.pdf. Accessed December 22, 2010.

Buell, Don Carlos. Telegram to William S. Rosecrans, November 14, 1862. William S. Rosecrans Papers (Collection 663, Box 7), Department of Special Collections, Charles E. Young Research Library, UCLA, Los Angeles, California.

———. "East Tennessee and the Campaign of Perryville." *Battles and Leaders of the Civil War: The Tide Shifts*. Edited by Robert Underwood Johnson and Clarence Clough Buel. Edison, NJ: Castle Books, 1995.

Carter, Hodding. *Lower Mississippi*. New York: Farrar and Rinehart, 1942.

Catton, Bruce. *Grant Takes Command*. Boston: Little, Brown, 1969.

Center of Military History, United States Army. *American Military History*. Washington, DC: Center of Military History, 1969.

Cist, Henry M. *The Army of the Cumberland*. New York: Charles Scribner's Sons, 1882.

Collins, Lewis. *History of Kentucky*. Lexington, KY: Henry Clay Press, 1968.

Cooper, Edward S. *William Babcock Hazen: The Best Hated Man*. Madison NJ: Fairleigh Dickinson University Press, 2005.

Cox, Jacob D. *Military Reminiscences of the Civil War, Vol. II*. Teddington, Middlesex, England: The Echo Library, 2008.

Cozzens, Peter. *No Better Place to Die: The Battle of Stones River*. Urbana: University of Illinois Press, 1990.

———. *The Shipwreck of Their Hopes: The Battles for Chattanooga*. Urbana: University of Illinois Press, 1994.

———. *This Terrible Sound: The Battle of Chickamauga*. Urbana: University of Illinois Press, 1992.

Crittenden, Thomas L. "The Union Left at Stone's River." *Battles and Leaders of the Civil War: The Tide Shifts*. Edited by Robert Underwood Johnson and Clarence Clough Buel. Edison, NJ: Castle Books, 1995.

Cunningham, O. Edward. *Shiloh and the Western Campaign of 1862*. Edited by Gary D. Joiner and Timothy B. Smith. New York: Savas Beatie, 2007.

Curtius, "Department of the Cumberland." *The New York Times*, December 26, 1862.

———. "Department of the Ohio." *The New York Times*, October 6, 1862.

Daeuble, John, and Gottfried Rentschler. *Two Germans in the Civil War*. Edited and translated by

Joseph R. Reinhart. Knoxville: University of Tennessee Press, 2004.

Dana, Charles A. Telegram to Edwin M. Stanton, November 26, 1863. Abraham Lincoln Papers at the Library of Congress. http://memory.loc.gov/cgi-bin/query/r?ammem/mal:@field(DOC ID+@lit(d1232400)). Accessed December 22, 2010.

Daniel, Larry J. *Days of Glory: The Army of the Cumberland, 1861–1865*. Baton Rouge: Louisiana State University Press, 2004.

Davidson, Donald. *The Tennessee: Civil War to TVA*. New York: Rinehart, 1948.

Davis, William C. *The Orphan Brigade: The Kentucky Confederates Who Couldn't Go Home*. Garden City, NY: Doubleday, 1980.

Davison, E.L. *Autobiography of E.L. Davison*. N.p.: n.p., 1901.

DiNardo, Richard L., and James R. Furquerson. "The Day After: Braxton Bragg and the Aftermath of Chickamauga." *North and South*, February 1998.

Dodge, William Sumner. *History of the Old Second Division, Army of the Cumberland*. Chicago: Church and Goodman, 1864.

Drury, A.W. *History of the City of Dayton and Montgomery County, Ohio*. Chicago: S.J. Clarke, 1909.

Durham, Walter T. *Nashville: The Occupied City, The First Seventeen Months, Feb. 16, 1862 to June 30, 1863*. Nashville: Tennessee Historical Society, 1985.

_____. *Reluctant Partners: Nashville and the Union, July 1, 1863 to June 30, 1865*. Nashville: Tennessee Historical Society, n.d.

Dykeman, Wilma. *The French Broad*. New York: Rinehart, 1955.

Ehrman, George P. Letter to B. Swart, 28 October 1861. Collection of the author.

Eisenhower, John S.D. *Agent of Destiny: The Life and Times of General Winfield Scott*. New York: The Free Press, 1997.

_____. *So Far From God: The U.S. War with Mexico, 1846–1848*. Norman: University of Nebraska Press, 2000.

Engle, Stephen D. *Don Carlos Buell: Most Promising of All*. Chapel Hill: University of North Carolina Press, 1999.

Esposito, Vincent J., ed. *The West Point Atlas of American Wars*. New York: Praeger, 1978.

Eubank, Damon R. *In the Shadow of the Patriarch: The John J. Crittenden Family in War and Peace*. Macon, GA: Mercer University Press, 2009.

Evans, David. *Sherman's Horsemen: Union Cavalry Operations in the Atlanta Campaign*. Bloomington: Indiana University Press, 1996.

Federal Writers Project. *Military History of Kentucky*. Frankfort: The State Journal Company, 1939.

Floyd, David Bittle. *History of the Seventy-Fifth Regiment of Indiana Volunteers*. Philadelphia: Lutheran Publication Society, 1893.

Foote, Shelby. *The Civil War, a Narrative: Fort Sumter to Perryville*. New York: Vintage Books, 1986.

_____. *The Civil War, a Narrative: Fredericksburg to Meridian*. New York: Vintage Books, 1986.

_____. *The Civil War, a Narrative: Red River to Appomattox*. New York: Vintage Books, 1986.

"The Freedmen — Reports of Col. Samuel Thomas." *The New York Times*, February 25, 1866.

Fullerton, Joseph S. "The Army of the Cumberland at Chattanooga." *Battles and Leaders of the Civil War: The Tide Shifts*. Edited by Robert Underwood Johnson and Clarence Clough Buel. Edison, NJ: Castle Books, 1995.

Fullerton, Joseph S. "Reinforcing Thomas at Chickamauga." *Battles and Leaders of the Civil War: The Tide Shifts*. Edited by Robert Underwood Johnson and Clarence Clough Buel. Edison, New Jersey: Castle Books, 1995.

Garner, James Wilford. *Reconstruction in Mississippi*. New York: Macmillan, 1902.

"Gen. T.J. Wood Relieved — Complimentary Note from Gen. Thomas." *The New York Times*, January 22, 1867.

"General Grant's Army." *The New York Times*, December 2, 1863.

"General Thomas' Army." *The New York Times*, December 24, 1864

"General William Jenkins Worth's General Orders after the Battle of Monterey." http://www.history.vt.edu/MxAmWar/Newspapers/Niles/Nilesd1846NovDec.htm#NR71.15November71846GenWilliam.

"General Zachary Taylor's Congratulatory Orders on the Capture of Monterrey." http://www.history.vt.edu/MxAmWar/Newspapers/Niles/Nilesd1846NovDec.htm#NR71.15November71846GenZachary.

Grant, Ulysses S. *Personal Memoirs of U.S. Grant*. New York: The Library of America, 1990.

Harp, Lucille. "Thomas J. Wood and the Civil War." Wood Family File, Collection of the Hart County Historical Society, Munfordville, Kentucky.

Harrison, Lowell H. *The Civil War in Kentucky*. Lexington: University Press of Kentucky, 1975.

Hazen, William B. *A Narrative of Military Services*. Boston: Ticknor and Co., 1885.

Hight, John J. *History of the Fifty-Eighth Regiment of Indiana Volunteer Infantry*. Princeton, IN: Press of the Clarion, 1895.

Hill, Daniel H. "Chickamauga: The Great Battle of the West." *Battles and Leaders of the Civil War: The Tide Shifts*. Edited by Robert Underwood Johnson and Clarence Clough Buel. Edison, NJ: Castle Books, 1995.

Horgan, Paul. *Great River: The Rio Grande in North American History, Volume II*. New York: Rinehart, 1954.

Horrall, Spillard. *History of the 42nd Indiana Volunteers.* Chicago: Spillard Horrall, 1892.

Howard, Oliver O. "The Struggle for Atlanta." *Battles and Leaders of the Civil War: Retreat With Honor.* Edited by Robert Underwood Johnson and Clarence Clough Buel. Edison, NJ: Castle Books, 1995.

"An Incident of the Capture of Lookout Mountain [sic]." *The New York Times,* December 6, 1863.

Johnson, Mark W. *That Body of Brave Men: The U.S. Regular Infantry and the Civil War in the West.* Cambridge, MA: Da Capo Press, 2003.

Jones, Howard. "Republic in Peril: The Threat of Foreign Intervention in the Civil War." *North and South,* November 2010.

Kleber, John E., editor-in-chief. *The Kentucky Encyclopedia.* Lexington: University Press of Kentucky, 1992.

Lafferty, Susan C. *Civil War in Hart County, Kentucky: A Different Perspective.* N.p: n.p., 2009.

_____, compiler. *1850 Hart County, Kentucky Slave Schedule.* N.p: n.p., 2003.

Lathrop, David. *History of the 59th Regiment Illinois Volunteers.* Indianapolis: Hall and Hutchinson, 1865.

Lavender, David S. *Climax at Buena Vista: The Decisive Battle of the Mexican-American War.* Philadelphia: University of Pennsylvania Press, 2003.

Lee, Dan. *The L&N Railroad in the Civil War.* Jefferson, NC: McFarland, 2011.

Legends of the Operations of the Army of the Cumberland. Washington, DC: Government Printing Office, 1869.

Leonard, John W. Letter to the Hancock *Jeffersonian,* October 20, 1861. Collection of Bowling Green State University, Bowling Green, Ohio.

"Letter from Camp Nevin." *The Louisville Daily Democrat,* October 18, 1861.

Lewis, Felice Flanery. *Trailing Clouds of Glory: Zachary Taylor's Mexican War Campaign and His Emerging Civil War Leaders.* Tuscaloosa: University of Alabama Press, 2010.

Longstreet, James. *From Manassas to Appomattox.* New York: Konecky & Konecky, 1992.

Lorant, Stefan. *The Presidency.* New York: Macmillan, 1952.

Lyles, Ian B. "Mixed Blessing: The Role of the Texas Rangers in the Mexican War, 1846–1848." Master's Thesis, U.S. Army Command and General Staff College, Fort Leavenworth, Kansas, 2003.

McClure, Alexander K. *Recollections of Half a Century.* Salem, MA: Salem Press, 1902.

McCook, Alexander McDowell. Letter to William Dennison, 15 November 1861. Collection of the Ohio Historical Society, Columbus, Ohio.

McDowell, Robert E. *City of Conflict: Louisville in the Civil War, 1861–1865.* Louisville: Louisville Civil War Roundtable, 1962.

"Major-Gen. T.J. Wood; Farewell Address to His Command." *The New York Times,* June 17, 1865.

Mallock, Daniel L. "For Want of a Primer: The Battle of Franklin, November 30, 1864." *North and South,* September 2008.

Mannville, Craig Julian. "The Limits of Obedience: Brigadier General Thomas J. Wood's Performance During the Battle of Chickamauga." Master's Thesis, U.S. Army Command and General Staff College, Fort Leavenworth, Kansas, 2005.

Mansfield, Edward Deering. *The Mexican War.* New York: A.S. Barnes, 1848.

Meiklejohn, G.D. Letter to Thomas J. Wood, May 7, 1900. Thomas J. Wood File, U.S. National Archives, RG-94/9W3/19/33/B/Box821.

Military Order of the Loyal Legion of the United States. "In Memoriam: Companion Thomas John Wood." Thomas J. Wood File, U.S. National Archives, RG-94/9W3/19/33/B/Box821.

Miller, John F. "Requisition for 29th Regt. Ind. Vol." Collection of the author.

"Mississippi: Education of the Freedmen — Circular from Gen. Wood." *The New York Times,* December 26, 1866

Monaghan, Jay. *Civil War on the Western Border, 1854–1865.* New York: Bonanza Books, 1955.

Morrison, James L. *The Best School: West Point 1833–1866.* Kent, OH: Kent State University Press, 1998.

"The Nashville Papers; Suspended." *The New York Times,* March 9, 1862.

Newton, Steven. "Joseph Johnston and Snake Creek Gap." *North and South,* March 2001.

_____. "Snake Creek Gap and the Campaign that Never Happened." *North and South,* August 2009.

Noe, Kenneth. *Perryville: This Grand Havoc of Battle.* Lexington: University Press of Kentucky, 2001.

Ohrt, Wallace. *Defiant Peacemaker: Nicholas Trist in the Mexican War.* College Station: Texas A&M University Press, 1997.

Opdyke, Emerson. *To Battle for God and the Right: The Civil War Letterbooks of Emerson Opdyke.* Edited by Glenn V. Longacre and John E. Haas. Urbana: University of Illinois Press, 2003.

"Our Army on Green River." *Harper's Weekly,* February 1, 1862.

Peskin, Allan. *Garfield: A Biography.* Kent, OH: Kent State University Press, 1978.

"The Rebel Enterprise in Kentucky." *Harper's Weekly,* November 1, 1862.

"Redstick." Letter to the *Fremont Journal,* November 22, 1861. Collection of Bowling Green State University, Bowling Green, Ohio.

"Redstick." Letter to the *Fremont Journal,* November 29, 1861. Collection of Bowling Green State University, Bowling Green, Ohio.

Reed, Billy. *Famous Kentuckians.* Louisville, KY: Data Courier, 1977.

Reid, Whitelaw. *Ohio in the War: Her Statesmen, Generals, and Soldiers.* Cincinnati: Robert Clarke & Co., 1895.

"The Removal of Rosecrans." *Harper's Weekly*, October 31, 1863.
"Richard W. Thompson to Abraham Lincoln, Sunday, October 06, 1861." Abraham Lincoln Papers at the Library of Congress. http://memory.loc.gov/cgi-bin/query/r?ammem/mal:@field(DOC ID+@lit(d1232400)). Accessed December 22, 2010.
Robertson, William Glenn. "The Battle of Chickamauga, Day One, September 19, 1863." *Blue & Gray Magazine*. Spring 2008.
———. "The Battle of Chickamauga, Day Two, September 20, 1863." *Blue & Gray Magazine*, Summer 2008.
Robinson, William C. Letter to Charlie, 17 October 1861. Collection of the Abraham Lincoln Presidential Library, Springfield, Illinois.
Schurz, Carl. "Report on the Condition of the South." http:www.gutenberg.org/dirs/etext05/cnsth10.txt. Accessed March 14, 2011.
Scribner, Benjamin F. *Camp Life of a Volunteer: A Campaign in Mexico*. Philadelphia: Grigg, Elliott, 1847.
———. Papers, Folders 2–4, SC 1322. Collection of the Eugene and Marilyn Glick History Center, Indiana Historical Society, Indianapolis, Indiana.
Senate Executive Journal, 30th Congress, 1st Session. http://memory.loc.gov/cgi-bini/ampage. Accessed May 17, 2010.
Senate Executive Journal, 32nd Congress, 1st Session. http://memory.loc.gov/cgi-bini/ampage. Accessed May 17, 2010.
Senate Executive Journal, 37th Congress, 1st Session. http://memory.loc.gov/cgi-bini/ampage. Accessed May 17, 2010.
Senate Executive Journal, 37th Congress, 2nd Session. http://memory.loc.gov/cgi-bini/ampage. Accessed May 17, 2010.
Senate Executive Journal, 38th Congress, 2nd Session. http://memory.loc.gov/cgi-bini/ampage. Accessed May 17, 2010.
Shanks, William F. G. *Personal Recollections of Distinguished Generals*. New York: Harper & Bros., 1866.
Sheridan, Philip H. *Personal Memoirs of P.H. Sheridan*. Cambridge, MA: Da Capo Press, 1992.
Sherman, William T. *Memoirs of General W.T. Sherman*. New York: Library of America, 1990.
Simpson, Brooks D., and Jean V. Berlin, eds. *Sherman's Civil War: Selected Correspondence of William T. Sherman, 1860–1865*. Chapel Hill: University of North Carolina Press, 1999.
Smith, William F. "Comments on General Grant's 'Chattanooga.'" *Battles and Leaders of the Civil War: The Tide Shifts*. Edited by Robert Underwood Johnson and Clarence Clough Buel. Edison, NJ: Castle Books, 1995.
Society of the Army of the Cumberland. *Society of the Army of the Cumberland, Fourth Reunion*. Cincinnati: Robert Clarke & Co., 1870.
———. *Society of the Army of the Cumberland, Sixth Reunion*. Cincinnati: Robert Clarke & Co., 1873.
———. *Society of the Army of the Cumberland, Seventh Reunion*. Cincinnati: Robert Clarke & Co., 1874.
———. *Society of the Army of the Cumberland, Eighteenth Reunion*. Cincinnati: Robert Clarke & Co., 1888.
———. *Society of the Army of the Cumberland, Twenty-First Reunion*. Cincinnati: Robert Clarke & Co., 1891.
———. *Society of the Army of the Cumberland, Twenty-First Reunion*. Cincinnati: Robert Clarke & Co., 1891.
———. *Society of the Army of the Cumberland, Thirty-Fourth Reunion*. Chattanooga: MacGowan-Cooke, 1907.
Stegner, Wallace. *The Gathering of Zion*. New York: McGraw-Hill, 1964.
Stickles, Arndt M. *Simon Bolivar Buckner: Borderland Knight*. Chapel Hill: University of North Carolina Press, 1940.
Stone, Henry. "Repelling Hood's Invasion of Tennessee." *Battles and Leaders of the Civil War: Retreat With Honor*. Edited by Robert Underwood Johnson and Clarence Clough Buel. Edison, NJ: Castle Books, 1995.
Streeter, Floyd Benjamin. *The Kaw: The Heart of a Nation*. New York: Farrar & Rinehart, 1941.
Taylor, Zachary. "Battle of Buena Vista, Official Report." http://www.dmwv.org/mexwar/documents/Bvista.htm. Accessed on May 31, 2008.
———. "Official Report (1) of the Battle for Monterrey." http://www.dmwv.org/mexwar/documents/monter1.htm. Accessed on December 9, 2010.
———. "Official Report (2) of the Battle for Monterrey." http://www.dmwv.org/mexwar/documents/monter1.htm. Accessed on December 9, 2010.
———. "Official Report (3) of the Battle for Monterrey." http://www.dmwv.org/mexwar/documents/monter1.htm. Accessed on December 9, 2010.
———. "Official Report of the Battle of Palo Alto." http://www.dmwv.org/mexwar/documents/paloalto.htm. Accessed on December 9, 2010.
———. "Official Report of the Battle of Resacadela Palma." http://www.dmwv.org/mexwar/documents/resaca.htm. Accessed on December 9, 2010
Thomas, Samuel O. Letter to the Hancock *Jeffersonian*, November 15, 1861. Collection of Bowling Green State University, Bowling Green, Ohio.
Thompson, Edwin P. *History of the Orphan Brigade*. Louisville, KY: L.N. Thompson, 1898.
Traas, Adrian. *From the Golden Gate to Mexico City: the U.S. Topographical Engineers in the Mexican War, 1846–1848*. Washington, DC: Corps of

Engineers and U.S. Army Center of Military History, 1993.

Truman, Benjamin C. "The War in Tennessee." The *New York Times*, December 12, 1864.

Tucker, Glenn. *The Battles for Chattanooga*. Jamestown, VA: Eastern Acorn Press, 1987.

_____. *The Battle of Chickamauga*. Jamestown, VA: Eastern Acorn Press, 1969.

Tuttle, John W. *The Union, the Civil War, and John W. Tuttle: A Kentucky Captain's Account*. Edited by Hambleton Tapp and James C. Klotter. Frankfort: The Kentucky Historical Society, 1980.

The United States Army and Navy Journal and Gazette of the Regular and Volunteer Forces, Vol. 3. New York: Army & Navy Journal, 1865.

United States Military Academy. "Address by Brigadier-General T.J. Wood, U.S. Army, Retired." *The Centennial of the United States Military Academy at West Point, New York, 1802–1902, Volume I: Addresses and Histories*. Washington, DC: Government Printing Office, 1904.

United States War Department. *The War of the Rebellion: A Compilation of the Official Records of the Union and Confederate Armies*. 129 Volumes. Washington, DC: Government Printing Office, 1880–1901.

Van Horne, Thomas B. *History of the Army of the Cumberland: Its Organization, Campaigns, and Battles*. Two Volumes. Cincinnati: Robert Clark & Co., 1875.

War Department Memorandum, December 24, 1897. Thomas J. Wood File, U.S. National Archives, RG-94/9W3/19/33/B/Box821.

Ward, Ezra. *Generals in Blue*. Baton Rouge: Louisiana State University Press, 2006.

_____. *Generals in Gray*. Baton Rouge: Louisiana State University Press, 2006.

Watkins, Sam. *Company Aytch*. New York: Plume, 1999.

Widney, Lyman S. *Campaigning with Uncle Billy*. Edited by Robert I. Girardi. Victoria, British Columbia: Trafford, 2008.

Wilcox, Cadmus Marcellus. *History of the Mexican War*. Washington, DC: Church News, 1892.

Wiley, Bell Irwin. *The Life of Billy Yank*. Baton Rouge: Louisiana State University Press, 1978.

"William T. Sherman to Abraham Lincoln, Wednesday, October 09, 1861." The Abraham Lincoln Papers at the Library of Congress. http://memory.loc.gov/cgi-bin/query/r?ammem/mal:@field(DOCID+@lit(d1238500)). Accessed June 23, 2010.

Wilson, James Harrison. *Under the Old Flag: Recollections of Military Operations in the War for the Union, the Spanish War, the Boxer Rebellion, Etc., Volume I*. New York: D. Appleton, 1912.

_____. "The Union Cavalry in the Hood Campaign." *Battles and Leaders of the Civil War: Retreat with Honor*. Edited by Robert Underwood Johnson and Clarence Clough Buel. Edison, NJ: Castle Books, 1995.

Wood George H. Letter to A.M. Stickles, April 30, 1935. Buckner Family File, Collection of the Hart County Historical Society, Munfordville, Kentucky.

Wood, George H. Telegram to the War Department, February 25, 1906. Thomas J. Wood File, U.S. National Archives, RG-94/9W3/19/33/B/Box821.

Wood, Thomas J. "The Battle of Missionary Ridge." *Sketches of War History, 1861–1865: Papers Read Before the Ohio Commandery*. Edited by Robert Hunter and William Henry Chamberlain. The Military Order of the Loyal Legion of the United States. Cincinnati: Robert Clarke & Co., 1896.

_____. "The Gaps at Chickamauga." *The New York Times*, November 19, 1882.

_____. "Kentucky and Slavery." *The New York Times*, February 12, 1865.

_____. Letter to E.D. Townsend, July 8, 1874. Thomas J. Wood File, U.S. National Archives, RG-94/9W3/19/33/B/Box821.

_____. Letter to Grover Cleveland, October 25, 1897. Thomas J. Wood File, U.S. National Archives, RG-94/9W3/19/33/B/Box821.

_____. Letter to J.W. Denver, May 16, 1858. Territorial Kansas Online, 1854 to 1861," Border Disputes and Warfare." http://www.territorialkansasonline.org/~imlskto/cgibin/index.php?SCREEN=border&topics_id+66&search+United%20States.%20Army. Accessed October 25, 2010.

_____. Letter to Lovell H. Rousseau, November 19, 1864. John A. McAllister Collection, Library Company of Philadelphia, Philadelphia, Pennsylvania.

_____. Letter to Simon Bolivar Buckner, May 2, 1840. Collection of the Hart County Historical Society.

_____. Letter to Simon Bolivar Buckner, May 29, 1840. Collection of the Hart County Historical Society.

_____. Letter to Simon Bolivar Buckner, June 30, 1840. Collection of the Hart County Historical Society.

_____. Letter to Simon Bolivar Buckner, September 29, 1840. Collection of the Hart County Historical Society.

_____. Letter to Simon Bolivar Buckner, January 2, 1841. Collection of the Hart County Historical Society.

_____. Letter to Simon Bolivar Buckner, March 9, 1841. Collection of the Hart County Historical Society.

_____. Letter to Simon Bolivar Buckner, March 19, 1841. Collection of the Hart County Historical Society.

_____. Letter to Simon Bolivar Buckner, August 22, 1841. Collection of the Hart County Historical Society.

_____. Letter to Simon Bolivar Buckner, August

29, 1841. Collection of the Hart County Historical Society.

_____. Letter to Simon Bolivar Buckner, July 2, 1843. Collection of the Hart County Historical Society.

_____. Letter to Simon Bolivar Buckner, July 19, 1843. Collection of the Hart County Historical Society.

_____. Letter to Simon Bolivar Buckner, August 1, 1843. Collection of the Hart County Historical Society.

_____. Letter to Simon Bolivar Buckner, November 18, 1896. Collection of the Hart County Historical Society.

_____. Letter to William S. Rosecrans, November 11, 1862. William S. Rosecrans Papers (Collection 663, Box 7). Department of Special Collections, Charles E. Young Research Library, UCLA, Los Angeles, CA.

_____. Letter to William S. Rosecrans, June 9, 1863. William S. Rosecrans Papers (Collection 663, Box 8). Department of Special Collections, Charles E. Young Research Library, UCLA, Los Angeles, CA.

_____. "A Thrilling War Chapter: The Battle of Missionary Ridge. Recollections of Gen. Thomas J. Wood." *The New York Times*, July 16, 1876.

_____. "Who Lost the Battle of Chickamauga? Notes on Gen. Rosecrans' Report By Gen. Wood." *The New York Times*, January 10, 1864.

_____. "Wood at Chickamauga." *The New York Times*, December 25, 1881.

Wood v. United States, 107 U.S. 414 (1883). http://www.chanrobles.com/usa/us_supremecourt/107/414/case/php. Accessed September 2, 2010.

Woodworth, Steven E. *Nothing But Victory: The Army of the Tennessee, 1861–1865*. New York: Alfred A. Knopf, 2005.

Wright, Steven L., ed. *Kentucky Soldiers and Their Regiments in the Civil War: Abstracted from the Pages of Contemporary Kentucky Newspapers, Volume I*. Utica, KY: McDowell Publications, 2009.

_____. *Kentucky Soldiers and Their Regiments in the Civil War: Abstracted from the Pages of Contemporary Kentucky Newspapers, Volume II*. Utica, KY: McDowell Publications, 2009.

_____. *Kentucky Soldiers and Their Regiments in the Civil War: Abstracted from the Pages of Contemporary Newspapers, Volume III*. Utica, KY: McDowell Publications, 2009.

_____. *Kentucky Soldiers and Their Regiments in the Civil War: Abstracted from the Pages of Contemporary Newspapers, Volume IV*. Utica, KY: McDowell Publications, 2009.

_____. *Kentucky Soldiers and Their Regiments in the Civil War: Abstracted from the Pages of Contemporary Newspapers, Volume V*. Utica, KY: McDowell Publications, 2009.

Index

Acklin, Adelicia 210–211
Acklin, Joseph 210
Acklin, Sallie 211
Adairsville, Georgia 187
Adams, Daniel W. 100
Adams, John Quincy 35
Agua Nueva, Mexico 29
Alabama (aka 290) 90
Alabama Troops: 24th Infantry 160; 28th Infantry 160
Alexander, E.P. 11
Alexandria, Egypt 41
Allatoona Pass 187, 188
Alston, Fielding 30
Altamont, Tennessee 70
Ammen, Jacob 73
Ampudia, Pedro de 19, 25, 28
Anderson, Robert 42, 43, 249
Anna 232
Apache Indians 47, 239
Arista, Mariano 21
Arkansas Troops: Arkansas Mounted Regiment (Mexican War) 31, 32, 33
Army of Mississippi (CSA) 113
Army of Northern Virginia (CSA) 17, 112, 131, 135, 173
Army of Occupation (Mexican War) 28
Army of Tennessee (CSA) 113, 156, 184, 185, 189, 195, 219, 224, 227
Army of the Cumberland 2, 47, 91, 98, 105, 107, 109, 112, 113, 114, 115, 118, 119, 126, 128, 137, 142, 144, 152, 153, 156, 157, 159, 162, 163, 182, 184, 185, 192, 194, 197, 198, 201, 202, 203, 226, 227, 229, 230, 231, 249
Army of the Mississippi 60, 64, 91
Army of the Mississippi (CSA) 68, 70, 75, 81, 88
Army of the Ohio 54, 57, 58, 59, 71, 73, 76, 77, 78, 80, 81, 89, 91, 107, 121, 154, 175, 176, 184, 185, 191, 194, 249
Army of the Potomac 15, 112, 157, 162, 173, 184, 230

Army of the Tennessee 57, 58, 59, 60, 154, 159, 162, 184, 185, 187, 191, 194, 197–198, 199
Atkins, S.D. 126, 127
Atlanta, Georgia 68, 185, 194, 195, 197, 198, 200, 201, 202, 223, 243; battle 196–197
Aunt Sarah (slave) 7
Avery, Captain 167

Bacon Creek, Kentucky 45, 52, 53, 79
Baird, Absalom 139, 141, 144, 165, 166, 172
Baltimore, Maryland 13
Bardstown, Kentucky 53, 79, 82
Barnes, Sidney P. 138, 140, 141, 144
Barren County, Kentucky 5
Bartleson, Frederick 149
Bass, Sion S. 49
Battle Creek, Tennessee 66
Bean's Station, Tennessee 183
Beatty, John 105, 112
Beatty, Samuel 156, 160, 161, 165, 166, 184, 186, 189, 209, 210, 214, 215, 216, 217, 221, 231, 251
Beauregard, P.G.T. 58, 62, 68
Bee, Bernard 14
Bell, John 55
Bell's Tavern, Kentucky 78
Belmont Mansion 210–211
Bickham, William D. 100, 102, 103, 104
Bierce, Ambrose 189, 190
Big Hill, Kentucky 73
Blain's Crossroads, Tennessee 179
Blair, W.W. 177
Bloomfield, Alpheus S. 50
Blue Springs, Tennessee 183
Blue Water Creek, Battle of (Indian Wars) 37
Board of Trade Battery 104
Board of Visitors (West Point) 14, 244
Bond, Frank 140
Boston Press 112
Bottom, Squire Henry 87
Bourbon County, Kentucky 7
Bowles, W.F. 31

267

Bowling Green, Kentucky 14, 44, 45, 52, 54, 72–73, 74, 75, 76, 77, 78, 90, 92
Boyle, Jeremiah T. 77
Boyle County, Kentucky 85
Bozeman Trail 239
Bradley, Cullen 104, 107, 108, 131, 134, 135, 140, 142–143, 156, 160, 184
Bragg, Braxton 31, 32, 33, 62, 68, 70, 71, 73, 74, 75, 76, 77, 78, 79, 81, 82, 86, 87, 88, 89, 90, 94, 97, 98, 103, 104, 105, 112, 113, 114, 115, 117, 121, 123, 128, 129, 133, 152, 159, 161, 163, 164, 168, 169, 173, 176, 184, 195
Bramlette, Thomas E. 178–179
Brannan, John 105, 138, 139, 140, 141, 145, 146, 147, 148, 153, 159, 173
Breckinridge, John C. 104, 112, 113, 133, 139
Breckinridge County, Kentucky 9
Brentwood, Tennessee 218
Bridgeport, Alabama 122, 156, 157, 158, 203, 225
Bridges, Lyman 251
Brown, Jacob 19, 20, 23
Brown, Lieutenant Colonel 79
Brown's Ferry, Tennessee 158
Brown's Mill Creek 188
Brownsville, Pennsylvania 13
Bryan, William Jennings 1, 2
Buckhead, Georgia 195
Buckner, Aylett 9
Buckner, Simon Bolivar 1–2, 3, 7–9, 12, 13, 14, 25, 34, 35, 45, 52, 75–76, 117, 127, 245, 246
Buell, Don Carlos 46, 51, 53, 54, 55–56, 57, 59, 60, 62, 64, 65, 66, 68, 69, 70, 71, 72, 73, 74, 75, 76–77, 78, 79, 80–81, 82, 85, 89, 90–91, 92, 93, 119, 175, 241, 249
Buell, George P. 92, 100, 101, 106, 107, 131, 133, 135–136, 137, 140, 141–142, 144, 145, 146, 147, 152, 156, 250
Buena Vista, Battle of (Mexican War) 30–33, 36, 247
Buford, Abraham 206
Bull Run, Virginia, First Battle of (see Manassas)
Bull's Gap, Tennessee 228
Bumpus, Mr. (spy) 72, 92–93
Bureau of Refugees, Freedman, and Abandoned Lands 233, 237
Burnside, Ambrose 121, 173, 174, 175–176
Butler, William O. 26
Buzzard's Roost Gap 185

Cable, George Washington 235
Calhoun, James 200, 201
Calhoun, Georgia 187
Camargo, Mexico 24, 25
Cameron, Simon 41, 43, 45, 46
Camp Nevin, Kentucky 46, 47–51, 79, 107, 156, 242
Camp Wood, Kentucky 52
Canby, Edward R.S. 226
Carlin, William P. 135
Carter, F.B. 208, 210

Cartersville, Georgia 202
Carthage, Tennessee 72
Cassville, Georgia 187
Catoosa Springs, Georgia 183
Cave City, Kentucky 74, 75
Centennial Exposition 245
Central District of Arkansas 233
Central District of Texas 232
Cerralvo, Mexico 25
Cerro Gordo, Mexico 33, 34
Chalmers, James 74–75, 99
Chalmette Plantation 232
Chamberlain, Joshua Lawrence 147
Champ de Mars, France 40
Chancellorsville, Virginia, Battle of 112, 162, 196
Chapultepec, Mexico 33
Charles XV, King of Norway 41
Chattahoochee River 191, 193, 194, 197, 201
Chattanooga, Tennessee 15, 64, 68, 69, 70, 81, 119, 120, 121, 123, 125, 126–127, 128, 129, 133, 143, 144, 147, 150, 152–153, 155, 156, 157, 158, 159, 169, 174, 175, 177, 178, 179, 184, 189, 203, 229, 243, 244
Cheatham, B.F. 196–197, 206, 207, 208, 216
Cherokee Indians 127
Cheyenne Indians 239
Chickamauga, Georgia, Battle of 15, 133–152, 154, 170, 178, 179, 181, 182, 196, 197, 224, 227, 242, 243, 247
Chickamauga Battlefield Park 243
Chickamauga Creek 122, 128, 129, 130, 131, 132, 133
Churchill, William H. 21
Churubusco, Mexico 33, 35, 46
Cincinnati, Ohio 5, 13
Clay, Henry 6, 9, 38, 78, 232
Clayton, Henry 218
Cleburne, Patrick 130, 139, 162, 164, 189, 190, 206, 208, 210, 217
Cleveland, Grover 244
Cleveland, Tennessee 183
Clinch Valley 183
Cochise 239
Columbia, Tennessee 65, 205, 220, 221
Columbus, Kentucky 44
Columbus Barracks, Ohio 246
Comanche Indians 239
Contreras, Mexico 33
Cooke, Philip St. George 37
Corinth, Mississippi 57, 58, 60, 64; battle 91
Corinth Campaign 60–63, 64, 80, 91, 108
Corpus Christi, Texas 16
Cox, Jacob D. 105, 178, 204, 205, 206, 207, 208, 209
Crab Orchard, Kentucky 88
Craddock, A.G. 76
Cram, Thomas J. 16–17
Crawfish Springs 138
Crittenden, George L. 81
Crittenden, John J. 81, 90, 118
Crittenden, Thomas L. 32, 64, 66, 72, 73,

Index

79–80, 81–82, 83–84, 85, 88, 90, 92, 94, 95, 96, 97, 99, 102, 103, 104–105, 106, 107, 110, 116, 118–119, 120–121, 122, 123–124, 127, 129, 130, 132, 133, 136–137, 138, 139, 142, 143–144, 148, 149, 150, 152, 153, 155–156, 181–182, 223, 242, 249, 250
Cruft, Charles 73, 104, 156, 225
Crutchfield House (Chattanooga) 126
Cumberland, Maryland 13
Cumberland Gap 45, 183
Cumberland River 55, 56, 72, 81, 93, 110, 212
Curtis, Samuel 108
"Curtius" 82, 93, 94
Cushing, Henry 143

Dallas, Georgia 188
Dalton, Georgia 127, 184, 186, 195, 202
Dana, Charles A. 137, 162, 171
Danville, Kentucky 6, 53, 88
Davis, Garrett 90
Davis, Jefferson 30, 31, 113, 169, 184, 194
Davis, Jefferson C. 80, 134, 135, 139, 140, 141–142, 143, 149, 162
Davison, E.L. 84
Dayton, Ohio 1, 2, 51, 105, 107, 181, 241, 242, 244, 245, 246–247
Dayton (Ohio) Literary Union 242
Decatur, Alabama 64, 65, 66, 67, 68, 203
Decatur, Georgia 195, 196
Decherd, Tennessee 68, 69, 70, 183, 225
Delafield, Richard 10–11
Democratic Party 1, 2, 28, 218, 242, 244
Denver, J.W. 39
Department of Arkansas and the Indian Territory 232
Department of Mississippi 57, 233, 234
Department of the Cumberland 42, 43, 51, 232
Department of the Gulf 232
Department of the Ohio 46, 51, 76, 173
Department of the Southwest 232
Department of the Trans-Mississippi 15
Dick's River 88
District of Mississippi 239
District of Tennessee 204
District of the Etowah 214
Dodge, William Sumner 49, 50, 100, 111
Donald's Church, Tennessee 116
Donelson, Daniel 99
Dougherty's Gap, Georgia 122
Douglas, Stephen A. 38
Dripping Springs, Kentucky 78
Duck River 65, 69, 205, 206, 220, 221
Dumont, Ebenezer 53
Duncan, James 25
Dunlap, H.C. 134

East Fork of Big Camp Creek 186
East Tennessee & Virginia Railroad 228
Eastport, Mississippi 227
Ehrman, George P. 50
Ehrman, Henry S. 50

Ehrman, John W. 50
El Camino del Rey, Mexico 35
Elisha (slave) 7
Elizabethtown, Kentucky 79, 225
Elk River 65, 66, 69, 117, 203, 222, 225
Elliott, Washington L. 214, 215, 216, 220, 221, 228, 231, 251
Emancipation Proclamation 111, 228
Embree, James T. 106
Emerson, Ralph Waldo 35
Estep, George 71, 99, 100, 104, 136, 142
Estill Springs, Tennessee 69
Etowah River 187, 188
Evansville, Indiana 59
Ezra Church, Georgia, Battle of 197–198

Fayetteville, Tennessee 69
Fern Creek, Kentucky 82
Florence, Alabama 58, 65, 66, 222
Forrest, Nathan Bedford 55, 56, 66, 71, 94, 112, 117, 131, 132, 133, 139, 146, 201, 205, 206, 208, 221
Fort Brown, Texas 23
Fort Donelson, Tennessee 54, 55, 153
Fort Henry, Tennessee 54
Fort Leavenworth, Kansas 37, 38, 39, 40
Fort McPherson, Nebraska 240
Fort Sanders, Tennessee 176
Fort Scott, Kansas 38–39
Fort Sumter, South Carolina 42
Fort Texas, Texas 18, 19, 20, 21, 23
Fort Washita, Indian Territory 41
Fort Wood, Tennessee 160
Fortress Rosecrans, Tennessee 110, 111, 179
Frankfort, Kentucky 2, 9, 72, 73, 77, 82
Franklin, Tennessee 206, 207–208; battle 208–210, 214, 217, 223, 229
Fredericksburg, Virginia, Battle of 173
Freedman's Bureau 236, 238, 239, 242
Frémont, John C. 43
French Broad River 175
Fullerton, Joseph S. 146–147, 167, 185, 187, 191, 193, 209, 220, 222
Fyffe, Edward P. 71

Gallatin, Tennessee 68, 72, 92
Galt House (Louisville) 42, 43, 45, 56, 80, 81, 134
Garfield, James A. 58, 61, 62–63, 108, 115, 149, 249
Garland, John 26
Garrard, Kenner 194, 219
Garrard, T.T. 183
Gaylesville, Alabama 203
Geary, John W. 196
George, John E. 136
Georgia Railroad 195, 196, 197, 201
Gettysburg, Pennsylvania, Battle of 118, 147, 166, 196
Gibson, William H. 187, 189, 190, 251
Gilbert, Charles C. 81, 82, 85, 90

Glasgow, Kentucky 14, 72, 73
Glendale, Kentucky 225
Glenn, Eliza 133, 137, 138
Goodspeed, Wilbur 251
Gorman, Willis A. 32
Grand Army of the Republic 247
Grand Review 230
Granger, Gordon 15, 108, 115, 121, 130, 146, 156, 159, 160, 161, 164–165, 167, 171, 174–175, 176–177, 179, 184, 241, 250
Grant, U.S. 13, 17, 18, 25, 26, 34, 54, 57, 58, 59, 60, 108, 112, 113, 115, 118, 153–154, 157, 158–159, 160, 161–162, 163–164, 165, 166, 167, 169, 171, 172, 173, 174, 175, 185, 192, 203, 212–213, 224, 226, 227, 242
Green, Willis 8, 9
Green River 2, 5, 7, 45, 48, 53, 54, 74, 75, 78, 79
Green River Iron Company 241
Greeneville, Tennessee 229
Greensburg, Kentucky 14
Greer, Caroline *see* Wood, Caroline Greer
Grose, William 99, 197
Guadalupe-Hidalgo, Treaty of 34–35
Gunter's Landing, Alabama 225
Guthrie, James 43, 90

Halleck, Henry W. 57, 60, 61, 62, 63, 64, 81, 91, 94, 108–110, 111, 114, 119, 123, 154, 155, 163, 202, 212
Hambleton, Charles A. 39–40
Hamilton, A.J. 233
Hancock Jeffersonian 50
Hanson, Roger W. 104
Hardee, William J. 74, 75, 104, 117, 196, 198
Hardin County, Kentucky 6, 49
Harker, Charles G. 53, 66, 68, 85–86, 87–88, 90, 92, 94, 95, 96–97, 98, 99, 102, 104, 107, 108, 120, 124, 125, 129–130, 131, 132, 133, 134–135, 136, 137, 138, 140, 141, 142, 144, 145, 146, 147, 152, 155, 156, 161, 185, 249, 250
Harney, William S. 37
Harper's Weekly 49, 54, 90, 154
Harpeth River 207, 220
Harpeth Shoals, Tennessee 93, 94
Harrison, Thomas J. 49, 136
Harrodsburg, Kentucky 88
Harrogate, Tennessee 242
Hart County, Kentucky 2, 3, 5, 6, 45
Hascall, Milo 57, 58–59, 65, 71, 92, 95, 96, 98, 99, 100, 101, 102, 107, 194, 249, 250
Hatch, R.R. 235
Hayes, Rutherford B. 243
Haysville, Kentucky 84, 106
Hazen, William B. 99, 100, 156, 158, 160–161, 165–166, 168, 173, 184, 186, 187, 188, 189–190, 193, 250, 251
Hébert, Louis 14–15
Heg, Hans C. 134, 135
Helm, Charles 6
Hembree, Richard 106, 111

Hickory Creek, Kansas 38
Hight, John J. 105, 106, 110, 121, 122
Hill, Daniel H. 136
Hillsboro, Tennessee 117, 120
Hindman, Thomas C. 130
Hiwassee River 174
Hodgenville, Kentucky 79
Holston River 175
Holt, Joseph 106, 235
Hood, John Bell 131–132, 135, 195, 196, 197, 198, 199, 200, 201, 202, 203, 204, 205, 206, 208, 211, 212, 215, 216, 217, 219, 223, 224, 225, 227, 231
Hooker, Joseph 115, 157, 158, 159, 160, 163, 164, 172, 186, 188, 191, 194, 196, 197
Horrall, Spillard 91
Hotchkiss, Charles T. 251
Howard, O.O. 157, 160, 161 162, 166–167, 184, 185, 186, 187, 188, 190, 191, 192, 193–194, 195, 197, 198, 199, 242, 250
Howard University 242
Hudson River 10, 12, 15, 244, 247
Humphreys, Benjamin G. 236, 238, 240
Huntsville, Alabama 64, 68, 203, 222, 223, 224, 226, 227–228

Illinois troops: Bridges' Independent Battery 251; 1st Volunteers (Mexican War) 31, 32, 33; 2nd Volunteers (Mexican War) 31; 25th Infantry 250, 251; 34th Infantry 50, 51, 110, 249; 35th Infantry 250, 251; 42nd Infantry; 59th Infantry 251; 89th Infantry 250, 251; 92nd Infantry 126; 100th Infantry 96, 135, 149, 250
Indiana Troops: 2nd Cavalry 250; 2nd Volunteers (Mexican War) 31, 32; 3rd Volunteers (Mexican War) 31, 32; 6th Artillery 249; 6th Infantry 251; 8th Artillery 71, 99, 100, 104, 152, 250; 10th Artillery 86, 249, 250; 13th Artillery 74; 15th Infantry 100, 136, 250; 17th Infantry 74, 249, 250; 29th Infantry 47, 49, 51, 249; 30th Infantry 49, 51, 249; 32nd Infantry 250, 251; 34th Infantry; 38th Infantry 49, 249; 39th Infantry 49, 136, 249; 40th Infantry 53, 249, 250; 42nd Infantry 91; 44th Infantry 145; 51st Infantry 53, 66, 94, 97, 249, 250, 251; 57th Infantry 53, 58, 100, 249, 250; 58th Infantry 53, 71, 99, 100, 105, 106, 121, 135, 142, 144, 195, 249, 250; 67th Infantry 74; 68th Infantry 250; 73rd Infantry 97, 250; 74th Infantry 74; 75th Infantry 115; 79th Infantry 160, 251; 86th Infantry 160, 251; 89th Infantry 74
Indianapolis, Indiana 42, 43, 51
Indianola, Texas 232
Island No. 10 232
Iuka, Mississippi, Battle of 91

Jackson, Andrew 232
Jackson, James S. 85, 86

Index

Jackson, John K. 100
Jackson, Thomas J. ("Stonewall") 14, 162, 184
Jackson, Mississippi 113
Jasper, Alabama 122
Jeffersonville, Indiana 43
Jewess 232
J.H. Baldwin 232
John (scout) 49
Johnson, Andrew 93, 233, 241
Johnson, Bushrod 131, 132, 142
Johnson, Richard W. 42, 107, 139, 165, 172, 188, 189, 190, 204, 242
Johnsonville, Tennessee 231, 232
Johnston, Albert Sidney 37, 44–45, 54, 55, 57, 58
Johnston, Joseph E. 113, 169, 184, 185, 186, 187, 188, 191, 192, 193, 194, 195, 216, 227, 230, 231
Jonesboro, Georgia 198, 199

Kalfus, H.F. 111–112, 179
Kansas Boundary Expedition 37
Kansas-Nebraska Act 38
Kansas Troops: 8th Infantry 250, 251
Kelley's Ferry, Tennessee 158
Kellogg, Sanford Cobb 140
Kennesaw Mountain, Georgia 191, 193, 202; battle 192, 208
Kentucky General Assembly 6, 9
Kentucky Military Board 52, 77
Kentucky Troops: 1st Artillery 251; 1st Cavalry 250; 1st Cavalry (Mexican War) 31; 1st Volunteers (Mexican War) 26; 2nd Volunteers (Mexican War) 31, 32, 33; 3rd Cavalry 250; 3rd Infantry 60, 66, 69, 70, 78, 96, 99, 122, 134, 135, 144, 178, 249, 250; 5th Infantry 250, 251; 6th Infantry 250, 251; 9th Infantry 160, 251; 12th Infantry 209; 15th Infantry 111, 179; 16th Infantry 209; 17th Infantry 251; 23rd Infantry 166, 251; 24th Infantry 249, 250; 26th Kentucky 112; 33rd Infantry 74
Kershaw, Joseph B. 142
Kilpatrick, Judson 198
Kimball, Nathan 197, 199, 202, 206, 207, 208, 214, 215, 216, 218, 220, 221, 228, 231, 251
King, Edward 155
Kingston, Georgia 187, 202, 203
Kiowa Indians 239
Kneffler, Frederick 189, 190, 251
Knoxville, Tennessee 70, 73, 121, 173, 174, 175, 176, 177, 178, 183, 228, 229

La Angostura, Mexico 30, 31
La Encarnación, Mexico 30
La Fayette, Georgia 203
La Hedionda, Mexico 29–30
Lane, Jim 40
Langdon, E. Bassett 168
Larkinsville, Alabama 225
Lavaca Bay 232
La Vergne, Tennessee 95–96, 100

Law, Evander M. 135, 142
Lawrence, Kansas 38
Lawrenceburg, Tennessee 57, 58, 205
Lebanon, Tennessee 92
Lee, Robert E. 17, 112, 118, 162, 196, 212, 230
Lee, Stephen D. 198, 199, 216, 217, 218
Lee and Gordon's Mills 129, 130, 131, 133, 150
Leonard, John W. 50
Lexington, Alabama 222
Lexington, Kentucky 73, 104
Liberty, Tennessee 113
Lightning Brigade, The 121, 132
Lincoln, Abraham 41, 42, 73, 81, 89, 90, 106, 107, 111, 113, 114, 154, 157, 174, 179, 180, 223, 227
Lincoln Memorial University 242
Linn County, Kansas 38
Little Tennessee River 175
London, Kentucky 89
Longchamps, France 41
Longstreet, James 17, 112, 131, 135, 142, 148, 150, 173, 175, 176, 177
Lookout Mountain, Tennessee 122, 123, 149, 150, 152, 155, 156, 158, 159; battle 163–164, 176
Los Angeles, California 242
Lost Mountain 191
Loudon, Tennessee 177
Louisiana Troops: 1st Cavalry (CSA) 73
Louisville, Kentucky 5, 6, 10, 13, 42, 43, 45, 46, 51, 56, 73, 75, 80, 82, 89, 90, 92, 107, 119, 156, 181, 204
Louisville & Nashville Railroad 43, 45, 46, 47, 50, 54, 55, 56, 68, 72, 74, 90, 93, 94, 225
Louisville and Nashville Turnpike 5, 10, 13, 47, 49, 74, 78, 79
Louisville Daily Democrat 52
Louisville Daily Journal 111, 112
Louisville Provost Guard 74
Lovejoy, Georgia 199, 202, 223, 227, 243
Lyman, Luke 110–11
Lynchburg, Kentucky 84
Lynnville, Tennessee 205, 222
Lyon, Arthur P. 225–226
Lyon, Hylan B. 225–226

Macon & Western Railroad 197, 198
Magoffin, Beriah 52
Mallory, Robert 90
Manassas, Virginia, Battle of (1861) 14, 47
Manchester, Tennessee 69, 113, 118
Manson, Mahlon 73
Marais des Cygnes Massacre 39–40
Marietta, Georgia 192, 194, 201
Marin, Mexico 25
Maryville, Tennessee 175
Mason, J.C. 235
Matagorda Bay 232
Matamoros, Mexico 17, 18, 19, 23, 24
Matthews, Shelburne (slave) 7
May, Charles 21, 22, 29, 30, 31, 32, 33

Maysville Dollar Weekly Bulletin 112
McClellan, George B. 56, 91, 154
McCook, Alexander McDowell 46, 47, 48, 49, 50, 51, 54, 64, 66, 73, 74, 77, 80, 82, 85, 92, 93, 95, 96, 97, 98, 102, 105, 107, 110, 115, 121, 122, 130, 133, 134, 138, 139, 141, 141, 142, 143, 144, 148, 149, 150, 153, 155, 156, 181–182, 249
McCook, Edward M. 88, 197, 250
McCulloch, Ben 29, 30
McKee, Samuel 99
McKibben, J.C. 81
McKinley, William 2
McLarty, John B. 9
McMinnville, Tennessee 68, 70, 113
McPherson, James B. 184, 185, 186, 191, 192, 193, 194, 195, 196, 197
Meade, George G. 16–17, 118
Medal of Honor 244
Meiklejohn, G.D. 244
Memphis & Charleston Railroad 60, 64, 65
Mendenhall, John 104–105, 143
Metcalfe, Leonidas 73
Mexico City, Mexico 28, 33, 34, 35, 36
Miami County, Kansas 38
Michigan Troops: 1st Michigan Engineers 250; 13th Infantry 97, 135, 249, 250; 15th Infantry 53
Middle Bass Island 243
Mier, Mexico 23, 25
Milan, Italy 41
Miles, Dixon S. 24
Military Department of the Mississippi 154, 158, 173, 184
Military Division of West Mississippi 226
Military Order of the Loyal Legion of the United States 170, 247
Mill Springs, Kentucky, Battle of 53, 54
Mill Springs, Tennessee 68
Miller, John F. 48, 49
Miñon, José Vincente 30
Minty, Robert H.G. 131, 132
Missionary Ridge, Tennessee 129, 130, 138, 152, 156, 159, 160, 161, 162, 163, 164; battle 164–169, 170, 171, 172–173, 176, 184, 219, 223, 227, 232, 247
Mississippi River 44, 112, 232
Mississippi troops: Mississippi Rifles (Mexican War) 30, 31, 32
Mitchel, Ormsby 54, 64
Mitchell, Robert B. 105, 138
Mitchellville, Tennessee 72, 93, 94
Mobile, Alabama 68, 224
Mobile & Ohio Railroad 60
Monongahela River 13
Monterrey, Battle of (Mexican War) 25–28
Montgomery, James 39, 40
Montgomery, Alabama 68, 197, 224, 226
Mooresville, Tennessee 69
Morgan, John Hunt 68, 92, 93, 94
Morgantown, Tennessee 174

Morton, Oliver P. 41, 42, 80
Mosler, Henry 49
Mud Creek 191
Munfordville, Kentucky 2, 3, 7, 9, 10, 13, 14, 15, 17, 37, 45, 52, 53, 54, 74–76, 77, 78, 79, 107, 152, 227, 245, 246, 247
Murfreesboro, Tennessee 66, 68, 70, 71, 94, 95, 96, 97, 105, 108, 109, 110, 113, 114, 115, 117, 149, 204

Nashville, Tennessee 9, 54, 55–57, 68, 69, 71, 72, 77, 90, 93, 94, 98, 99, 100, 101, 102, 103, 105, 110, 203, 204, 205, 206, 210, 221, 225, 227, 229, 231, 232; battle 210–218, 219, 223, 225, 227, 244, 247
Nashville & Chattanooga Railroad 66, 68, 111, 122, 125
Nashville & Decatur Railroad 66, 68
Nashville Banner 56
Negley, James S. 130, 138, 139, 140, 143, 149–150, 152, 153, 155, 181–182, 242
Nelson, William "Bull" 62, 64, 68, 69, 70, 80, 81, 134
Nelson County, Kentucky 82
Nevin, David 47
New England Emigrant Aid Company 38
New Hope Church, Georgia, Battle of 188
New Market, Tennessee 228
New Orleans, Louisiana 5, 228, 231, 232; battle (War of 1812) 232
New York City 10, 13, 34, 37, 41, 243
New York Times 57, 82, 93, 151, 164, 166, 168, 172, 211, 215, 216, 228, 231, 235–236, 237, 242
New York Tribune 46
Newport, Tennessee 175
Newton, John 184, 186, 187, 188, 191, 193, 194, 196, 199, 202
Nolin, Kentucky 45, 46, 47, 225
Nolin River 47
North Alabama Campaign 64–68, 177
Nueces River 15, 16, 17

Oates, William C. 166
O'Brien, John Paul Jones 31, 32
Ohio River 41, 43, 45, 112, 142, 212, 232
Ohio troops: Ohio National Guard 247; 1st Artillery 50, 251; 1st Cavalry 67, 250; 1st Infantry 168, 251; 2nd Cavalry 65, 249, 250; 3rd Infantry 105; 5th Artillery 249; 6th Artillery 135, 250, 251; 6th Infantry 99, 100, 251; 13th Infantry 251; 15th Infantry 250, 251; 19th Infantry 160, 161, 251; 20th Artillery 251; 26th Infantry 71, 99, 100, 127, 135, 250; 41st Infantry 251; 49th Infantry 50–51, 250, 251; 59th Infantry 251; 64th Infantry 53, 144, 249, 250; 65th Infantry 53, 144, 249, 250; 71st Infantry 251; 93rd Infantry 251; 97th Infantry 99, 127, 250; 124th Infantry 251; 125th Infantry 120, 129, 144, 185, 209, 250

Index

Old Soldier's Home (Washington, D.C.) 242
Oostenaula River 187
Opdyke, Emerson 120, 129, 130, 144, 145, 153, 154, 185, 197, 198, 206, 207, 208, 209, 226, 227, 229, 232
Orchard Knob 160–162, 163, 165, 166, 169, 184, 247
Ormsby, Stephen 26
Orphan Brigade (CSA) 104

Pace's Ferry, Georgia 193, 194, 195
Paducah, Kentucky 232
Paint Rock 174
Paint Rock, Alabama 225
Palmer, J.B. 100
Palmer, John M. 1, 2, 95, 96, 97, 99, 104, 107, 116, 119, 120, 127, 128, 130, 133, 136, 137, 139, 150, 152, 165, 188, 191
Palmer, William J. 225
Palo Alto, Battle of (Mexican War) 20–21, 33, 150
Paris, France 41
Parks, Zingu 105–106
Peachtree Creek 196
Pelham, Tennessee 117
Pemberton, James C. 113
Pennsylvania troops: Independent Battery B, Pennsylvania Artillery 251; 7th Cavalry 250; 15th Cavalry 225; 77th Infantry 51, 249
Perryville, Kentucky, Battle of 82, 85–87, 90, 91
Petersburg, Virginia, Siege of 212
Phelps, A.J. 168
Philadelphia, Pennsylvania 10, 245
Pickett, George 166
Pickett's Mill, Georgia, Battle of 188–190, 192, 227
Pike, Albert 32, 33
Pine Mountain 191, 202
Pinhook Town, Alabama 222
Pittsburg Landing, Tennessee 58, 59, 60
Pittsburgh, Pennsylvania 13
Poinsett, Joel 10
Point Isabel, Texas 17, 19, 20, 21
Polk, James K. 19, 28, 34, 35, 36, 55, 211
Polk, Leonidas 44, 71–72, 74, 75, 103, 117, 191
Polk, Sarah 55, 210–211
Pope, John 60, 64, 91
Populist Party 1, 2
Porter, Fitz John 15
Post, P. Sidney 202, 206, 209, 214, 215, 217, 251
Pottawatomie Creek, Kansas 38
Powder Springs, Tennessee 177
Powers' Ferry, Georgia 194, 195
Preston, William B. 100
Prewitt's Knob, Kentucky 78
Prohibition Party 2
Pulaski, Tennessee 65, 203–204, 205, 222

Rancho Carricitos, Texas 19
Red Clay, Georgia 183
Red Cloud 239
Red Hill, Alabama 225
"Redstick" 49
Reed, B.L. 40
Republican Party 2
Resaca, Georgia 202; battle 186–187, 192
Resaca de la Palma, Battle of (Mexican War) 21–22, 23, 25, 29
Reynolds, Joseph J. 111–112, 126, 138–139, 140, 141, 148, 155, 181, 232
Reynosa, Mexico 23, 24
Richland Creek 222
Richmond, Kentucky 73
Richmond, Virginia 103, 194, 195, 197
Ridgely, Randolph 20, 22
Ringgold, Samuel 20, 21, 22
Ringgold, Georgia 127
Rio Grande 17, 19, 20, 21, 22, 23, 24, 33, 34, 220
Robinson, William C. 49
Rocky Face Ridge 185, 192
Rogersville, Tennessee 229
Rolling Fork River 84
Rosecrans, William S. 91, 92, 93, 94, 96, 97, 98, 101, 102–103, 105, 106, 107, 108–110, 111, 112, 113–114, 115–116, 117, 118, 119, 120, 122–123, 124, 125, 126, 128, 130, 133, 137, 138, 139–140, 141, 143, 147, 148, 149, 150, 151, 152, 153, 154, 155, 157, 175, 182, 223, 241–242, 243, 250
Rossville, Georgia 126, 127, 131, 142, 143, 146, 147, 150, 155
Roswell, Georgia 194
Rousseau, Lovell Harrison 32, 47, 72, 76, 85, 86, 107, 197, 198, 204, 242
Ruger, Thomas H. 205, 208
Rutherford Creek 206, 220, 221
Rutledge, Tennessee 177

Safety Powder Company 242
St. Cloud Hotel (Nashville) 56
St. Louis, Missouri 43, 59
Salem Church, Georgia 183, 185
Saltillo, Mexico 25, 28, 29, 30, 31, 32, 33
San Antonio, Texas 232–233
San Antonio Springs 233
San Juan River 24
San Luis Potosi, Mexico 29
San Patricio, Texas 16, 17
San Pedro Springs 233
Santa Anna, Antonio Lopez de 29, 30, 31, 34
Santa Fe Trail 38
Savannah, Georgia 197
Savannah, Tennessee 57, 58, 59, 60
Schofield, John M. 184, 185, 191, 192, 194, 195, 196–197, 198, 203, 204–205, 206, 207, 209, 210, 212, 214, 215, 216, 217, 220, 226, 251
Schurz, Carl 238
Scott, John 74
Scott, Thomas A. 46
Scott, Winfield 28, 29, 33, 34, 38, 46

Scribner, Benjamin F. 31, 49
Selma, Alabama 226
Seminole War 46
Sequatchie Valley 70, 121
Seven Pines, Virginia, Battle of 184
Shanks, W.F.G. 88, 91, 105
Shelbyville, Tennessee 68, 69
Shellmound, Alabama 122, 149
Sheridan, Philip H. 85–86, 110, 133, 136, 138, 139, 143, 149, 156, 160, 161, 165, 166, 167, 168, 169, 173, 174, 177, 232, 241
Sherman, John 244
Sherman, Thomas W. 31, 32
Sherman, William T. 42, 43, 44- 46, 47, 48, 49, 51, 154, 159, 162, 163, 164, 172, 173, 174, 175–176, 177, 183, 184, 185, 186, 187, 188, 189, 190, 191, 192, 193–194, 195, 196, 197, 198, 202, 203, 204, 208, 226, 227, 230, 241, 249
Sherman, Willie 159
Shiloh, Tennessee, Battle of 57–58, 59, 60, 77, 80, 86, 156, 235
Sill, Joshua 82
Sioux Indians 37, 239
Slocum, Henry W. 157, 234
Smith, A.J. 204, 214, 215, 216, 217, 219, 226
Smith, Edmund Kirby 15, 70, 73, 74, 77, 90, 233
Smith, William Farrar 15, 157, 158, 159
Smith, William S. 65, 85, 86
Smyrna, Georgia 193, 202
Snake Creek Gap 185, 186, 202
Society of the Army of the Cumberland 41, 52, 242, 245, 246
Soldiers' and Sailors' Monument (Dayton) 242–243
Soldiers' Home (Dayton) 245
Somers, Orlando A. 41, 246
Somerset, Kentucky 53
Song, Paul J. 244
Sonora, Kentucky 79
Sope Creek 194
Spanish American War 246
Sparta, Tennessee 70
Speed, Frederick 234–235
Speed, James 107
Speed Brothers 204
Spring Hill, Tennessee 206, 207, 208, 220
Springfield, Kentucky 84
Stanley, David S. 115, 184, 186, 188, 193, 194, 196, 197, 200, 201, 202, 203, 207, 209, 226, 227, 231, 242, 245, 251
Stanton, Edwin M. 107, 111, 118, 119, 137, 154, 157, 171, 179, 227, 235
Stark County, Ohio 156
Starling, Lyne 140–141
Steedman, James B. 146, 147, 214, 216, 217, 218, 225
Stevens' Gap 122, 130
Stevenson, Alabama 68
Stewart, Alexander P. 142, 214, 215, 216, 244

Stokes, James 104
Stone, Edward 7
Stoneman, George 197
Stones River, Tennessee, Battle of 97–101, 102–103, 107, 108, 112, 131, 143, 150, 178, 199, 243
Strawberry Plains, Tennessee 177
Streight, Abel D. 66–68, 77, 97, 180, 209, 217, 221, 223, 251
Sugar Creek 222
Sultana 234–235
Summerseat Knob 5, 9–10, 79
Summerville, Georgia 203

Taylor, Mr. (planter) 237
Taylor, Zachary 15, 16, 17–18, 19–20, 21, 22, 23, 25, 26, 27, 28–29, 30, 31–32, 33, 80
Tennessee River 54, 57, 59, 60, 64, 66, 67, 68, 70, 119, 121, 122, 127, 149, 158, 203, 222, 224, 225, 231, 232
Tennessee Troops: 1st Infantry (CSA) 195, 208
Texas Rangers 25, 26, 27, 29, 30, 31
Thatcher, Mr. (spy) 70
Therman, Tennessee 121, 122
Thomas, George H. 45, 53, 54, 60, 70, 73, 82, 84, 85, 86, 91, 92, 95, 96, 97, 107, 115, 121, 122, 126, 130, 133, 138, 139, 140, 141, 144, 145, 145, 146, 148, 153, 154, 162, 164, 167, 171, 172, 184, 185, 186, 191, 192, 193–194, 196, 197, 200, 201, 203, 204, 210, 211–213, 216, 218, 221, 222, 223, 225, 226, 227, 229, 239, 241, 250, 251
Thomas, Lorenzo 233
Thomas, Samuel 238–239
Thomas, Samuel O. 51
Thomas J. Wood vs. the United States 243
Thompson, Richard W. 42
Thoreau, Henry David 35
Thornton, Seth 19
Tod, David 107
Torrejón, Anastasio 19, 20, 25, 32
Trail of Tears 127
Trenton, Georgia 122
Trenton & Chattanooga Railroad 122
Trist, Nicholas 34–35
Truman, Benjamin C. 211
Tullahoma, Tennessee 69, 113, 116, 117, 119
Tullahoma Campaign 115–118, 119, 141, 220
Tunnel Hill 159, 162–163, 164, 185
Tupelo, Mississippi 68
Turchin, John Basil 149, 158
Tuscaloosa, Alabama 224
Tuscumbia, Alabama 64, 65, 66, 224
Tuttle, John W. 60, 61, 62, 65, 66, 69–70, 78, 87, 122
Twiggs, David E. 26
Tyler, G.B. 8

United States Colored Troops 204, 214, 217, 218, 235–237
United States House of Representatives 90, 242

Index

United States Military Academy 7, 8, 9, 10–13, 14, 15, 25, 35, 37, 46, 47, 63, 81, 91, 153, 157, 195, 208, 243, 245, 246, 247
United States Senate 35, 90, 204, 227, 238
United States troops: 1st Cavalry 37, 41; 1st Infantry (Mexican War) 26; 2nd Cavalry 240; 2nd Dragoons (Mexican War) 29, 30, 31, 33, 36; 3rd Infantry 247; 3rd Infantry (Mexican War) 26; 4th Artillery 250, 251; 4th Infantry (Mexican War) 21, 26; 5th Infantry (Mexican War) 20, 21, 26; 7th Infantry (Mexican War) 19, 24, 26; 15th Infantry 239; 16th Infantry; 18th Infantry 74, 143
University of Kentucky 241
University of Minnesota 242
University of Missouri 242
Upton, Kentucky 79
Utah (Mormon) Expedition 37, 45

Valley Head, Georgia 122
Van Buren, Martin 10
Van Cleve, Horatio P. 85, 86, 89, 92, 97, 98, 99, 103, 104, 127, 130, 133, 134, 136, 138, 139, 155
Vega, R.D. de la 22
Veracruz, Mexico 29, 33, 35
Vicksburg, Mississppi 112, 113, 118, 154, 232, 233, 234, 239
Vicksburg Herald 239–240
Victoria, Texas 232
Villanow, Georgia 202
Vining's Station, Georgia 193

Wagner, George D. 53, 58, 61, 69, 85–86, 92, 95, 98, 99, 100, 103, 104, 107, 108, 120, 121, 126, 128, 147, 156, 161, 205, 206, 207, 208, 209, 214, 249, 250
Walden's Ridge 152–153, 157, 158
Walker, William H.T. 132
Walnut Springs, Mexico 25
Ward, William T. 196
Warren, William B. 30
Warren County, Kentucky 72
Warren County, Mississippi 239
Wartrace, Tennessee 69
Washington, George 154
Washington, John 31
Washington County, Kentucky 84
Washington, D.C. 10, 34, 41, 43, 46, 49, 56, 89, 113, 119, 157, 178, 230, 242
Watkins, Sam 195–196, 208–209, 210, 219
Wauhatchie, Tennessee 123
West Point, Kentucky 79

West Point, New York *see* United States Military Academy
Western & Atlantic Railroad 187, 193, 197, 201
W.F. Curtis 232
Wharton, John 82, 89
Wheeler, Joseph 78–79, 84, 85, 89, 94, 105, 112, 196
Wheeling, Virginia 10
Whig Party 28
Whitesides, Tennessee 156
Widney, Lyman S. 51, 52, 110, 112, 113
Wilder, John T. 74, 75–76, 77, 78, 107, 112–113, 121, 126, 132, 135
Willard, J.P. 139
Willard Hotel (Washington, D.C.) 56
Williams, Alpheus 196
Williams, Isaac 241
Willich, August 156, 160, 161, 165, 166, 168, 184, 186, 187, 231, 232, 233, 250
Wilson, James H. 159, 203, 204, 206, 207, 211, 212, 213–214, 216, 217, 219, 220, 221–222, 226
Winchester, Tennessee 69
Winston Gap 122
Wisconsin Troops: 15th Infantry 250, 251
Wood, Caroline Greer (wife) 51, 105, 155, 180–181, 228, 241, 246
Wood, Elizabeth Helm (mother) 6, 79
Wood, George H. (son) 2, 241, 244, 245, 246
Wood, George Tyman (father) 5–7, 8, 14, 52, 77, 79, 245
Wood, Henry C. (brother) 6
Wood, Major General Thomas J.: ambition 36, 37, 80, 107, 119, 150, 179, 223, 226, 233–234, 244; appearance 1, 42–43; birth 6; boyhood and schooling 7; death 246; friendships 2, 34, 107, 120, 212, 245, 246; promotions 36, 37, 41, 42, 227, 233–234; religion 11, 121, 243; at the United States Military Academy 10, 11, 12, 13, 14, 15, 25, 35, 37, 244, 245; wit 98, 169; wounds 1, 100, 105, 199, 202, 240, 243
Wood, Thomas J., Jr. (son) 241, 246
Wood, William (son) 181
Wool, John E. 30, 31
Worth, William J. 17, 26–27, 28
Wright, Horatio G. 76
Wright Brothers 246
Writer, Stephen C. 67

Yell, Archibald 31, 32

Zahm, Lewis 92
Zollicoffer, Felix 45, 53

www.ingramcontent.com/pod-product-compliance
Ingram Content Group UK Ltd.
Pitfield, Milton Keynes, MK11 3LW, UK
UKHW041930140426
52171PUK00014B/403